From the Lost Land

From the Lost Land

Schizo-poem

André Spears

Station Hill Press
BARRYTOWN, NY

Published by Station Hill Press, the publishing project of the Institute for Publish-ing Arts, Inc., 120 Station Hill Road, Barrytown, NY 12507, a not-for-profit, Feder-ally tax-exempt organization [501(c)(3)].

Online catalogue: www.stationhill.org
E-mail: publishers@stationhill.org

Acknowledgements
The author wishes to thank the editors of the following publications, in which parts of this work first appeared: *First Intensity, Voix Editions, Pierogi Press, FoArm Magazine, COUGH, Sibila, House Organ, Dispatches from the Poetry Wars, BlazeVOX Journal, Blazing Stadium, Salt, Caesura.*

Portions of *From the Lost Land* were published under the titles *Letters from Mu (Part I)* (2000), *Fragments from Mu: A Sequel* (2007), *Nexus of Evil: Late Frag-ments, 1-7* (2009), *XIII: Ship of State* (2019), and *From the Lost Land (I-XII)* (2020).

Cover photo by Anne Rosēn

Library of Congress Catalog Card Number: available
ISBN: 978-1-58177-234-0

Land Acknowledgment
In the spirit of truth and equity, it is with gratitude and humility that we acknowl-edge that the Institute for Publishing Arts, Inc. and Station Hill Press reside on the sacred homelands of the Munsee and Muhheaconneok people, who are the orig-inal stewards of this land. Today, due to forced removal, the community resides in Northeast Wisconsin and is known as the Stockbridge-Munsee Community.

for AER

Contents

Fore-words 1

The Illusionist 9
The Seeress 13
The Queen 26
The King 33
The Philosopher 47
The Lovers 55
The War Machine 66
The Scales 77
The Mendicant 88
The Wheel Of Chance 94
The Strong Force 100
The Hanged One 120
The Skeleton 129
The Arts 211
The Devil 226
The God's House 253
The Star 272
The Moon 301
The Sun 341
The Aeon 366
The Universe 462
The Fool 483

About the Author 504

Fore-words

In 1950, Hannah Arendt had this to say about the state of western societies:

> We can no longer afford to take that which was good in the past and simply call it our heritage, to discard the bad and simply think of it as a dead load which by itself time will bury in oblivion. The subterranean stream of Western history has finally come to the surface and usurped the dignity of our tradition. This is the reality in which we live. And this is why all efforts to escape from the grimness of the present into nostalgia for a still intact past, or into the anticipated oblivion of a better future, are vain. (*Origins of Totalitarianism* ix.)

All of Euro-American modernism is implicit in this comment. The world wars had shattered what was left of faith in a Christian humanist order as well as any semblance of cultural common ground. Hence James Joyce, rummaging through the rubble, or Ezra Pound repeating Odysseus's journey to the underworld in order to find out what might still be of use. In "'Deep Time,' Archaeology and the Post-Romantic Paradigm," André Spears makes a case for the significance of the modernist dive into the past, particularly the archaic or deep past in post-romantic writings—Freud, Joyce, and Bataille in this essay (348). The point was to "[advance] the vision of a coherent society that would cease to produce the type of large-scale systematic contradictions of which world war seemed the expression" (351).

Fast forward to the present and that reach for a "vision of a coherent society" has foundered on multiple crises: the globalizing of supply chains, environmental degradation, the financialization of economies and the consequent democratic deficit, a seemingly endless succession of wars, and rapid technological change. In *Poetry and Finance*, Franco Berardi writes that we are now experiencing an "overcrowded infosphere and ... chaotic flows of financial microtrading" (10) at speeds too great for individuals to process; hence a hypercomplexity that stymies popular agency. Protest strategies, such as those of the Civil Rights era in the U.S. or the May 1968 student movement and general strike in France, fail to move economically entangled, socially hetereogeneous and heavily mediated societies. The "global machine" seemingly cannot be turned off by the rational will because the zone of possible change has been set by the techno-financial systems that created the machine. The difference between the 20th-century moderns and more contemporary writers is that the moderns had a political imaginary in socialism or fascism or direct democracy; contemporaries must contend with its loss or relegation to science fiction, where, as we know, myth hides out in these skeptical times.

It seems fitting, then, that Spears's *From the Lost Land* starts off with loss. Mu, a legendary Atlantean world, now under the ocean, was "discovered" by Colonel James Churchward (1851–1936) on tablets he claimed to have accessed in India (*The Lost Continent of Mu*). Churchward made Mu the cradle of the world's great civilizations. The Greek alphabet, he thought, referred symbolically to this lost continent. Churchward's claim and others like it have been discredited on scientific grounds, but Mu, like Atlantis or Eden, has lived on in imagination. Alongside this opening reference to a lost land, Spears poses a lost child, "our beloved child, Es." The speaker here is S, Navigator on a space ship, and she is writing to A, player in a game of Tarot cards. The poem unfolds through letters that pass between these two lovers, each one an episode. In the next letter, A responds that the loss of Es "seems now to have its echo / in the world": "The truth—regardless / of whether Es fell / in the Limbo Abyss / or the ones at Eden / or Ur—/ is that together / we have gone on. // And our world has gone on, / despite the unpromising signs." To push the allegory a little, we may go on, but we have lost it—lost the homeliness of the world and an imagination for it.

If the stickiness of world problems can be attributed at least partly to a narrow framing of possible responses, a lack of political will, and a fast-moving multiverse as Berardi suggests, then imagining things otherwise may require strategies of commensurate complexity. Spears's poem is written in two columns, a series of quotations on one side of the page and the letters on the other. The letters carry the narrative; the quotations bring a chorus to bear on it. The two columns complement and complicate each other. As well, each episode unfolds under the sign of a card from the Higher Arcana of the Tarot. Read conventionally, these cards appear to be western archetypes, but as Spears presents them, they work more like magnetic fields that attract various events, characters and objects. In "The Strong Force" ("Strength" in the A.E. Waite deck, "La Force" in the Marseille), for instance, the ship's crew engage with an Alien fleet and lose their companion vessels. These latter have names drawn from classical and biblical sources and American history, so one possible reading of this "plot-hole" (Negarestani's term) seems to be the sinking of western civilizations. However, the downed ships are also associated with "a complement of / World-Cup Theorists / and Analysands," while the phrase, "strong force," brings to mind that term in particle physics for the interaction between quarks which holds an atom together. So are we reading cultural history, psychoanalysis, or nuclear physics? It isn't that the divinatory meanings of the card are denied—creativity, new beginnings, energy, strength, heroism as well as their reverse in repression, inhibition, or anger, for instance (Jodorowsky 191)—but rather that various "forces" have been set in motion by the card. We are invited to imagine ourselves post-nuclear in physical, psychic, and cultural dimensions.

Multi-dimensionality, in fact, is a prominent feature of the poem. As well as the quotations, the two narratives, and the Tarot cards, there is a host of characters with names drawn from history, fiction, myth, music, or pop culture and a generous use of Joycean malapropisms and puns—all of which send the reader scrambling after allusion. "The Moon" episode for instance, begins with a retelling of Revelations in a vision of "U.U. Knucklehead / the Mad Boy: / he is dressed in a long / robe with a Red girdle / around his breast, / his feet are shining / like White Metal, and / his eyes are radiant Blue." This is the apocalypse "re-taled," as Joyce "re-taled" the Fall at the beginning of *Finnegans Wake*. Then there is the jazz factor. Ornette Coleman's harmolodics turn up by name, but Coleman's style is also present in method. In harmolodics, there is no element of the music (melody, rhythm, harmony, pacing) that is predetermined or dominant. Similarly, there is no tonal center to *Lost Land*, and no definitive beginning or ending. In Deleuzean language, it is a textual smooth space.

Gilles Deleuze and Félix Guattari, in fact, are present throughout the poem, not only in direct quotation and vocabulary, but in Spears's mobilization of strategies developed in *Anti-Oedipus* and *A Thousand Plateaus*. The point of schizoanalysis was to change the framing of the possible. Rather than lock into Freudian neurosis (the Oedipus complex), Deleuze and Guattari look to schizophrenia for a vision of pre-formal ("molecular") processes that produce the real. As they speak of it, flows, intensities, and part objects—"desiring machines"—precede "molar" forms that come together and then fall apart into new combinations. This de- and re-territorializing process applies to psychic and social formations as well as capitalist flows of money, but it may modalize any field. In *From the Lost Land*, Deleuzian becomings set in motion the social and psychic fields, but also aesthetic, historical, philosophical, and even scientific ranges of cognition and affect. Inner and outer worlds—the psyche and the cosmos, the individual and the historical—twist together in moebius fashion: outside is inside and vice versa.

The effect of these strategies is to create what Deleuze and Guattari would call a plane of consistency (smooth space) or a body without organs, where machinic couplings make possible new connections that may potentially alter the real. It seems to me crucial to remember at a distance of more than 50 years since the French publication of *Anti-Oedipus* (Les Editions de Minuit, 1972; English translation, Viking Penguin, 1977), that the aim of schizoanalysis was liberation. In his introduction to that volume, Michel Foucault says that the book hits three targets: political purism (ideologies); psychoanalysis as lack (castration complex); and fascism, psychological or historical. "I would say," Foucault writes, "that *Anti-Oedipus* (may its authors forgive me) is a book of ethics... " (xiii). And Mark Seem in his Preface to this volume explicitly connects psychic and political revolution: "Once we forget about our egos a non-neurotic form of politics becomes possible, where singularity and collectivity are no longer at odds with each other, and where collective expressions of desire are possible" (xxi). Change the mind and change the world? I would call this a necessary, if not sufficient, condition; certainly it is where a poet (as opposed to a political, military or corporate operative) might begin to re-vision the world out of its stuckness.

If we are indeed mired in the endgame of western civilization as we know it, where better to begin a re-visioning than at the beginning, with an odyssey. As in Homeric epic, there is much of the weird and wonderful in *Lost Land*—a massive Sea Jelly, a giant, free-floating Faucet, a Fold that brings the sub- and super-conscious minds together, a descent to Hell on a bicycle, a strange recurrent luminescence on the horizon. These adventures are freighted with allegorical commentary, often comedic, on world happenings and intellectual history. The ship's crew and the card player typically find themselves in dire straits and try to escape in absurdist ways. One persistent push, both on the ship and in the card game, is toward an outside to wherever the characters happen to be stuck. For instance in "The Skeleton" (episode 13, the Death card), the Navigator turns on "Atomatic pilot" and can't turn it off again because no one knows the password. This episode plunges the crew into "methodological turmoil" in their efforts to regain control over the direction of the ship. The details of this passage suggest a lack of agency in both psychic and political dimensions. No one can experience the outside of perception this side of madness or death, which is perhaps why crew members regularly go mad and jump overboard. Analogously, no one seems capable of turning around a ship sailing under a "Doubloon-Bind," a blue-red haze, an accelerating infosphere, or a micro-traded dollar. When the ship runs finally aground, the crew decide to hold a symposium to map the Heavens in hopes of discovering some "Guiding Spirit" to get them moving again. Unfortunately, their first find is Mor-o-Log-on and we are into the Trump era, covid, online shopping (more log-ons), climate change, QAnon, and the alt-right. By the end of episode 17, the ship is on the floor of a Silver Sea; in episode 19 they churn their way through the mud only to face an existential crisis: "For each of us, / all at once, grief followed / ecstasy, as Sovereignty collapsed / under the weight of its own / Crown, and Economics silenced / Laughter; admiration gave way / to loathing, as Victory over / meaninglessness succumbed / to the Death of Empathy, and / serenity and pensiveness / suffered the Ordeal of Politics ..."

We have lost It. Spears's card player makes a mad descent to Hell on a Holy Davidson bicycle, during which the bike and his body fuse in various states of decrepitude that should logically end in death but do not. The point of the descent is to beat the game—one with life and death stakes—that A cannot not play, just as the ship's crew cannot turn off Atomatic pilot. How to decenter the ego, extend the imagination, or overcome binary logic without entirely fading away? As A descends, he meditates on possible outcomes—win-win, lose-lose, or the more ominous zero sum, win-lose, lose-win. Is it possible to win by losing oneself? "You have to keep enough of the organism for it to reform each dawn"; Deleuze and Guattari warn, "you have to keep small supplies of significance and subjectification, if only to turn them against their own systems when the circumstances demand it ... " (TP 60).

On the historical record, utopias systematized have tended to harden into their opposites and from there we know the story. The last episode of *From the Lost Land* takes place under the sign of The Fool, the Zero card that enables everything and nothing. The quotations disappear and the two letter writers, S and A, come together in two columns, each reiterating their stories, each borrowing from the other certain narrative elements. Both characters experience apocalyptic visions, both relent into various becomings. Captain Anna-O achieves "Bio-political Enlightenment," crew members engage in erotic couplings, Leviathan appears (shades of Melville's *Moby Dick*), and a single cosmic blast of Sound sends the ship to a "Bottomless Rift" "between a Submarine lake / and a forest / of Coral." Both the Navigator and card player embrace resurrection into nomadism. In "Proprioception," Olson says that America is the "inheritor" of "a secularization which not only loses nothing of the divine but by seeing process in reality redeems all idealism fr theocracy or mobocracy, whether it is rational or superstitious, whether it is democratic or socialism" (CPr 190). On this proposition, one does not retrieve Mu, one mu(ses).

So does this mean subversion or exit? Among contemporary speculative writers, there are plenty of proponents of both. Reza Negarestani, a philosopher in the Deleuzean line, imagines resistance to power (Wholeness) through a poetics of decay (()holes) that degrades and ungrounds power formations by softening them from within—a "poromechanics" he calls the corrupting processes that subvert the coherence of entities whether they are organic, imaginal, or socio-political (*Cyclonopedia*). The logic is Deleuzean, but the quality of the vision recalls the horrors of H.P. Lovecraft. Leprosy, in this context, is a metaphor for ungovernable creativity. Negarestani makes an appearance in Spears's *Lost Land* ("The Scales") as does a leprosarium, and there is plenty of subversive molecular action in Spears's poem. What I don't hear, however, is zombified deterritorialization and weaponized theory-fiction. Instead, I hear something like Bataille's wonderment before eroticism and death as he came to it in prehistoric art—the awful / awe-full enigma of humanity as it appears in the caves of Lascaux (*Tears of Eros* 53). The "animated archaic" turns up in Spears's "Fool" episode, as if the Zero of this card were an egg that might someday hatch the human universe again.

From the Lost Land combines epic range and comic littleness, but it is also lyrical. One has to love the world to learn how to stay inside it, and one learns to love a thing by extending one's view of it. A great accomplishment of the poem is its insistence on cultural memory through quotation and allusion. Arendt writes that "[t]he triumph of memory is that in presenting the past and thus depriving it, in a sense, of its bygone quality, memory transforms the past into a future possibility" (*Love and Saint Augustine* 48). Memory keeps thought alive and moving and this is particularly important at a historical moment when it is tempting to shut it all down—to choose sides on the big issues and insist. The remedy that poetry can offer is an enlarged view of things. Long before the advent of "theory," Emerson proposed a double consciousness as a possible response to misfortune and dark times: "So when a man is the victim of his fate... he is to rally on his relation to the Universe, which his ruin benefits" (389). A case of winning while losing, perhaps? Spears's poem ends with an embrace of outwardness that transforms loss—the loss of "It"—into a harrowing, death-defying, world-loving look-around the globe, "from the Barricades / onto Elysium Plains" and so forth "Outward / over the sea ... "

— Miriam Nichols

Works Cited

Arendt, Hannah. Preface to the First Edition. *The Origins of Totalitarianism*. Orlando, Florida: Harcourt Brace, 1951. vii–ix.

______. *Love and Saint Augustine*. Ed. Joanna Vecchiarelli Scott and Judith Chelius Stark. Chicago and London: U of Chicago P, 1996.

Bataille, Georges. *The Tears of Eros*. Trans. Peter Connor. San Francisco: City Lights, 1989.

Berardi, Franco "Bifo." *On Poetry and Finance*. South Pasadena, CA: Semiotext(e) Intervention Series, 2012.

Churchward, Colonel James. *The Lost Continent of Mu*. 1926; Kempton, Illinois: Adventures Unlimited Press, 2007.

Deleuze, Gilles and Félix Guattari. *Anti-Oedipus: Capitalism and Schizophrenia*. Trans. Robert Hurley, Mark Seem, Helen R. Lane. Minneapolis: U of Minnesota P, 1983.

______. *A Thousand Plateaus: Capitalism and Schizophrenia*. Trans. Brian Massumi. Minneapolis, London: U of Minnesota P, 1987.

Emerson, Ralph Waldo. "Fate." In *Selected Essays*. Ed. Larzer Ziff. New York, Middlesex, UK: Penguin, 1982. 361–391.

Foucault, Michel. "Preface." *Anti-Oedipus*. xi-xiv.

Jodorowsky, Alejandro. And Marianne Costa. *The Way of the Tarot: The Spiritual Teacher in the Cards.* Trans. Jon E. Graham. Rochester, Vermont: Destiny Books, 2009.

Negarestani, Reza. *Cyclonopedia: Complicity with Anonymous Materials.* Melbourne, Australia: re.press, 2008.

Olson, Charles. *Collected Prose*. Eds. Donald Allen and Benjamin Friedlander. Berkeley: U of California P, 1997.

Seem, Mark. "Introduction." *Anti-Oedipus*. xv–xxiv.

Spears, André. "'Deep Time,' Archaeology and the Post-Romantic Paradigm." Comparative Literature Vol. 48, No. 4 (Autumn 1996): 343–358.

______. "Warlords of Atlantis: Chasing the Demon of Analogy in the America(s) of Lawrence, Artaud and Olson." *Canadian Review of Comparative Literature / Revue Canadienne de Littérature Comparée*, Vol. 8, No. 2-3 (2001): 245–270.

The Illusionist

My love,

"A... Heavily break
the waters
B... extending
over the plains
Γ... they cover
the land
Δ... in low places,
where
there are no
obstructions,
shores form
and whirlpools
Z... strike the earth
H... with water.
Θ... The waters spread
I... on all that lives
and moves,
K... obstructions
give way and
Λ... submerged is
the land of
M... Mu.
N... Peaks only
Ξ... appear above

It was at this same time
in a distant past
that we first mourned
our beloved child, Es.

Then, as now,
Delta, Neutron and Playtex
were aligned in the sign
of The Cross-Eye, Colors
brightened and sadness
touched our souls.

How well I remember
this brilliant Red sky, and
the sea so glossy White...

If the Porno continues to
blow as it has, even with
the Nirvana against us,
we should be reaching
the Waters of Torus
in six Days.

the waters,
O... whirlwinds
blow around
Π... and little by little,
Ρ... until there comes
Σ... cold air. Before
where valleys
existed, are
Υ... now abysses,
cold depths.
In circular places
Φ... mud formed.
Χ... A mouth
Ψ... opens, vapors
Ω... come forth and
volcanic sediments."
Col. James Churchward,
The Lost Continent of Mu,
"The Greek Alphabet
and its Esoteric Meanings."

"A monk asked Jōshū,
'Does a dog have
the Buddha nature?'
Jōshū answered: 'Mu.'"
Zen koan.

"Etnean gasps! /
Vesuvian acclamations!"
Melvin Tolson,
Harlem Gallery, "Mu."

"'While you are sheltered

The crew's morale
for the most part
is holding up well,
although Don Juan,
the Chief Mate,
was recently seized
with Madness and jumped
over the side, screaming.

Two Prayer Flags were
flown in remembrance:
S'un (Number 9)
and *C'iao* (Number 33).

Our linkup with the Indian
fleet seems likely to occur
in the Georgian Sea.

There is still no explanation
for the sudden alien presence
in the Orionis Ripple.

Latest readings
from the S\S MARU,
the Byzantine scout vessel
furthest afar of our forces,
indicate that the alien ships
are engaged in what appears
to be a Defensive maneuver.

here, the magnificent city
of Puhar... is being swallowed
into the belly of the ocean.
I will explain why.'"
Chithalai Chathanar,
Manimekalai, Canto XXV.

"The fall (bababadalgha-
raghtakamminarronn-
konnbronntonnerronn-
tuonnthunnnawnskawn-
toohoohoordenenthurnuk!)
...retaled..."
James Joyce,
Finnegans Wake.

"I find letters from God
dropped in the street."
Walt Whitman,
Leaves of Grass.

"Here is the alchemist's key,
it unlocks secret doors."
H. D.,
The Walls Do Not Fall.

"Several billion years
from now, there will be
a last perfect day. Then,
over a period of millions
of years, the sun will swell...
Eventually the sun will fill
most of the sky."

Their armada presents
four different fronts,
equal in length, positioned
along two lines.

These lines, according
to the S\S MARU, bisect
each other and continue
to revolve in opposite
directions, periodically
forming a single row.

Other reports claim
the ships are equipped
with oars as well as sails.

Intelligence is divided
on this matter.

Tarzan believes
such findings are true,
but Venus and Maria,
her colleagues, disagree.

With the growing sense
that Fate is deep at work
my love becomes stronger.

The memory returns
of our time together
by Panama Crater,

Carl Sagan,

Cosmos.

"My Life had stood –

a Loaded Gun –"

Emily Dickinson (764).

on the eve of the last

New Age.

I hope to read you soon.

Your lover,

S.

The Seeress

"Let us learn that we are
nothing and the Tarot will
have divulged its last secret."
Oswald Wirth,
The Tarot of Medieval
Image-Makers.

"...There is this angel who's coming
toward you as you are coming
toward him. And there's a moment
when you pass through your angel
and become the fact that you are
without any chance involved with
another figure who is you,
who is coming toward you in time
as you proceed forward in time.
And at the moment that you pass,
you then are something that
that angel was, and you're
no longer that thing you were."
Charles Olson,
Muthologos, "On History."

"After us the Savage God."

Dear S.,

No sooner were you off
at sea than phantoms came
to visit me, wearing skeleton
costumes and masks.

"What? No cool buttocks to pet
but your own?" they'd say,
and puff on cigarettes.

I sent them away
with a three-fingered curse,
but the knot in my heart
quickly tightened.

The signs have arrived
that tell of new times.

Since your departure
for the Orionis Ripple, events
have followed a disturbing course.

The Youth especially

have been causing alarm.

They flaunt their nakedness.

They take to the streets in
unruly gangs, where they strike
obscene poses and scream.

No longer sweet-tempered
and dear to behold, they perform
Masturbation while uttering poems.

They dance on the Sabbath,
euphoric and wild, cursing
their parents and Elders,
declaring themselves
"Masters of the Last Word."

The Youth of Valium,
long famed for the beauty
of their rear ends, are making
more havoc than most.

Their leader is an arrogant boy
by the name of McDonalds,
whose Sex is said
to be high all the time.

Invoking the theme
of "Violent Green Freeze,"
he calls for an order based

William B. Yeats,
The Trembling of the Veil.

"Load up on guns, bring your friends /
It's fun to lose and to pretend."
Nirvana, "Smells like Teen Spirit."

"The simplest Surrealist act consists
of dashing down the street, pistol in
hand, and firing blindly, as fast as you
can pull the trigger, into the crowd."
André Breton,
Manifesto of Surrealism.

"It is difficult to write a Paradiso,
when all the superficial
indications are that you ought
to write an Apocalypse."
Ezra Pound, in D.G. Bridson,
"A.B.C. interview with Ezra Pound,"
New Directions 17.

"I am certain of nothing
but of the holiness of
the Heart's affections and
the truth of Imagination."
John Keats, "Letter to Benjamin
Bailey" (22 Nov. 1817).

"There is further an art
which imitates by language
alone, without melody, in prose
or in verse, and if in verse, either

on their law and exhorts
his companions to riot.

Though little is known
of their ultimate goals,
they gather on beaches
in secret groups
and wait for new Youth
to rise from the sea.

It remains to be seen
if this practice will spread.

Nor is it clear
if the new arrivals conspire
in a larger scheme.

Everywhere,
their number is increasing,
as is their beauty.

According to rumor,
the Initiation of Youth
is now taking place
on a clandestine basis.

More troubling still,
the few Initiations held of late
have met with odd results,
a development lending support
to the view that outsiders

in some one or in a plurality of
meters. This form of imitation
is to this day without a name."
Aristotle,
Poetics.

"As a wife has a cow,
as a wife has a cow,
a love story. Has to be
as a wife has a cow
a love story. Has made as
to be as a wife has
a cow a love story. When
he can, and for that when
he can, for that. When he
can and for that when he
can. For that. When he can...
And to and in and six
and another. And to and in
and six and another. And to
in six and and to and
in and six and another. And
to and in and six and
another. And to and six and
in and another and and to
and six and another and and
to and in and six and
and to and six and in
and another. In came in there,
came in there come out of
there. In came in come out
of there. Come out there in
came in there. Come out of

are tampering with mysteries
of the flesh.

It was only recently that
I saw the problem firsthand.

I had lost 19 cents playing
Cards at a saloon called
the *Joie de Vivre*,
and was on my way
to the Wetlands.

Near Marienbad
I reached a temple
where a crowd was gathered,
and the rites had just begun.

In keeping with custom,
the associate officer read
from *The Book of Jiminy*,
while the assistant officers
poured bottles of sparkling water
into a large basin
lined with mosaic.

Family and close friends
looked down from a balcony,
while off to one side
a fiddler and piper
created a dreamlike Sound
through the ongoing patterns

there and in and come out
of there. Came in there, come
out of there. Feeling or for
it, as feeling or for it,
came in or come in, or
come out of there or feeling
as feeling or feeling as for
it. As a wife has a
cow. Came in and come out."
Gertrude Stein,
"As a Wife Has a Cow: A Love Story."

"Just as all fiction first found
extensive embodiment in poetry,
so is it in poetry that we first
encounter the permanent entry of
the weird into standard literature."
H. P. Lovecraft,
Supernatural Horror in Literature.

"Evening paper, second edition /
Evening paper, third edition /
Evening paper, latest edition /
Tomorrow morning's paper /
Read about the new end
of the world! / The latest news
of the world's end! /
World's end tomorrow! /
World's end day after tomorrow! /
...Evening papers, evening papers!
The night at noon, the noon
at night / The night at noon!
Eight o'clock edition /

they played.

At first, nothing unusual
marked the proceedings.

The lovers waited
in separate chambers
at opposite ends of the hall,
remaining unseen
till the pool was full
and the music had stopped.

Then they came into view
and began their approach—
he, Kirkor by name,
handsome, tall and able-bodied;
she, Sumella, equally fine,
with healthy breasts
and a slender waist.

Walking in step,
they reached a halt
and stood face-to-face
with the water between them.

The priestess and priest
followed next, blessing them
with incense.

Nine o'clock edition /
Ten o'clock edition /
Eleven o'clock edition /
Midnight edition...
1:00 A.M. morning edition /
1:00 A.M. morning edition...
Third evening edition /
One o'clock morning paper /
Panic in Berlin! /
The New York Press coming
to witness the word's end!"
Kurt Schwitters and Kate Steinitz,
"Collision: A Science-Fiction
Opera Libretto in Banalities."

"A child must exist, so be it."
David Henderson, in Ornette
Coleman, "Science Fiction."

"When you meet a Gethenian
you cannot and must not do what
a bisexual naturally does, which is
to cast him in the role of Man or
Woman, while adopting towards him
a corresponding role dependent on
your expectation of the patterned or
possible interactions between persons
of the same or the opposite sex.
Our entire pattern of sociosexual
interaction is nonexistent here.
They cannot play the game. They
do not see one another as men or
women. This is almost impossible for

Before they had even embraced,
there was an ominous sign.

When Kirkor and Sumella entered
the water, its sparkle went flat.

They immersed themselves
nonetheless, ignoring the trouble;
as soon as their bodies
made contact, the water
was fizzing once more.

Foreplay, however,
took no time at all,
and the water
quickly came to a boil.

Propped up against the side
of the basin, the girl encircling
the boy with her legs,
they heaved and panted intensely,
without respite, venting
their passion at a frantic pace.

It was only a little while
later that smoke began to appear.

In a matter of moments,
it thickened into a velvety cloud
that poured from the basin,
forming a strange mass from
which long strands were escaping.

our imagination to accept. What is
the first question we ask about
a newborn baby? Yet you cannot
think of a Gethenian as 'it.' They are
not neuters. They are potentials,
or integrals... One is respected
and judged only as a human being.
It is an appalling experience."
Ursula Le Guin,
The Left Hand of Darkness.

"Become who you are!"
Friedrich Nietzsche,
Thus Spake Zarathustra.

"Poetry is not knowledge of oneself,
and still less the experience of
a distant possibility (of that which
previously was not), but the simple
evocation with words of
possibilities beyond reach."
George Bataille,
Hatred of Poetry (The Impossible).

"Forgive her Lord and forgive
all of us / for our 20th Century /
for this Colossal Super-Production
in which we all had a hand."
Ernesto Cardenal,
"Prayer For Marilyn Monroe."

"I was clothed with confusion."
H. D.,

The lovers, hidden from view
and letting out wild cries of
rapture, were near the height
of their enjoyment when a ghastly
Sound ripped through the air.

Climax came almost at once,
with a billow of smoke
so huge that it plunged
the whole room in a Fog!

There was silence while
the haze slowly dispersed.

The tension kept building—
until all eyes were fixed on
the site where this odd event
had occurred, and where
the last of the smoke hovered
like a large bubble.

Finally, out of the pool
stepped a dark man
with a thin mustache.

He surveyed his surroundings
with an air of indifference,
then stood with his arms crossed.

In the usual manner, after having
been offered a towel, the man

End to Torment:
A Memoir of Ezra Pound.

"When we do escape,
it is of immense importance
that we know the language."
Charlotte Perkins Gilman,
Herland.

"She was all charm, beauty, and
perfect grace, with a forehead
like the new moon, eyes like
those of a deer or wild heifer,
eyebrows like the first crescent
in the month of Sha'ban, cheeks
like red anemones, mouth
like the seal of Solomon, lips
like red carnelian, teeth like a row
of pearls set in coral, neck
like a cake for a king, bosom
like a fountain, breasts like a pair
of big pomegranates resembling
a rabbit with uplifted ears, and belly
with a navel like a cup that holds
a pound of benzoin ointment."
Tales of the 1001 Nights.

"Fay ce que tu vouldras..."
("Do what thou wilt.")
François Rabelais,
Gargantua.

"We pulled off our clothes

was told of his previous form
as the maiden Sumella.

He showed little response,
occasionally glancing to and fro.

His wife was slow to follow.

She was ugly and squat, with
short fair hair and fair skin.

She moved awkwardly,
making her way out
of the water and coming up
next to the man.

She was welcomed as an Elder,
reborn of Kirkor, after which
the two of them stood
surrounded by silence—
he, beginning to fidget;
she, timidly looking around.

The bundles were then
brought forth, six in all.

It was a rare case,
part of Southern tradition,
when for reasons unknown
a leprosarium offers both
Initiates an extra choice.

and pushed naked together
in Bacchic fury."
Apuleius,
The Golden Ass.

"Thus, says Suvarnanabha,
these different ways of
lying down, sitting, and standing
should be practiced in water,
because it is easy to do so therein.
But Vatsyayana is of opinion
that congress in water
is improper, because it is
prohibited by the religious law."
Vatsyayana,
Kama Sutra.

"The only destiny with which
we are born is the destiny of ritual."
Clarice Lispector,
The Passion According to G. H.

"Insistence on birth at the wrong
season is the trick of evil."
Alfred North Whitehead,
Process and Reality.

"Albi. I'll be, You'll be. Al'll be. /
Eventually we'll all be."
Ed Dorn, "Albi, a Day Trip."

"Then she opened up a book
of poems / And handed it to me /

They were thus presented
with three bundles each,
and the woman was asked
to choose her clothing first.

Confused and hesitant,
she pointed to the bundle
on her right, which was found
to contain a T-shirt and jeans.

After dressing to general
applause she said nothing,
but stared at the floor
and sucked on her fingers.

Then the man exclaimed
it was his turn to choose.

He wanted the bundle
on the left, and signaled
to have it undone.

It contained a uniform:
matching shirt, pants and
a visored cap, plus a belt
onto which was fastened
some sort of club—
a sinister stick, not straight
but curved in shape,
rounded and smooth at the end.

Written by an Italian poet / From the thirteenth century. / And every one of them words rang true / And glowed like burnin' coal / Pourin' off of every page / Like it was written in my soul / From me to you."
Bob Dylan,
"Tangled Up in Blue."

"Every epoch dreams its successor."
Jules Michelet, "Future! Future!"

"Was not: Bacchus born from Jupiter's thigh? – Rocquetaillade born from his mother's heel? – Croquemouche from his nurse's slipper? Was not Minerva born through the ear from the brain of Jupiter? – Adonis from the bark of a myrtle-tree? – Castor and Pollux from the shell of an egg laid and hatched out by Leda?"
Rabelais,
Gargantua.

"When you set out for Ithaka / pray that your road's a long one, / full of adventure, full of discovery. / Laistrygonians, Cyclops, angry Poseidon—don't be scared of them… you won't encounter them / unless you bring them along inside you / unless your soul

He put on the clothes,
and, raising his arms
in a gesture of greeting,
announced that his name
was Monroe.

He honored thereafter
the dictates of custom,
thanking the congregation,
although a certain unnaturalness
about him was peculiar.

Before leaving, Monroe declared
his joy on becoming an Elder,
then turned and kissed his wife.

"The woman's name,"
he added, "is Lee."

As they walked from the temple,
the husband went first
with a swaggering air, while
his barefooted wife wobbled along,
following him at a distance.

They continued down to the valley,
toward the Silicon Lagoon.

The common feature
that seemed to mark them

raises them up in front of you."
Constantin P. Cavafy, "Ithaka."

"polis is / eyes"
C. Olson,
The Maximus Poems.

"Zeus, the god of gods, who rules
according to law, and is able to see
into such things, perceiving that
an honourable race was in a woeful
plight, and wanting to inflict
punishment on them, that they
might be chastened and improve,
collected all the gods into their most
holy habitation, which, being
placed in the centre of the world,
beholds all created things.
And when he had called them
together, he spake as follows—"
Plato,
Critias.

"On the shores of Gitche Gumee, /
Of the shining Big-Sea-Water, /
Stood Nokomis, the old woman, /
Pointing with her finger westward, /
O'er the water pointing westward, /
To the purple clouds of sunset. /
Fiercely the red sun descending /
Burned his way along the heavens, /
Set the sky on fire behind him, /
As war-parties, when retreating, /

was in their eyes.

Neither Lee nor Monroe
upon coming to life
had the Colorless eyes of Youth;
but despite their Color,
the eyes appeared dull
and less than human.

No light shone from within.

According to H. Ecolagicus
the Proconsul,
this was an unfavorable omen.

The emergence of Elders
like Lee and Monroe,
with their shallow gaze
and deviant manner,
seems to coincide
with another development
that I learned about from Pleiades.

We were in the *Rendez-Vous*,
a saloon where the ouzo is
excellent and Card Players gather.

During our talk Pleiades told me
that he had recently noticed
on a statue of Armstrong,
overlooking Bayrouth,

Burn the prairies on their war-trail..."
Henry Wadsworth Longfellow,
The Song of Hiawatha.

"Holderlin called the lyric /
'the continuous metaphor of
a feeling,' / the epic, 'the metaphor /
of an intellectual point of view.'"
Ken Irby *(RIP)*,
"Jed Smith and the Way."

"Inanna placed the *shugurra*,
the crown of the steppe,
on her head... When she leaned
against the apple tree,
her vulva was wondrous to behold. /
Rejoicing at her wondrous vulva,
the young woman Inanna
applauded herself."
"Inanna and the God of Wisdom," in
Inanna: Queen of Heaven and Earth
(ed. D. Wolkstein and S. Kramer).

"It was as if something
unbelievably strange and fierce—
like the holy temper—lifted her
to where she could not breathe
or walk: she choked in the ether,
a scrambling seraph, tumbling
aflame and alien, powerful
beyond belief, hideous and
frightening and beautiful
beyond the reach of the human.

a small glowing object stuck
to the side of her neck.

More are being discovered,
although I have not seen them.

Solid and round and soft
to the touch, they are often
spotted on ceilings or walls,
hidden or just out of reach;
yet of their origins, or
the means by which they
stay fixed, nothing is known.

They may be able to travel.

For the Muthologists
these mysterious beads
are tears—the tears of Atlas,
filtering into our land—
though whether they stem
from her joy or her sorrow
is uncertain.

Between the recent quirks
in nature's order and
an alien fleet on the far
reaches of the sea
looms the specter of Death.

A screaming child, an angel
howling in the Godly sphere:
she churned without delicacy,
as wild as an angel bearing threats;
her body lifted from the sheets,
fell back, lifted again; her hands
beat on the bed; she made
very loud hoarse tearing noises."
Harold Brodkey, "Innocence."

"Coming into this matter
is hard. My way of telling about
these things is raw."
G. Bataille,
Madame Edwarda.

"Nine at the beginning means: /
Hidden dragon. Do not act."
I Ching (tr. R. Wilhelm).

"Venerandam, / In the Cretan's
phrase, with the golden crown,
Aphrodite, / Cypri munimenta
sortita est, mirthful, orichalchi,
with golden / Girdles and
breastbands, thou with dark
eyelids / Bearing the golden
bough of Argicida. So that: / "
E. Pound,
Cantos, I.

"It is hard to say to what extent

That we as parents should
find our thoughts turning
to the memory of one
we loved so completely
makes conditions more painful.

What failed in us then,
when the idea took hold
that our child would never
be seen or heard from again,
seems now to have its echo
in the world.

The truth—regardless
of whether Es fell
in the Limbo Abyss
or the ones at Eden
or Ur—is that together
we have gone on.

And our world will go on,
despite the unpromising signs.

I wait to hear from you.

Your lover,

A.

Moses de Leon expected
his work in the Zohar actually
to be accepted as an ancient
and authoritative Midrash, or
how far he intended to create
a compendium of Kabbalah
in a suitable literary form."
Gershom Scholem,
Kabbalah.

"All art is essentially poetry."
Martin Heidegger,
"The Origin of the Work of Art."

"Art is the only twin life has—
its only valid metaphysic."
C. Olson, "Human Universe."

"But look where sadly
the poor wretch comes reading."
William Shakespeare,
Hamlet.

The Queen

Dear A.,

"I moved the chair up
to the shelves. I took
down a book I knew
only too well—
the second volume
of Hughes and Eugel's
old *History of Solaris*—
and started flipping
through it, resting the thick,
stiff spine on my lap.
Solaris had been discovered
almost a hundred years
before I was born.
The planet orbits two suns,
a red one and a blue one.
For over forty years
no spaceship came near to it."
Stanislav Lem,
Solaris.

"You would have thought
the craft had two keels—
one cleaving the water,
the other the air—

We have crossed
the Waters of Torus
and are sailing
onto parts of the sea
untraveled since the time
of our ancestors.

I think of you often.

You are my only refuge
from the fear that I feel
as we venture
so far from home.

The alien nature
of our surroundings,
however subtle,
is unmistakable.

The sky seems almost violent
in its Redness.

The sea looks different too:
its surface more active,

as the boat churned on
through both opposing
elements at once."
Herman Melville,
Moby Dick.

"For archaeological analysis,
contradictions are neither
appearances to be overcome,
nor secret principles to be
uncovered. They are objects
to be described for themselves,
without any attempt being
made to discover from what
point of view they can be
dissipated, or at what level
they can be radicalized and
effects become cause."
Michel Foucault,
The Archaeology of Knowledge.

"Nature loves to hide."
Herakleitos, in *7 Greeks*
(tr. G. Davenport).

"Look into ether and holy sea."
Friedrich Hölderlin,
Hyperion.

"Where are we? / and what is
the answer? /... 'The sea-roads lie
between / you and the answer.'"
H. D.,

as if stirred by wilder forces.

Even the stars are more Fiery.

The Aura of strangeness,
as well as the fear
felt by the crew,
are not likely to last; but
judging from our recent transit
a hazardous course lies ahead.

Of immediate concern to me
as Navigator is the tension
between Möbius the Mapper
and Occam the Weatherwoman.

Both are still novices,
having served for
just a few journeys.

Tempers began to rise
as we were nearing
the Omega Line
and about to go past
the Maya Whirlpool.

The quarrel between them
involved the issue of a port
versus starboard approach.

Occam argued for starboard,

Helen in Egypt.

"It is not down in any map;
true places never are."
H. Melville,
Moby Dick.

"We have no map."
H. D.,
The Walls Do Not Fall.

"...We are now in mid-sea,
surrounded by untried
possibilities and things
undiscovered—we can
no longer choose,
we must be conquerors,
now that we have no land
in which we feel at home
and in which we would fain
survive. A concealed 'yea'
is driving us forward,
and it is stronger than all
our 'nays.' Even our strength
no longer bears with us
in the old swampy land:
we venture out into the open,
we attempt the task.
The world is still rich and
undiscovered, and even
to perish were better than
to take to be half-men or
poisonous men. Our very

on the grounds that the wind
was more dependable
and the chance of meteors
not as great.

Möbius, on the other hand,
maintained that the charts
for a starboard approach
were by now obsolete.

I referred the dispute
to the Captain,
who sided with Occam.

There is still disagreement
regarding what happened.

We kept close
to the Omega Line, sailing
alongside it; as we entered
the pass, with the whirlpool
virtually behind us, an easy
crossing seemed assured.

Yet suddenly,
as if by a will
of its own,
the ship veered away
and turned back
toward the whirlpool.

strength itself urges us to
take to the sea; there where
all suns have hitherto sunk
we know of a new world..."
Friedrich Nietzsche,
The Will to Power, quoted
by Frances Boldereff,
in *Charles Olson and*
Frances Boldereff:
A Modern Correspondence
(ed. R. Maud and S. Thesen).

"The end of artistic activity is not
the finished work but freedom."
Octavio Paz,
Marcel Duchamp.

"Freedom's just another word
for nothin' left to lose."
Janis Joplin,
"Me and Bobby McGee."

"Whatever you have to say,
leave / the roots on, let them /
dangle / And the dirt /
Just to make clear /
where they come from"
Charles Olson,
"These Days."

"These go to *eleven.*"
Rob Reiner (dir.),
This is Spinal Tap.

All attempts to alter our course
seemed hopeless.

We started to circle,
slowly at first,
then faster and faster.

For one frightful round
we were trapped
on the edge of that hole—
when, as unexpectedly as before,
the ship made an abrupt turn,
breaking free.

We went straight toward the pass,
propelled by the force
of the water, and soon after
were heading onto the open sea.

No harm befell either ship
or crew, to the credit
of Anna-O; and van Rr'Ubik
proved her worth at the helm.

Furthermore, as I explained to
the Captain, our data files showed
that the North-West quadrant, and
Pass XI especially, were optimal
under the circumstances.

Möbius and Occam, however,

"With respect to the requirements
of art, a probable impossibility
is to be preferred to a thing
improbable and yet possible."
Aristotle,
Poetics.

"A dizzy figure in the days of figures."
Samuel Beckett,
How It Is.

"The eight Sentiments (*rasa*)
recognised in drama are
as follows: Erotic (*srhgam*),
Comic (*hanya*), Pathetic
(*lcarunn*), Furious (*ramlra*),
Heroic (*fira*), Terrible
(*bhaijanalca*), Odious
(*biblmtsa*) and Marvellous
(*adbhula*). These eight are
the Sentiments named
by Brahman... Paralysis,
Perspiration, Horripilation,
Change of Voice, Trembling,
Change of Color, Weeping
and Fainting are the eight
Temperamental States."
Bharata Muni,
Natya Shastra.

"It is only when the emotions
illumine the perceptive powers

are not on speaking terms.

I hope they resolve
their differences soon.

The crew's morale
otherwise seems all right,
and in this respect
credit must go to Avon,
one of the new recruits.

She serves as the ship's Poetess.

On several occasions recently,
as the constellation Bigfoot
was rising, Avon has inspired us
with her verse.

She recites in a rich,
exotic Voice, usually
to the accompaniment
of claves.

She is able to span
all the moods:
Wonder, Courage,
Laughter and Love
are those she most often
returns to, but there are
times when she achieves
Peace of Mind,

that we see reality."
Ezra Pound,
Translations.

"When fury rages in the breast, /
Watch the reiterating heart."
Sappho, in *7 Greeks*
(tr. G. Davenport).

"What poetry supported
her existence?"
Clarice Lispector,
"Lídia."

"In the northern Pacific,
floating in a swirling vortex,
is a mass of plastic debris
the size of Texas."
City Sierran, 2008.

"Purification practically
unknown to Olympian
worship is the keynote
of the lower stratum."
Jane Harrison,
*Prolegomena to the Study
of Greek Religion.*

"The cycle of fate encircled
the abyss of nothingness."
Hermann Broch,
The Death of Virgil.

evoking all of them at once.

With the exception of
the Commander, who has yet
to leave his cabin,
everyone gathers on deck
when Avon works her art.

There has been no news
from either Intelligence
or Communications
regarding the other fleets,
or the alien armada.

This is not unexpected,
and represents
according to the files
a transitional out-of-sync
phase between "inner"
and "outer" wavelengths.

As soon as contact is
reestablished, our surroundings
should take on new life,
and their beauty will increase.

I was alone
on the fo'c's'le deck
just a while ago, when
a shooting star fell overhead;
and the echo it made

“A chain of facts is like
a barrier reef: on one side,
there is wreckage, and beyond it
harbourage and safety.”
Alfred North Whitehead,
Process and Reality.

“And now farewell,
all you Olympians, /
You islands and mainlands
and salt sea between.”
Hesiod,
Theogony.

“And never quite lost... /
and never quite lost till the end”
Ezra Pound,
Cantos, VIII.

seemed as clear to me,
as pure and profound,
as the Red of the sky
or the Whiteness of the sea.

I felt the delight
of continual pleasure
fulfilling me, consuming me
down to the bone...
until the sea, the sky,
the silence were there again,
returning me to my solitude.

I miss you and want you,
and I know that our hearts
are forever as one.

Love,

S.

The King

My love,

I imagine, contained in my heart,
a teardrop that revolves
on a tautly drawn thread.

Pierced through its center,
it ceaselessly turns.

I write by the yew trees
of Saxe and Zildjian—
such memories come to life!

Of a time when our love
was new, and Es
not yet of the world,
not yet absent from it...

But I find myself haunted now
by an added sense of grief,
for I recently witnessed a Death.

It was at the *Carte Blanche*
in Alcatraz Province,

"'Slave, is that man your king?
—That man is not my king!
Were that man my king,
were that his fearsome brow,
were those his bison eyes,
were that his beard of lapis lazuli,
were those his fingers fine,
would a myriad not fall, a myriad
not rise, would all the nations
thereby not be overwhelmed,
would the mouths of the land
not be filled with dust, would
he not cut down the horns
of the boat?'—They hit him
and they beat him. They battered
[him] from head to toe."
The Epic of Gilgamesh,
"Bilgames and Akka:
The envoys of Akka,"
in *The Babylonian Epic Poem*
and Other Texts in Akkadian
and Sumerian (tr. A. George).

"Fortune-telling is a parascience...

beside the Bikini Oasis.

I like the ouzo they serve:
fruity and rich in aroma,
drier than at *Trompe L'Oeil*,
but less dry
than at the *Déjà Vu* nearby.

The site is as beautiful
as ever.

Especially the contrast it offers
between the Shadows below
and the open sky overhead,
with the sea barely visible
in the distance.

Because the saloon is spacious
and perched on a hill,
the Monochrome there
has a finer quality,
one I prefer, since it tends
to soften Color
in the opponent's eyes.

About twenty people were present,
including Sophia, Psychê and Brigit,
with whom I was seated,
plus others whose names
you may recognize: Ahab, Freytag,
Góngora and Thoth, Ramus,
Racter, Bombario the Dwarf.

A parascience is not a science—
it is a mixture of rules of thumb,
half-truths, and fanciful lies
painfully yoked to each other
by centuries of experience;
but a parascience can become
a science; alchemy can become
chemistry; astrology can become
astronomy; fortune-telling,
after a century of patient scientific
observation, could become a new
means of understanding time and
necessity in the universe."
Jack Spicer, "Introduction,"
in *A Plan for a Book on Tarot*
(ed. R. Blaser and J. Granger).

"Translucent planes of color
shuffled like a trick deck. Take
a card, he thought, any card."
William Gibson,
Neuromancer.

"In one sentence... the whole idea:
*Mutual cooperation can
emerge in a world of egoists
without control, by starting
with a cluster of individuals
who rely on reciprocity."*
Douglas Hofstadter, "The Prisoner's
Dilemma Computer Tournaments
and the Evolution of Cooperation,"
in *Metamagical Themas.*

The four of us
were off to the right
by the window, talking.

Rumors are plentiful,
you hardly know what to believe.

There are stories
of rampant Madness,
phantoms with Sexes
and angels in the flesh,
cash machines up in Flames,
whole leprosariums empty...

For my part
I had never observed
a Death at Cards,
but have heard
of several recent ones.

And this, with no taxes due
until The Freemason's Day.

What I saw will always
be with me, like a scar.

I remember the sudden blank
expression on the faces around me,
the silence, the Rattling
of the glasses on the tables.

"Who gives a damn for losers?"
Archie Shepp, "Un Croque Monsieur
(Poem: For Losers)."

"If you have tears,
prepare to shed them now."
William Shakespeare,
Julius Caesar.

"And the staggering Gongorisms!
...Oh eyes, no eyes,
but fountains fraught with tears!"
Aldous Huxley,
Beyond the Mexique Bay.

"Having been born
was to be full of errors
that needed correcting."
Clarice Lispector,
"The Misfortunes of Sophia."

"All men think."
Herakleitos (tr. G. Davenport).

"Well, my telephone rang
it would not stop / It's President
Kennedy callin' me up /
He said, My friend, Bob, what
do we need to make the country
grow? / I said my friend, John,
Brigitte Bardot / Anita Ekberg /
Sophia Loren / Country'll grow."

The Players in question,
two big fat men,
both of them bald,
were at the back
of the room
by a large mirror
on the other side
of the Bar.

The one who had bet
a Dollar and won
wore slippers and a robe;
his name was Koo.

His opponent, Judd,
in an undershirt and trousers,
sat motionless, staring at the table.

By the time the others
and I approached,
it was clear
that he was lost.

As for the Cards,
there were five left,
arranged in the shape
of a cross.

The seven in the first row
were gone
and in the second row

Bob Dylan, "I shall be free."

"I must create a system, or
be enslaved by another man's; /
I will not reason and compare:
my business is to create."
William Blake,
Jerusalem.

"And the running form, naked
Blake, / Shouting, whirling his arms,
the swift limbs, / Howling against
the evil, / his eyes rolling, / Whirling
like flaming cart-wheels, / and
his head held backward to gaze
on the evil / As he ran from it..."
E. Pound,
Cantos, XVI.

"What fresh hell can this be?"
Dorothy Parker, quoted in
John Keats, *You Might as Well Live.*

"What in the devil's name is this?
Do you call it squitters, pooh, crap,
turds, shit, ordure, droppings, faeces,
excrement, wolf-muck, scumber,
mute, fumets, turds, *scybala* or
spyrathia? It is, I believe, saffron
of Hibernia: / Ho, ho, hee, / Safran
d'Hibernie. / Selah! Let us drink!"
François Rabelais,
The Fourth Book of Pantagruel.

only the middle Card remained.

It was the Queen of Spades.

Along the third row
were the Five, the Four
and the Three of Hearts;
in the fourth row
was the King of Spades.

The wagers, they say,
were high from the start.

Judd had made the opening move.

Quiet and slumped in his chair,
like some true-to-life statue,
the man looked unreal—a huge,
useless thing on which was stuck
a haggard face.

In the matter of a short
while, with everyone gathered
nearby, Judd showed
the first symptom: sweat.

It formed in small patches—
on his brow, his scalp,
under his nose—and broke
into larger drops that coursed
down his face and neck.

"You shall possess your body;
you shall not become corrupt,
you shall not have worms,
you shall not be distended,
you shall not stink,
you shall not become putrid,
you shall not become worms."
The Egyptian Book of the Dead.

"Whatever opinion we may be
pleased to hold on the subject
of death, we may be sure that
it is meaningless and valueless."
Samuel Beckett,
Proust.

"If community is revealed in
the death of others, it is because
death itself is the true community
of *I's* that are not *EGOS*. It is not
a communion that fuses the *EGOS*
into an *EGO* or a higher *WE*."
Jean-Luc Nancy,
The Inoperative Community.

"And so from hour to hour
we ripe and ripe, /
And then from hour to hour
we rot and rot; /
And thereby hangs a tale."
W. Shakespeare,
As You Like It.

More drops followed,
together with tears that flowed
from his stunned eyes.

Before long, continuous streams
of tears and sweat were pouring
down his head, drenching him
and dripping onto the floor.

His gaze was unflinching,
his body paralyzed—
then came a twitch
in his lip.

Infrequent at first, it took on
a life of its own—
until a new twitch occurred,
in one eye, then in both.

It was as if the parts
of his face were being touched
by a terrible current.

While his eyes kept blinking
wildly, his mouth, his cheeks
and his ears were seized
by a series of spasms.

The tears and sweat receded.

Finally his entire head started
to tremble, and what remained

"Story, like perspective in
painting, may be an invention
to satisfy a need in experience
for design, to build a house
for feeling in time or space."
Robert Duncan,
The H. D. Book
(ed. M. Boughn and V. Coleman).

"Quéribus Castle tops
a rocky peak which is 728
metres high. It thus controls
the Garu de Maury pass and
overlooks the Roussillon Plain.
The viewpoint that it offers
from its ramparts includes
Peyrepeteus to the north-west
and stretches as far as the sea
to the south-east and the Canigou
to the south. The shape of the land
lent itself to the building of
a *castellum*... It is not out of
the question that it was built at
an earlier date than the occupation
of the castle by the Cathars."
Michèle Aué,
Cathar Country.

"I have seen Stethelos that is
below the great cataract,
and have gazed on the marsh
where Sarnath once stood.

of the sweat turned into smoke.

When the smoke had passed,
he let out a scream.

During his scream
the figures on the Cards faded
and eventually vanished.

His mouth yawned
and out came his tongue,
darting from side to side
to the Sound of a hum
in his throat.

The new Cards appeared:
The Devil above,
The Moon, *The Star*, *The Sun*
across the middle,
The Devil // reversed below.

He fell silent again,
his face as blank as before,
his body motionless.

Tragic and dreamlike,
Judd's doom unfolded
on the table.

First *The Star* turned
into *The Universe // reversed*;

I have been to Thraa, Ilarnek,
and Kadatheron on the winding
river Ai, and have dwelt long in
Olathoe in the land of Lomar...
'Canst thou tell me where
I may find Aira, the city
of marble and beryl, where
flows the hyaline Nithra and
where the falls of the tiny Kra
sing to verdant valleys and
hills forested with yath tree?'"
H. P. Lovecraft,
"The Quest of Iranon."

"Even if there is no story,
there will have been a movement,
a movement of liberation."
Hélène Cixous,
Reading with Clarice Lispector.

"Spread out the paper
and break the pen.
The wine-server has arrived."
Rumi, ghazal #1,
in Brad Gooch, *Rumi's Secret.*

"There is something to be
told about us for the telling
of which we all wait.
In our unwilling ignorance
we hurry to listen to stories of
old human life, new human life,
fancied human life, avid

next came the simultaneous
change of *The Devil*
into *The Aeon // reversed*
and *The Devil // reversed*
into *The God's House*.

Once under way,
the changes never stopped.

With the arrival of *The Skeleton*,
Judd showed new signs of life
and a pattern emerged.

After a long period of silence,
he exclaimed "Suck! Suck!
The War Cry!" and
"Remember the sharp smiles!"

He started weeping and mumbling
to himself, and all at once
the five Cards showed *The Fool*.

Overcome by grief and confusion,
often babbling incomprehensibly,
he continued to weep,
while the Cards in unison
turned blank, then into *The Fool*,
then blank—repeating
the process dozens of times.

Then *The Illusionist* came up,

of something to while away
the time of unanswered curiosity.
We know we are explainable,
and not explained. Many of
the lesser things concerning us
have been told but the greater
things have not been told;
and nothing can fill their place."
Laura Riding Jackson,
The Telling.

"I have carried you from gate
to gate... My pen halts, though
I do not. Reader, you will walk
no more with me. It is time we both
take up our lives. To this account,
I, Severian the Lame, Autarch,
do set my hand in what shall be
called the last year of the old sun."
Gene Wolfe,
The Book of the New Sun.

"They froze me into silence."
W. Shakespeare,
Timon of Athens.

"Hot and torpid, our thoughts
revolve endlessly in a kind
of maniacal abstraction,
an abstraction so involuted,
so dangerously valiant,
that my own energies seem
perilously close to exhaustion,

announcing the start of Judd's
final agony.

The Cards followed in succession,
turning blank each time in between.

Seized with terror,
Judd described a Beast
part-human and part-machine,
walking toward him with a limp.

As the Cards pursued their course
and the Beast drew near,
Judd became obsessed
by the mask it wore,
a mask "shaped like a Y,"
that was "screwed to its nose."

He shouted "No! No! No!"
as Number X,
The Wheel of Chance,
came and went.

With Number XII,
The Hanged One,
his fear reached its peak.

"It's turning upside down!"
he screamed.

In his final utterance,
he described a "huge, long tooth..."
and "Ping-Pong balls... for eyes...

to morbid termination. Well,
have we reached a crisis?
Which way do we turn?
Which way do we travel?
...Doubtless my changes are
matched by your own. You.
But you are a person, a human
being. I am silicon and epoxy,
energy enlightened by
line current. What distances,
what chasms, are to be bridged
here? Leave me alone, and
what can happen? This."
The Policeman's Beard Is Half
Constructed: Computer Prose
and Poetry by Racter.

"Great God! His yellow skin
scarcely covered the work of
muscles and arteries beneath...
I beheld the wretch—
the miserable monster whom
I had created... his eyes,
if eyes they be called,
were fixed on me. His jaws
opened, and he muttered
some inarticulate sounds, while
a grin wrinkled his cheeks.
He might have spoken,
but I did not hear; one hand
was stretched out, seemingly
to detain me, but I escaped,
and rushed down the stairs."

with Toothpicks through them!"

He began to laugh,
and fell off his chair
onto the floor.

Five copies of *The Skeleton*,
Number XIII, were in place.

As the Cards turned blank again,
the laughter gave way to Coughing.

His face swelled and grew dark.

When *The Skeleton // reversed*
suddenly appeared,
his body stiffened,
his eyes bulged, and he fell
flat on his back,
letting out a long squeal.

A last faint cry,
and then silence.

Judd was Dead;
the Cards on the table
were blank.

Despite the horror
of what we had witnessed,
a sense of relief

Mary Shelley,
Frankenstein.

"Now I am ready to tell
how bodies are changed /
Into different bodies."
Ted Hughes,
Tales from Ovid.

"Dionysus... was hailed as
the god-begotten, virgin-born
Anointed One (*Christos*)
whose mother seems to have
been all three forms
of the Triple Goddess...
He was also a Horned God,
with such forms as bull, goat,
and stag. According to the classic
story of his dismemberment,
the god took such animal forms
in rapid succession to avoid
the onslaught of the Titans... who
eventually caught him, tore him
to pieces and devoured him."
Barbara G. Walker,
*The Woman's Encyclopedia of
Myths and Secrets,* "Dionysus."

"As men's prayers are a disease
of the will, so are their creeds
a disease of the intellect."
Ralph Waldo Emerson,
"Self-Reliance."

came over the room.

In due course, the figures
returned to the Cards
(the King of Spades,
Queen of Spades,
the three Hearts).

Patches of Ice developed here
and there: nature was taking over.

The various patches spread
and proceeded to merge,
coating Judd's body
with a thin film
that gradually thickened
into a bloc.

He remained encased for some time,
his features indistinguishable.

I stood by only as long
as it took for the Shit
to manifest.

It first began to show through
in the regions of his forehead,
belly and knees—
small dark clusters beneath the Ice,
growing, as if coming to life.

"Mirth cannot move
a soul in agony."
W. Shakespeare,
Love's Labour Lost.

"And now distill your mind /
to its airiest essence, allowing
the subtle elixirs of thought to
permeate and penetrate every pore
of the problem. Then Analyze,
Refine, Synthesize, Define."
Aristophanes,
The Clouds.

"I am flatly taking Socrates as
the progenitor, his methodology
still the RULE: 'I'll stick my logic up,
and classify, boy, classify you
right out of existence.'"
C. Olson,
"The Gate and the Center."

"It is here, in the imagery of
alchemical art, that some
commentators see a possible
connection with the imagery
of Tarot... A very simplified
version of these connections
would place The Fool
as the *prima materia* and
The Magician as the alchemist.
The Papess and The Empress

Judd's Mutation into Shit was
slow at first, according to Thoth.

As noted in *The Chixulub Field Guide,* the Ice stopped
melting three Days later.

To no one's surprise the saloon
was quickly abandoned.

There is one further detail
I should mention.

The Bartender at the *Carte Blanche*,
a woman by the name of
Mazda, was a former Essentialist
who had just turned Liquidationist.

Liquidationists, like Gastanoans
and 'Pataphysicians, consider
the nature and ultimate
Fate of Shit undecidable.

Such ironies currently seem the rule.

Not only has the incidence
of Death by fear reached
extraordinary proportions,
but most cases reveal
a pattern of sorts.

would be the spiritual
and material versions of
the feminine principle.
The Pope and the Emperor
would fill the same roles
for the masculine principle,
and The Lovers would be
the 'chemical marriage.'"
Cynthia Giles,
The Tarot.

"In a now lost piece, the young
Aristotle makes a reference to
the torture practiced by
the Etruscan pirates. In that text,
Aristotle draws a comparison
between the soul tethered to
the body and the living chained
to a dead corpse (*nekrous*):
'Aristotle says, that we are
punished much as those who
once upon a time, when they had
fallen into the hands of Etruscan
robbers, were slain with elaborate
cruelty; their bodies, the living
(*corporaviva*) with the dead,
were bound so exactly as possible
one against another: so our souls,
tied together with our bodies as
the living fixed upon the dead
[quoted by Cicero, in *Hortensius*].'
...This fragment subtly points to

In the suburbs of Occident,
for example, only saloons
associated with Continuists,
Assymetrists and Cleanheads
have been affected—
three schools with a shared belief
that the Aura of Shit decreases
but never disappears.

In the Province of Neume,
where Triumphalists and
Neo-Alarmists predominate,
Death has occurred in all
the saloons save for two,
the *Raison d'Etre*
and the *Fait Accompli*,
both of which have strong
Harmolodeon ties.

There are other examples
just as bizarre.

The fact remains that Death
has struck nearly everywhere.

That profound forces are at work
can no longer be doubted.

So I wait.

a moment in philosophy when
both the philosophy of Ideas and
the science of being qua being
are fundamentally built upon
putrefaction and act in accordance
with the chemistry of decay."
Reza Negarestani,
"The Corpse Bride:
Thinking with Nigredo."

"Taking myself the exact
dimensions of Jehovah and
laying them away, / Lithographing
Kronos and Zeus his son, and
Hercules his grandson, / Buying
drafts of Osiris and Isis and Belus
and Brahma and Adonai, /
In my portfolio placing Manito
loose, and Allah on a leaf, and
the crucifix engraved, / With Odin,
and the hideous-faced Mexitli,
and all idols and images, /
Honestly taking them all for what
they are worth, and not a cent
more, / Admitting they were alive
and did the work of their day."
W. Whitman,
Leaves of Grass.

"Three thousand years ago I lost
my head, and all that was left
were phonetic fragments of me."

C. Lispector,

Remembering you, desiring you. *The Passion According to G. H.*

Your lover,

A.

The Philosopher

Dear A.,

"Athos fenced with as much
calmness and method as if he had
been practicing in a fencing school. /
Porthos... played with skill
and prudence. Aramis, who had
the third canto of his poem to finish,
behaved like a man in haste. /
Athos killed his adversary first."
Alexandre Dumas (*père*),
The Three Musketeers.

"I'm so happy because today /
I've found my friends /
They're in my head."
Nirvana, "Lithium."

"We know that there is no help
for us but from one another,
that no hand will save us
if we do not reach out our hand.
And the hand that you reach out
is empty, as mine is. You have nothing.
You possess nothing. You own
nothing. You are free. All you have

As I write,
we sail with the ABARIS
and the SOLARIS
toward Oops, the fabled region
where four seas come together:
the Meridian, the Rarian,
the Koppa and the Stigma.

Tragically, a third Indian vessel,
the ARAMIS, is gone,
destroyed by a violent explosion.

The disaster occurred soon after
the fleet had drawn into view.

All of us were on deck
at the time, except
for the Commander.

The three ships
lay on the horizon
at equal intervals,
with the ship on the left
nearest to us and

is what you are, and what you give."
Ursula Le Guin,
The Dispossessed.

"Comprehension does not mean
denying the outrageous, deducing
the unprecedented from precedents,
or explaining phenomenas by such
analogies and generalizations that
the impact of reality and the shock
of experience are no longer felt...
Comprehension, in short, means
the unpremeditated, attentive
facing up to, and resisting of reality
—whatever it may be."
Hannah Arendt,
The Origins of Totalitarianism.

"The fireworks have gone off.
Gray is the absolute color
of the present tense."
Alice Rahon,
"Despair, *to Pablo Picasso."*

"So quick bright things
come to confusion."
William Shakespeare,
A Midsummer Night's Dream.

"Such is also the truceless warfare
of the waves on the surface of
the sea, whilst profound peace
reigns in the depths below.

the one on the right,
the ARAMIS, furthest away.

I was aft, by the mizzenmast,
and I remember Marlboro saying:
"Lo! There's *doom* there!"

Then came a Sound
that none of us recognized,
like the Sound you imagine
wind would make,
if the wind had Sound—
and suddenly on the horizon,
where the ARAMIS had been,
an intense flash of light.

It was clear
that the ARAMIS
had met a terrible Fate.

According to Finn the Stammerer,
Captain of the ABARIS,
whose ship was next in line,
what he and his crew witnessed
prior to the explosion
was the ARAMIS
beginning to slip out of view,
becoming ethereal.

Voices from the crew
of the doomed ship

The billows clash and collide with
each other, as they strive to find
their level. A fringe of snow-white
foam, feathery and frolicsome,
follows their changing outlines.
From time to time, the receding
wave leaves behind a remnant
of foam on the sandy beach.
The child, who plays hard by,
picks up a handful, and, the next
moment, is astonished to find
that nothing remains in his grasp
but a few drops of water, water
that is far more brackish, far more
bitter than that of the wave which
brought it. Laughter comes into
being in the selfsame fashion.
It indicates a slight revolt
on the surface of social life.
It instantly adopts the changing
forms of the disturbance. It, also,
is a froth with a saline base.
Like froth, it sparkles. It is gaiety
itself. But the philosopher who
gathers a handful to taste may
find that the substance is scanty,
and the after-taste bitter."
Henry Bergson,
Laughter.

"For in the sea, nothing is lost.
One dies, another lives,
as the precious elements

seemed to rise
and inhabit the air
before drifting away.

Then the ABARIS heard
the same strange Sound
that we ourselves had heard.

And without further warning,
the blast.

As if the entire Crystal
structure, all at once, had
disintegrated into a brilliant
ball of shards and Dust.

Pure in its Fiery Whiteness,
meteoric, the explosion was over
before anyone realized
what had happened.

Only haze and
a blanket of Fog remained.

Yet the water was marked.

The figure on the water
was almost the size
of the Rorschach Straits,
and took the appearance
of a large disk,

of life are passed on and on
in endless chains."
Rachel Carson,
Under the Sea Wind.

"The crystal ship is being filled /
A thousand girls, a thousand thrills."
The Doors, "The Crystal Ship."

"If on this ship I'm number one /
For special reasons that was done, /
Yes, I'm the first one here you see /
Because I like my library."
Sebastian Brant,
The Ship of Fools.

"I pored over the electronic
catalogue, asking it questions
to which it responded... by spitting
out a slip of paper... The library
was located in the very center
of the Station; as such it had
no windows and was the most
isolated place inside the steel shell...
I wandered about the large space
till finally I came to a stop in front
of a huge bookcase, reaching up
to the ceiling and filled with books.
It wasn't so much an indulgence
and a very dubious one at that,
as a respectful memorial to
the pioneers of solaristic exploration:
the shelves, on which there were

with a prominent inward-
curving stem or tail.

Over its total surface, except
for a small central whirlpool,
the sea was boiling wildly—
a state likely to last, according
to readings taken by the ABARIS
in its circumnavigation of the area.

The Sound produced by
the bubbles, audible even to us,
was measured at 6 point 9.

As for the presence of echoes,
nothing was heard or registered,
although they seem sure to emerge.

Both the SOLARIS and
the ABARIS remain in mourning
for one more Day,
as is the custom in Indiana.

We look forward to
the end of the lamentations.

Our close formation,
as we approach Nazca Pass,
plus the strangeness
of their Voices, have made
the gloom on board unremitting.

perhaps six hundred volumes,
contained all the classics of
the discipline... I took out the tomes,
so heavy they made my hand droop,
and flipped through them idly
as I perched on the arm of a chair."
Stanislav Lem,
Solaris.

"I would be an historian
as Herodotus was, looking /
for oneself for the evidence of /
what is said"
Charles Olson,
The Maximus Poems.

"It has always seemed to me
a rare privilege, this, of being
an American, a real American, one
whose tradition it has taken scarcely
sixty years to create. We need only
realize our parents, remember
our grandparents and know ourselves
and our history is complete."
Gertrude Stein,
The Making of Americans.

"One will recall that in 1500
the earth's population is on the order
of some 400 million, of which 80
inhabit the Americas. In the middle
of the sixteenth century, of those
80 million, 10 remain. Or to limit

In fact, not only morale,
but also the ship's performance
have suffered a serious reversal,
for reasons hard to explain.

Part of the trouble seems
due to a change of wind,
the ion-rich Nommo
having yielded of late
to its contrary
out of the West, the Jinx.

How distant that spell
of good feeling appears,
before the ARAMIS exploded!

I remember (all of us do)
the elation, the sense of beauty
in the world.

Poetry seemed the rule.

Ben-Cnopee danced at the bow
of the ship, while Sony played
the concertina.

Lensmen as happy as could be!

Sinbad the Steward
told joke after joke,

oneself to Mexico: on the eve of
the Conquest, its population is about
25 million; in 1600 it is 1 million."
Tzvetan Todorov,
The Conquest of America.

"Through the round numbers /
and the colored nerves /
the stars are made /
and the worlds are sounds."
Frida Kahlo,
The Diary of Frida Kahlo.

"I do not believe that our era
and the results of our civilization
will be as predicted; I feel certain
we are in the presence of an immense
gathering for a "new"—however
intense the rapid disintegration
of the past approach to knowledge
may be, concomitant as it is with
a vast break-up in social forms,
there appears to be a sensitive stir
abroad in the world which, with
the powerful leverage of despair,
may boil into a new concoction.
From such an immense accumulation
as our civilization represents
must necessarily flow a torrent
of disintegration."
Frances M. Boldereff,
Hermes to his Son Thoth.

amusing the crew
as the ship sailed along.

It was as if past thrills
kept being renewed,
and were ours to share.

I sat in the galley
with Kodak and Wang, and
described to them our tryst,
long ago, in Xerox Grove
by the Esperanto Abyss,
and how the angels
whispered through the pines
and the palm trees.

I knew that the pleasure
I had in reliving that time
was theirs too as they listened,
for such was the feeling
on board, the exhilaration
that seemed to prevail.

Now, much has changed.

Tempers are short.

There have been tantrums
and bizarre outbursts.

Leiningen shows signs of going Mad,
along with others in Engineering:
Mazüka, Fiat, Finnegan, Meade...

"I see it feelingly."
W. Shakespeare,
King Lear.

"Fire in water, / air in earth /
water in air / and earth in the sea."
Antonin Artaud,
The New Revelations of Being.

"Let me conclude my account of
the Hyperboreans, for I shall not tell
the story of Abaris, said to have been
a Hyperborean who went around
the whole world carrying an arrow
and eating nothing... It makes
me laugh when I see so many
people nowadays drawing maps of
the earth and not one of them giving
an intelligent representation of it.
They draw Ocean flowing around
the whole earth, portray the earth
to be more perfectly circular than if
it were drawn with a compass, and
make Asia the same size as Europe."
Herodotus,
The Histories.

"Linear A and Linear B scripts...
were both lost and forgotten
for centuries. In historical times,
the Greeks lost three other letters
that they had taken on a trial basis
from the Phoenicians: *san, koppa,*

Part of the problem
is that several of the ship's
systems are malfunctioning.

After the ARAMIS blew up,
a multi-headed
probe \ deflector device
triggered gradimetric
and gradometric oscillations
in the phaser bank,
causing automobiline leaks
in the diatransmeta.

Sensor and tricorder readings
showed Absolüt zero.

Segmentometers
and stratometers
stayed virtually flat.

In succession,
the anticipator mechanism,
the interval analyzer and
the Wilson-Lincoln system
underwent brief Energizing delays.

A series of glitches ensued,
in the course of which
a mysterious noise was heard,
a noise that gives way
with each new malfunction
to a different noise

and *digamma* (also known as *vau*)."
Alexander & Nicholas Humez,
Alpha to Omega.

"Language is one
of humanity's errors."
Marcel Duchamp,
interview with Otto Hahn
in *L'Express*, #684 (23 Jul. 1964).

"Tao begets One; one begets two;
two begets three; three begets
all things. All things are backed
by the Shade (yin) and faced by
the Light (yang), and harmonized
by the immaterial Breath (ch'i)."
Tao Tê Ching.

"I find what connects and leads,
to an encounter. / I find something—
like language—immaterial, yet
terrestrial, something circular that
returns to itself across both poles
while—cheerfully—even crossing
the tropics: I find... a *meridian*."
Paul Celan,
"The Meridian."

elsewhere in the ship.

From the gas cylinder,
it has just passed
to the #2 lithium mold.

Despite the setbacks, and barring
the unforeseen, our rendezvous
with the Zen and Jovian fleets
seems likely to occur on schedule.

Perhaps this is so
because we are sailing
toward Oops, and benefit
from some influence that
helps us resist our fear.

I try to be strong,
as when this weïrd voyage
began, and the memory
of our loss returned.

You are alive within me.

Your love,

S.

The Lovers

Dear S.,

If you were not alive
within me, I would be
in Philadelphia,
with those who read
Miscellanies in their wish
to go Mad.

Consider that Lesbos,
Xanadu, Patmos, Babel
have pearls on their shores
as far as the eye
can see; that Mecca Bay
lies empty, open land
before a wall of water
from Monte Carlo to Punjab;
that a great wave,
worse than any since the Flood,
has poisoned Chernobyl
and Cape Town;
that the Shaded waters
off Telstar are probably
bottomless now...

I write from Apple,

"The way of the world is to bloom
and flower and die but in the affairs
of men there is no waning and
the moon of his expression signals
the onset of night... His meridian
is at once his darkening and
the evening of his day. He loves
games? Let him play for stakes."
Cormac McCarthy,
Blood Meridian.

"Consider the well-known
card trick, 'forced choice.'
You want to make someone choose,
for example, the king of hearts.
You say first of all: 'Do you prefer
red or black?' If he answers
'Red,' you withdraw the black
cards from the table; if he replies
'Black' you take the red cards
and again you withdraw them.
You have only to continue: 'Do you
prefer hearts or diamonds?' Until
'Do you prefer the king or the queen

between Times Square
and Our Lady of Lucifer.

My only solace,
when I think of you
and where you are,
is the stubborn belief
that the turmoil here
is no different.

Nature seems a prison;
yet what reappears
is a vision of absence,
our own cells unoccupied.

Word is spreading that Madness
has struck both Rex-King
and Dexter-King, and the Queen
has fallen Asleep in Orient.

Worse still, those who say so
are themselves Mad, or at least
the story can be traced
to someone who is.

These events came
to my Attention
through 'eccO the Actor.

It was after a difficult hand
at the *Avant-Garde*

of hearts?' The binary machine
works in this way… The point is
that the machine goes beyond us
and serves other ends… In fact
the binary machine is an important
component of apparatuses of power.
So many dichotomies will be
established that there will be
enough for everyone to be pinned
to the wall, sunk in a hole."
Gilles Deleuze and Claire Parnet,
Dialogues.

"That completed, the cards would
be brought out—not for play but
to learn from them hundreds of little
delights and novelties all of which
derived from arithmetic."
François Rabelais,
Gargantua.

"I sing the body electric, /
The armies of those I love
engirth me and I engirth them, /
They will not let me off till I go
with them, respond to them, / And
discorrupt them, and charge them
full with the charge of the soul."
Walt Whitman,
Leaves of Grass.

"Voice is a kind of sound
characteristic of what has

in Rhetro Province,
beside the Pool of Dreamings.

(The ouzo there has balance,
light-bodied with a soft
bouquet, like at the former
Tic Douloureux.)

Death felt imminent,
closer than ever.

I faced the Polychrome
statue of a masked figure,
larger than life, whose phallus
poked straight through
the top of a bald head
impaled in its lap.

Rounded and smooth
at the end, the phallus,
like a rod about which
the head continued to
rotate, shone a White beam
that lit Dollar signs
on the ceiling.

To either side of the statue,
gazing out from the wall,
were monstrous eyes
as wide as doors,
one of which (the left?
the right?) blinked periodically.

soul in it; nothing that is
without soul utters voice."
Aristotle,
On the Soul.

"We may define colour as the limit
of the Translucent in the body."
Aristotle,
On Sense and the Sensible.

"A propos of sleep, that sinister
adventure of all our nights,
we may say that men go to bed
daily with an audacity that would
be incomprehensible if we did
not know that it is the result
of ignorance of the danger."
Charles Baudelaire, quoted in
H. P. Lovecraft, "Hypnos."

"No one here gets to transcend
out of this landscape."
Kip Hanrahan, "No one gets
to transcend anything
(No One Except Oil Company
Executives)," in *Coup de Tête.*

"Transcendence is always
a product of immanence."
G. Deleuze,
"Immanence: A Life."

"There are many kinds of open. /

Beneath a grid on the floor
lay a Red patch of sky.

The air smelled of sulfur.

Voices babbled.

I knew that my only hope
was the memory
of the last wager
—13 cents—
yet Number XIII,
in its correspondence
with *The Skeleton*,
interfered with my knowledge
of the ruling hand: whether
five Cards remained or six.

Then, to the far left,
a Bluish form glimmered
momentarily.

The setup became clear to me:
a vertical Rhomboid,
consisting of six Cards
on four rows.

The impaled head
turned into a skull,
the eyes on the wall closed,
and the light from the phallus
went out, obscuring
the Dollar signs on the ceiling.

How a diamond comes into a knot
of flame / How a sound comes
into a word, coloured /
By who pays what for speaking."
Audre Lorde, "Coal."

"Commodity, the bias
of the world; / the world,
who of itself is piezed well, / Made to
run even upon even ground, /
Till this advantage, this vile-drawing
bias, / This sway of motion,
this Commodity, / Makes it take head
from all indifferency, / From all
direction, purpose, course, intent."
William Shakespeare,
King John.

"Nine in the second place means: /
Dragon appearing in the field. /
It furthers one to see the great man."
I Ching (tr. R. Wilhelm).

"I squeezed that sperm till a strange
sort of insanity came over me."
H. Melville,
Moby Dick.

"The fateful process of civilization
would thus have set in with man's
adoption of an erect posture.
From that point the chain of
events would have proceeded

Intuiting my wager, I exclaimed:
"21!"

After the brief Sound
of wind chimes,
and severe Nausea,
I found myself
in the saloon once again,
alone opposite my double.

S/he removed *The Scales* and
The Arts from the third line,
and repeated the wager.

At which point
the original Cards returned,
and I was out
of the dreamscape.

Before me, in loincloth,
cuirass and running shoes,
sat my opponent, Daedalus
of Lascô Province.

I played the Queen and King
of Coins off the third line,
as foreseen in *The Scales*
and *The Arts*.

Daedalus went on to win,

through the devaluation of olfactory
stimuli and the isolation of
the menstrual period to the time
when visual stimuli were paramount
and the genitals became visible,
and thence to the continuity of
sexual excitation, the founding of
the family and so to the threshold
of human civilization."
Sigmund Freud,
Civilization and Its Discontents.

"In the state of degeneration,
in which we live, it is through
the skin that metaphysics will
be made to reenter our minds."
Antonin Artaud, "The Theater
of Cruelty (First Manifesto)."

"Chrysippus connects Zeus, reason,
semen, and matter in the following
allegory: in an erotic painting
portraying Hera performing a sexual
act—apparently fellatio—with Zeus
(Origen [*Contra Celsum*],
Theophilius [*Ad Autolycum*]...).
According to Origen, Chryssipus
discussed this painting to illustrate
how 'matter receives the generative
principles of God, and contains
them in itself for the ordering
of the universe.' So understood,
the allegory seems to present Zeus'

but with the loss
on my last Card
at 61 cents
I count my blessings.

semen as the origin of the whole
cosmos, and Hera as the matter.
But how exactly should we interpret
this illustration? In particular: how
should we understand the relationship
between Zeus and Hera?"
Malin Grahn-Wilder,
Gender and Sexuality
in Stoic Philosophy.

It was because of 'eccO
that my course changed.

The Blue specter glimpsed
from the corner of my eye
—before the layout of
the Cards reoccurred to me—
was the emanation from 'eccO
at the moment he walked
into the saloon.

"Truth has nothing in common
with *allegorical figures*,
with the figures of *nude women*:
but that foot, belonging to a man
alive just a short while ago,
that foot had the violence—
the negative violence—of truth."
George Bataille, fragment
from a manuscript preface to
The Dead Man (in Lucette Finas,
La Toise et le Vertige).

Through a twist of Fate,
his entrance was the signal
from outside.

I found him at the Bar
afterward, and during our talk
learned about the Queen's
Sleep and the Kings' Madness.

"Into his muscles, into his feet
the terror flooded, his aura of
terror flooded, / (Bilgames)
could not *move* his foot from
the ground. / His foot was *held fast*
by his big toe. / In his flank,
in his... it flooded."
The Epic of Gilgamesh,
"Bilgames and Huwawa:
The Lord to the Living One's
Mountain" (tr. A. George).

But I could tell he himself
was not well, especially
from the way he interrupted
his sentences with a click
of the tongue and a slap
on the forehead.

When he finally left,
smiling and serene, he was
"bound for the soothing
waters of Baalbec."

Almost certainly
he will enter the sea there
and sleep.

What I saw earlier
was no less troubling.

I was with Libra
and a small crowd of others,
among whom Romeo and
Gwenhwyvar, Gilgamesh,
Go-go, Video and Robot.

Before me stood a cash machine.

It was of Proto-Futurist type,
with Depression and Rococo
elements, more common
to meteor country.

And pointing up at the sky,
protruding from the controls,
was a man's leg!

The Camouflage pattern

"A figure materialized on
the landing just below where
Valentinus lay. The being grinned
up at him. Speech returned
to him, in a shocked whisper.
'Not Achamoth, but you!
The *antiminon pneuma*,
my Counterfeit Spirit!
My psyche feigning the glory of
my spark.' His double, not fully
materialized, continued to smile
triumphantly... and Valentinus
painfully scrambled up to confront
this mockery of himself...
The double, still smiling, bent down
to retrieve a jagged chunk of stone
that Valentinus had broken away.
Straightened up again,
the Counterfeit Spirit mounted
toward Valentinus, the stone
held high over its head
by both hands, ready to strike.
'Elaborated error,' Valentin
unflinchingly cried. 'Dissolve
back into ether!' The stone fell
and crumbled upon the lower stairs.
Valentinus peered into the half
light, but his double was gone."
Harold Bloom,
The Flight to Lucifer.

"The divine names Bran, Saturn,

on the pants phased in
and out of the background,
against the Iridescence
enwrapping the machine,
and the large dark boot
held high seemed the center
of an unworldly form.

(Even now, a mist seems to
veil the machine, setting it
apart within the courtyard.)

When I arrived at the scene,
I overheard the name "Monroe,"
and that of his wife, "Lee."

I did not immediately notice
the woman, short and plump,
lying face down on the ground
in a T-shirt and jeans.

Next to her Pesos and
Y'en sat cross-legged,
in dark glasses.

From what I could gather
they alone saw
what had happened.

According to Pesos and Y'en,
Monroe, dressed in a uniform,
with a strange curved club
fixed to his belt,

Cronos... are applied to the ghost
of Hercules that floats off
in the alder-wood boat
after his mid-summer sacrifice.
His tanist, or other self, appearing
in Greek legend as Poeas
who lighted Hercules' pyre and
inherited his arrows, succeeds
him for the second half of
the year, having acquired royal
virtue by marriage with the queen...
He is in turn succeeded
by the New Year Hercules."
Robert Graves,
The White Goddess.

"Leave the boy alone, wild boar /
Whether you haunt the lush pasture
lands / Or the intricate corners
of hanging woods on the hills /
Don't whet your tusks for the fight /
But send him back safe to me."
Sulpicia, "Cerinthus Goes
Pig-Sticking," in *The Poems of Sulpicia*
(tr. J. Heath-Stubbs).

"When we come to Chretien's
poem we find... there are, not
one, but two, disabled kings;
one suffering from the effects of
a wound, the other in extreme
old age. Chretien's poem being
incomplete we do not know

marched into the courtyard
followed by Lee
several paces behind.

Monroe went over
to the cash machine,
as if to pay taxes.

Then he reached for his club,
and, raising it with the back
of his hand turned inward,
appeared to shove it
through the panel.

They said they saw the club
"go into the screen."

The machine began
to "engulf the man."

Currents of electricity
coursed over it,
to the Sound of screams.

Vibrating strongly,
the cash machine
"pulled him in,"
consuming first Monroe's
arm, then his head and torso,
until all but one foot
had passed beyond.

Lee collapsed.

what he intended to be the result
of the achieved Quest...
The Parzival of von Eschenbach
follows the same tradition...
Here we find the wounded King
was healed, but what becomes of
the aged man... we are not told."
Jesse Weston,
From Ritual to Romance.

"Gwenhwyfar felt
the familiar nausea gripping
the pit of her stomach."
Marion Zimmer Bradley,
The Mists of Avalon.

"If one gets indignant about certain
impartial descriptions of the world
and man, it is not, as one claims,
because they are 'depressing'...
It is because the evil that they reveal
comes out of man's freedom.
The 'bastards' of *La Nausée* chose
to be that way; it is completely
up to them to be lucid and honest,
and to repudiate the lie behind
which they shelter themselves."
Simone de Beauvoir, "Existentialism
and Popular Wisdom."

"Artaud Rewrites his Letter:
When I saw O, I wanted
to protect her because

Finally, the boot began to rise,
revealing the leg in full.

There was silence, and
soon after came the echoes.

Such at least was Pesos's
and Y'en's account of
what they had witnessed.

The echoes exist
as surely as the leg itself.

I could hear them well.

And I still hear them
from here, however faintly.

Their intermittent Sound
is no mere illusion.

They are loud and clear,
unfathomably distant,
like the Sound of shooting stars;
yet they issue from down below...
darker, hollower, more Metallic.

A falling into place.

she worships her cunt."
Kathy Acker,
Pussy, King of the Pirates.

"The origins of the tarot are
shrouded in mystery. It seems that
the high priests of ancient Egypt
transmitted their secret knowledge
by means of pictorial symbols and
that these symbols were the twenty-
two Major Arcana of the tarot pack.
It is believed that Moses brought
these cards with him to Israel,
having received them from
the high priests of Egypt. That
explains why the Hebrew cabala
is linked to the twenty-two cards
(tarot – tora – rota)... The first
tarot cards we know of were found
in Italy, designed by Bonifacio
Bembo in the fifteenth century
for the Visconti family of Milan
...It was not until the eighteenth
century that Antoine Court de
Gébelin rediscovered their
esoteric meaning... The Major
Arcana are engraved in stone
inside the dome of Siena."
Niki de Saint Phalle,
The Tarot Garden.

"Ah, the minutes twinkle in and
out / And in and out come and go /

You are the heart and soul
of my life, now and always.

Love,

A.

One by one, none by none, / What
we know, what we don't know."
Laura Riding, "Yes And No."

The War Machine

"In the church of my heart
the choir's in flames!"
Vladimir Mayakovsky,
"Cloud in Trousers."

"Near and / Hard to grasp, the god."
Friedrich Hölderlin,
"Patmos."

"One needs to be blind to some extent
in order to perceive certain things."
Clarice Lispector,
Near to the Wild Heart.

"There are gods here too."
Herakleitos (tr. G. Davenport).

"'—And how do you know
the gods exist?
—Simple: just look at the way
they're treating me.'"
Aristophanes,
Knights.

Dear A.,

Since our most recent adventure,
the memory of a bad dream
has stirred in the hollow
of my soul, like the dark
Metallic echoes said to haunt
bottomless rifts in the sea.

I was suspended
off the ground
by a Magnetic Field
that pressed me against a wall.

I felt exhilarated.

There was an uncanny Sound,
like the constant echo
of a great meteor.

I remember closing my eyes.

The pleasure grew more extreme.

Patterns of Shade appeared,
one after the other; slower, faster,

"The prototypical Roman hero-
charioteer was the god Mars,
son of the Blessed Virgin Juno.
The twelfth-century *Liber Imaginum*
Deorum said Mars in his chariot
symbolized leadership, glory, war,
and death... He in turn might be
traced back to the pre-Vedic
'red god' Rudra... In his native land,
Rudra merged with both Shiva
and Krishna, who expounded
the secrets of Fate to prince Arjuna
in the guise of a divine charioteer."
Barbara G. Walker,
The Secrets of the Tarot.

"God is neither good / nor evil, /
neither loving / nor hating
God is Power. God is change."
Octavia E. Butler,
Parable of the Sower.

"You don't need a weatherman /
to know which way the wind blows."
Bob Dylan,
"Subterranean Homesick Blues."

"In the thinly populated desert area
north of Tamaghis a portentous event
occurred. Some say it was a meteor
that fell to earth leaving a crater
twenty miles across. Others say
that the crater was caused by what

like Apokalyptic signs.

Then I tried to open
my eyes... and discovered
that I was blind!

I found myself split apart,
torn between a surge of panic,
as I struggled against
my blindness, and the bliss
that still possessed me.

The schism felt unbearable.

I thought it was Death.

Later, I told my dream
to Intelligence: to Tarzan,
who discussed it with Venus.

They agreed it was pure illusion,
because of conditions here
in the Meridian Sea,
outside the Waters of Oops.

Maria was uncommitted;
she too was bothered
by a bad dream.

Furthermore, I was sixth in line
to be heard (after Bismark,

modern physicists call a black hole. / After this occurrence the whole northern sky lit up red at night, like the reflection from a vast furnace."
William Burroughs,
Cities of the Red Night.

"We define the 'war machine' as a linear assemblage which is constructed on lines of flight. In this sense, the war machine does not at all have war as its object; it has as its object a very special space, *smooth space*, which it composes, occupies, and propagates. *Nomadism* is precisely this combination 'war machine—smooth space...'"
Gilles Deleuze,
Negotiations.

"We are imprisoned in the realm of life, like a sailor on his tiny boat, on an infinite ocean."
Anna Freud, in E. Young-Bruehl,
Anna Freud: A Biography.

"I'll trace the wake of vessels in the air, the pathway over the waters, the pupil's mirage."
Claude Cahun, "Disavowals."

"In the literary machine that Proust's *In Search of Lost Time* constitutes,

Cîpher, Bedlam, Q'bal
and ben-Cnopee),
and with others still waiting.

Events had already taken a bad
turn, when a shooting star fell
into the Waters of Oops,
the legendary sea between
the Digamma, the Koppa,
the Rarian and the Meridian.

The column of Fire was
visible from our position
in the central sector
of the Meridian.

We had been scheduled
to link up at Absolüt Point
with the combined fleets
of the Jovians and Zen.

The Jovian Commander,
still in the Koppa, described
the disaster as follows:
"As per Maxwell's
Last Compendium, Volume II,
Part ii, Section 123, Subsection 345,
Lines 56-67 and 78-89."

As you can imagine, we watched
the meteor's fall closely.

we are struck by the fact that all
the parts are produced as asymmetrical
sections, paths that suddenly come
to an end, hermetically sealed boxes,
non-communicating vessels, water-
tight compartments in which there
are gaps even between things that are
contiguous, gaps that are affirmations,
pieces of a puzzle belonging not to any
one puzzle but many, pieces assembled
by forcing them into a certain place
where they may or may not belong,
their unmatched edges violently forced
out of shape, forcibly made to fit
together, to interlock, with a number
of pieces always left over. It is a schizoid
work par excellence: it is almost
as though the author's guilt,
his confessions of guilt are merely
a sort of joke. (In Kleinian terms,
it might be said that the depressive
position is only a cover-up for a more
deeply rooted schizoid attitude.)"
Gilles Deleuze and Felix Guattari,
Anti-Oedipus.

"Aeschylus shows in a magnified form
an aspect of normal development
...When the depressive position
is reached and worked through...
guilt becomes predominant
and persecution diminishes."
Melanie Klein, "Some Reflections

The shockwaves
from the time of its standstill
over the water
until the whirlpool's opening
(since called: "High Holy
of High Holies")
sent a full-scale tremor
through the ship.

The situation here is tense.

Since our transit of Nazca Pass,
an unexplained noise
on board has traveled from
the Atomatic convertor, to
the recyclotron, to the keyboard
of Möbius the Mapper,
where I can hear it now.

Möbius, overcome by Sleep,
lies in the Engine room
by the propeller shaft,
in a pool of water.

And hanging directly
above Möbius, upside down,
with her foreleg stuck
through a hole in the ceiling,
is Occam the Weatherwoman,
cursing and shouting for help...

on 'The Oresteia.'"

"The water I taste is warm and
salt, like the sea, / And comes
from a country far away as health."
Sylvia Plath, "Tulips."

"do domi not passi do not dominate /
do not dominate / your passive
passions not / ...do devouring not
not dominate / your rats your rations /
your rats rations not not..."
Gherasim Luca, *"The Carp's Song,"*
(tr. B. Massumi), quoted in G. Deleuze
and F. Guattari, *A Thousand Plateaus.*

"Some of us... never meant anything
less by women's liberation than
the creation of a society without
domination; we never meant less than
the making new of all relationships."
Adrienne Rich, "Notes
Toward a Politics of Location."

"In the period which geologists
call the Glacial Period, the waters
of earth must have been gathered
up in a vast body on the higher
places of our globe, vast worlds
of ice... So that the Azores rose up
mountainous from the plain of
Atlantis, where the Atlantic now
washes, and the Easter Isles and

We are temporarily stalled
here in the Meridian, until
the right course of action
is determined—
either by Captain Anna-O,
who walks with a limp
and refrains from ouzo,
or Commander Exprès
(who remains in his cabin).

Our predicament
is not easily analyzed.

We were entering the channel
and Möbius was reading a chart.

The last record
of a transit dated back
to the Reggaen era,
when the TITANIC
was pulled under; the fear,
for us, was that portions
of the seaweed had shifted
through the ages.

I heard Möbius gasp.

What Occam and I saw,
as we turned to look,
were Möbius's forearms

the Marquesas and the rest rose
lofty from the marvelous great
continent of the Pacific. / In that
world men lived and taught and
knew, and were in one complete
correspondence over all the earth."
D. H. Lawrence, "Foreword,"
in *Fantasia of the Unconscious.*

"the road which leads me to you
is safe / even when it runs into oceans"
Edmond Jabès,
The Book of Questions, Vol. 1.

"And now we rushed into
the embraces of the cataract
where a chasm threw itself open
to receive us."
Edgar Allan Poe,
*The Narrative of Arthur
Gordon Pym of Nantucket.*

"Where are the peoples that have
gone before, and serve as a lesson
for those who can learn? Where are
the kings of China, the masters
of might and power? Where is 'Ad,
son of Shaddad, and the buildings
he raised up? Where is Nimrod,
the mighty tyrant? Where is Pharaoh,
who refused to believe his God?"
Tales of the 1001 Nights.

inserted past his elbows,
beyond the main control panel,
into the sea.

The Crystal seemed ethereal;
his forearms penetrated the hull.

And when Möbius
withdrew his arms,
they were wet.

To our dismay, not only did
he suffer contamination,
but his symptoms
worsened immediately.

The whole course of the sickness
accelerated before us:
his teeth and hair fell out,
marks appeared on his skin,
he became tired, was speechless
and confused, etc...

He staggered off, moaning,
and wandered in a daze,
putting the ship on alert.

Making his way
to the Engine room,
by the propeller shaft
he succumbed to Sleep.

As in the Mysteries of E. P.,

"He—for there could be no doubt
of his sex, though the fashion
of the time did something
to disguise it—was in the act
of slicing at the head of a Moor
which swung from the rafter.
It was the colour of an old football,
and more or less the shape of one,
save for the sunken cheeks and
a strand or two of coarse, dry hair,
like the hair on a cocoanut."
Virginia Woolf,
Orlando.

"Snow on his beard.
But he had no beard..."
H. D.
End to Torment:
A Memoir of Ezra Pound.

"What remains intact is what
was there in the beginning:
space and the spirit of fiction."
Jean Baudrillard,
America.

"For an instant I think I *saw.*
I *saw* the loneliness of man as
a gigantic wave which had been
frozen in front of me, held back
by the invisible wall of a metaphor...
Don Juan... stood up and gently
put his hand on my shoulder."

the water started seeping
from his body soon after,
forming the pool
in which he lies.

The location of the body
and the presence of water
seemed to call
for a group chant,
to hasten the disappearance
of Möbius's flesh and
the shrinking of the puddle.

It was also believed
that his bones would have
oracular powers.

So Greenwich, Neanderthal,
Soho, Thebes and Woodstock,
began chanting
around Möbius's body.

They continue to chant
as I write.

Their success
is all the more urgent,
with Occam
hanging above them
by her foot.

Carlos Castaneda,
Journey to Ixtlan.

"I moved further down and reached
out my hand to the next wave...
It hesitated, withdrew, then flowed
over my hand yet without touching it,
in such a way that a narrow layer
of air remained between the surface
of my gauntlet and the inside
of the covering, which instantly
changed consistency, turning
from liquid to almost fleshy."
Stanislav Lem,
Solaris.

"The fifth dimension's a tesseract.
You add to the other four
dimensions and you can travel
through space without having
to go the long way around.
In other words, to put it into Euclid,
or old-fashioned plane geometry,
a straight line is *not* the shortest
distance between two points."
Madeleine L'Engle,
A Wrinkle in Time.

"**absolute** *Philosophy*
19th century idealists... were heavily
influenced by Immanuel Kant (1724 -
1804)... These idealists concluded
that the world as we see it is some-

When the meteor struck,
Occam was in the Quietist room,
just above the propeller vault.

She was trying to communicate
with the presumed origin
of the noise haunting the ship,
the ghost of a drowned sailor.

Incredibly, while the meteor
hovered near sea level,
the floor seemed to melt away
and disintegrate.

As Occam sank through,
her foot got caught
in the fibers of the Crystal,
until she went tumbling
head over heels.

There was no contact with
Möbius's body or the water below,
so Occam escaped contamination;
but the Crystal quickly hardened,
leaving her hanging.

As we wait
for the situation to change,
the Jovian fleet is sailing

how derivative, apparent, relative,
incomplete, and even contradictory...
They used 'the absolute' as a term
for reality as it really is, free from
these limitations but unknowable
by us. Spinoza (1632-77) and
the Greek philosopher Parmenides
(early 5th century BC...) have been
seen as forerunners of this doctrine."
Jennifer Bothamley,
Dictionary of Theories.

"It's the one who starts who wins. /
You have to take an even number. /
The lowest whole uneven number. /
It's a logarithmic series. /
You have to pick a different
row each time. / Divided by three. /
Seven times seven forty-nine."
Alain Robbe-Grillet,
Last Year at Marienbad.

"Those discords, / I don't think, /
Will reach the sky."
Sappho (tr. G. Davenport).

"There are seven vowels,
seven strings to the scale,
seven Pleiades... The interval
from alpha to omega in the alphabet
is equal to that from the lowest
note of a flute to the highest,
whose number is equal to that of

toward our present position,
under the general command of
Kooch on the Flagship METIS.

Their ships are the largest
in the world,
and next to those
of the Vandals, the fastest.

They include,
in addition to
the METIS,
the DEIMOS,
the PHOBOS,
the CHIRON,
the CHARON,
the ANANKE,
the TITAN,
the TRITON,
the TITANIA,
the IO
and the EUROPA.

The Jovians had no sooner
rendezvoused with
the Zen at the foot of
the Platonic Iceberg
when the meteor
pierced through the sky.

The meteor's descent
and prolonged standstill
forced the Jovians and

the whole system of the universe."
Aristotle,
Metaphysics.

"The seven inner circles revolved gently in the opposite direction to the whole... And the spindle turned on the knees of Necessity, and up above on each of the rims of the circles a Siren stood, borne around in its revolution and uttering one sound, one note, and from all eight there was the concord of a single harmony."
Plato,
The Republic.

"in a Time of Wars seeking
the end of Time / the Song
of What War shall I sing?"
Robert Duncan,
Ground Work II: In the Dark,
"The Five Songs."

"Until the Jaunte Age dawned, the three Inner Planets (and the Moon) had lived in delicate economic balance with the seven inhabited Outer Satellites: Io, Europa, Ganymede, and Callisto of Jupiter; Rhea and Titan of Saturn; and Lassell of Neptune."
Alfred Bester,
The Stars My Destination.

Zen to break rank:
the vibrations in the aether,
triggering an alchemical
reaction, affected the Crystal
of the two fleets differently.

Waves erupted over the sea.

As a result,
while the Zen follow
the Digamma-Rarian border,
the Jovians are proceeding
in our direction,
and will loop around
for a scheduled linkup
with the Zombis,
South of the Thorn Mists
in the Ocean of Reading.

Latest readings
from the S\S MARU,
the Byzantine scout vessel
furthest afar of our forces,
indicate that the alien armada,
still inside the Orionis Ripple,
consists of sixteen different
squadrons disposed along four
rows, in units of one, three,
five and seven squadrons.

Other reports claim

"I hunt among stones."
Charles Olson, "The Kingfishers."

"The light clung around him
like a skin, lit the dark hangings
behind the stage. He was projecting."
William Gibson,
Neuromancer.

"Nothing says anything /
but that which it wishes /
would come true, fears /
what else might happen in /
some other place, some /
other time not this one."
Robert Creeley, "For Love."

the vessels are built
of Bluestone, and
have fylfot propellers
like our own.

There is no index
of the Years
they have crossed
to get here.

I hunger for love;
and ask for your Fire,
so that I am safe
from the dark.

Your lover,

S.

The Scales

Dear S.,

You came in a Flame,
across the Years
that separate Hel
from the Shade
and the Shadows of Edh.

I was at the *Qui Vive*
in the Province of Hunter,
after traveling from Olympus
to Viaduct View,
by way of Point Blanks
and the Chasm Atlantl.

The sky was a vast dome
of White glass.

Below, smooth sheets
of Bluestone unfurled
in all directions, through
Shadows and fields of ivy.

I sat in a circle
of Thrones, and watched
in the near distance

"I, Hermes, stand here
by the windy row of trees /
in the crossroads,
near the white-edged beach, /
with rest for people exhausted
by their road; / and the spring
murmurs cold and clear."
Anyte (c. 300 BCE),
"Epigrams" (tr. I. M. Plant).

"For here an empty echo
reaches into Hades. / But there is
silence among the dead
and darkness closes their eyes."
Erinna (c. 350 BCE), "The Distaff."

"As Dawn leaves ocean's / seas,
she drags from heaven /
the holy light of the moon, /
while the Seasons take life
from ambrosial Zeus /
among the flowers of spring..."
Corinna (c. 200 BCE), "Orestes."

the light from a Red Chasm,
as it danced on the face
of an overhanging cliff.

My fear was that the sky
would shatter.

I hesitated, tempted by the Chasm.

I could run at once
over the smooth open stone,
and leap.

Or I could wait,
and trust my hand.

Then I saw you coming
across the way, wrapped in Fire.

You spoke in a deep Voice
that was loud and garbled.

In the moment thereafter,
I understood
that my triad of Cards
fell on two different lines.

But with 89 cents at stake—
on *The Strong Force // reversed*,
The War Machine,
The Mendicant—
the danger felt closer than ever.

"It was an age of freaks, monsters,
and grotesques. All the world
was misshapen in marvelous and
malevolent ways. The Classicists
and Romantics who hated it were
unaware of the potential greatness
of the twenty-fifth century."
Alfred Bester,
The Stars My Destination.

"It's prodigies held in time's amber /
old destructions / and the theme
of revival the heart asks for. /
The past and futures are / full of
disasters, splendors / shaken to earth,
seas rising to overshadow /
shores and roaring in."
Robert Duncan, "Atlantis."

"I created, O holy Zarathustra,
a place, a Creation of delight,
[but] nowhere was created
a possibility [of approach]."
The Avesta (tr. A. H. Bleeck).

"Our lord, the lord of the near,
of the nigh, is made to laugh.
He is arbitrary, he is capricious...
We make him laugh;
he is making a mockery of us."
Florentine Codex,
in Inga Clendinnen, *Aztecs.*

Earlier, I was with Baboozas
and Jykks at *Fin-de-Siècle*
in Genome Province,
where the angels
are said to play music.

I can see *Fin-de-Siècle*
from here, where I write,
by the cedars of Saxe
and Zildjian—and behind
the saloon the vapors
rising from the ground.

The ouzo there is lush
and medium-bodied,
not too spicy,
but not flabby or soft either;
it has a delightful aftertaste.

(The ouzo I had had earlier
at the *Qui Vive* was less
structured, "so goddamn mellow,"
Rem had said after the Game,
"I raised the goddamn stakes
too goddamn high.")

I was aware of rumors
concerning the coupling
of Youth in JuJw Forest
by the ancient Tar Pits
of Rom.

"And I beheld the Spirit
of the Lord, that it was upon
the Gentiles, and they did
prosper and obtain the land for
their inheritance; and I beheld that
they were white, and they were
exceedingly fair and beautiful..."
The Book of Mormon,
1 Nephi 13.

"We had come to our decision.
Ancient history told long ago,
old sorrows long since healed...
And though... the gruesomeness of
the present was irrefutably conveyed
by the beggars's words, we laughed
and shook our heads and refused
to listen any longer. So eager are
our people to obliterate the present."
Franz Kafka,
"The Great Wall of China."

"All of Kafka's work is the search
for a would-be affirmation—
an affirmation which, as soon as
it comes into view, slips away,
seems a lie, and therefore rules
itself out as affirmation, making
affirmation once again possible."
Maurice Blanchot, "Reading Kafka."

"The sun shone, having no
alternative, on the nothing new."

At Fort 'Qinx I heard
two Antipodeans,
Xòxòthròs and Râ,
discussing the incident.

I heard a similar story from
Jeez, our friend, and Mosads,
of the Foreskin Generation,
at Acid Pond.

From the Crater of Led,
there were also reports
of a drowned Youth,
whose last word was:
"Bird-Dog!"

In fact, the rumors had started
with Baboozas and Jykks,
who both saw what happened
and confirmed the news.

Baboozas, who hails from Krylon,
sat in a velvet tunic
and gloves
by the Bar next to Jykks.

He was dreaming.

So Jykks did the talking
at first.

Samuel Beckett,
Murphy.

"We are just now seeing,
amidst the fads and distractions,
the strange fact that what has
been most modern in our time was
what was most archaic."
Guy Davenport,
"The Symbol of the Archaic."

"On desperate seas long wont
to roam... / Thy Naiad airs
have brought me home /
To the glory that was Greece, /
And the grandeur that was Rome."
Edgar Allan Poe, "To Helen."

"Two nations have been
essential for our culture: Greece
(since Rome is a Hellenistic
extension) and Israel, an Eastern
country. Both are combined into
what we call Western civilization."
Jorge Luis Borges,
"The Thousand and One Nights."

"With the flow of the centuries
I have lost the secret of Egypt..."
Clarice Lispector,
Água Viva.

"And Moses stretched out his hand

They were passing from
Vaudeville to the Valley
of The Wind of Knives,
when they overheard
the nearby revelry of Youth.

Together, they took
an abandoned stairway
down to the beach,
where they hid in a cave.

About twenty Youth
were making their way
along the shore,
in the company
of a tall fair-headed boy,
whose erect phallus
seemed the totem
urging them onward.

The Youth were laughing
and singing and dancing,
until they stopped near the cave...

At this point, however,
Jykks's eyes turned White,
and the dreamscape set in.

I was about to go,
when Baboozas awoke

over the sea; and the Lord caused
the sea to go back by a strong east wind
all that night, and made the sea
dry land and the waters were divided."
Exodus 14.

"At the end of Odysseus'
recounting of his voyages,
at the exact center of *The Odyssey*
(the conclusion of Book XII),
there occurs the most uncanny
of episodes, that of the Oxen of
the Sun. It is uncanny because
there seems to be a transformation
—or phantom translation—
of another celebrated sequence in
the West's core repertory of episodes:
that of the Golden Calf and its sequel
in Exodus 32... The book of
Skylla and Charybdis... [is] in
substantial contact not only with
the episodes of the Golden Calf
and the Levite purge, but also
perhaps with that of the crossing of
the Red Sea... The most suggestive
fragment of the Greek text
in relation to the Exodus episode
is the celebrated suggestion that
it will be Odysseus's destiny to die
after a trip 'where men have lived
with meat unsalted, never known
the sea, nor seen seagoing ships'
(11, 127-137). There his oar,

from his dream.

In the dream, he said,
angels writhed in pain
on a mound of ears.

After a few drinks,
he resumed Jykks's story.

The Youth were gathered
beside McDonalds,
their Sex-aroused guide
with the curly hair,
when Gucci emerged
from the sea.

Shapely and firm of flesh,
Gucci had pale skin
and a pretty face,
with short dark hair
and small darkish teeth.

As she stood on the sand,
resplendent with new life,
they offered her poems
and blessed her with myrtle.

Then, arm in arm,
McDonalds and Gucci
led the others
in a joyous procession
by the sea, past the cave,
toward JuJw Forest—

borne aloft, will be confused with
a 'winnowing fan'... This supplement
...is an inexplicable (...) oscillation
between the maritime world
of *The Odyssey* and the parched
desert world of Exodus."
Jeffrey Mehlman, "Core of the Core:
A Phantasmagoria in Translation."

"There are no records
outside the Bible which indicate
Merneptah, or any Pharoah,
to have drowned in the Red Sea."
Isaac Asimov,
Asimov's Guide to the Bible.

"All of these unholy powers are
delivered unto the judgment of
the Kingdom, which is called
'the great sea,' in order that they
may be uprooted each in his own
grade, and be utterly cast down,
and when they are broken above,
all their counterparts below are also
broken and lost in the 'lower sea.'"
Zohar, "Beshalach" (ed. M. Berg).

"It is at the level of the interference
of many practices that things
happen, beings, images, concepts,
all kinds of events."
Gilles Deleuze,
Cinema 2.

each rear end
more beautiful than the next,
according to Baboozas.

The Youth made their way
to the Colossus of Jersey,
outside the Pillars of Plymouth;
then, inland, beyond
the flying megaliths
in the Salt Flats of Ut,
to the Great Wall.

The party reached
its destination
on a hillside
near the Rom Pits.

Amid a grove
where the bristlecone pines
chime in the wind,
Baboozas and Jykks
were amazed to discover
a new pool...

They quickly hid behind
a large rock, to behold
the secret rite of passage.

Seven sisters prepared
the ceremony by
making the Tremolo.

"Men on Earth have had
the presentiment of a superior being
who may one day succeed them
but... no scientist, philosopher, or
poet has ever imagined this super-
human in the guise of an ape."
Pierre Boule,
Planet of the Apes.

"The air got too full once, of
chemicals, rays, radiation, the water
swarmed with toxic molecules,
all that takes years to clean up...
Who knows, your very flesh may be
polluted, dirty as an oily beach..."
Margaret Atwood,
The Handmaid's Tale.

"The mayor... lists the disasters,
the droughts, the storms, the fires,
the encroaching seas that swallowed up
so much of the land, the brutal war for
what little sustenance remained."
Suzanne Collins,
The Hunger Games.

"The brain-pan of the New Tower of
Babel was Peopled with numbers."
Thea von Harbou,
Metropolis.

"Ubik talks to us from the future,

All of the Youth assembled
around the pool, in a pattern
of circles within circles,
before sitting down
in the Lotus position.

When the Tremolo ceased,
Gucci and McDonalds
approached, separated
by the water and
the surrounding congregation.

They stood face-to-face,
and after declaring
Murphy's Law climbed
into the pool together.

To hear the rest,
you would think
that *The Book of The Angels*
had come true.

While strong gusts of wind
rattled the pines,
the pool's bubbling water
began to part down the middle,
forming two separate walls
that grew higher and higher,
until a trail of mud
was cleared across the bottom.

from the end state toward
which everything is moving."
Philip K. Dick,
The Exegesis.

"One can speak of the good mental
health of van Gogh... in a world
in which every day one eats vagina
cooked in green sauce or penis of
newborn child whipped and beaten
to a pulp... And this is not just
an image, but a fact abundantly
and daily repeated and cultivated
throughout the world."
Antonin Artaud, "Van Gogh,
the Man Suicided by Society."

"In the absence of grounding tyranny
of the Whole the worm-function
(( )hole function) internally re-
configures its modules and turns itself
into a more versatile line through
participation with the complex
whose recesses are interconnected."
Reza Negarestani,
Cyclonopedia.

"What is the poet for, if not
to scream / himself into a hernia
of admiration for all paradoxical
integuments: the kiss, the / bomb,
cathedrals and the zeppelin
anchored / to the hill of dreams?"

Frank O'Hara,
"Ashes on Saturday Afternoon."

"Johnny is a joker that's a' tryin'
to steal my baby (he's a bird dog)."
The Everly Brothers, "Bird Dog."

"O they are holy days when
our heart first tests its wings."
Friedrich Hölderlin,
Hyperion.

"I remember my first birth in
water. All round me a sulphurous
transparency... I sway and float,
stand on boneless toes listening
for distant sounds, sounds beyond
the reach of human ears, see things
beyond the reach of human eyes.
Born full of memories of the bells
of the Atlantide... I cut the air with
wide-slicing fins and swim through
wall-less rooms... Ejected from
a paradise of soundlessness,
cathedrals wavering at the passage
of a body, like soundless music."
Anaïs Nin.
The House of Incest.

"When the individual finds
a partner in kemmer, hormonal
secretion is further stimulated...
until in one partner either a male

With the wind gusting violently,
two Elders—the man
"Bird-Dog" and the woman
"Rainbow"—got up from the mud,
and stepping into the walls of water
rinsed themselves clean.

They climbed out
and joined the others.

Then the waters collapsed
in a downpour,
and the wind became still.

During the subsequent rites,
the crowd offered Rainbow—
the reborn McDonalds,
who was blind—a "badge";
and they gave the gap-toothed
Bird-Dog, formerly Gucci,
a "striped towel"
and a "pair of Plastic thongs."

Baboozas, however,
seemed increasingly lost
in the memory of the event,
speaking by fits and starts
and mumbling incoherently.

As far as I could tell,
his confusion centered
around two fragments

of Crystal that Jykks
had later discovered
at the site.

They bore the inscriptions
"AM" and "IS."

But suddenly a dream interfered,
leaving Baboozas in mid-sentence.

I am reminded of a dream
I had forgotten.

It was in a Green,
with a panorama that gave
on the Chasm Atlantl.

There, the Shadows climb
to a Colorless sky
inside a crater, whose walls,
set with remnants of old brick,
surround me.

From an abandoned stairway
coated with seaweed, I look
down at a mass of bones
that covers the ground.

The surface keeps changing,
because a portion of the bones
disappears at odd intervals.

or female hormonal dominance
is established. The genitals
engorge or shrink accordingly,
foreplay intensifies, and the partner,
triggered by the change,
takes on the other sexual role..."
Ursula Le Guin,
The Left Hand of Darkness.

"Eroticism, it may be said,
is assenting to life
up to the point of death."
George Bataille, "Eroticism."

"He stood upright in complete
nakedness before us, and while
the trumpets pealed Truth! Truth!
Truth! we have no choice left but
confess—he was a woman...
Let biologists and psychologists
determine. It is enough for us
to state the simple fact; Orlando
was a man till the age of thirty;
when he became a woman and
has remained so ever since."
Virginia Woolf,
Orlando.

"What love lays bare in me is energy."
Roland Barthes,
A Lover's Discourse.

"It's a new generation /

Although, in real time,
they would remain invisible,
I know that in my dream
these are the bones of Youth—
fading now and again
above the bones of the parents.

Perhaps I am waiting;
as if for an answer
from you...

Your lover,

A.

Looking for a peace of mind /
New generation / Groovin' it
down the line. / New generation /
Groovin' it all the time."
Albert Ayler,
"New Generation."

"And beneath: the clear bones
far down, / Thousand on thousand..."
Ezra Pound
Cantos, XX.

The Mendicant

Dear A.,

"It had been a [dream,]
he shuddered... He [rubbed]
his eyes with his hands,
there was desolate [silence.] /
The dream........ / The dream........"
The Epic of Gilgamesh,
"The Death of Bilgames."

"So when did archaeology begin?
And who was the first
archaeologist?... Nabodinus,
the last king of Babylon, dug
and restored Ur. Nabodinus
was delighted to find at Ur
'the inscriptions of former
ancient kings,' and his daughter
En-nigaldi-Nanna (her name was
formerly transcribed incorrectly
as Belshalti-Nanner) had dug
for years at the temple of Agade.
When a heavy downpour of rain
opened a great gallery revealing
the temple it is recorded that this
discovery 'made the king's heart

Commander Exprès
had a dream, and told it
to the Poetess Avon,
who told it in verse
after breakfast, below deck.

In the dream, it was
the Day of the Unborn.

Distant whistles echoed
on the sea; the water
flashed, non-stop, with
deep and brilliant bursts
of Phosphorescence.

Scud and Ducs, robots,
cursed the surf at the edge
of our homeland
as the Thorn Mists
receded toward the jungle
of the Ziggurats...

glad and caused his countenance
to brighten.' The princess seemed
to have a room in her house for
her collection of local antiquities."
Glyn Daniel,
A Short History of Archaeology.

"History, which interprets
the present to understand
the past and confront the future,
is the least rewarding discipline
for a dying species."
P. D. James,
Children of Men.

"Underlined in red pencil was
a name that meant nothing to me:
André Berton. It appeared on two
different pages. I found the first of
these and learned that Berton had
been the co-pilot on Shannahan's
ship. The next mention of his name
was over a hundred pages later."
Stanislav Lem,
Solaris.

"There is no Frigate like a Book /
To take us Lands away..."
Emily Dickinson (1286).

"In navigation it is not
the cleverest who are fortunate,
but (just as in throwing dice

By order of the Commander,
the Engine room has been sealed
as two guards stand watch—
first, Nobadinus and Rosetta,
then Cowabunga and Kongō.

Möbius hangs by his toes
over the spare shaft,
in the place of Occam,
whose bones have been
tossed overboard.

Van Rr'Ubik is Dead;
the profile of her Shadow
covers half the figurehead,
port-side.

The chant of Greenwich,
Neanderthal, Soho, Thebes,
and Woodstock is non-stop,
almost a motor's murmur,
as if encompassing
the conundrum-that-binds
both in our Fate
and Jupiter's Kâ Ma.

At times, the Voice of Möbius
can be heard to echo
beyond the bulkhead,
shouting at them to *Be free!*

one man throws a blank and
another a six) a man is fortunate
according as things were arranged
by nature. Or is it because he is
loved by God, as the phrase goes,
and because success is something
from outside? As for instance
a badly built ship often gets through
a voyage better, though not owing
to itself, but because it has a good
man at the helm. But on this showing
the fortunate man has the deity
as steersman. But it is strange
that a god or deity should love
a man of this sort, and not the best
and most prudent."
Aristotle,
Eudemian Ethics.

"At last, the boat still passing on,
was forced into another world,
for it is impossible to round this
world's globe from Pole to Pole,
so as we do from East to West;
because the Poles of the other
world, joining to the Poles of this,
do not allow any further passage
to surround the world that way."
Margaret Cavendish,
The Blazing World.

"Why had I not thought of
this simple solution before?...

The general strategy,
planned by Inspector 17,
involves a multiplex
power base, deployed
in two matching flanks
along the perimeter
of the alien theater.

Latest readings from
the S\S MARU of Byzantium
indicate that the alien fleet,
still inside the Orionis Ripple,
is engaged in an offensive
maneuver: their formation
presents four parallel lines
of seven, five, three and
one squadron, respectively.

According to the Zombis,
the scout vessel MILES
proceeds full steam past
Lenin's Loop to the Sampi Sea,
where the Vandal Superships
A-1, K-1, B-2, T-2, U-2, B-3,
D-3, D-4 and the Flagship
DOUBLE ZERO
have already arrived.

The Zombis also report that
the VALHALLAH, the AOLIAN,
the BARAQA, the TANTRA
and the YUCATAN
have formed a crescent line

I drew the geometrical figure
illustrating the theorem of
Pythagoras… I had even discussed
this during the voyage with
Professor Antelle, who approved
of the method. He had added,
I distinctly remembered, that
the Euclidean rules, being
completely false, were no doubt
for that very reason universal."
Pierre Boule,
Planet of the Apes.

"Never do anything which
you do not understand."
The Golden Verses of Pythagoras.

"Let it be said at the beginning
that no woman has ever more
completely given herself to man's
ideas, or felt less antagonism
towards him than I."
Frances Boldereff,
in *Charles Olson and*
Frances Boldereff:
A Modern Correspondence.
(ed. R. Maud and S. Thesen.)

"His head passed down a sky
(as suns the circle of a year). /
His other shoulder, open side
and thigh maintained, / by law
of conservation of / the graveness

with a reconnaissance force
of five Zen vessels:
the ST. LAWRENCE,
the GLOUCESTER,
the MOUND CITY,
the METACOMET
and the LEVIATHAN.

Once assembled,
the Zen-Zombi Holy League
will have a center under
the joint command of Mandala
aboard the BIOTA and Nemo
aboard the BOUNTY.

The remainder of the Alliance
is to be distributed between
a van co-led by Capts. America
of the TANG and Lucy
of the DETERMINATOR.

On the advice of
the Byzantines, who are
now in "the Rain under
the Sea," the split mantras
of Auto-da-fè will power
the juggernath (with
pre-selected mantras Bo
(Sony) and Wiki-Wiki
(ben-Cnopee) for back up,
after switch to left eye).

of his center, / their clockwise
fall. / Then he knew, so came
to apogee / and earned and
wore himself as amulet."
Charles Olson,
"The Moebius Strip."

"If I have time! Time /
is a shell love breaks."
C. Olson,
in *Charles Olson and*
Frances Boldereff:
A Modern Correspondence.

"Ayla tasted the primordial forest
again, then felt it turn to warm salt."
Jean M. Auel,
Clan of the Cave Bear.

"Nothing the peoples of
Europe have produced
is worth the first known poem
that appeared among them.
Perhaps they will yet rediscover
the epic genius, when they
learn that there is no refuge
from fate, learn not to admire
force, not to hate the enemy,
not to scorn the unfortunate.
How soon this will happen
is another question."
Simone Weil,
The Iliad, or *The Poem of Force.*

So Sony and ben-Cnopee
received Salt and Wax
for the wickerwork,
while in the bunker
the Captain's spyglass,
Areopagiticus, was pulled
from the stones.

Scard'nelli the Bo'sun
(who replaces Sokrates
the Librarian, who replaces
van Rr'Ubik at the helm) was
assigned to Urim-Thummin
by Remote Commander CD,
and will give another reading
from Monte Fan Tan's
Dātā-Dādā-Bābā-Bāvā.

For the Byzantines
"the Rain under the Sea"
is a natural state of suspension
that can last indefinitely.

In virtual silence,
the Byzantine crew
succumbs to the glamour
of Sex, as the vessel
rides at the tip of
a speeding current,
whose course it controls

"Quand partons-nous
pour le bonheur?"
("When do we set sail
for happiness?")
Charles Baudelaire, in
Katherine Anne Porter,
Ship of Fools, epigraph.

with fourfold lock
on Atomatic pilot.

A good omen, they say.

As perverse as it is timely.

Now and always.

Love,

S.

"shipwreck this / / pertaining
to man / without vessel /
no matter / where vain"
Stéphane Mallarmé, "A Throw of
the Dice Will Never Abolish Chance"
(tr. H. Weinfield).

P.S. *Mayday!*

S\S MARU.

Byzantines unable to surface,
Zen are on standby.

The Wheel of Chance

Dear S.,

They all dream;
fifteen bodies in all.

In the Shade, the White
of their eyes takes on
a life of its own:
Tristis, Histrix,
Haema, Tyro, Coronatu...
face up on the bench,
mouth open.

Beyond the door the Red
seems radiant against
the darkness of the saloon.

At the *Passé* the ouzo
addresses the palate
powerfully, and yet manages
its dramatic girth with supple
and buoyant grace,
so that the impact
in the mouth is large
but not ponderous,
while the aftertaste fades with

"Beginning, before it becomes
a historical event, is the supreme
capacity of man: politically it is
identical with man's freedom."
Hannah Arendt,
The Origins of Totalitarianism.

"Canst thou draw out leviathan
with an hook? Or his tongue with
a cord which thou lettest down?"
The Book of Job 41:1.

"The dreamer is in the center,
the 'I' or Eye of the Dream."
Robert Duncan,
The H. D. Book
(ed. M. Boughn & V. Coleman).

"No, / no, / no, / no, / no, / no, /
that was a dream."
H. D.,
Hippolytus Temporizes.

"I think mebbe he's troubling

haunting slowness, releasing
a last emanation of flavor—

(I have just heard a Sound
that I have heard before.

Déjà vu, from a dream...

I am in a Card Game.

Hiva, the *Risqué*.

One Dollar:
on *The Mendicant*
and *The Wheel*.

Like the Sound of waves,
if the waves had Sound.)

Decoded from the Gnostic
and Indo-Californian,
these "beads" are the Post-
Torture tears of Atlas.

"A Saint's torment
for All / or for None
but the Dead."

Here, in this saloon,

her dreams."
Ezra Pound (tr.),
Elektra.

"Beasts wild with hunger
shall swim the rivers: /
Most of the host
shall move against Ister: /
He'll have the great one
dragged in iron cage, /
When the child
the German Rhine surveys."
Nostradamus,
The Prophecies (tr. R. Sieburth).

"I wonder why the oracle would write
a novel. Did you ever think of asking it
that? And why one about the Germans
and the Japanese losing the war?"
Philip K. Dick,
The Man in the High Castle.

"'If you saw Atlas, the giant who holds
the world on his shoulders, if you saw
that he stood, blood running down
his chest, his knees buckling, his arms
trembling but still trying to hold
the world aloft with the last of
his strength, and the greater his effort
the heavier the world bore down
upon his shoulders—What would you
tell him? / I... don't know. What... could
he do? What would you tell him? /

a mass of hundreds,
thousands of them,
everywhere.

On the floor and ceiling,
along the wooden Bar
and the old mirrors
on the wall,
even on the bodies:
a face, covered with them;
and in the corner,
like a sand dune,
across the European
in a paper dress.

The Book of Hister's
Meditations,
or *A Child's Within*,
describes their Color
as "God-like."

I am alone,
called to the threshold
that they adorn.

It was no different
when I arrived.

The Dust stirred in the richness
of this same light.

To shrug.'"
Ayn Rand,
Atlas Shrugged.

"The dews drop slowly and
dreams gather: unknown
spears / Suddenly hurtle before
my dream-awakened eyes...."
W. B. Yeats,
"The Valley of the Black Pig."

"Who sacrifices pigs
to the god of war?"
Aristophanes,
The Acharnians.

"Why should the tides of Tahiti
follow the sun rather than the moon?"
Rachel Carson,
The Sea Around Us.

"They say that... if a wooden cup
is thrown into the Alpheus
in Greece, it will reappear
in Arethusa's well in Sicily."
Edith Hamilton,
Mythology.

"a peri-Mediterranean syllabary
neither Greek nor Egyptian
nor Semitic / but in between them
such as the lines Eratosthenes ran
before Pytheas / were as good

At the *Sang-Froid*
they stuck to the Ice
on Cuculc's body, and
to a map-of-the-world
on the wall.

They line the Stone Age
riverbed nearby,
in Arathussa,
and the phantom waterfalls
at the end of Graecia's Land.

The Book of Days says
they were last seen in
the Blow-Up Days of C'crete,
when O'Nasa's Towers
served as center of the Trades.

as all the distances of the globe
then turned out to / be—as rivers
run under seas and bays to come up /
Meander under Piryne as / Alpheus
under the Adriatic to / Latinum"
Charles Olson,
The Maximus Poems: Volume Three
(posthumous).

"'And from this out,' he said, 'your name
will be Cuchulain, the Hound of Culain.'
'I am better pleased with my own
name of Setanta, son of Sualtim,' said
the boy. 'Do not say that,' said Cathbad,
'for all the men in the whole world
will some day have the name of
Cuchulain in their mouths.'"
Lady Gregory,
Cuchulain of Muirthemne.

Suspended before me,
a single new bead
is crossing the room
like a pearl of pure light,
slowly traveling
from the window,
where I saw it leave,
to the opposite wall
on my left, toward
the Bar and the tables.

It moves as I write.

"(...reference: constellations, Venus
included (which here I will show can be
called KuKulCan... discovering
this man's death, April 5, 1208 AD,
who 'rose' with Venus, 8 days later,
was sufficient unto itself...)"
C. Olson
Mayan Letters (ed. R. Creeley).

"In the period before his final retirement
he would accept twelve cases.
And those twelve cases should
be selected with special reference to

When the movement
is complete, and
the thing comes to rest,
the writing will have ended,
so that you know.

the twelve labors of ancient Hercules.
Yes, that would not only be amusing,
it would be artistic, it would be *spiritual*."
Agatha Christie,
The Labors of Hercules.

My love—

A stranger, Bird-Dog
of Megidon, arrives from
the Gardens of Pangaea,
after *Fin-de-Siècle*,
and asks to play Cards.

He stands at the Bar, sipping
ouzo as I end this letter.

Bird-Dog wears a striped towel
around his waist,
and walks in Plastic thongs.

He is slim and virile,
gap-toothed,
with big pectorals
and biceps.

"1400 BC—exactly / 60 years later
than 2 generations birth /
Hercules / was born the / Greek
Hercules thereabouts / Tiryns or
Thebes of My / cenae /
took all of the lineage of Tyre
or Zeus / away / and buried them
under themselves and their cities /
Europe was beautiful /
800 AD to 1250—Java was also,
Iceland was, Greenland, Vinelanda /
Boston was 1637"
C. Olson,
The Maximus Poems: Volume Three.

"It'll never be known how
this has to be told, in the first
person or in the second, using
the third person plural or
continually inventing modes

that will serve for nothing."
Julio Cortázar,
"Blow-up" (tr. P. Blackburn).

More, later—

Your lover,

A.

The Strong Force

"Ethereal root and cheer and boo /
The billioned all-time attendance /
The Zeusian pandemonium /
Hermes racing Owens /
The Spitball of Buddha /
Christ striking out /
Luther stealing third /
Planetarium Death Hosannah Bomb /
Gush the final rose O Spring Bomb"
Gregory Corso, "Bomb."

"I've seen the future,
brother / It is murder."
Leonard Cohen,
"The Future."

"I am deliberate /
and afraid / of nothing."
Audre Lorde, "New Year's Day."

"I do believe / (Statist though
I am none, nor like to be) /
That this will prove a war."
William Shakespeare,

Dear A.,

Somewhere, behind us now,
beyond the Doubloon-Bind
on La Renaixença Hills,
we have left a holocaust
to answer for the Breath
of the Lord.

We are alone and
presume the others destroyed.

Commander Exprès
is in shock, subject to seizures
during which he spits
on Glass Ingots, in patterns
that Venus interprets.

Despite his own odd
spells of cursing,
Venus thus guides us,
the survivors, across
the Mercurial waters
of a new Silver Sea,
"under starry Heavens
Black as Ink."

Cymbeline.

"Our mission is one of suicide:
we present ourselves
as volunteers for the future."
Clarice Lispector,
Chronicles.

"Without war no stability."
Antonin Artaud,
The New Revelations of Being.

"...The Mare Tenebrarum—
an ocean well described by
the Nubian geographer, Ptolemy
Hephestion, but little frequented
in modern days unless by
the Transcendentalists and some
other divers for crotchets..."
Edgar Allan Poe,
Eureka.

"Paranoid-critical activity
organizes and objectifies
in an exclusivist manner
the unlimited and unknown
possibilities of the systematic
association of subjective and
objective phenomena presenting
themselves to us as irrational
concerns, to the exclusive
advantage of the obsessive
idea. Paranoid-critical

Only Avon is Dead.

Or half-Dead?

The torso lives—the head,
the eyes, the mouth—
while the lower part,
the legs and feet, have
passed through the hull
and are bone in the water.

Minimal seepage so far.

The Valley of the Centaurs
at Orion traverses
the highest known crests
in the ocean.

A sort of overload
must have brought Avon
to her Poet's Death.

Legend and seafaring tales
from unchartered points
on the far perimeter,
compounded by the surreal
displays in the zigzag
corridor of the waters,

activity thus reveals new
and objective 'meanings'
of the irrational; it tangibly
makes the very world of delirium
pass to the level of reality."
Salvador Dalí,
The Conquest of the Irrational.

"Since the Surrealists constantly
confuse moral nonconformism
with proletarian revolution,
they attempt, instead of following
the course of the modern world,
to relocate themselves to a historical
moment when this confusion was
still possible… And that is certainly
no accident. For, on the one hand,
we have here elements—anthropo-
logical materialism, hostility toward
progress—which are refractory
to Marxism, while, on the other hand,
the will to apokatastasis speaks here,
the resolve to gather again,
in revolutionary action and
in revolutionary thinking, precisely
the elements of the 'too early'
and the 'too late,' of the first
beginning and the final decay."
Walter Benjamin,
The Arcades Project.

"Old Heraclitus… discovered
the most marvelous of all

weighed her down,
until she crawled on
her hands and knees,
on her stomach, into
the depths of the hull—
and sung, chanted,
whistled the agonized
melody of her euphoria.

Second in line, single file
through the Skyscrapers,
our ship was aglow to
the eyes of Indians and
Jovians, as if lit from within
by the Crystal mound
of Avon's remains.

("J-junctions of
the Last Word?" asked
the phantoms on board,
who puffed on cigarettes,
gesturing to the cool
Green artifacts buried
in the Orionis walls.)

Within the Zen fleet,
nine ships at the center—
the CONSTELLATION,
the CONSTELLATION II,
the ENTERPRISE III,
the CHALLENGER,

psychological laws: the regulative
function of opposites. He called
it enantiodromia, a running
contrariwise, by which he meant
that sooner or later everything
runs into its opposite."
Carl G. Jung,
Psychological Types.

"The first metamorphosis of fire
is to become the sea, and half
of the sea becomes the earth,
half the flash of lightning."
Herakleitos (tr. G. Davenport).

"The earth is surrounded by water,
just as that is by the sphere of air,
and that again by the sphere
called that of fire."
Aristotle,
On Meteorology.

"Lamentings heard i' the air;
strange screams of death, /
And prophesying with accents
terrible / Of dire combustion
and confus'd events."
W. Shakespeare,
Macbeth.

"O gods! O holy gods!
Oh! Ohhhh! Ohhhhhhh!"
Seamus Heaney,

the WASHINGTON,
the BUNKER HILL,
the NEW ARK
the LONG BEACH
the SURPRISE—
together with
the CONSTITUTION
under the command
of En'Antidromia,
were simulcasting to
the Jovian central command
all Zen-Zombi business
stored by the Holy League
on a Zombi information
"subway" in the Zombis'
rear guard, and
in their center aboard
the WANDERER,
the SPEEDWELL,
the PROGRESS,
the PEQUOD,
the NANTUCKET,
the GLOBE,
the FUWALDA
and the ARCTIC.

The Jovian central command
—Maui on the RHEA,
Negafok on the LEDA,
Inuit on the CALLISTO,
Bella Bella on the GANYMEDE,
False Face on the THEBE,
Geronimo on the AMALTHEA,

The Cure at Troy: A Version
of Sophocles' Philoctetes.

"then laughter mingled with fury, /
as host encountered host"
H. D.,
Helen in Egypt.

"Comedy brought with it too great
a contrast to the inner despair:
when such were attempted, it was
not unfrequent for a comedian,
in the midst of the laughter occasioned
by his disproportioned buffoonery,
to find a word or thought in his part
that jarred with his own sense of
wretchedness, and burst from mimic
merriment into sobs and tears,
while the spectators, seized with
irresistible sympathy, wept, and
the pantomimic revelry was changed
to a real exhibition of tragic passion."
Mary Shelley,
The Last Man.

"Let us stress once more
that for the Renaissance (...)
the characteristic trait of laughter
was precisely the recognition
of its positive, regenerating,
creative meaning. This clearly
distinguishes it from the later
theories of the philosophy of

and Montezuma on
the ADRASTEA—relayed
to all ships via Satellite Dish
the Zen-Zombi Holy League's
88th key: "GOD! OH GOD!
OH! GOD! OH GOD!"

The Vandals took the lead in
forming a crescent line that
drew within Firing range
by arching half-way round
the opposing fleet
along an East \ West axis.

The alien ships, by contrast,
ran North \ South, and
consisted of four parallel
lines of one, three, five
and seven squadrons
respectively—the last and
largest line squaring off
with the Vandals.

The final bulletin from
the doomed Byzantines
regarding the structure
and movement of
the enemy ships—
broken off by the MARU's
implosion on impact with
the Cannabis sea floor—

laughter, including Bergson's
conception, which bring out
mostly its negative functions."
Mikhail Bakhtin,
Rabelais and his World.

"And now let all the ships
come in... / —and the mind go
forth to the end of the world"
Charles Olson,
Maximus Poems IV, V, VI.

"Both sides have artfully
avoided the escalation to SACPOP
that often takes both super-
combatants right out of the game;
and AMNAT's president LaMont
Chu has used the excuse of
Gopnick's emotional strikes
against the U.S. South, plus Penn's
a-rational lobbing at an Israel
that at the summit was explicitly
placed under AMNAT's mutual-
defense umbrella, has used these
as golden tactical geese, racking up
serious INDDIR-points against
a SOUTHAT and INDPAK
whose hasty defensive alliance
and shaky aim produce nothing
more than a lot of irradiated cod
off Gloucester."
David Foster Wallace,
Infinite Jest.

had just confirmed
an earlier report that
the entire alien fleet
showed Bluestone hulls
of varying size and design,
all of them fitted with
fylfot propellers and semi-
soft rigs, with Organic sails
made of Nail.

This finding, plus
indications that
their weaponry was
based on a system
of Diorite gongs
and hammerstones,
immediately struck
a deep chord with
the Zombis and Zen,
who agreed to dispatch
the CAGE
under Capt. John E. Cage,
the MILES
under Capt. Ironman,
the SHOEMAKER
under Capt. Juvernal,
and the LIVI X
under Capt. Macedon—
each with a complement of
World-Cup Theorists
and Analysands, including
Rwandan, Ptolemayan,
Babelonian and Solutrion

"Then the Lady Principal
with her two thousand students
marched to the battlefield,
and arriving there directed
all rays of the concentrated
sun light and heat
toward the enemy."
Rokeya Sakhawat Hossain,
Sultana's Dream.

"But those were not
ordinary projectiles!"
E. E. "Doc" Smith,
First Lensman.

"Between one instant and the next,
between the past and the future,
the white uncertainty of an interval."
Clarice Lispector, "The Man."

"Some died without speaking:
others spoke without dying; some
died speaking; others spoke dying."
François Rabelais,
Gargantua.

"For now in truth the whole land
of Asia, dispeopled, maketh moan:
Xerxes led forth (woe!), Xerxes
laid low (woe!), Xerxes disposed
all things imprudently with his sea-
faring barques... For landsmen

among the Zombis, and
the families of Tsimpsons
and Flintstons among the Zen.

The SHOEMAKER and
LIVI X, side by side,
were approaching
the foremost cluster
of some twenty alien

and seamen both, the ships, dark-
eyed and linen-winged, led forth
(woe!), the ships laid them low
(woe!), the ships under the deadly
impact of the foe and by the hands
of the Ionians... And they who were
first to meet their doom (alas!), left
behind perforce (alas!) are swept
along about the Cychrean strand
(woe!). Groan and gnash your teeth;
in grievous strain shout forth
our woes till they reach the heavens
(alas!), raise high your wailing
clamor in cries of misery.
Lacerated by the swirling waters
(alas!) they are gnawed (alas!) by
the voiceless children of the stainless
sea (alas!). The home, bereaved
of his presence, lamenteth its head;
and parents, reft of their children,
in their old age bewail their heaven-
sent woes (alas!), now that they learn
the full measure of their affliction."
Aeschylus,
The Trojans.

"Violence can destroy power:
out of the barrel of a gun grows
the most effective command
resulting in instant and perfect
obedience. What can never
grow out of it is power."
Hannah Arendt,

On Violence.

“From the middle of the northern
coast juts out the Crimean peninsula
where the savage Taurians live,
who delight in human sacrifice
and fix the heads of strangers upon
stakes about their houses. Behind
the Taurians live the Cimmerians,
a small, dark, excitable people,
famous for their singing and
valiant in war, but addicted to
sodomy; and both to the east
and west of these Cimmerians live
the long-lived, equitable Scythians,
who have no homes but their
wheeled carts, drink mares’ milk
and are wonderful archers. Behind
these, again, live the black-cloaked
cannibal Finns; and the Neurians,
many of whom become were-wolves
by night; and the hunting Budinians,
who paint themselves with red and
blue dye, build stockaded wooden
cities, and wear beaver-skin caps
and tunics; and the Issedonians,
who esteem it an act of piety to eat
the dead flesh of their parents and
make goblets from their skulls;
and a bald-headed priestly tribe,
the Argippians, who ride on white
horses, carry no arms, and feed on
milk curdled with cherry juice into

gap off Absolüt Point.

Dead silence followed
on the Far Western front.

The Zen-Zombi Theorists
and Analysands
attributed the sudden silence
to Brainwashing.

Their assessment was
in the process of verification

a thick paste. On the western coast
live the Thynians and Bithynians,
who speak the Thracian language;
and the lusty beer-swilling Goths;
and the agricultural Scythians; and
the Brygian fishermen, who wear
sealskin breeches; and the tattooed,
gold-getting Agathyrsians, who
still worship the Triple Goddess
with primitive simplicity."
Robert Graves,
Hercules, My Shipmate.

"Without surprise, watching
from her pillow, she saw herself
run swiftly down this gangplank
to the slanting deck, and standing
there, she leaned on the rail and
waved gaily to herself in bed, and
the slender ship spread its wings
and sailed away into the jungle.
The air trembled with the shattering
scream and the hoarse bellow of
voices all crying together, rolling
and colliding above her like ragged
storm-clouds, and the words became
two words only rising and falling
and clamoring about her head.
Danger, danger, danger, the voices
said, and War, war, war."
Katherine Anne Porter
Pale Horse, Pale Rider.

by the Circuit of Sovereignty
—Capt. Pacific on the J-I,
Capt. Cervantes and Aeschylus
on the DAEMON, Capt. Agrippa
and Severian the Grammarian
on the JUGGLER, and
Sequoia the Deep-Minded on
the POOL OF DREAMINGS—
when the S\S MARU hit bottom.

On the Eastern flank,
the PARALLAX advanced,
while the SOL under
Capt. Carbon and the LUNA
under Capt. Blood
dropped back and fell
into a Y-formation, together
with the ASTRAL BODY
under Capt. Tauhid.

It was the Jovians who
suffered the frontal assault
in full, against an immense
blast of Sound, as first
the ADRASTEA
went down in a ghost-like
Cloud of Dust, followed
by the AMALTHEA,
the LEDA,
the THEBE,
the GANYMEDE,
the CALLISTO,
and moments later—

"Transcendence of sexuality
is the human contribution to
the universe; and this is much
more clearly foreshown in
the personal nature of women
than it is in that of men..."
Laura Riding,
"How Now to Think of Women."

"'I've taken my fun where
I found it. / I've rogued and
I've ranged in my time... /
The things that I learned from
the yellow and black, / They 'ave
helped me a 'eap with the white.'"
Charlotte Perkins Gilman,
Herland.

"...And as for the ordinary sort
of men in that part of the world
where the Emperor resided, they
were of several complexions; not
white, black, tawny, olive or ash-
coloured; but some appeared of
an azure, some of a deep purple,
some of a grass-green, some of
a scarlet, some of an orange-colour,
etc... The rest of the inhabitants
of that world, were men of several
different sorts, shapes, figures,
dispositions, and humours, as I have
already made mention before...
The bear-men were to be

as if in a Cosmic Echo
of life's extermination—
all the Jovian ships.

Like the Sound of a billion
drums in the distance,
the beating continued.

The smell of Shit was everywhere.

The polyrhythmic Sounds
from the alien fleet intensified,
causing the LIVI X,
the SHOEMAKER, the MILES
and the CAGE to shatter.

The Holy League took action,
as did the Vandals
on the ZERO and
DOUBLE ZERO, preparing
for full-scale deployment.

To our despair, however,
no sooner were the first
beams on their way than
huge waves started rising
on all sides, isolating
our ships between surging
walls of water, fragmenting
the fleet within a maze.

her experimental philosophers,
the bird-men her astronomers,
the fly-, worm- and fish-men
her natural philosophers, the ape-
men her chemists, the satyrs
her Galenic physicians, the fox-
men her politicians, the spider-
and lice-men her mathematicians,
the jackdaw-, magpie- and parrot-
men her orators and logicians,
the giants her architects, etc."
Margaret Cavendish,
The Blazing World.

"the silent giver of worlds, what /
is most important is the nonillusion. /
Morning breaks, the friendly reds, /
the big blues /... a rare understanding
of human struggle / simplicity of
the senseless song / the folly of
the wind in my heart... sweet xocolatl
of ancient Mexico, storm of the blood
that comes through the mouth—"
Frida Kahlo,
"the silent life-giver of worlds."

"The book from which Felix
instructed Safie was Volney's
Ruins of Empires... It gave me
an insight into the manners,
governments, and religions of
the different nations of the earth.
I heard of the slothful Asiatics;

We knew we were Dead.

The pounding seemed to
redouble, as Zen and Zombi
ships, hidden from view,
could be heard to explode.

Our decimation was
accelerating, lighting up
the sky with explosions near
and far, reaching deeper
into the Holy League—
the SALAMI,
the ECONOMU,
the ACTION,
the RAGNAROK,
the LEPANTO,
the CISCO,
the SANTA,
the NUESTRO,
the DEFENCE,
the GUERRIERE,
the DREADNOUGHT,
the GOLIATH,
the THESES,
the BELLEROPHONE,
the NEPTUNE,
the MERCURE
—when Capts. Nafta
and Gatt of the Vandal
High Command,
without warning,
launched the nomad fleet

of the stupendous genius and
mental activity of the Grecians;
of the wars and wonderful virtue
of the early Romans—of their
subsequent degeneration—
of the decline of that mighty
empire; of chivalry, Christianity,
and kings. I heard of the discovery
of the American hemisphere, and
wept with Safie over the hapless
fate of its original inhabitants."
Mary Shelley,
The Last Man.

"The Cherokees came out
of the Creek campaign firm
in the conviction that, having
helped America in its need,
they had forever established
in American eyes their right
to perfect their government
and improve their land in peace."
Marion Starkey,
The Cherokee Nation.

"And now my book
of Crazy Horse is done...
I have used the simplest words
possible, hoping by idiom
and figures and the underlying
rhythm pattern to say some
things of the Indian for which
there are no white-man words,

on a suicide run.

Already in overdrive, and
heating up past the point of
no return, a massive force
of Iridescent ships,
set to crack in chain reaction,
charged through the waves
from the North.

It was the ZERO
that blew first,
releasing the Big Bang.

For an instant
the sky turned White.

In the tumult that followed,
as the sea and sky succumbed
to blast after blast
in deafening flashes of light,
the waves surged upward,
streaming higher and higher—
until the last, ungodly moment,
when the boundless power
of a Rainstorm heaved
the waves up to the sky...

The pouring Rain

suggest something of his innate
nature, something of his
relationship to the earth and
the sky and all that is between.
I hope I have not failed too
miserably, for they were a great
people, the old buffalo-hunting
Sioux, and some day their greatness
will reach full flowering again
in their children as they walk
the hard new road of the white man."
Mari Sandoz,
Crazy Horse.

"All that can be said is that
the laws of interior preparation
revealed by Quetzalcoatl were
used by the Aztecs to prop up
their bloody state... We are here
dealing with low witch-craft:
the material transmission of human
energy to the sun. The exalted
revelation of the eternal unity
of the spirit was converted into
a principle of cosmic anthropophagy.
The liberation of the individual,
the separate 'I', came to be under-
stood with crude literalness only,
and achieved through ritual killings
which in their turn fomented wars."
Laurette Séjourné,
Burning Water.

left no ship unscathed.

The Vandals, like the Jovians
before them, were gone.

But the ocean was calm again;
and half the alien fleet
had been destroyed.

The Clouds above us flashed
with silent blasts of lightning.

In their wake, below,
the radiant Green band
of the Doubloon-Bind
was manifest against
the Whiteness of the sea.

Twilight ruled the Orionis waters.

The pounding persisted,
growing stronger,
as the A. POCATAZZ's
Lenses were lit,
followed by the twenty-two
ships under Prof. Parmenides
on the SEPHIROT.

Before the first rays
from our ships could
reach their mark, Voices

"This relatively modern attitude
of cultural autarky for Europe,
of demonstrating her cultural and
racial supremacy at the expense
of everyone else, can best be
described as the conversion
of Classical Studies into
Aryan Studies... The relationship
between Classical Antiquity
and its neighbors to the East
was viewed in this period
not as a cultural continuity but
a *Kulturkampf*—a struggle for
survival between West and East.
The high-points of this eternal
and undeclared war: Achaean
versus Trojan, Greek against
Persian, Alexander against
the East, Rome against Carthage,
Byzantium against Islam."
Charles Doria, "Pound, Olson
and the Classical Tradition."

"The world was all revenge
and thou hadst said: / 'It is
a seething sea!' Earth had
no room / For walking, air
was ambushed by the spears; /
The stars began to fray,
and time and earth /
Washed hands in mischief."
Ferdowsi, *Shahnameh*
("*The Book of Kings*"), quoted

came bursting in the air—new
commands, canceled orders,
secret codes—jamming our
communications systems with
a false flow of information.

In their confusion,
the REPRISAL,
the REPULSE,
the RESOLUTION
and the RETALIATION
misread the PARALLAX
for an enemy vessel, Fired
in error, and destroyed it.

Moments later,
the Zombis responded
by Firing on each other.

The pace of our annihilation
quickened, as if reflected
in the flashes
of the Clouds overhead.

Visibility deteriorated,
while gusts and whirlwinds
stirred the dark air with
the specter of Astral Corpses.

What could still be recognized
was the dim aura

in Giorgio de Santillana and
Hertha von Dechend, *Hamlet's Mill.*

"Let Greeks be Greeks, and
Women what they are."
Anne Bradstreet, "Prologue."

"The argument of the Odyssey
is not a long one. A certain
man has been abroad many
years; Poseidon is ever on
the watch for him, and he is
all alone. Matters at home too
have come to this, that his
substance is being wasted and
his son's death plotted by suitors
to his wife. Then he arrives
there himself after his grievous
sufferings; reveals himself,
and falls on his enemies."
Aristotle,
Poetics.

"It is for the other world that
the madman sets sail in his fools'
boat; it is from the other world
that he comes when he disembarks."
Michel Foucault,
Madness and Civilization.

"Six hundred thousand men
in all, / Not counting wives and
children small, / Were led by God

of the Doubloon-Bind.

Alone, in the end, our ship
reached the Green water
above La Renaixença Hills.

The Captain mounted
the wicker-work,
and, after the blessing
of Areopagiticus
with Toothpick, gave
ben-Cnopee and Sony
the signal to unwind
the eightfold plexus
of Backward Speech,
in accordance with
the "Time Pills
of the Stageguard"
described by Terran.

No sooner had she asked
Mach the Lookout,
"Do you copy?" while Vico
and Chauvée sang
the Battle Hymn in Re,
than the light from the Lens
began to Materialize.

On impact,
the Fire spread instantly
to port and starboard.

Rising on either side,

across the sand, / Two only
reached the Promised Land."
Sebastian Brant,
Ship of Fools.

"There is a nightmare
at the core of Exodus."
Jeffrey Mehlman,
"Core of the Core:
A Phantasmagoria in Translation."

"...If your majesty were resolved
to make a cabbala, I would
advise you, rather to make
a poetical or romancical cabbala,
wherein you can use metaphors,
allegories, similitudes, etc. and
interpret them as you please."
Margaret Cavendish,
The Blazing World.

"The text, in its mass, is
comparable to a sky, at once
flat and smooth, deep, without
edges and without landmarks;
like the soothsayer drawing
on it with the tip of his staff
an imaginary rectangle wherein
to consult, according to certain
principles, the flight of birds,
the commentator traces through
the text certain zones of reading,
in order to observe therein

it formed a great archway
that closed above us,
sealing us in a chamber
of Flames.

Beyond, the whole
Orionis Ripple
was consumed by Fire,
vast Inferno
that we had created.

Rosetta has no way
of knowing how long
we were there.

The ship's timepieces
eventually reverted
to a t-zero loop.

Throughout our seclusion,
only ghost-like outlines
were discernible, Red and
Pink contours feeding off
the Whiteness of the light.

As the heat increased,
cracks in the ship's Crystal
echoed faintly at first,
then more violently.

The vessel was rising,

the migration of meanings,
the outcropping of codes,
the passage of citations."
Roland Barthes,
A Lover's Discourse.

"Space and Time the saliva /
in the mouth"
C. Olson,
The Maximus Poems: Volume Three
(posthumous).

"Like cures like; and for this hunt,
my malady becomes my most
desired health... but methinks
like-cures-like applies to him too,
he grows so sane again."
Herman Melville,
Moby Dick.

"Progress and Doom are two
sides of the same medal."
Hannah Arendt,
The Origins of Totalitarianism.

"So that the life of a writer,
whatever he might fancy to
the contrary, was not so much
a state of composition, as a state
of warfare; and his probation
in it, precisely that of any other
man militant upon earth,—
both depending alike, not half

lifting itself into the air...

The hull and sails cracked
intermittently, until
a long Sound seemed
to Rip through the Crystal.

After it passed, we were back
on the surface, realigned,
joined to the water again—
as if the sea had shifted
into place beneath us.

The immediate sign
of structural damage
was a fissure down
the length of the mast, and
across the propeller shaft.

The other signs appeared later,
once the vault of the Flames
had opened overhead,
parting on either side of us,
to reveal the stars and
the Blackness of our new sky,
and the Silver water.

Here on board the calm
is overwhelming—as if
rooted to an infinitesimal
cushion of air,

so much upon the degrees of
his WIT—as his RESISTANCE."
Lawrence Sterne,
Tristram Shandy.

"From here on it will be
a trip of thrills and despair."
Hiromu Arakawa,
Fullmetal Alchemist.

"beloved Child, we are together, /
weary of War, /
only the Quest remains"
H. D.,
Helen in Egypt.

"Many mouths empty their waters /
into the Godavari of Art— / a river
that flows / across the Decan trap
of the age / with its lava-scarred
plateaux; / and, in the selfheal of
the river, / pilgrims lave the bruises
of the Rain of woes."
Melvin Tolson,
Harlem Gallery, "Omega."

"That's how Don Quixote
decided to save the world."
Kathy Acker,
Don Quixote.

"I've seen the future /
and boy it's rough."

over which the ship glides
by a will of its own.

Our new Mare Tenebrarum
is like a dreamscape.

The Silver water reflects
the stars in pools of Shade,
like an Antique mirror.

Small waves rise
like sand dunes—
and collapse
like crumpled paper.

The Sound of shooting stars
is gentler, less vibrant,
less electric: both conch
and flute of Pan, in one.

Soft bursts of light across
the unknown constellations
of Black space...

Something basic may be
wrong, however,
in our dreamlike tranquility,
beyond the holocaust
raging under a timeless
cover of Clouds.

Prince, "The Future,"
in *Batman* (soundtrack).

"In his boredom and annoyance
he took out a Japanese koto
and pleasantly hummed
'The Field in Hitachi.'"
Murasaki Shikibu,
The Tale of Genji.

Do you read me,
or will you ever again?

From the lookout
there is word
of luminescence
on the horizon.

I will try again from there.

Love,

S.

The Hanged One

My love,

When I close my eyes,
I see the damp walls
and the graffiti.

Walls of silence,
Untranscendable...

As in:

"Teh sez:
'Sign-language'S
VOID!'"

Or,

"Power Control
shut down!

SHUT UP!"

Or,

"Qi is the commander of Blood,
Blood is the mother of Qi."
Song Shi,
Lingshu Jing.

"Such a perceptive entanglement, /
beyond crucifixion, /
gives / wings to our rhythm."
Jay Wright, "Cursus Ensemble."

"The middle of the road is trying to
find me / I'm standing in the middle
of life with my plans behind me..."
The Pretenders,
"Middle of the Road."

"Observe due measure."
Hesiod,
Works and Days.

"It often happens that, though
a person cannot recollect at
the moment, yet by seeking he can
do so, and discover what he seeks...

"MêMe sez :

SUICIDE
IS
D-O-U-B-L-I-N-G.

...CONDITION :
un-STOPPABLE...

Do

YOU

read

ME?"

As if I were the last
of many souls
to pass through here—
in this unreal space
between a closed gate,
unlocked, and a stairway
leading nowhere.

In contrast to the graffiti
there is the sculpture
of a Nude, untouched
and resplendent,

But one must get hold of a starting
point. This explains why it is that
persons are supposed to recollect
sometimes by starting from mnemonic
loci... It seems true in general that
the middle point also among all things
is a good mnemonic starting-point
from which to reach any of them."
Aristotle,
On Memory and Recollection.

"Perish the man whose
mind is backward now."
William Shakespeare,
Henry V.

"...Cool reflections never occur until
after the event. And one of the most
important and generally acknowledged
truths is stifled and useless in
the vortex of our absurd manners."
Choderlos de Laclos,
Dangerous Liaisons.

"You can't go... back home to
the escapes of Time and Memory."
Thomas Wolfe,
You Can't Go Home Again.

"A cell of graffiti
is merely aphoristic."
Lyn Hejinian, "The Guard."

at the center of a pool.

The figure sits on a log
with legs crossed
and feet arched, smiling
at the walls and at me.

I am reminded of
the Sacrificial Victim
in "The Nature Theater
of Oklahoma."

On the stone wall
beyond the gate
there is the bas-relief
of a Saint, in Lotus
position, meditating.

I cannot be sure
the Saint was there
before the moment
of my vision.

Since then, it seems clear
the graffiti have multiplied.

The walls are less bare,
and I do not remember reading:

" *Message co-signed*

'DOUBLE-TALK'

"Short seemd too night. L K."
Ron Silliman,
Tjanting.

"'This is the Sibyl's cave;
these are Sibylline leaves.'
On examination, we found that
all the leaves, bark, and other
substances, were traced with
written characters... I have
been employed in deciphering
these sacred remains."
Mary Shelley,
The Last Man.

"Mary was Frankenstein's
creator / his yellow eye /
before her husband was
to drown / Created the monster
nights / after Byron,
Shelley / talked the candle down. /
Who was Mary Shelley? /
She read Greek, Italian /
She bore a child / Who died /
and yet another child who died."
Lorine Niedecker,
"Who was Mary Shelley?"

"(what the skull can endure!)"
H. D.,
The Walls Do Not Fall.

"Significance is never without

'DOUBLE-BIND'

One-way...

Pre-set...

IM-movable!

A s A b o v e

S o B e l o w

WIND-

up-

IN-

the-

HOLE : "

When the vision came,
I was sitting against
the opposite wall,
between the gate
on the left
and the stairway
on the right.

a white wall upon which it inscribes
its signs and redundancies.
Subjectivation is never without
a black hole in which it lodges
its consciousness, passion, and
redundancies. Since all semiotics
are mixed and strata come at least
in twos, it should come as
no surprise that a very special
mechanism is situated at their
intersection. Oddly enough, it is
a face: the *white wall / black hole*
system. A broad face with white
cheeks, a chalk face with eyes cut
in for a black hole. Clown head,
white clown, moon-white mime,
angel of death, Holy Shroud."
Gilles Deleuze and Félix Guattari,
A Thousand Plateaus.

"I will instruct men or women who
are intelligent and for the briefest
period, patient, to become masters
of their facial destiny. I understand
the skull with its muscular sheath
as a sphere whose superficies
can be voluntarily energized.
And the foundations of beauty as
embedded in the three inter-
connected zones of energy encircling
this sphere: the centers of control
being at the base of the skull
and highest point of the cranium.

Near the floor,
next to me, I saw
the drawing of a Wheel
and a pair of Scales,
and the formula:

" HEAVEN'S ENERGY'S ~ <u>SEA</u>
MOMENTUM = *PHANTOM* + ——
^ <u>ICE</u> "

No sooner had I read
the inscription
than the chamber's walls
began to decompose.

They seemed to pour down
all around me, foaming
in slow, thick streams.

My teeth and jaws
clamped shut,
as if my skull
were being crushed.

And just as suddenly,
the motion was reversed.

The liquid walls
passed back into matter,
returning as before.

Mina Loy,
"Auto-Facial Construction."

"...He fled forward still,
toward your face."
W. Shakespeare,
Cymbeline.

"and again Plotinus / To the door, /
Keep your eyes on the mirror"
Ezra Pound,
Cantos, XV.

"Mirror is not something created
but something born. You don't
need many to have the sparkling
and the sleepwalking mine:
two are enough, and one reflects
the reflection of what the other
reflected, in a trembling that
is transmitted in an intense and
mute telegraphic message,
insistent, liquidity in which
you can plunge a fascinated
hand and pull it out dripping
with the reflections of that hard
water that is the mirror."
Clarice Lispector,
Água Viva.

"'Where are the new frontiers?'
the Romantics cried, unaware
that the frontier of the mind had

New changes followed.

The graffiti appeared to slip
out of focus, under a layer
of Ice that covered the walls.

The words receded
and grew illegible
behind a radiant surface.

As the luminescence
increased, the water
in the pool darkened,
reflecting the statue's
inverted gaze.

Its blank face and empty eyes
stared back at me.

Then a different face emerged,
replacing the first:
the bodiless face
of our Departed child.

As if across the Years
of pain and loss...
looking at me,
and glancing at the gate.

I sat in contemplation

opened in a laboratory on
Callisto at the turn of the twenty-
fourth century... Teleportation...
the transportation of oneself
through space by an effort of
the mind alone... had long
been a theoretic concept...
Twelve psychologists, para-
psychologists, and neurometrists
of varying specialization were
called in as observers....
The experimenters sealed Jaunte
into an unbreakable crystal tank.
They opened a water valve,
feeding water into the tank...
It was impossible to open
the tank; it was impossible
to stop the flow of water...
The tank filled quickly...
Jaunte began to drown. Then
he was outside the tank, dripping
and coughing explosively. He'd
teleported again... The body
of knowledge grew rapidly...
They had learned how to teach
man to recognize, discipline,
and exploit yet another resource
of his limitless mind."
Alfred Bester,
The Stars My Destination.

"'The great Theater of Oklahoma
is calling you! It is calling only

of Es's face—until the walls
became clear again,
and the graffiti resurfaced.

Of the Magick deck,
I know that *The Fool,*
The Scales,
The Hanged One,
and *The Universe*
are in play;
I cannot be sure what
other Cards are here.

I know the stakes
have been raised
to a Dollar:
one of us is saved,
the other lost.

And I remember
my opponent's name:
"Bird-Dog."

I fear that Bird-Dog
is *The Lovers // reversed—*
in which case I am lost
in this netherworld forever.

The presence of *The Fool*

today, only this once! Anyone who
misses this opportunity shall miss it
forever! Anyone who is thinking
of his future belongs in our midst!
All are welcome! Anyone who
wants to become an artist should
contact us! We are a theater that
can make use of everyone, each
in his place! And we congratulate
here and now those who have
decided in our favor. At twelve
o'clock everything shall close and
won't open again! Accursed
be those who don't believe us!'"
Franz Kafka,
Amerika: The Missing Person.

"We're living through a time /
That needs to be lived through us."
Adrienne Rich,
"The Will To Change."

"Rising harmonies to a level
of blissful stability at end."
John Coltrane, from a manuscript
to *A Love Supreme.*

"On the mornings that had once
throbbed with the dawn chorus
of robins, catbirds, doves, jays,
wrens, and scores of other bird
voices, there was now no sound."
Rachel Carson,

marks the two walls
to my left—in the direction
toward which Es's face
kept turning.

Either *The Fool* corresponds to
the outside wall beyond the gate,
or to the near wall
that contains the gate.

The truth of the one lies
in the graffiti of the other.

Both walls bear the inscription:
" : -) Very Romantic) - : ."

Common to the walls,
in addition, there is a mass
of strange symbols—
lines, dots, and spirals,
together with handprints—
below which a human figure
in headdress is shaking a spear.

The caption reads:
"AFTER THE FLOOD."

"Alpha" and *"Beta"*
appear to the left
and right of the gate.

On the outer wall,
"Omega" is canceled,

Silent Spring.

"The false dawn came over the flats,
bringing nothing with it. / She sat and
considered her sins. / That they were
vast was undeniably true, a mental
land as flat and bare as a world-sized
table, and yet with here and there
those disturbing dips and slides;
concave surfaces that somehow
remained flat, hills that slid the other
way, like the squares on a chessboard
which bend and produce nausea."
Joanna Russ,
Picnic on Paradise.

"...Of this one thing we may
be sure, the Grail is a living force,
it will never die; it may indeed
sink out of sight, and, for centuries
even, disappear from the field
of literature, but it will rise to
the surface again, and become once
more a theme of vital inspiration."
Jesse Weston,
From Ritual to Romance.

"I am not familiar with the exact
constitution of the Tarot pack of cards,
from which I have obviously departed
to suit my own convenience."
T. S. Eliot,
Notes on "The Waste Land."

replaced by a Dollar sign:
"$."

"Sophistication! Sophistication! /
You are the idol of our nation /
Each fellow has / Fallen for jazz /
And we'll give the past a merry razz /
Thro' the ghoul-guarded gateways
of slumber / And fellow-guestship
with the glutless worm."
H. P. Lovecraft, "Waste Paper:
A Poem of Profound Insignificance."

A woman with
Cuneiform breasts
speaks the word:
"*GENESIS.*"

On the inner wall,
another Dollar sign—
but backward,
as in a mirror.

"The first level or statement of three
an open field of question, how large
it ought or ought not to be."
Cecil Taylor, liner notes,
Unit Structures.

"I love tomorrow."
Conrad Roberts, "Inamorata,"
in Miles Davis, *Live / Evil.*

"Oh, Death, why canst thou
not sometimes be timely?"
Herman Melville,
Moby Dick.

I see myself as
The Hanged One
in the wall facing me,
with each of the other walls
representing a Card:
The Universe to my right,
The Scales behind me.

Regardless of the outcome,
The Fool spells Khaos.

Your lover,

A.

The Skeleton

My love,

"I wish that I'd sail
the darkened seas /
On a great big clipper ship /
Going from this land
here to that /
In a sailor's suit and cap."
Nico and the Velvet Underground,
"Heroin" (*RIP* Lou Reed).

"The river is within us,
the sea is all about us."
T. S. Eliot, "The Dry Salvages,"
in *Four Quartets.*

"The river we stepped
into is not the river
in which we stand."
Herakleitos (tr. G. Davenport).

"A branch of Ocean, allotted
a tenth of its waters. /
Nine parts circle earth
and the sea's broad back /
In silvery currents returning

I think the luminescence
on the horizon, *which leads me
back to you,* continues to recede
as we head in its direction
because the Elders of
Kohiba, commenting on
the NOSTROMO's passage
through the Straits
of the Scarlet Sea
in Chapter X, Book II,
from *The Pedagogue's Handbook*,
describe conditions similar
to our own, given:
1) the recent overboard fall
into the Pelagic Omega of
Finnegan and Leiningen,
Mazüka, Meade and Fiat,
from Engineering,
who jumped into the ocean
or pushed each other
like Sun, Li and company;
and 2) the gaseous Dust Cloud
of the Username nebula, in which
"the Light loves to hide"—

to Ocean's brine."
Hesiod,
Theogony.

"I looked out at the ocean.
I liked that ocean. You always
knew there was going to be
another wave. It had always
been there, and more
than likely it always would."
S. E. Hinton,
Rumble Fish.

"'TO THE SEA
YE MYSTICS,'
the cry that heralded
the act of purification..."
Jane Harrison,
*Prolegomena to the Study
of Greek Religion.*

"In regards death
everybody's a mystic."
Stephen Rodefer,
Four Lectures,
"Words in Work in Russian."

"All of a sudden /
killer-squalls attacked us,
screaming out of the west /
a murderous blast shearing
the two forestays off /
so the mast toppled backward,

as if clothing, un-clothing,
re-clothing itself in successive
layers of Spiritual cover,
yet shrinking nonetheless.

Neither Venus's reading
of the spit projected
by Commander Exprès
onto the first Glass Ingot
inside the Cauldron's
nestled Metal bowls,
nor *Tōran-Ba*,
the Spirit of the Keel
following the so-called
"Big Fart," agrees with me.

Thus, we sail ahead toward
the light, over Murmuring waters,
to a constant Ringing
of the Bells, with the feeling
of being watched;
here in a Morphic field
of Rubber cylinders floating
like tall, alcove-riddled towers
in a web of Black slime;
the deck furniture secured, but
the ouzo in the jars polluted
with Canaanite Seashells;
the Bluestone anchor encrusted
with Sea Weed and Dead moss,
the fissure down the mast and
the crack along the propeller shaft
sprouting radio-active Plant Life,

its running tackle spilling /
into the bilge. The mast itself
went crashing into the stern, /
it struck the helmsman's head
and crushed his skull to pulp /
and down from his deck
the man flipped like a diver— /
his hardy life spirit left
his bones behind. / Then, then
in the same breath Zeus hit
the craft / with a lightning bolt
and thunder. Round she spun, /
reeling under the impact,
filled with reeking brimstone, /
shipmates pitching out of her,
bobbing round like seahawks /
swept along by the whitecaps
past the trim black hull— /
and the god cut short
their journey home forever."
The Odyssey, Book XII.

"And Moses stood in the gate
of the camp and said, 'Whoever
is for YHWH: to me!' And all
the children of Levi were gathered
to him. And he said to them,
'YHWH, God of Israel, said this:
Set, each man, his sword on
his thigh; cross over and come back
from gate to gate in the camp;
and kill, each man, his brother,
and, each man, his neighbor,

the arcade's stained glass
melted away, the Flag poles
inscribed with Flaming Letters,
the Lens out of joint
with the light of new stars;
our sights set on Absolüt Point,
to which we now theoretically
return under the pure,
stop-and-go movement
of a meteor advancing
with its tail pointing forward.

Stories of gas "passed" by
a whole crew simultaneously
are collected in Helikon's
Pamphlet on Ultrathin Borderlines
based on the logbooks of
the WINCHESTER, the ESSEX,
the LUXOR, the LYNCEE,
the ULUBURUN and the ALERT;
in our case, however,
the Black sky and
the Silver sea had opened
the field of *Dasein,*
so the situation was different.

Following the Alien debacle
and our arrival
in the Mare Tenebrarum—
just after Captain Anna-O,
cursing in chronic fits
beside a dumbfounded
Commander Exprès,

and, each man, his relative.'
And the children of Levi did
according to Moses' word, and
about three thousand men fell
from the people in that day."
Exodus 32.

"And when in his wide
courtyards Odysseus
had cut down / the insolent
youths, he hung on high
his sated bow / and strode
to the warm bath to cleanse
his blood-stained body."
Nikos Kazantzakis,
The Odyssey: A Modern Sequel.

"Then, I must ask you again,
Virgil, toward which goal
have you been striving
with your poetry, since
it seems it was not toward
an understanding of life?"
Hermann Broch,
The Death of Virgil.

"if the seas of cities should crash
against each other / and break
the chains / and break the walls
holding down the cargo / and break
the sides of the seas / and all
the waters of the earth wash
together / in a rush of breaking /

had assembled the crew
between the Third level
of the ship's First bottom
and the Middle level
of the Middle bottom,
above the head and torso
of Avon the Poetess—
the "Big Fart" became manifest
through a gas-induced
chain reaction of signs.

All at once, we stood still
and started talking fast,
until the random moment
when the Diving Bell cracked
and the velvet pipeline
filtered the Sound,
the spokes on the Omnicycle
appeared to spin in reverse,
and we found ourselves pacing
to-and-fro, humming in unison,
creating a background Drone
over which could be heard,
from beyond the Quietist room,
the timbrel, the cymbal and gong
—until the next random moment,
when an auxiliary ladder
crossed through the air
from starboard to port,
and some of us stopped,
while others kept moving,
and Communications and
Intelligence put their foreheads

where will the captains
run and / to what harbor?"
Lucille Clifton,
"if something should happen."

"With its coherent artifact
assemblage and extant
hull remains, the wreck
is considered the world's
oldest sea-going ship...
The Uluburun ship had
a carrying capacity of
at least 20 tons' burden.
This minimum capacity
was calculated by tallying
the recovered objects,
which included more than
10 tons of copper and one
ton of tin ingots, Canaanite
jars, large ceramic storage
jars (pithoi), stone anchors,
and approximately one ton
of cobblestone ballast."
Cemal Pular,
"The Uluburun Shipwreck
and Late Bronze Age Trade,"
in *Beyond Babylon* (ed. J. Aruz,
K. Benzel and J. Evans).

"Oh build your ship
of death, oh build it! /
for you will need it. /
For the voyage

to the bulkheads, and together
dreamed the same dream.

By their own account,
they dreamed of Red Dots,
like dominoes, Mutating
under Cosmic Rays
into thirteen Open Hands,
then into nine Dancing Heads,
then into twelve Heads-on-Sticks,
exchanging kisses...

The Waves of Fear
hit only later,
because, paradoxically,
when the signs of Passed Gas
subsided, a good measure
of calm settled over the ship
into the crew's Lower Elixir,
and like others—
Maria, Soho and Greenwich,
Marlboro and Wang—
I experienced a tingling
in my breasts,
my Sex felt lusty and wet,
while the phalluses
of Chauvée and Venus,
Sinbad the Steward
and Kodak the Second Mate
stood fully erect—
a seemingly clear indication
that jubilation and
self-renewal were in order,

of oblivion awaits you."
D. H. Lawrence,
"The Ship of Death."

"I recommend to you
the making of my epitaph;
for I perceive I will die confected
in the very stench of farts."
Francois Rabelais,
The Third Book of Pantagruel.

"The poet as poet
is the one who points,
thus something that shows,
and is thereby a 'sign.'
The poet is a sign that has
a soul in which a 'mind' is
appropriate, in which it bears
the stars of the heavens...
The sign, the demi-god,
the river, the poet: all these
name poetically the one
and singular ground of
the becoming homely
of human beings as
historical and the founding
of this ground by the poet."
Martin Heidegger,
Hölderlin's Hymn "The Ister."

"I'm baffled by the Muse's
state of mind: / she looks
at me and doesn't say

as on the STARMAN
or the SATELLITE OF LOVE
in the abandoned gloss
to the Senzar Almanac.

Yet new sensations
followed, from the moment
the matrix codes
in the Majic Lantern
of the depth gauge
confronted the crew's
generalized Sexual arousal
with the nomadic,
Poromechanical spectacle
of bottomless Abysses
opening, closing, re-opening
across the ocean floor,
as the ship made its way
through random Fog Clusters
of variable densities.

The change of mood
and weather recalled
the Abyssal Time, when
New York came into view
for the LANCASTER II,
and the twin figure(s)
of Smashed Tablet
and Burned Manuscript
replaced the Azreal-Asmath
equation (Ocean = Lubricant)
in *The Catalogue of Men*.

a word, / And lays her head,
in its dark wreath, /
exhausted on my breast."
Anna Akhmatova,
"All Has Been Taken Away"
(tr. S. Kunitz, M. Hayward).

"And some grew weary
of the ghastly dance /
And fell, as I have fallen
by the way side, /
Those soonest
from whose forms
most shadows past /
And least of strength
& beauty did abide. /
— 'Then, what is Life?'
I said... [T]he cripple cast /
His eye upon the car
which now had rolled /
Onward, as if that look must
be the last, / And answered...
'Happy those for whom
the fold / '"
P. Bysshe Shelley,
"The Triumph of Life."

"It takes wings to seize /
The nearest things /
Immediately /
And reach the other side."
Friedrich Hölderlin,
"The Ister."

It was the Abyssal Time
in which distress
took hold of our souls
at the Cutting Edge
of the ship's Crystal body,
and anxiety kept us on alert
before the cryptogenic emergence
of new constellations;
it was the Time of mysterious
seething and the Tracelessness
of the figurehead
after the recombination of
van Rr'Ubik's Half-Shadow;
the Time of the Movement-
that-transports-being during
the Dormition of Möbius;
it was the multi-functional
Abyssal Time of Sing-Along
Songs for Yusef and Madiba,
when the struggle
between opposing powers
in the First Testament
of the Old War impaired
the ability to traverse
incompatible dimensions,
and when the lapses,
wounds, pains and
rewards-after-appeasement
in the Second Testament
of the New War
foreclosed undiscovered
territories of the "new."

"I often stand at this height...
but a moment of reflection
hurls me down."
F. Hölderlin,
Hyperion.

"The need to climb
is too widespread.
To feel it no longer
is a rare deliverance."
Samuel Beckett,
The Lost Ones.

"If I cannot sway the Heavens,
I'll stir the Netherworld."
Virgil, *Aeneid*;
quoted by Sigmund Freud
in *The Interpretation of Dreams.*

"Power comes from below."
Michel Foucault,
The History of Sexuality.

"The axis of my writing
does not run from death
to life or from life to death,
but rather from death
to truth and from truth
to death. I think that
the alternative to death
isn't life but truth.
What we have to rediscover

Finally, inevitably,
after emerging from
the 21st Fog Cluster,
we beheld *starboard side*
at Three O'Clock,
like the Isle of Blessèd Wounds
in Yax Passage's Torn Letters
from *Manifesto of*
the Unconscious and Random,
a monstrous mound of Sea Jelly
rising from the ocean's surface,
as if from the Underground depths
of a River of Light
or a Lake of Fire.

Temporarily enlightened by
the spectacular event,
like us all, Captain Anna-O
became our Model of Moderation
along the split, schizo-warped
Axis of the Ephesians—
Dead to the stings-of-life
and stronger-than-Herself
in the game of Pleasure Relations
—while Kongō and Thebes
of the Syracuse School
immediately theorized about
the Sea-Flower Brain or
Watery Eyeball of Super Mind
as "Bell Jar,"
and Avon rhapsodized
about her legs-turned-to-bone
floating under the Ark of Millions

through the whiteness
and inertia of death isn't
the lost shudder of life,
it's the meticulous
deployment of truth."
M. Foucault, in conversation
with Claude Bonnefoy.

"all is not dead
one drinks
one gives to drink
goodbye"
S. Beckett,
How It Is.

"Now choose, /
right, left, / win, lose."
H. D.,
Hermetic Definition.

"The Soul selects
her own Society – /
Then – shuts the Door – "
Emily Dickinson (409).

"The genuine poet
chooses to lose...
This is the deeper
meaning of that tough-luck,
of that curse with which
he always claims
kinship and which
he always attributes

and reaching down
as "long super feelers"
in an Electro-magnetic
helical thread of Love Fuel,
that opened the way
through an "uncanny" mode of
recirculation back to Malaysian,
Mazlum and Palmyra.

The logbook shows that
the second mound of Sea Jelly,
turned upside down on its back,
appeared *portside* at Nine O'Clock
in the spot of time before
the ship was again enveloped
in a cosmodromic Fog Cluster—
just as Neanderthal shouted,
"Something happening here..."
and Commander Exprès
started spitting in the wind.

During the conversation
that followed under
the penumbra of the Fog,
Woodstock and Soho,
who had witnessed the second
Mutation of the Silver sea,
discussed with Kongō and Thebes,
who had not, the Theoretical-
Poetic significance of what
had taken place, *viz.* whether,
relative to the Soft Metal Machine
of the crew's collective Mind,

to an intervention
from without; whereas
it is his deepest choice,
the source, and not
the consequence of his poetry."
Jean-Paul Sartre,
What Is Literature?

"I found in this myth
situated at the confines
of the world the theories
of philosophers I had
made my own:
every man must forever
choose, in his short life,
between indefatigable
hope and the wise absence
of hope, between
the delights of chaos
and those of stability,
between the Titan
and the Olympian."
Marguerite Yourcenar,
Memories of Hadrian.

"Above all,
don't fool yourself,
don't say / it was
a dream, your ears
deceived you: / don't
degrade yourself with
empty hopes like these."
C. P. Cavafy,

the upside-down sea mound,
and the long, life-like
coils of Silver water
that reached up from it
and seemed to probe the stars—
taken as the Mind's
complemental Sub-Conscious
together with the first sea mound
as Mind's Super-Conscious—
functioned either as
an Analytic or Histrionic
assemblage; or as an Academic
composite of both; or
as the vectorial White Light
\ White Heat of neither.

When the Fog Cluster lifted again,
it settled as a Blue-Red haze
high above the ship and
revealed, directly astern,
right side up, a third mound
of gelatinous water, as massive
as the previous two combined...
both of which were now gone.

According to Mazüka,
who was sitting with her head
between her knees
and her legs in her arms
against the bulkhead between
the photo-polarimeter and
the Stelae of Tesla and Tlaloc,
under the boom, this giant mound

"The God Abandons Antony."

"I have had to learn
the simplest things / last."
Charles Olson,
The Maximus Poems,
"Maximus, to himself."

"The Light is easy to move,
but difficult to fix."
The Secret of the Golden Flower
(tr. R. Wilhelm).

"Poetry / is this."
C. Olson,
The Secret of the Black
Chrysanthemum.

"It is considered
more lucky to dream
of a vulva as open."
Sheikh Nefzaoui,
The Perfumed Garden,
"The Names Given
to a Woman's Sexual Organs."

"His finest work
is his use of time."
Henri Pierre Roché,
"Souvenirs de
Marcel Duchamp."

"Time, perfect

represented the appearance
of the third oceanic Dot
in an Archaean three-Dot pattern
identified as the Renowned
Philosopher's Hieroglyphic Triad
of Unlocalizability—a pattern
whose manifestation at sea
Mazüka, her eyes bulging
in an early sign of Madness,
dubbed "Plataforma of
the Moist Principle."

Despite naming the event,
however, and opening
theoretical access into
the Heavenly Arms of truth,
through the love of truth,
within a hermeneutics of Erojan
Otherness, her words acted
as Penetralia to Madness
in the Mind(s) of Meade and
Leiningen, Finnegan and Fiat,
all of whom save Fiat
found their short- and mid-
term memory wiped out.

In an archetypal instance of
Synchronicity, when the order
was given to accelerate
and put maximum distance
between ourselves and
the giant mound behind us,
two more gelatinous mounds

or syncopated time,
is when a faucet dribbles
from a leaky washer."
Charles Mingus, liner notes,
The Black Saint
and the Sinner Lady.

"I am. I am. I am."
Sylvia Plath,
The Bell Jar.

"I am myself alone."
William Shakespeare,
Henry VI, Part 3.

"I am a thousand times
the richest, let us be
as greedy as the sea."
Arthur Rimbaud,
A Season in Hell.

"He felt a sudden little
shock of awakening,
a tremor, when he found
that his memory had
failed to account for
the war years. Then
he totted up the years
and, for an instant,
everything inside him
stopped functioning."
Colette,
The Last of Chéri.

surfaced directly ahead,
as if reborn side-by-side
from their earlier incarnations
—one *right side up,*
the other *upside down*
with its long coils of water
wildly reaching for the sky.

So the counter-order was issued
to stop the ship immediately,
moving the members of Engineering
to abandon their posts
and follow their Spiritual call to
transformation on the "Horizon
of Purity" beyond the "Gateway
of Concealment" by taking
a walk on the Wild Side
to the Alcove of the Panel
of the Close-Up, which
they no longer remembered
was on the fo'c's'le deck...
until reminded by Fiat,
who led the way.

As in the Great Disturbance
at Sov-Ar-Dee described
by Hadron the Circle-Drawer,
an invisible scythe seemed
to slice through the water,
which started bubbling
all around us, just as
the Silver coils of the inverted
mound reached over and

"Many men have
related hideous things,
not mentioned in print,
which happened
on the battle fields
of the Great War."
H. P. Lovecraft,
"Herbert West: Reanimator."

"The love-region
takes on its character
of mind, becomes
this womb-brain
or love-brain
that I have visualized
as a jellyfish."
H. D.,
Notes on Thought and Vision.

"It was the unnamable!"
H. P. Lovecraft,
"The Unnamable."

"This is not quite accurate."
S. Beckett,
The Lost Ones.

"The best way out
is always through."
Robert Frost,
"A Servant to Servants";
restated as, "The way

seized the mound beside it—
then lifted it in the air
completely out of the ocean
and turned it upside down,
setting the second mound,
with its life-like coils reaching
for the stars, on top of
the coils of the first.

Towering before us,
like a Gothic Tree of Life
at the intersection of the Control
and Conception Meridians
on the Ionic Grid in N'ikon's
Fund of Funds, the double upside-
down Cuhthulic phaenomenon
polluted the Art of Pleasure in
the Know-How of Anna-O, and
brought deep Dread to the ship.

The Captain issued the command
to veer to starboard, and ordered
Engineering to their stations;
but Fiat and Meade, Mazüka
and Leiningen, led by Finnegan,
scrambling from the fo'c's'le deck
in the grip of Madness, searched
in vain throughout the ship
for the Engine room, whereupon
Scard'nelli, Nobadinus and I,
like the Swift Nudes of Anatis,
had the Presence of Mind
to act on Engineering's behalf

out is the way through,"
in *Star Trek,*
"To Attain the All."

"I am boring into
a mountain from two sides.
The question is, how
to meet in the middle."
James Joyce on *Finnegans*
Wake; in Frank Budgen,
James Joyce and the Making
of Ulysses.

"I have come that I may greet
myself with myself."
The Egyptian Amduat,
"First Hour" (tr. D. Warburton).

"And Xibalba is packed
with tests, heaps
and piles of tests."
Popul Vuh (tr. D. Tedlock).

"Today, as in the time
of Pliny and Columelle,
the hyacinth thrives
in Wales, the periwinkle
in Illyria, the daisy
on the ruins of Numantia,
and while the cities
around them have
changed masters
and names, several having

and tend to the binnacle magnets,
adjust drainage levels on the draft
pistons, and secure the cassettes
in the cyberspace sockets.

We pulled away to starboard,
gaining speed as the wind
Energized the jib, the flying
jib and the spanker; but,
as we sailed to safer waters,
the towering phaenomenon
from which we escaped,
and the long Shadow it cast,
Mutated: the two sets
of watery coils merged
and formed a single column
of two intertwining strands.

At the same time,
during the process of Mutation,
the mass of Sea Jelly
hovering in mid-air dissolved
and continued to shrink,
while its Image \ Movement
underwent dissemination
and transference onto
the column's Mystical summit.

All hands were on deck,
when the Silver waters of
the column's twin strands,
rising to a height of some
2000 cubits, portside

passed into nothingness,
civilizations having
clashed and broken,
their peaceful generations
have crossed the ages
and come down to us,
fresh and laughing,
as in days of battle."
Edgar Quinet, "Introduction,"
in J. G. Herder,
Reflections on the Philosophy
of the History of Humanity.

"the saying that grass
mocks catastrophe /
is a whim of the inconsolable
and fickle"
Zbigniew Herbert,
"The Hill Facing the Palace."

"...the spring, the summer, /
The childing autumn,
angry winter change /
Their wonted liveries,
and the mazèd world /
By their increase now
knows not which is which."
W. Shakespeare,
A Midsummer Night's Dream.

"The sea's / boiling
the land's / boiling
all the winds / of the earth

behind us, converged
to form the Simulacrum
of a culminating Faucet—
like the Hardware on the Thigh
of the Goth Colossus—
creating the miraculous apparition
of a Colossal free-floating Faucet
running water into the sea.

In the visionary Fold
of that moment, Sub-Conscious
and Super-Conscious
Mind(s) came together,
and the Open Call was heard
to take a closer look;
so we turned back
and resumed our course toward
the luminescence on the horizon,
with the Faucet off to port.

What could not be foreseen
was the change of Weather
we saw next: a Force 11
gust of wind swept in, and
blew across the Faucet's stream,
projecting a massive body
of sea water in our direction,
that kept approaching
like a long sinister cloud—
the Weather Event whose impact
was to wreak such havoc
with the ship...

are turning /
the snow into sand—"
C. Olson,
The Maximus Poems: Volume Three
(posthumous).

"As man advanced
in control over nature,
the mystery and
the godhead of things
natural faded into science.
Only the mystery of life,
and love that begets life,
remained, intimately
realized and utterly
unexplained; hence
Aphrodite keeps
her godhead to the end."
J. Harrison,
Prolegomena to the Study
of Greek Religion.

"Inside the Music /
The Devil cant get in."
Amiri Baraka,
Un Poco Low Coup.

"A blackened shroud,
a hand-me-down gown /
Of rags and silks,
a costume / Fit for one
who sits and cries /
For all tomorrow's parties."

Amid the ensuing commotion,
the order was given to activate
the Ventilation system,
but before the photon fans,
the tachyon fans, the trilithon fans,
and the pyramidion fans
could be engaged, Meade, falling
from the Belvedere, cried out,
"The end of Theory!"
and plunged into the sea,
followed soon after by Finnegan,
who took a running jump.

Moments later, along the portside
bulwarks, Fiat, Mazüka and
Leiningen did the same, jumping
overboard one after the other.

Strangely, as if refusing to sink,
Leiningen's legs continued
to kick in the air, which
prompted Cîpher, beside me
on the quarterdeck by the paddle,
to remark that the spectacle
seemed an "ironic" re-
presentation of the legs
turned-to-bone dragged below
the hull by Avon the Poetess;
while Chauvée, overcome
with emotion, recalled
how our lost crewmates
"were exquisite... the most Youthful
and elegant among us...

Nico and the Velvet Underground,
"All tomorrow's parties."

beautiful of body... the sweetness
of their thighs, their lips

"Ocean, you wanna be my bro?"
Lautréamont,
Maldoror.

"I no longer said to the flower,
you are my sister."
F. Hölderlin,
Hyperion.

"Poetry was a word used
by grown-ups. And their distrust
was enormous, like that
of animals. Whose instinct
warns them that one day
they will be hunted down."
Clarice Lispector,
"The Message."

"'*Ygnaiih.... Ygnaiih...*
thflthkh'ngba... Yog-Sothoth...'
rang the hideous croaking
out of space. '*Y'bthnk...*
h'ehye—n'grkdl'lh.'"
H. P. Lovecraft,

My love—
since I broke off
this letter to you,
Action-adventure and Death
have bent and twisted time.

We are now stuck,
here in the Shoals
with the light finally aligned
behind us.

Different Wave Types
continue to pound us,
no doubt as the direct result
of the furious Whipping-of-
the-Sea commanded by Anna-O
during our second go-around
after the Accidental thrust
of Mutiny: Internal Waves
at Two and Three O'Clock,
"*Rebirth*'s Magnetizer"
behind the hallucination
of the all-swallowing gate
at the Edge of Night

"The Dunwich Horror."

"I take SPACE to be
the central fact to man
born in America,
from Folsom cave to now.
I spell it large because
it comes large here.
Large and without mercy."
C. Olson,
Call Me Ishmael.

"Since then more countries
far away / We've found
past Thule, past Norway, /
As Iceland and
Pilappenland, /
Which ancient writers
never scanned. /
They've found
in Portugal since then /
And in Hispania
naked men, / And sparkling
gold and islands too /
Whereof no mortal ever knew."
Sebastian Brant,
The Ship of Fools.

"Don't you think that
the true captain will be
called a real stargazer,
a babbler, and a good-
for-nothing by those

in *Introduction to Cosmos*
by Capt. Ursula; Constructive
and Destructive Waves at Four
and Five O'Clock, respectively,
both preserving and spending
the Memory-Images
of *Comedy* and *Tragedy*
in the "Maat.Daat Chiasmus"
of Eleusis and Isis's
Labyrinth \ Asylum;
Standing Waves, alternately
at Six and Twelve O'Clock,
whose silence is final and
criss-crossed with oblique,
horizontal Sounds from
the most primitive vibrations
of Underworld, before
"*the Monster* is overcome,"
according to Cabu's
Tarot Manifesto; Breaking
Waves at Seven O'Clock
and Progressive Waves on
the Orthogonal Axis of Eight,
where *Quest*, *Voyage* and *Return*
are "Sheets of the Past in
the Cone of a Fool's cap,"
as explained in Dr. Starbük's
Treatise on Phosphenes;
Refracted Waves at Nine
and \ or Ten O' Clock,
Instruments of Creation
for the Colored glass shards
of the Smashed Mirror—

who sail in ships
governed in this way?"
Plato,
The Republic.

"Doomsday is near:
die all, die merrily."
W. Shakespeare,
Henry IV, Part I.

"One would think a writer
would be happy here—if a writer
is ever happy anywhere."
Raymond Chandler,
The Long Goodbye.

"That for which we find
words is something already
dead in our hearts."
Friedrich Nietzsche,
Twilight of the Idols.

"A Pen has so many
inflections and
a Voice but one."
E. Dickinson (L 470).

"For there is a rose,
and then there is a rose!"
Zohar (tr. D. Matt), "Introduction"
("Haqdamat Sefer ha-Zohar").

"I like anything that

"from the *Riches* of Gloucester
to the *Rags* of Machiavel"—
in Prosper's Chain of Spectacles,
quoted by Maria from
The Adonis View of Polytics,
before Maria fell Asleep... Maria,
whose constrained clockwise path
channeled Geulincx, whose bones
left a spiral of Death glyphs...
Maria... *Maria!*

Maria... blew out
Red Alert on her Sleepwalk:
the Din of Ringing Bells,
that had enveloped us
since the Storm Cloud disaster,
stopped, and a deep silence
stilled the Murmuring sea;
then, from bow to stern,
the alarms of Red Alert
went off, one by one,
just as the distorted Voice
of Scard'nelli from the Library
blared over the loudspeakers
that Maria had fallen Asleep
and "the Sleeper was walking."

I broke off my letter
to you and went
to the ambulatory,
where I was joined

a word can do. And words
do do all they do
and then they can do
what they never do do."
Gertrude Stein,
Everybody's Autobiography.

"When attempt is made to
arrange a large number of facts
in diagrammatic order for
the sake of easy comprehension,
exact truth frequently suffers
in the interests of simplicity."
Vilhjalmur Stefanson,
The Friendly Arctic.

"...à Thelonius, /
qui s'y entendait"
("for Thelonius, /
who heard it all")
Gérard Genette,
Palimpsests, dedication.

"Lead off, my lyre, /
And we shall sing together."
Sappho,
Fragments.

"You too, in response,
now tune within yourselves
your interior lyres
for the Divine Musician."
Hermes Trismegistus:

by twin sisters
Thebes and Rosetta.

Maria moved forward
with indolent grace,
as if to showcase
her distinctive uniform
from the leprosarium at Carnak
—a stylish ensemble consisting
of small Feathered Slippers,
trousers embroidered
in a pattern of Lotus
and Mandrake, a scarf
falling over her shoulders
caught up at her waist
by a girdle of fretted Metal,
and a drapery of filmy gauze
that veiled her head and throat,
through which could be seen
her tiny ears, arched eyebrows
and closed eyes.

She continued to advance,
until the moment she arrived
at the bexium tubes and
the site of the Pinball alarm,
where she removed her veil...
to begin her Dance of Death.

Her slender feet tiptoed
through the glass cage, the crypt
and the hall of mirrors,
as if to the polyrhythmic Sounds

Corpus Hermeticum,
"Poimandres."

"I saw Dionysus
as an instinctive attempt
to express what Bergson
called *durée.*"
J. Harrison,
Introduction to Themis.

"When you do dance, I wish
you / A wave o' th' sea, that
you might ever do / Nothing
but that, move still, still so, /
And own no other function..."
W. Shakespeare,
The Winter's Tale.

"When I think of the moment
before revelation I think of
Salome... dancing before Herod
and receiving the prophet's head
in her indifferent hands, and wonder
if what seems to us decadence
was not in reality the exultation
of the muscular flesh and of
civilization perfectly achieved."
W. B. Yeats,
A Vision (1925).

"The superimposition of
the Logos Plan pattern
causes all material reality,

of the Chime and Doorbell alarms;
her sculpted arms seemed
ever-beckoning and striving
to entice to her side
Death-in-Life, who was fleeing
from her allurements,
and who she appeared to pursue
while walking on air,
in a nostalgic re-enactment of
Floating Dollar emerging
from the mists of Breton Woods;
she continued past the waterfall,
while other crewmembers
looked on, and reached the jars
of "Special Reserve" ouzo
(ouzo which has lost its aroma,
and strikes the palate with
a blast of volatile acidity,
producing an astringent flavor
that turns insipid and lifeless,
with a raspy, cloying finish).

On the fore'tween deck,
where the Sound of the Doorbell
alarm was replaced by the plaintive
Sound of the Time Passing alarm,
Maria's attitudes in her Dance
denoted an overpowering lassitude;
as her chest heaved with sighs,
her whole being expressed
a profound languor...
although it was unclear whether
the anxiogenous flow of her sighs

this entire space-time universe,
to experience a certain stress
to be other than it is,
a certain urging to become."
Philip K. Dick,
The Exegesis.

"With a leap (she said
it was an arabesque /
I made, off the porch... /
into the snow."
C. Olson,
The Maximus Poems,
"Letter # 41 [broken off]."

"Rushing out into the snow,
he had flung his arms aloft
and commenced a series
of leaps directly upward
in the air."
H. P. Lovecraft,
"Beyond the Wall of Sleep."

"The Poet is like that wild
inheritor of the cloud, / A rider
of storms, above the range of
arrows and slings; / Exiled
on earth, at bay amid the jeering
crowd, / He cannot walk for
his unmanageable wings."
Charles Baudelaire,
"The Albatross"; quoted
in M. Gardener (ed.),

derived from the pollution of
the psychosphere at the limit
of Commodity, or whether
she was expiring of Love
from the embrace of Death-in-
Life, the object of her seduction.

Eyes closed, her form quivering,
the Sleepwalker's body undulated,
while her face remained impassive
and her twinkling feet still moved
in their intricate steps toward
the Urim-Thummin, the gas cylinder,
the #1 lithium mold, and
the Sound of the Descent alarm;
onward, to the Anticipate alarm,
beyond the anticipator mechanism,
the diatransmeta, the interval
analyzer; to the propeller shaft
overgrown with Plants, to the melted
stained glass of the arcade and
the Sound of the Ascending alarm;
her yearning to bust loose—
be free, fly—her will
to *go! go! go!* was irreversible;
by embracing Death-in-Life
she welcomed the infinite
acceleration of the infosphere,
the financial flow of
the micro-traded Dollar,
the deterritorializing effect of Tarot;
she invited Deregulation, hyper-
complexity, she wanted to turn Life

The Annotated Rime
of the Ancient Mariner.

"Is there something that prevents
a passenger in a boat which is
taking him westwards at great
speed from heading eastwards
in the boat? Thus it is that God's
will directs all things... but
without anything standing in
the way of what we attempted..."
Arnold Geulincx,
Ethics, Book III.

"Nothing to be done."
S. Beckett,
Waiting for Godot.

"No-one / bears witness
for the / witness."
Paul Celan,
"Ashglory" (tr. P. Joris).

"O body swayed to music,
O brightening glance, /
How can we know
the dancer from the dance?"
W. B. Yeats,
"Among School Children."

"He stretched out
his arms toward Zion;
and, standing tall,

into repayment of the Metaphysical
debt she would absolve.

Between the Swoosh and Swish
alarms, in the Engine room
by the spare propeller shaft—
above which Möbius stills hangs
by his toes in suspended animation
—the dancing Sleepwalker seemed
transported by a delirium of
Love and Passion; she danced
as the Boolean embodiment
of leper consciousness,
as the religious incarnation
of suffering in an Engine
of Leper Creativity; open
to the enigma of openness,
she whirled in a labyrinthine voyage
of becoming-Hanged Woman,
toward the Sound of the digital
and electronic alarms by the keel,
before the presiding Spirit
of *Sanbon-Sugi*, along non-escapist
Sorcerous lines toward the schizo-
strategic plane of Pelagic openness,
the openness associated
with Love as the stronger
closure of the outside world;
to the Sound of the Boing
alarm in the promenade, between
the purifier and the trap-door,
her swift movements made the folds
of her draperies blur into

his head drawn back
and his fists clenched,
he hurled an anathema
against it, believing
that words had the power
to be effective."
Gustave Flaubert,
"Herodias."

"Oh, Time, Strength,
Cash, and Patience!"
Herman Melville,
Moby-Dick.

"Karl Marx never
in his life saw
the inside of a factory."
David Markson,
Vanishing Point.

"Thus the Hegelian proposition
turns into its opposite through
Hegelian dialectics itself:
All that is real in the sphere of
human history becomes irrational
in the process of time..."
Friedrich Engels,
Ludwig Feuerbach and the End
of Classical German Philosophy.

"The art of storytelling is reaching
its end because the epic side
of truth, wisdom, is dying out.

a social and instinctual body
emerging from a field of bodies
within the war machine of
Over-health, within the Hygiene-
complex of Death and taxes,
Dollarism and Tarot, competition,
leprosy, clothing...

All the crewmembers who
watched Maria's Dance of Death
felt drawn in solidarity toward
a re-opening of the Indefinite,
transported by the Khaosmic flow
of a collective Intelligence
in which closure remained
entangled with Impossibility
and the exteriority of an outside;
her arms, her feet, her garments
reactivated sensuousness
in harmony with the exhaustibility
of her psychic resources,
to a rhythm that invited
slowness and withdrawal
beyond the frontiers of suffering,
at the threshold of freedom's
new landscape.

To the thrilling Sound
of the Suspense alarm, between
the luminary and the net—
with a symbolic flourish that
signaled an insurrectional halt
to the disastrous acceleration of

This, however, is a process that
has been going for a long time.
And nothing would be more
fatuous than to want to see in it
merely a "symptom of decay,"
let alone a "modern" symptom.
It is rather, only a concomitant
symptom of the secular productive
forces of history, a concomitant
that has quite gradually removed
narrative from the realm of living
speech and at the same time is
making it possible to see a new
beauty in what is vanishing."
Walter Benjamin,
"The Storyteller."

"You know that the waves
are only waves, and the sea
is only the sea, and you can't
put god in a boat."
C. Olson,
cited by Robert Duncan in
Charles Olson Memorial Lecture.

"My mother is a fish."
William Faulkner,
As I Lay Dying.

"ecstasy ? fantasy ? insanity ?"
H. D.,
Hermetic Definition.

semio-inflation across the ship—
she came to a pause,
placed her feet wide apart,
and without bending her knees
swayed her lithe torso downward
until her chin touched the deck;
then, as if releasing magnetine
streams of Meaning and Affection,
Friendship and Love
above and against overproduction
in the field of attention, against
the mathematization of language,
her body slowly rose again; and,
standing tall, with ease and grace,
she let the embroidered trousers
that enveloped her legs fall
to the ground, and stepped out
of her slippers as seminude Bride
in a world made safe
for de-automation and poetry.

The reference to the Chymical
Marriage of Anthropoëme
in Laffer's *Critique of Pure Mercy*
was clear: Maria whirled on,
while the music of the Tri-
Tone alarm grew louder and
the faces in her audience began
to shine; she paused again at
the foot of the Grand Spiral
stairway, under the Tweet alarm,
and, like Geulincx the Fumist
on the Stairway of Destinies in

"...Come, my friends. /
'Tis not too late to seek
a newer world. / Push off,
and sitting well in order smite /
the sounding furrows;
for my purpose holds /
To sail beyond the sunset, /
And the baths / Of all
the western stars, until I die."
Alfred Tennyson, "Ulysses."

"Six decks I gave her,
dividing her thus into seven, /
Into nine compartments
I divided her interior / I struck
the bilge plugs into her middle. /
I saw to the punting-poles and
put in the tackle / Poured pitch
into her furnace... / Tar... /
Oil... / Oil for libations."
Gilgamesh, Tablet XI.

"...Weep your tears /
Into the channel,
till the lowest stream /
Do kiss the most exalted
shore of all."
W. Shakespeare,
Julius Caesar.

"It is no accident that those
who die are said to have
passed since those who have

Guide for the Dazed and Confused,
threw herself into a handstand;
her feet rose straight
in the air, and, holding
the Archetypal pose of
Nomad-Monad, she climbed
on her hands up the stairs
to the deck, behind the spanker,
and arrived motionless
in front of the Lens.

The nape of her neck
formed a Right Angle
with the bones of her Spine,
her veils fell around her face
like a headdress; as she arched
her back and angled her Pubic
Triangle toward the Malic panel
in the alcove, her eyes opened
and glowed with radiant
Sensibility, as if drawing Energy
from the stars through the Lens...
while, one by one, from signal
to signal, the alarms
of Red Alert shut down.

Seemingly whisked out from under,
by a Refrain beyond the Noösphere,
across a Slippery Deck,
she dropped on her side, Dead.

PASSED are PAST."
Sun Ra, "The Dead Past,"
liner notes, *Atlantis.*

"Life will show you masks that
are worth all your carnivals."
Ralph Waldo Emerson,
Conduct of Life, "Illusions."

"*Dif-tor heh smusma.*"
("Live long and prosper.")
Star Trek, "Amok Time"
(*RIP* Leonard Nimoy).

"Everything changes
it is extraordinary how
everything does change."
G. Stein,
Everybody's Autobiography.

"Heraclitus was right; change
is real, all right. But there is
a theos, as Parmenides
realized, an *it* which changes."
P. K. Dick,
The Exegesis.

"These contraries
such unity do hold."
W. Shakespeare,
The Rape of Lucrece.

"Sobriety diminishes,

At 13.0.0.0.0
'15 Solmōnath 13 Frig'edaeg'
the end-that-is-not-end
of Maria's Dance of Death
disseminated her flesh and
exposed her skeletal remains.

The skeleton's Silver bones
curled inward, following
a clockwise spiral—
with the skull aligned
along the axis of the ship—
and proceeded to release
a dark stream of smoke,
as the bones became
absorbed and embedded
in the main deck's Crystal.

The skeletal coil began
to migrate within the Crystal
across the length of the ship,
giving rise to an Atlantean
column of smoke that twisted
toward the Heavens like the trunk
of the World-Direction Tree
at the intersection of the Red,
White, Blue and Black Rivers
in the *Baroque Prophecies*
of Cod'z Poop.

The column of smoke
seemed to send a signal
up to the Blue-Red haze

discriminates, and says no;
drunkenness expands,
unites and says yes."
William James,
"The Varieties of
Religious Experience."

"One must always be drunk."
C. Baudelaire, "Get Drunk."

"Enthusiastic Admiration
is the first Principle
of Knowledge and its last."
William Blake,
Annotations to the Works
of Sir Joshua Reynolds.

"The devil can cite Scripture
for his purpose."
W. Shakespeare,
The Merchant of Venice.

"And the man said: 'This one
at last, bone of my bones, flesh
of my flesh, this one shall be
called woman, for from man
this one was taken.'"
Genesis 2: 23, in R. Crumb,
The Book of Genesis Illustrated
(tr. R. Alter).

"... Judicious books enlarge the mind
and improve the heart."

that still hovered over the ship
after our close encounter
with the third gelatinous
Mound of Consciousness;
it eventually dissipated, when
the bones came to a stop
by the so-called "Large
Collapse" of the melted arcade.

Sinbad the Steward,
claiming his right to act
as Public Entertainer—
by virtue of his crossed eyes
and crooked teeth—
took a deep Breath
through his nostrils and
observed that the distance
traveled by the bones,
from the Lens, across the deck,
to the "Large Collapse,"
appeared equal to twice the height
of the Belvedere from which
Meade had jumped into the sea...
and three times the distance
from the Lens to the spot
near the drainage slopes
where Finnegan had jumped;
similarly, he suggested
that the distance traveled
by the bones measured four times
the distance from the Lens
to where Mazüka in her Madness
had tossed herself overboard;

Mary Wollstonecraft,
Thoughts on the Education
of Daughters.

"Given! A way a lone
a last a loved along the /
riverrun, past Eve
and Adam's, from swerve
of shore to bend of bay..."
J. Joyce,
Finnegans Wake.

"309 miles is the length
of this field; 120 is its breadth."
The Egyptian Amduat,
"Second Hour."

"13..., /
13...stones, ...13 bundles, /
13..., 13..., /
13...bundles, 13...bundles, /
13..., 13..., /
13...stones, 13...stones, /
13...stones, 13...stones, /
13...stones, 13...stones, /
13...stones, 13...lord stones, /
13 ended bundles,
13 higher bundles, / 13 bundles,
no score of stones, /
no single stones,
no scores of days, /
no single days, on 4 Lord; /
the ninth lord of the night

and, respectively, five times
the distance, and seven times
the distance, from the Lens
to where Leiningen and Fiat
had plunged over the side.

No sooner had Sinbad
concluded his observations
than he threw his wide-
brimmed hat into the sea;
and like Master Quicken
on the Hal Deck,
standing with his legs apart,
pointing one finger at his rib
and the other overhead
at the starry Black sky,
he uttered the percipient
remark that the spiral design
of Maria's Silver bones
now ran *counter-clockwise*;
which was quickly confirmed.

The shift of the remains'
orientation, from Deasil
to Widdershins, like the switch
from positive to negative
in the Red-Panel Hands of
Sexiwôman on Nimrud's Eve of
Destruction, divided the crew
and "doubled the Double Talk."

Measurements were verified:
from the figurehead

wore the headband, /
and 3 days ago
the moon had arrived, /
...in the name of the new /
month of a score and 9 days; /
it was on 8 Kiln."
Stela I, Cobá (Yucatan);
in *2000 Years of Mayan Literature*
(tr. D. Tedlock.)

"The world is never ready /
for the birth of a child. /
Our ships are not yet back
from Vinland. / We still
have to get over the St. Gotthard
pass. / We've got to outwit
the watchmen on the desert
of Thor, / fight our way
through the sewers to Warsaw's
center, / gain access to King
Harold the Butterpat / and wait
until the downfall of Minister
Fouché. / Only in Acapulco /
can we begin anew."
Wislawa Szymborska,
"A Tale Begun."

"Knetch consulted
the oracle from the Book
of Changes by means of
the yarrow stick ceremony,
and met with the symbol Yu,
which signifies 'The Wanderer,'

to the Crystal skull rack...
from the Plumed Shell
to the Domino recess...
to the Xibonachi Chandelier...
from the re-charging station to
the Sacred Heart... the Whirling
Sword... the Burning Deck...

The recurring presence
of the Vague Number
and the Majic Number
occulted in the measurements,
and the complex array
of mysterious symmetries
linked to the Death sites
for the lost members of
Engineering, compelled a re-
examination of our heading
toward the light.

Then came a great sign:
seven stars shot across the sky
to the melodic Sound
of *New Starway Rundown.*

Like the charismatic Lady Tongue,
whose thick and laughing speech
dispelled the Wingèd Sphinx's
curse over the land
between Ixt'lan and Eden,
Captain Anna-O gave the order
to turn the ship around.

along with the judgment:
'Success through humility.
Salvation comes to the wanderer
through perseverance.'"
Hermann Hesse,
Magister Ludi.

"Even people who dislike each
other, if in the same boat will
help each other out in trouble."
Sun Tzu,
The Art of War.

"Life is the poem."
Vincent Ferrini,
Hermit of the Clouds.

"As we know, man
is represented—and then
merely by certain schematic
features—only in the scene
at the bottom of the well:
there he lies, stretched out
between a charging bison
and a rhinoceros that is
turned the other way.
Is he dead? Is he asleep?
Is he feigning a magical
immobility? Will he come
back to life?... It seems
to me that the meaning
of this obscure drawing
is nonetheless clear:

Although there is still general
agreement that Anna-O's
Fateful decision to reverse course
was correct, the consequences
of that decision were not good.

The logic that best explains
the Mutiny of Woodstock,
Greenwich and Soho
centers on the phallic pillar
of seawater that poured from
the Miraculous Faucet floating
in mid-air, and pre-supposes
the exposure of ship and crew
to ocean's Lethal content,
after the weïrd Weather Event
that blew the Large Cloud
of sea-spray our way;
indeed, the collision's impact
on the ship's Crystal body
left a line of demarcation
that replicates, across the deck
from bow to stern,
the coastline of Yonaguni,
as first seen through the eyes
of Andrea Diva on the S\S
EASTERLAND in Skylock's
1001 Argunot Poems: de-crypted
Crystal vision of Mythic shores,
in conjunction with which
the Blue-Red haze, suspended

it is the first signature
of the first painting,
the mark left modestly
in a corner, the furtive,
fearful, indelible trace
of a man who is
for the first time born
of his work, but who also
feels seriously threatened
by this work and perhaps
already struck with death."
Maurice Blanchot,
Friendship,
"The Birth of Art."

"The dead have become
ever more distinct for me
as the voices of the un-
answered, unresolved
and unredeemed."
Carl G. Jung,
The Red Book.

"So shalt thou feed on
Death, that feeds on men, /
And Death once dead,
there's no more dying then."
W. Shakespeare,
Sonnet 146.

"I do not believe that
Shakespeare can be set
alongside any other poet.

overhead like a rhizomatic
Cloud, seemed to offer
an unfathomable analog map.

When they later realized,
with hindsight, that Greenwich,
Soho and Woodstock had been
at the front of the seawater's
Impact Zone, Venus and Tarzan,
the remaining Intelligence officers
after Maria's Death,
explained that first contact with
the Faucet's wind-swept stream
cast the Mutineers as phantom
observers of the 16 Trump-card
landmarks on a Poematic seaboard
that was always already
sealing their Fate—
from the Big Wheel of Cope,
above the Lost Tower of Pay,
by the Hanging Gardens of Même
at the foot of Mount Persepolis,
Hill of the Hierophant...
to the Lover's Leap on either
side of the Giza-Rider Abyss...
to the Clashing Rocks of Justice
and Judgment, and the Column
of Aha the Big-Nosed Hermit
from New Yazidi.

It was Captain Anna-O's order
to turn about,
after the Deaths of Maria...

Was he perhaps
a *creator of language*
rather than a poet? I could
only stare in wonder
at Shakespeare; never do
anything with him.
I am *deeply* suspicious
of most of Shakespeare's
admirers. The misfortune is,
I believe, that he stands by
himself, at least in the culture
of the west, so that one can
only place him by placing
him wrongly. It is *not*
as though Shakespeare
portrayed human types well
and were in that respect *true*
to life. He is not true to life...
'Beethoven's great heart'—
nobody could speak of
'Shakespeare's great heart.'
'The supple hand that created
new natural linguistic forms'
would seem to me nearer
the mark. A poet can not
really say of himself
'I sing as the birds sing'—
but perhaps Shakespeare
could have said this
of himself."
Ludwig Wittgenstein,
Culture and Value.

Leiningen, Mazüka, Finnegan,
Fiat, Meade... that set
Greenwich, Soho, Woodstock...
on their own Death-track;
the 180° change of
direction—that would put
the light on the horizon
behind us—revealed itself
to be more over-determined
than imagined, multiplying
the physical quanta
whose continued observation
and measurement
pointed the whole crew
to the figure of *STUPID*
writ large.

The doubts, mysteries, uncertainties
raised by the unfolding spectacle
of Death's encryption of the hull
were compounded by snafu
conditions at sea that justified
my decision, as Navigator,
to engage Atomatic pilot as soon
as the U-turn was ordered;
we were sailing into
three separate headwinds—
1) a mild, fair Yin wind
at Two O'Clock,
like the Ishmael,
the Lemuel or the Sam,
that filled the flying jib,
the jib and the stunsail,

"Shahrazad had read books
and histories, accounts
of past kings and stories
of earlier peoples, having
collected, it was said,
a thousand volumes
of these covering peoples,
kings and poets."
Tales of 1001 Nights.

"The artistic problem
is to objectify the mythic
plane satisfactorily—
so that it produces
those benefits of
therapeutic catharsis,
social bonding and
psychological renewal—
without becoming
unintelligible, and without
spoiling the audience
for adaptive, practical life
on the realistic plane."
Ted Hughes,
Shakespeare and the Goddess
of Complete Being.

"And we sit here...
there in the arena..."
Ezra Pound,
Cantos, IV.

"The man who's careful

2) a hot, high Yang wind
at Ten O'Clock,
like the Oxib' Xk'ub',
that engaged the Central and
Left-Hand papyrus columns
3) a cold, light wind
at Twelve O'Clock,
like the Shariahr, that made
the flying buttresses shiver—
three headwinds that
blew concurrently against
a violent Icy tailwind,
like the Kain
in B'alam and Laman's
Abridged Explorations
of the Pyramid Wilderness.

Together they formed a fourfold
Crosswind force field,
whose epicenter was located
behind the foremast
(above the radar, the Application
Gallery, the hydopath, and
the stratacaster) and seemed
to correspond to the nexus
of "S\he-who-Weeps,
S\he-who-Praises,
S\he-who-Mourns,
S\he-who-Wails"
in Wa-Wa's *Orientalist Guide*
to Majical Thinking.

Moreover, in combination

when he borrows / Has but
few cares and fewer sorrows;
Trust not the men,
they are not true, / Who'd sign
your bond and lend to you."
S. Brant,
The Ship of Fools.

"What defines industrial art
is not mechanical reproduction
but the internalized relation
with money... Money is
the obverse of all the images
that the cinema shows and
sets in place, so that films
about money are already,
if implicitly, films within
the film or about the film."
Gilles Deleuze,
Cinema 2.

"What an uproar the light brings!"
J. W. Goethe,
Faust, Part II.

"The strange, upheaving,
lifting tendency of the taffrail
breeze filling the hollows
of so many sails, made
the buoyant, hovering deck
to feel like air beneath the feet;
while still she rushed along,
as if two antagonistic influences
with the churning, rising waters
of a larboard current
that carried us forward, and
an equally strong starboard current
that pushed us back, the Ecologic
Forces acting on the ship—
winds-plus-currents as
a Synergetic Whole greater-
than-the-sum-of-its-parts—
suggested the outline
of a Peace Symbol, facing
backward as seen from above,
but *forward* as seen from
the luminescence on the horizon,
that marked the ship as
we advanced, and framed
Ayasugi-Hada, Spirit of the Keel,
as "crucified" Hanged Man
at 12 Manik' 1 Tox
on the Jefferson Plane
of the Zodiac cycle.

(I am saying what I believe
on the basis of Article 184
in the Episcopal Charter
from the Navigation Plates
of 'Istorian-Prophetess
the Marquise of O...
and what is,
I, Navigator,
see with certainty,
and what is not
I will do, if I must,

were struggling in her—
one to mount direct to heaven,
the other to drive yawingly
to some horizontal goal."
H. Melville,
Moby Dick.

"The sails that drove
the ship and the spars
that supported them were
balanced in a complex and
dynamic system of opposing
forces. Some sails lifted,
while others depressed
the vessel as they drove her
forward, each sail affecting
the flow of air upon the next.
The masts were raked
at slightly increasing angles,
and the yards were corkscrewed
in subtle ascending spirals."
Gregory Gibson,
Demon of the Waters:
The True Story of the Mutiny
on the Whaleship Globe.

"The long wake shone
ever white behind them,
like some / track seen
dwindling away across
the green savannah."
Apollonius Rhodios,
Argonautika, Book I.

because since that time
I have felt the Void,
but I refuse to throw myself
into the Void, even if,
between a Blue-Red haze
that hovers overhead
and a collective "Big Fart"
that still haunts the ship,
I was fooled by a powerful
illusion in all I saw...
and, while I thought
I refused FIRST FACT,
I know now
I was refusing the Void,
because I understand
that FIRST FACT
is *not,* and I know *HOW*
it is *not*... and what
I have suffered from,
since opting for Atomatic pilot,
is to have denied the Void,
the Void always already
within me... within Woodstock,
Greenwich and Soho... within
the Dead of Engineering, whose
place they were ordered to take...
within Möbius, for whose
Dormant body they chanted—
all of them, Spirit companions
meant to enlighten me
in the way(s) of the Void,
and who I refused
to be enlightened by,

"Behold I have dreamed
a dream; or, in other words,
I have seen a vision..."
The Book of Mormon,
1 Nephi 7.

"Even sleeping men
are doing the world's business
and helping it along."
Herakleitos (tr. G. Davenport).

"The Sphinx knows everything,
the Centaur feels everything."
H. D.,
Notes on Thought and Vision.

"The Holy Spirit is in time,
and moving: retrograde."
P. K. Dick,
The Exegesis.

"O, 'Tis most sweet /
When in one line
two crafts directly meet."
W. Shakespeare,
Hamlet.

"Poetry makes nothing happen."
W. H. Auden,
"In Memory of W. B. Yeats."

"...Let it be, Horatio. I am dead."

until the Mutiny of the Void
played itself out,
as in the Lost Memory Theater
of Arnaut... from password,
to printer, to remote control.)

The Silver seas
were dim and dull
on our curved and narrow
path, as we veered
through starboard Shadows,
keel to breakers,
struggling through one wave,
as the next one tossed us
backward half as far
as we progressed, the lights
holding steady, the arras
in the booby hatch swaying
to and fro, and the pendulum
on the quarterdeck leaning
sideways, as on the ARGOT,
when Blimey braved
Deukalion's Flood
after the Mikrosoft campaign,
in Kulchur's *Book On Useless*
Books, Useless Study, and
Useless Wishing; we came into
a Whirlwind at 45 degrees,
the sky opened wide,
and the parking space split open
—as on the KISMET,
in Orphic's *Tale of the Tribe*,
when the angels stepped aside—

W. Shakespeare,
Hamlet.

"Know the masculine,
hold to the feminine /
Be the watercourse
of the world."
Lao-Tse,
Tai Te Ching, 28.

"The silvery water glazes
the upturned nipple..."
E. Pound,
Cantos, III.

"...I tried to demonstrate
that justice, in the most
un-heard-of sense
of the word, was un-
deconstructible itself,
thus another name
of deconstruction
(de-construction?
deconstruction *is* justice)."
Jacques Derrida,
"The Time is Out of Joint."

"Nature is not just,
but nature is exact."
Aleister Crowley,
The Book of Thot.

"Free man, you will

and we found ourselves sailing
parallel to the luminous horizon;
our new heading drew closer
as we glided on a Cord—
like the Aether Rod that guided
King Tahiti on the WÜRM
across the Great Middle Sea,
"from Troynovant to Botany Bay"
—through the Fiery Arabesques
of sparkling water that resisted
our will to change,
to go on despite all...
until our wake was Arrow-
straight, the light *behind* us
at last—and there was silence,
pre-historic and hyper-real,
returning us to ourselves
like the Skin of Nail
on the Celestial Bodies
of the AM-DUAT's crew,
as per Bru-nel and Mo-rel's
Median Days Before
The Long Count...
deep and beautiful silence.

Then a burst of Sound,
like the Duquesne Whistle
cut short, plunged us all
into dreamtime.

I was part of the first

always cherish the sea! /
The sea is your mirror;
you contemplate your soul /
In the infinite unrolling
of its billows; /
Your mind is an abyss
that is no less bitter."
C. Baudelaire,
"Man and the Sea."

"They are not yet
mad enough, not yet
crashing one against
the other, and all the more
furious, all the more
enraged the nearer
and dearer they are."
Antonin Artaud,
The New Revelations of Being.

"Only the dying understand
COMMUNION.
Understand Love,
understand the interrealm."
H. Broch,
The Death of Virgil.

"You should have
considered the terror
that has hallucinated
and haunted me
since prehistoric times."
C. Lispector, "Vengeance

wave in the crew's 3-phase
awakening from dreamtime,
when Captain Anna-O ordered
Woodstock, then Soho, and
Greenwich—our Emergency
substitute crew for the Dead
of Engineering—to initiate
the remote control and turn off
Atomatic pilot ASAP, because
during our collective dreams
the Crystal ship continued to swerve
in a starboard loop, and was
coming full circle, re-headed
toward the light on the horizon.

Soho responded
immediately, like S\he-Who-
Cuts-With-Shining-Face
in the Posterior Analytics of
The Histriomatrix by Ananke
the "Eunuch Slave," and tried
to locate the remote control
beyond the step stool,
the air pump and the hammock,
between the narrow gate
and the Magdeburg Jars,
down the Seven Steps
to the Heavy Metal cage,
from which began to emanate
the Gurgling Sound of
Gaga fluid in the Baba Hole;
and I, Navigator, could tell that
after the search to find

and Painful Reconciliation."

"I speak the password primeval..."
Walt Whitman,
Leaves of Grass.

"Praise be I, writing, dead
already and dead again."
Jack Kerouac,
"The Ocean."

"Who are the Muses?
Who but the Maenads
repentant... clothed
and in their right minds...
The shift of Maenad
to Muse is like the change
of Bacchic rites to Orphic;
it is the informing
of savage rites with
the spirit of music, order
and peace... The grace
Orpheus sought was not
physical intoxication
but spiritual ecstasy,
the means he adopted not
drunkenness but abstinence
and rites of purification...
the possibility of attaining
divine life."
J. Harrison,
Prolegomena to the Study
of Greek Religion.

the missing remote control—
in order to stop Atomatic pilot
and reset our course *away*
from the light—Mutiny would
follow, because in my dream
I was a Flaming vortex,
curing myself of a remote control
that was making me struggle
to exist as Navigator, taking all
the *ethos, logos* and *pathos*
I had... in the same way
that Woodstock, then Soho and
finally Greenwich—from what
I recognized—were struggling
to resist the forms with which
the Poly-encephalic Illusion of
being 1st-, 2nd- and 3rd-substitute
Engineers clothed their reality
and continued to function as
that which flowed forth
in our Replacement World.

(I, Navigator, will stop
henceforth being Deluded:
I have a body
which suffers this ship
and disgorges reality;
I will be done with
the Protocols of the ship,
which make me invoke
what I reject, and reject
what I invoke.)

"Sexy motherfucker
shakin' that ass, /
shakin' that ass,
shakin' that ass."
Prince *(RIP),*
"Sexy M. F."

"Readers, disinfect your brains!"
Saşa Pană, "Manisfesto,"
in *Burning Cities*
(ed. J. Rasula, T. Conley).

"Don't stir / The trash."
Sappho (tr. G. Davenport).

"Every action must be due
to one or other of seven
causes: chance, nature,
compulsion, habit, reasoning,
anger, or appetite."
Aristotle,
Rhetoric.

"When I lifted my eyes
a little higher, I saw the Master
of those who know, Aristotle,
sitting amongst the company
of philosophers. All gaze
at him: all show him honor.
There I saw Socrates, and Plato,
who stand nearest to him
of all of them; Democritus,

It was the total input from
the dreams of those of us
who woke up first
that led to Woodstock's
moment of Krisis, after
Woodstock remembered having
dreamed of books on Fire
under the Mammon panel...
after Soho in her dream
heard "the Sound of Blood
from the Restless Sea of Nod,
west of Eden," and searched
for the remote control at
the Kalashnikov console,
where Woodstock was stationed...
after Woodstock left
the Khalishnikov console, and
went to where Greenwich had
searched for the remote control,
down the Seven Steps
to the Heavy Metal cage,
along the "Redeemer Axis"
received in Woodstock's dream
from the Bataclan Boys
by the melting Ice at Ecbatan.

As the ship returned
on its ineluctable heading
toward the light, a sevenfold
Backlash of Repressed anger,
due to the continued failure
to find the remote control
and turn off Atomatic pilot,

who ascribes the world to
chance, Diogenes, Anaxogoras,
and Thales; Empedocles,
Heraclitus, and Zeno…
Orpheus… Avicenna…
and Averroës, who wrote
the vast commentary."
Dante Alighieri,
The Divine Comedy: Inferno.

"We have decided to illustrate
for you today the truth…
that it is the symbolic order
which is constitutive for
the subject—by demonstrating
in a story the decisive
orientation which the subject
receives from the itinerary of
a signifier. It is that truth,
let us note, which makes
the very existence of fiction
possible. And in that case,
a fable is as appropriate
as any other narrative
for bringing it to light…
A fictive tale even has
the advantage of manifesting
symbolic necessity more
purely to the extent
that we may believe
its conception arbitrary."
Jacques Lacan, Seminar
on *The Purloined Letter.*

led to a period of Mixture
during which, in their bid
to help find the missing remote,
our other shipmates—of those
who woke up first—introjected
their visionary dreams as
Psycho-dramatic Chimera
in the Waiting Room
to the Shi'ite Gardens.

In keeping with the *Spartan
Protocols* of the Realpolitik
Institute for Arrière-Garde Studies,
they held hands and blew
Proskynetic kisses at the bulkheads
like the Princes of Araby
on the PARIS and
the VIRGINS OF LAHORE…
the total effects of which
combined to momentarily arrest
Woodstock in a Freeze Frame.

Then Woodstock fell into Krisis,
gesticulating madly during
an obsessive-compulsive post-
visionary recital of the 72
Ways to Curse the Darkness,
from Dido's *Pragmatics.*

After Curse #1 ("Against
The Poëtiks of Darkness"),
Kodak the Second Mate,
who had dreamed he was

"All that is needed is a sign,
pure and simple."
F. Holderlin, "The Ister."

"I went to work /
like the horns of a snail"
C. Olson,
Maximus IV, V, VI,
"Maximus, at the Harbor."

"... like the hydra's vile leap,
at having once
heard the angel /
give a purer meaning
to the words of the tribe."
Stéphane Mallarmé,
"The Tomb of Edgar Poe."

"you must dream patiently /
hoping the content will be
completed / that the missing
words / enter crippled sentences
and the certainty we are
waiting for / casts anchor"
Z. Herbert,
Inscription,
"We fall asleep on words."

"From third he has become
tenth. To the Time
of his stupor that he must
redeem corresponds

midway on the path
from Aleppo to Damascus
in search of a new Juddeca,
projected his Future Body as
supplemental-4th Engineer, and
went to calm Woodstock down,
explaining that the missing
remote would inevitably
manifest its Fate as Light-spatter
on the Time-landscape
of the Minor Domination.

Similarly, when Woodstock
was at Curse #11 ("Against
The Oubliette of Darkness"),
Sinbad and Tarzan,
who both awoke terrified
in the secret passageway to
the Queen's Bicameral quarters
—he, Sinbad, from a dream
of Laughing-to-Death at
a Cash Machine; she, Tarzan,
of trying to pay Taxes
on a Pleasure \ Pain Scale
from Old Media—progressed
to their Future Bodies as
supplemental-5th and -6th Engineers
and exhorted Woodstock to stop
in the name of Love
before the Power of Nothing.

Woodstock cursed on;
at Curse #14

the emanation of the seven
other Intelligences which
are called the seven Cherubim
or the seven Divine Words."
Henry Corbin, "Cyclical Time
in Mazdaism and Ismailism."

"...A spirit I saw, cleft
from the chin down to
the part that gives out
the foulest sound: the entrails
hung between his legs:
the organs appeared,
and the miserable gut
that makes excrement
of what is swallowed.
While I stood looking wholly
at him, he gazed at me,
and opened his chest
with his hands, saying:
'See how I tear myself:
see how Mahomet is ripped!
In front of me, Ali goes,
weeping, his face split
from chin to scalp...'"
Dante,
The Divine Comedy: Inferno.

"And, strange to tell,
among that Earthen Lot /
Some could articulate,
while others not: /
And suddenly one

("Against The Chocolate
Darkness"), Vico,
who woke up with
the Mutant gift of seeing
around corners... Bismark,
on Anchor Watch, who managed,
while dreaming, to lose the ship's
Crystal anchor to the sea...
and Kongō, who got
instantly Fat dreaming
of an undiscovered leak
aboard ship—proceeded
toward their Being as
supplemental-7th, -8th and -9th
Engineers.

In a Fateful twist,
they wrestled Woodstock
to the ground at the very
Moment of Stupor, when—
to the Sound of rocks
on the ocean's floor being Torn
beneath the hull—the ship was
violently shaken, and the three
of them found themselves
wrestling Cowabunga instead,
as if Cowabunga, during
the actuation of his archetypal
emergence as supplemental-
10th Engineer, had traveled
in a Spiral Waltz through
the *dense time* of his dream
to take Woodstock's place...

more impatient cried— /
'Who is the Potter, pray,
and who the Pot?'"
Omar Khayyám,
Rubáiyát (tr. E. Fitzgerald).

"Who are these dummies,
these ogres of a past age,
these fearful effigies
that wrecked our world,
these devils, these dolls?
Who are they?
We put away childish things.
It is we who walked
into another dimension."
H. D.,
End to Torment.

"As though awakened from
a dream / The Muse opened
her eyes / This time as Queen."
Prince,
The Rainbow Children,
"Deconstruction."

"Let be be finale of seem."
Wallace Stevens,
"The Emperor of Ice-Cream."

"Magical password that
conceals death and life
in its simple syllable."
F. Hölderlin,

while Woodstock, now
completely calmed down, was
over by the Mammon panel,
where the remote control
was hiding in plain sight
on the mantelpiece, between
the logbook and the Spinning-
Rainbow Disk of Zoro.

Despite its eventual recovery,
for the ten replacement Engineers
the traumatic experience of
the remote control's temporary loss
had henceforth been written
"on the corners of their eyes"
with the proverbial
needle of Mithridas.

Having passed through
the successive emanations
of Engineer Intelligence,
they seemed predisposed
to hold the rest of us,
who were awake, as Scapegoats
for the debacle—Captain Anna-O,
Commander Exprès, Venus
the Interpreter of the Spit,
Sokrates and myself.

(A cruel irony... because
I, Navigator, like them,
the ten Engineers, knew
that it had to be ended,

Hyperion.

"Rabbi Shim'on rose
and said, 'I was gazing.'"
Zohar, "Be-Reshit."

"'Tis a pageant / To keep us
in a false gaze."
W. Shakespeare,
Othello.

"The 'phenomenon of
the mirror'... is a general
mode of perception which,
instead of putting man in
the presence of what is for us
the brutal and compact reality
of the empirically real, which
we violate in order to exploit,
puts man before an image
appearing in a mirror. One does
not get closer to the image by
breaking it... A similar view
is suggested by the central water
basin of the traditional Iranian
garden ('paradise') or that
of the traditional mosque...
like the water basin in the vast
enclave of the royal mosque
at Esfahan. The mirroring water
gathers the image of the immense
surfaces of blue-enamel faience
that surround it; at night these

a final wrenching away from
the Nautical Order-of-things had
to happen; I can no longer
deal with this Primordial
Hypostasis within me,
this Being-that-is-not-Being—
because as it advances,
I fall into the Gap
this same Order-of-things
is always already negating.)

And to make matters worse,
the last post on the logbook
indicated that the password
to unlock the remote control
from its Hermetic Seal
was incorrect.

The second group in the crew's
awakening from dreamtime—
Sony, Cîpher, Nobadinus,
Chauvée, Mach, Bedlam,
Marlboro and Wang—presented
a passive-aggressive common
front that deployed the Silent
Treatment as an ambiguous and
manipulative "wait and see"
strategy for contending with
the power politics of Mutiny...
a strategy presumably suggested
by the dreams themselves.

are followed by a gathering
of stars. To plunge into the basin
in order to 'touch' the image
would be as vain as breaking
the mirror. The reflective
surface is the site of
an apparition (*mazhar*),
but the image is not *there*."
H. Corbin,
In Iranian Islam, "Preface."

"We are the first generation
in the West able to read
the Koran, if we are able
to read *Finnegans Wake*."
Norman O. Brown,
Apocalypse and/or
Metamorphosis.
"The Apocalypse of Islam."

"The warships / Got together
for a gossip. The oldest
whoreship, the madam, said, /
'Know what's happening,
girls? / He wants to send
a hundred of us out /
To Africa...' / One of them
(one, never shipped a man)
said, / 'He won't spread
my sail! I'd rather not.' /
Another said 'It's rape,
not business, girls. / Let's sail
to the Akropolis for sanctuary.'"

The silent, neutral presence
of the newly awakened crew
heightened tensions,
as the ten incipient Mutineers
\ substitute Engineers,
under the direction of Soho,
scanned Engineering's
rollerdex for the password
to unlock the remote control
and disengage Atomatic pilot.

But after a thousand and one
trials, and the ultimate failure of
Hèteronymus1YHY49,
Hêteronymus11ΛAY44,
Héteronymus14MBH55
(discovered by Greenwich
scrawled in Majic marker
behind the Red-tipped Phallus
next to the Emerald Tablet
of Apollo Exeğesus),
Soho had the Big Idea to
search the memory banks
of the *printer*.

Faced with the urgency of
de-activating Atomatic pilot
and changing course, because
the ship was coming full circle
and turning back again
toward the light on the horizon,
Anna-O gave Soho the go-ahead

Aristophanes,
Knights.

"Rabelais and his contemporaries
were also familiar with the saying
of Pliny that only one man,
Zoroaster, began to laugh
at the time of his birth;
this was interpreted as an omen
of his divine wisdom."
Mikhail Bakhtin,
Rabelais and his World.

"I have imposed this penance
upon the lady... to rebuke
a vicious taste, neither out
of wantonness or cruelty,
but from the best of motives
which has crept into thousands
besides herself, —of reading
straight forwards, more in
quest of the adventures,
than of the deep erudition
and knowledge which a book
of this cast, if read over
as it should be, would infallibly
impart with them. — The mind
should be accustomed to make
wise reflections, and draw
curious conclusions as it goes
along; the habitude of which
made Pliny the younger affirm
'That he never read a book so bad,

to initialize the printer.

The machine was turned on,
but after the fast blinking
of the Multicolored lights
in the Troubleshooter
there followed an immediate
Error Message, and
the printer started trembling
to a low-pitched Sound,
like the Rumble
in *The Robots of Quad*
by Serpentarius the Short.

Then the woodblock and
triangle Icons *popped up*
on the Diagnostics Bar of
the print queue's Uninstaller,
and suddenly the printer pulled
away from the system settings
and flew Telekinetically
across the control room,
just as the portside porthole
unlatched and swung open.

The traveling printer
pursued a line-of-flight
across the area
in front of the porthole,
that Soho described as
"symbolic": it hovered
at a point outside and
above it, to the left; dropped

but he drew some profit from it.'"
Lawrence Sterne,
Tristram Shandy.

"Benjamin's ideal of producing
a work consisting entirely
of quotations, one that
was mounted so masterfully
that it could dispense
with any accompanying text,
may strike one as whimsical
in the extreme and self-destructive
to boot, but it was not, any more
than were the contemporaneous
surrealistic experiments
which arose from similar
impulses. To the extent
that an accompanying text
by the author proved
unavoidable, it was a matter
of fashioning it in such a way
as to preserve 'the intention
of such investigations,'
namely, 'to plumb the depths
of language and thought...
by drilling rather than
excavating...' (*Briefe, I, 329).*"
Hannah Arendt,
"Walter Benjamin: 1892-1940."

"Art is the underground
of the world, and
we will win in the end."

down to the porthole's lower
left; and moved diagonally
to the upper right
along an ascending path that
veered around the porthole,
as if to avoid passing
in front of it.

From its position outside
the porthole, on the upper
right, the printer repeated
a similar line-of-flight:
it moved directly across to
the left; dropped diagonally
toward the lower right, again
circumventing the porthole
with a quick swerve
on its way down.

It continued to repeat the same
two-vector movement around
the porthole, obeying a pattern
that rotated clockwise.

As the printer pursued
its vectorial flight path
in the Mutinous heat
of the crew's hermeneutic
deliberations—framing
the porthole's circular opening
within an imaginary square—
Soho explained that
the encrypted symbol traced

Maria Martins,
"Underground Art,"
in *Time* (6 May 1946).

"Resistance is never
in a position of exteriority
in relation to power."
M. Foucault,
The Archaeology of Knowledge.

"A rebellion... gripped
him when he discovered
that the handful of instructions
he had received
included no explanation."
C. Lispector,
"The Egg and the Chicken."

"You know, sometimes
we're not prepared
for adversity. When
it happens, sometimes
we're caught short.
We don't know exactly
how to handle it,
when it comes up.
Sometimes we don't know
just what's to do,
when adversity takes over."
Cannonball Adderley,
"*Mercy, Mercy, Mercy.*"

"There is no death. Only music."

by the printer's movements
corresponded to the Ninja Star of
Nijū-Ba, Spirit of the Keel.

Captain Anna-O was disputing
Soho's Mutinous interpretation,
arguing that the *rosette* traced
by the line-of-flight was
Tuthmosian, when the printer
broke out of its pattern and
headed straight for the opening;
but instead of flying through,
it rammed into the hole,
and got stuck inside it.

Following the impact,
Woodstock was the first
to succumb to Madness:
grabbing the Vice-Cu't-Sin
mechanism of the Black box
on the ceiling, in a move
that recalled the dice toss
of Pseudo-Bacchus in
The Song of O'Hio'Wa'Chi'Gan!,
Woodstock kicked the printer-
lodged-in-the-porthole out,
and in a second maneuver
plunged after it, backward,
falling into the sea feet-first.

From that *Klein-bottled* moment,
the terms of the Mutiny changed.

Samuel Delaney,
The Einstein Intersection.

"I start in the middle of a sentence and move both directions at once."
John Coltrane, in conversation with Wayne Shorter *(RIP),* c. 1960.

"A line of becoming has only a middle."
G. Deleuze and F. Guattari,
A Thousand Plateaus.

"The unconscious is structured like a language."
J. Lacan,
Seminar XX.

"A fantastic and brilliant regression... But it is like the story of the Resistance fighters who, wanting to destroy a pylon, balanced the plastic charges so well that the pylon blew up and fell back into its hole."
G. Deleuze and F. Guattari,
Anti-Oedipus.

"All space is flat, clearly there are mathematicians who have said as much."

During the complicated time of the printer's symbolic flight and the Mutiny implicated therein, before the imaginary plunge into the "hole" of Real Denial, the schizo-analytic explanation suggested by the Texas instruments failed to anticipate the Paranoid fear of a Khaotic inundation by Castration Complex empowering the technological phantasm of a ship-wide Mathesis.

According to the Mutineers, the nature of the light on the horizon and the question of how to "deal with it," pro-actively or re-actively, involved the Atomatic pilot's re-presentation of the "conceptual" failure of language discussed in the *Enthymeme Commentaries* of Cartheuze the Silent.

Woodstock, Soho and Greenwich resisted what they saw as the vacuous definition of Identity operated by a mathematized, panoptic code that controlled and organized Psycho-Political life on the ship, as it had come to be expressed by the half-skeleton of Avon the Poetess

J. Lacan,
Seminar (14 Jan. 1975).

"The players (1, 2, 3, 4)
pace the given area,
each following
his particular course...
Course 1: AC, CB, BA, AD,
DB, BC, CD, DA."
Samuel Beckett.
Quad.

"Don't know if it's day
or night... / Is it tomorrow,"
or just the end of time?"
Jimi Hendrix, "Purple Haze."

"Could this be night
or is it day? / did mankind
fashion monkeys, pray?"
S. Brant,
The Ship of Fools.

"Human anatomy contains
a key to the anatomy of the ape."
Karl Marx,
Grundrisse.

"By what miracle does
le marriage du ciel
et de la terre
find consummation?
It filled my fantasies

dragged under the hull, and
by Maria's bones absorbed in
the ship's deck; by van Rr'Ubik's
Half-Shadow and her profile
imprinted on the figurehead;
by the Dormant body of Möbius
suspended upside down in
the Engine room—all of which
in retrospect masked
a Death Wish beyond the limits
the Mutineers had imagined.

When Woodstock forced
the printer through the porthole
into the sea, and succumbed
to Death by jumping after it,
Mutiny became a topological circle
whose center was everywhere and
whose circumference was nowhere:
mis-recognized by the Mutineers,
a tunnel-like libidinal torsion
had cut-and-pasted onto
their Mutiny a flattened projective
field of consistency, which
functioned for the Time-Being
as the unilateral space of
a False Imaginary that equated
the coherence of a *spacetime*
Signifier ("money vector")
with the Death of a *lifetime*
Signified ("language vector")—
re-placing Desire, Phantasm and
Anguish with Payback, Hatred

and dreams, poetry
and prose for ten years.
But in the end, intellectual
and physical perfection,
the laurel wreath of
the acclaimed achievement
must be tempered,
balanced, re-lived,
re-focused or even sustained
by the unpredictable,
the inchoate, challenged
by a myth, a legend—
the poet (...), changed
to Wolf or Panther,
hunted down and captured."
H. D.,
End to Torment.

"You wanted to be historic,
Yorick."
C. Olson,
"A Lustrum for You, E. P."

"We fall asleep
on words / and wake up
with words / sometimes
congenial / simple nouns /
forest or ship /
they break away
from us / the forest
rushes off /
across the horizon /
the ship sails away /

and Ignorance, as predicted
in *The Prokol Harum Book of
Secret Knowledge and Thanksgiving*
by Bildungsberg and Brexxit.

The intensive de-territorialization
of the Mutineers' war-machine
on a plane of immanence
became obvious with infinite speed
for all non-dreaming crew.

(I, Navigator, have to resist
this ship and be done
with it once and for all.

But I have already fallen
into the ocean, since everything,
everything about this ship,
has finally pushed me
over the edge.

You know you are no longer
on the ship, when you can
see it sailing without you.)

With the active crew in
methodological turmoil,
the crack-up of the Mutiny
happened fast: radically
self-divided, yet overwhelmed
by the Will-to-Power,

without trace or cause"
Z. Herbert,
"We fall asleep on words."

"The readiness is all."
W. Shakespeare,
Hamlet.

"True life is absent.
We are not in the world."
A. Rimbaud,
A Season in Hell.

"The world is elsewhere."
W. Shakespeare,
Coriolanus.

"The terrestrial Angels
form two groups.
One occupies the right side:
they are the Angels
who know and who order.
In front of them, a group
occupies the left side:
these are the Angels
who obey and who act...
It is said that the two Angels
to which a human being
is entrusted belong to
this order, the ones called
'Guardians and Noble Writers'
—one on the right and one
on the left. The one who

Greenwich found herself
obsessed with the control and
command of a Transcendent Ship,
and her obsession located
its Double in Soho's compulsion
to break the Hermetic Seal on
the remote control *manually*,
given the Absúrd absence
of an operative password.

Greenwich and Soho were
thus resurrected as Dyad in
the field of becoming: Greenwich
(*noös*) as She-Who-*KNEW*-and-
Put-in-Good-Order, 'Dictator'
to Soho (*psychê)* as She-Who-
Would-*OBEY*-and-Act, 'Writer.'

As glossed in the Catheotheist
Hieroglyphs of Philo the Wizard,
the order given by Greenwich,
Guardian of the Planemon, to Soho,
Noble Writer of the Ecumenon,
translated the Art of Writing
as the act of breaking
the remote control's Hermetic
Seal in order to seize control
of the ship's navigation.

Re-conceived in such terms,
it follows that the Mutiny
would necessarily self-destruct with
the advent of Soho's Package Rage.

stands on the right belongs
to the Angels who order;
it is incumbent upon him
to dictate. The one who
stands on the left belongs
to the Angels who act;
it is incumbent upon him
to write."
H. Corbin (tr.), "The Tale of
Hayy Ibn Yaqzân," in *Avicenna
and the Visionary Recital.*

"He cultivated the power
of dreaming himself
momentarily Earthward."
H. P. Lovecraft,
"Through the Gates
of the Silver Key."

"Mean while through
duskie deepe / On seas
discovered bed, / Where
none thy trace could view, /
A path by thee was wrought."
Psalms 77, tr. Mary Sidney.

"The tension was aggravated
by the disappearance
of Müller and Zimmer,
who undoubtedly committed
suicide as a result of
the fears which had seemed
to harass them, though

At first, calm and self-assured,
standing still, Soho tried to pry
the Seal open, turning it over
in her hands, pausing and
adjusting her grip, renewing
her angle of approach, her stance;
then she clenched her teeth
and started swearing.

Cursing more intensely,
out of mounting frustration,
she was soon stomping back and
forth across the control room
in a Rage, lowering and raising
the Sealed remote, jumping up and
down, then falling to her knees,
shaking it with increasing violence,
and finally collapsing on the ground,
where she rolled around, pounding it
against the floor, harder and harder,
hollering incomprehensibly.

What happened next
came to light after the fact:
Soho in her Package Rage became
the object of different hallucinations
for different observers.

In my case—as for Vico,
Bismark and Kongō—Soho, while

they were not observed in
the act of jumping overboard."
H. P. Lovecraft, "From Beyond."

"Alas, thou hast
misconstrued everything."
W. Shakespeare,
Julius Caesar.

"It is, of course, a translation.
There was an Hypoborean
original millions of years earlier
in the primal tongue of Tsath-yo."
H. P. Lovecraft,
"Through the Gates
of the Silver Key."

"Thus it appears that Rhetoric
is, as it were, an offshoot
of Dialectic and the science
of Ethics, which may reasonably
be called Politics."
Aristotle,
Rhetoric.

"When I left to come here
to your market, / They were
debating in the assembly /
How long it would take
to go to Hell."
Aristophanes,
The Acharnians.

rolling around on the deck pounding
the remote, took the form of
Yug-Sathoth, the Webbed-handed
Keeper of Energy from
the Malodorous Jungles of Nyl;
for Sinbad and Tarzan, she appeared
in the shape of Tsuthaggui, Keeper
of Treasure, dripping with Blue Ooze
by the Sloping Meadows of Nohng.

Cowabunga saw her as Nyerthalup,
the Fungoid Keeper of Health
on the Desert Plateau of Klang;
to Kodak, she manifested
as Zozoath of the Fire Mist,
Keeper of Strategy, Labor and Law.

At the same time,
the various hallucinations that
each of us saw separately were
being experienced sequentially
by Greenwich, who beheld,
in the progress of Soho's Package
Rage, figures from the seven Floats
in the Apprentice's Pageant,
described by the Nameless Poet
in *Monster Handbook for
the Seven Stages of Poetic Justice
in "Tarot-Trump Madness."*

Shrieking wildly, she rose
to her feet like Mi-Go,
the Bleached, Star-headed

"We must renounce,
as the most puerile
delusion, the hope
that art can ever again
perform a social function."
Herbert Read, "The Artist
in the Modern World."
in *Clé* #2 (1939).

"Art extracted from
the most familiar reality
does indeed exist and
its domain is perhaps
the largest of any.
But it is nonetheless true
that considerable interest,
not to say beauty,
may be found in actions
inspired by a cast of mind
so remote from anything
we feel, from anything
we believe, that they remain
incomprehensible to us,
displaying themselves
before our eyes like
a spectacle without rhyme
or reason. What could
be more poetic than
Xerxes, son of Darius,
ordering the sea to be
scourged with rods for
having engulfed his fleet?"
Marcel Proust,

Keeper of Environments
on the ARCKHAM THE RED,
before it sank into the Sea
of Pleasures Unsustained.

In a final spasm of Rage,
she hurled the Hermetically Sealed
remote control to the ground,
breaking her spell on us
and regaining her appearance;
then, she jumped to her Death
head-first out of the porthole.

Greenwich, for her part, in keeping
with the Gay Science of
the Manchurian Pirate Code on
the ARDEN in the Guccifer Sea,
realized that her Triumvir's
Despotic regime had been captured
by a Genus-1 Abstrakt Machine
of Mutation, and that the Spirit
of Misrule was now actualized as
the becoming-minoritarian of
a Kenoma-Creatura assemblage.

Picking up the remote,
its Seal intact, she tossed it
out of the porthole, and then
she, too, plunged to her Death
head-first, with the cry:
"Mi-Go! Wait for me!"

In Search of Lost Time:
The Captive.

"The soul has moments
of Escape – / When bursting
all the doors – / She dances
like a Bomb, abroad, /
And swings upon the hours."
E. Dickinson (360).

"And it came to pass after
we had all gone down
into the ship, and had taken
with us our provisions and
things which had been
commanded us, we did put
forth into the sea and were
driven forth before the wind
towards the promised land."
The Book of Mormon,
1 Nephi 18.

"Life is like getting in
a boat that is about to set sail
out to sea and sink."
Zen koan (Shunryu Suzuki).

"Do not mourn the dead.
They know what they are doing."
C. Lispector,
The Hour of the Star.

"Thomas Mann, in his

Being no more,
I see what is.

All of us on board
see what is,
and what is not.

We are now identified
with that Being, the Being
that has never ceased to exist.

And that Being
has revealed all.

I knew it,
but I could not say it;
and if I can start
to say it, and to speak
for all the crew,
that is because, as Navigator,
I have left reality behind.

It is one of the Hopeless
who writes to you,
and who knows
the happiness of being
here on board, ever since
she has taken leave
of this ship, and separated
herself Absolütely.

Those who have left us

essay on Freud, has spoken
of the 'quotation-like life'
of the men of mythological
times... Archaic man,
he said, stepped back a pace
before doing anything,
like the toreador poising
himself for the death-strike."
C. Kerényi, "Prolegomena,"
in C. G. Jung and C. Kerényi,
Introduction to a Science
of Mythology.

"Myth and action
form a pair always
associated with the duality
of patient and healer.
In the schizophrenic cure
the healer performs actions
and the patient produces
his myth; in the shamanistic
cure the healer supplies
the myth and the patient
performs the actions."
Claude Levi-Strauss,
Structural Anthropology.

"In front of the ocean /
under the cliff / on the face
of the granite /... those open /
hands... / Man came alone
into the cave / facing the ocean
All the hands are the same size /

did not separate themselves:
Dead—Don Juan, Occam,
van Rr'Ubik, Maria,
Finnegan, Fiat, Leiningen,
Meade, Mazüka, Woodstock,
Greenwich, Soho, Kodak—
they still circle around their bodies.

We are not Dead,
but we are separated.

The third group in the crew's
awakening from dreamtime
experienced the proverbial
"Nightmare in Hell," except
perhaps for Avon the Poetess,
whose legs still drag
beneath the hull
as bone in the water.

Neanderthal dreamed of trees;
of being towed
by Ptah the El Daoud
on a stretcher
as Concealed Corpse,
whose "pain was hard,"
through the Corrupt Forest
of Perpetual Evil,
that "grew Monstrous"
in the Dieback circle of
self-amplified "Green air."

He was alone.../
And he cried out to me /
You who are named
you who are granted identity /
I love you... / I love you
beyond you / I will love anyone
who will hear me cry out
that I love you /
Thirty thousand years /
I cry out / I cry out to the one
who will answer me /
I want to love you
I love you /
For thirty thousand years
I cry out before the sea
the white specter / I am
the one who cried out
that he loved you, you"
Marguerite Duras,
"The Negative Hands."

"Man cannot understand
without images."
Thomas Aquinas,
On Memory and Recollection.

"That controversy led them
naturally into Thomas Aquinas,
and Thomas Aquinas to the devil."
Lawrence Sterne,
Tristram Shandy.

"The soul never thinks

She suffered as if from
Trauma at Birth,
witness to massive waves
of Moisture outflow
in the Airstream,
and to the undulations of
Vegetation-Atmosphere
feedback collapse,
that destroyed the yew trees,
the hemlocks, the junipers,
the Red, White and Blue pines
across the Mother Forest
of Ardennes, and caused
the Pools of Sexual Renewal
to go dry.

Dressed as the Men
of Malatestes, twin sisters
Rosetta and Thebes, whose hair
reaches down to the ground,
had Traumatic visions of Mu
disappearing under the ocean.

Rosetta saw the waters
advancing in zig-zag waves
of Phlegm and Bile, Choler
and Blood, as prophesied
on the Narrow Seas
by Captain Newborne of
the VORTEX in *Encyclopaedia
of the Common People;*
Thebes's Nightmare vision was

without images."
Aristotle,
On the Soul.

"...Remember that there's no /
Bottom to the universe where
the atoms / Might stand tight,
since the limitless span of space /
Stretches unmeasured forever
in all directions."
Lucretius,
On the Nature of Things.

"Comparisons are odorous..."
W. Shakespeare,
As You Like It.

"The end of politics
is the best of ends;
and the main concern
of politics is to engender
a certain character
in the citizens and to make
them good and disposed
to perform noble actions."
Aristotle,
Nicomachean Ethics.

"But the Cosmi are
worse than the Ephors."
Aristotle,
Politics.

of water everywhere, become
a vast sheet of melting Ice,
that broke apart across the Void.

In their dreams, ben-Cnopee,
Scard'nelli and Q'bal relived
the Trauma of our disastrous war
against Aliens at Absolüt point,
"head-waters of the Eternities";
and had climactic visions of us,
the survivors, as lepers.

Emerging from the horror
of Nightmare, the horror
of dreamtime's private Hell,
all of them confronted
a dream-awakened crew that
was in deep psychic disarray,
still reeling from the after-effects
of a failed Mutiny...
and headed once again toward
what we assumed was the light
of Absolüt Point—weïrd light
that continued to recede
on the horizon, as the ship
advanced in its direction.

After awaking from dreamtime with
the last group of dreamers, Avon
the Poetess began to improvise,
as soon as Captain Anna-O

"I can't go on. I'll go on."
Samuel Beckett,
The Unnamable.

"As far as I can remember
there are no books in the world
which are concerned with the fate
of a woman's soul, but only
concerned with woman as
a tool, whereby man destroys
or saves his own soul."
Frances Bolderoff, in
Charles Olson and Frances Boldereff:
A Modern Correspondence.

"No one simply turns on a light."
Robert Creeley,
"Caves 6."

"One / looks and looks and time /
is the variable, the determined /
as ever river, lost on the way, /
drifted on, laps and continues."
R. Creeley,
"Caves 5."

"You think it's funny? To have
prospect / of being last creature
on earth or at best a / company
of rats and cockroaches?"
R. Creeley,
"Caves 2."

ordered the portside porthole—
through which Woodstock, Soho
and Greenwich had leaped to
their Deaths—shut and Holistically
sealed with 4-Color Borromean lines;
but her poetry, first received
on Kodak the Handsome Sailor's
communicator in the Abstrakt
Workshop's frontispherion,
was strangely incomprehensible
to the rest of us.

In a relaxed Monotone,
periodically puffing her cheeks,
then pushing her tongue through
her lips, Avon projected soft,
gentle bursts of Sound into the air—
a performative act reminiscent of
Dunnoldini's extreme Slo-Mo "Bronx
Cheer" in Eranos the Scholiast's
Black Rain of Maxam.

Her poetry of freakish Sounds
seemed intended as commentary
on a series of different signs
she made with her hands
and fingers: an open angle,
a triangle, circle or semi-circle,
oval, spiral, or hashtag, and
other geometric figures that were
Claviform or Tectiform, Pectiform,
Reniform, Cordiform, Unciform,
or Cruciform, as catalogued in

"Even as Macbeth watched
the approach of Birnam Wood
in the hands of his enemies,
Leiningen saw the tamarind
wood move nearer and nearer
in the mandibles of the ants."
Carl Stephenson,
"Leiningen versus the ants."

"The revolution
will not be televised."
Gil Scott-Heron,
Small Talk at 125th and Lenox.

"And a scene like one
from Dante lay around him;
for miles in every direction
there was nothing but a black,
glittering multitude,
a multitude of rested, sated,
but none the less voracious ants."
C. Stephenson,
"Leiningen versus the ants."

"Ants and bees are not *it.*
They are *shes*... The air is *it.*"
C. Lispector,
Água Viva.

"Mother Nature seems
to love us so / When she
smiles there is a subtle glow /
And with tears of joy,

*Hieroglyphic Intensities of
the Paree Apokalypse* by D. J.
Logos the Conceptual Amerikan.

At stake in the Lost Speech
of Avon's new poetry,
according to Kodak,
were the Laws of Poetry
in their opposition to Khaos,
as mediated by the Neutral.

But, as Kodak continued
to enlighten the crew with
hermeneutic interpretations
of Avon's ongoing recital,
he fell Asleep.

Because the ship seemed out
of control, as if moved by
a will of its own, Captain
Anna-O quickly gave the order
to throw Kodak's body
overboard, as part of a larger
ritual effort to steer the ship
away from the light, yet again.

(What Big Head guards our way
and does not go
to any other place
at any other time—guards us,
of the righteous 7th Generation,

the happiness flows / I see
red and orange and purple /
Yellow and blue and green."
Leon Thomas, "Colors,"
in Pharoah Sanders, *Karma.*

"One must therefore be a fox
to recognize traps, and a lion
to frighten wolves."
Niccolò Machiavelli,
The Prince.

"And now I have
stray cats to feed and
my class at the Leprosarium."
William Burroughs,
"Doing Easy."

"If time is constantly
subtracted from
a limited extent of time,
one will obviously
come to the present."
Aristotle,
Metaphysics.

"To be a *famous* American
poet is not the same thing
as *being famous*."
John Ashbery *(RIP).*

"For "IS" and "IS-NOT"
though with Rule and Line, /

who once reveled in tongue-
twisters and phallic song,
and climbed the smoky ropes
of ritualized argument and
shouting matches; who did
the right things for the wrong
reasons, and the wrong things
for the right reasons, while some
shook their heads to mean *no,*
and others nodded *yes,* from
a higher sense of moral virtue;
who confronted the conditions
of responsibility for action
with courage and temperance,
honor and anger; whose intellect,
both contemplative and calculative,
embraced practical wisdom,
intuitive reason, political science
and art; who championed *mythos*
against *logos* in the Spirit of
friendship and practiced Neoteric
sex "off the radar" of rationalism,
in Exoceanist freedom from
allegory, to Rashomon effect,
only to look at each other, amid
the wreckage of our Astrology,
and ask: how did this happen?)

The Death of Kodak
the Handsome Sailor
and Second Mate,

And "UP-AND-DOWN"
without, I could define, /
I yet in all only cared to know, /
Was never deep in anything
but— / Wine."
Omar Khayyam,
Rubaiyat (tr. E. Fitzgerald).

"'Quantum' means
that which is divisible
into two or more constituent
parts of which each is
by nature a 'one' and a 'this.'
A quantum is a plurality
if it is numerable, a magnitude
if it is measurable."
Aristotle,
Metaphysics.

"At that time it was assumed,
intuitively as it were,
on the basis of 'common
sense,' that the ocean
was a lifeless chemical
conglomerate, a monstrous
mass of jelly covering
the globe, which produced
extraordinary formations
as a consequence of its
'quasi-volcanic' activity...
From time to time more
daring and intriguing
conceptualizations emerged,

as he was explaining Avon's
new poetry, provided the necessary
shock for bringing psychological
understanding to the Captain
in the aftermath of failed Mutiny,
given the absence of recognizable
constellations in our Stygian sky.

Anna-O's post-Mutiny
Politics of Sorcery, and her refusal
of Revenge, represented
a becoming-worthy of Mythic
Ordeal that acknowledged
a shipwide entrapment in
the Static, and understood Mutiny
as a mode of therapeutic activity.

Her self-transformative insight,
which she communicated
to the entire crew, and
her new knowledge of Nature's
Oneness with a Cosmic
process of psychic renewal,
identified the becoming-
schizoid of the ship
as the work of Nature's Revolt,
as a field of Emergence
that released the autonomous
partial systems of its creative force
through the hazardous daemons
of an Alien / Alienated sea
cathected in the vessel Itself...
as if, in our hypomanic frenzy,

but they all seemed to pass
judgment on the ocean,
which came to be seen as
the final stage of a development
which long ago, thousands of
years back, had had its period
of supreme organization and
now, having survived only
physically, was disintegrating
into a multitude of unnecessary,
nonsensical agonal formations...
But it was impossible to deny
the existence of its mind,
whatever could be understood
by the term. It had become
quite clear that it was only
too aware of our presence...
It existed then,
it lived, thought, acted."
Stanislav Lem,
Solaris.

"Whether the wind gave
rise to rippling waves,
or the rain riddled it
with holes and covered it
with small bursting bubbles,
the boat kept moving North,
from dawn to dusk.
The bellow of deer,
the trumpet of the mammoth,
the roaring voice of lions
greeted in passing the small

rather than *seeing*, we had read
the Otherness of our environment
despotically, as Underworld,
and the misreading had been
ritually repeated and intensified
as the Mutiny of prisoners on
a Daemon Ship from Xibalba.

The "Majic moment,"
the moment of Metamorphosis,
came when Anno-O understood
that Mutiny had not been
a form of Judgment rendered
against the ship, but of Healing...
that the Mutineers were not
acting as Judges, but as Medics
tending to a dysfunctional,
malevolent vessel that was
resistant to joy, love and
laughter, estranged from nature
on a Hieroglyphic sea.

For this reason,
Anna-O ordered that the old
Purification Rites be performed
—starting with the jettison of
Kodak's body—in an effort
to reset the ship's systems.

The will to make shipshape
proceeded with the naming
of Wang the Third Mate
as replacement for Don Juan

frail vessel and man the enemy.
It went, they went, along
the stretches of islands, under
the shadow of trees, through
vast clear waterways."
J.- H. Rosny (*aîné*),
Vamireh:
A Novel of Primitive Times.

"where is the spark that /
promises stars?"
Wanda Coleman,
"Essay on Language 3."

"For Plato, too,
was right in... asking,
as he used to do,
'Are we on the way from
or to the first principles?'"
Aristotle,
Nichomean Ethics.

"Every sharp is always
already a flat."
Michael Boughn,
Cosmographia.

"Kepler, in later life,
became convinced that
the planets play music along
their paths. In his 1619 book
Harmony of the World
he derived the planet's tunes

the Chief Mate, by having her
recite the mantra "Abrāhādābrā"
three times above a bowl of
sparkling water, by the gash
in the bulkhead of the Quietist
room—which also confirmed
her and Kodak's replacement by
Able-Bodied Sailors Nobadinus
and Marloboro as Second
and Third Mates, respectively.

By the same token, Ordinary
Sailors Neanderthal, Thebes and
Rosetta chanted, "It is...
all good," "It is... all good,"
while being walked through
the smoke and washed with
the ashes from the Mutoscope
—like Pyongyang, Pokémon and
General Tso in *Notes toward*
a Love Machine Supreme—
during their ritual appointment
as substitutes for Möbius
the Mapper, who hung,
Unconscious, upside-down
in the Engine room; for Occam
the Weatherwoman, Drowned;
and for Scard'nelli, whose position
as Bo'sun was left vacant,
when Scard'nelli became Librarian,
after taking over for Sokrates, who
replaced van Rr'Ubik at the helm.

and concluded that
'the Earth sings Mi-Fa-Mi.'"
Sabine Hossenfelder,
Lost in Math.

"Anyone who has ever
experienced the pleasure
of Socratic insight and
felt how, spreading in ever-
widening circles, it seeks
to embrace the whole world
of appearances, will never
again find any stimulus
toward existence more
violent than the craving
to complete this conquest
and to weave the net
impenetrably tight...
But now science,
spurred by its powerful
illusion, speeds irresistibly
toward its limits where
its optimism, concealed
in the essence of logic,
suffers shipwreck."
F. Nietzsche,
The Birth of Tragedy.

"The shipwreck is
Shakespeare's final symbol."
Mark Van Doren,
Shakespeare.

Van Rr' Ubik's superimposed
profile on the port side
of the figurehead,
like the spiral design of
Maria's bones on the deck
near the Large Collapse,
were exorcized by ceremonies
of Mystic pantomime and
by the processional display
of the sacred Liohana's
flap and balancer, at the same
time that the Flaming Scalp,
the Smileless Stone and
the Sock Puppets of The Quincunx
were tossed into the sea.

Further cleansing rites
were devoted to the geoglyphic
inscription of the Tarot Trumps
along the Yonaguni shoreline
reproduced on the deck by
the Storm, and to the lingering
effect of the crew's so-called
"Big Fart," that occurred after
our entry onto the Silver sea:
the Exchanging of Clothes,
the Festival of Laughter and
the Contest of Abusive Language
and Scurrilous Jests... all of which
culminated with the Opening
of the Jars, at the ship's bow

"I dreamt about... the hull
of the ship of state... /
I was in the Assembly.
A flock of sheep, / with walking
sticks and cloaks. Listening.
In rows, / And who was
doing the talking? A great
fanged whale / haranguing
these poor sheep a booming
bellow, the bloated blatting
of a swollen sow..."
Aristophanes,
The Wasps.

"We don't want honest
men, who can read a bit, /
to lead the people.
We want lowdown scum /
And swine. It's all yours.
Grab your chance!"
Aristophanes,
Knights.

"We must admire the depth
of Aristophanes in having
recognized the dialectic side
in Socrates as being a negative."
G. W. F. Hegel,
Lectures on the History
of Philosophy.

"At this time, bridges
were being built across

and stern, and the Sacrificial
Outpouring into the sea of
the ouzo—which had become
increasingly thin, sharp, pungent
and astringent on the palate,
like a wall of acidity, with
a musty, deeply unpleasant,
vaguely chemical bouquet and
an insipid, lifeless finish that
left a fizziness on the tongue.

With the purification rituals
completed, all ship systems
were engaged to help steer
the ship away from the light
on a second go-around.

At Twelve O'Clock
the self-guiding ship,
responding to the supplemental
action of the wheel
and the steering paddle,
and to the extra power boost
in the propeller,
the fore and aft top-sails,
the t'gallants and the Burtons,
started turning away
from the light.

But at Three O'Clock,
the ship once again continued

the Hellespont from Asia
to Europe... But in fact after
these bridges had been built,
a violent storm descended
upon them, broke them up,
and tore apart all that work...
Xerxes was infuriated when
he learned of this; he ordered
that the Hellespont was to
receive 300 lashes under
the whip, and that a pair
of shackles was to be dropped
into the sea... He instructed
his men to say barbarian and
insolent things as they were
striking the Hellespont:
'Bitter water, your master
is imposing this penalty on
you for wrongdoing him,
even though you had suffered
no injustice from him...'
Thus he ordered that
the sea was to be punished
and also that the supervisors
of the bridge
were to be beheaded."
Herodotus,
The Histories.

"'Chaunt in his ear delusions
magical, / That he may fight
the horses of the sea.' /
The Druids took them to

to swerve on a starboard course,
as if initiating a loop
back toward the light.

At which point Captain Anna-O
forgot what she had understood;
psychologically, she blamed
the sea for the ship's failure
to maintain its new heading.

In reaction, seized by
the fury of her frustration,
she invoked the Nazions Edicts
and gave the order that
the Wands of Klan be retrieved
from the Power-Knowledge Center,
and that Neanderthal, Q'bal,
Thebes, Bedlam, Rosetta,
on the larboard side,
and Scard'nelli, Mach,
ben-Cnopee, Sokrates, Sony,
on the starboard side, station
themselves at the portholes
on the C-level deck,
in order to beat the sea
with the Wands and seal
the beating with Narrative Lubes.

Almost at once,
Commander Exprès had
a Coughing Fit, and Venus
read the projection of
his spit on the Glass Ingots

their mystery, / And chaunted for three days. / Cuchulain stirred, / Stared on the horses of the sea, and heard / The cars of battle and his own name cried; / And fought with the invulnerable tide."
W. B. Yeats,
"Cuchulain's Fight with the Sea."

"Extreme states are contrary both to the intermediate state and to each other... Hence he who aims at the intermediate must first depart from what is the more contrary to it, as Calypso advises—Hold the ship out beyond that surf and spray."
Aristotle,
Nichomean Ethics.

"Anyone can run to excesses, / It is easy to shoot past the mark, / It is hard to stand firm in the middle."
E. Pound,
Cantos, XIII.

"There are two sides to every issue: one side is right and the other is wrong, but the middle is always evil."

as a bad omen.

The beating and the Narratives began nonetheless... and just as Bismark started reading from The Book of Proper Distance—comparing Ωceanic to

- Tarquin the Persecutor of Mutabilitie the Suppliant;
- Yorick, Executioner of Toby, who was Friend to Tubal the Witness;
- Ha'm the Threatener of Thelema's Rescue—

six shooting stars passing overhead played the Sounds of the Mystic Chord first heard by the legendary crew of the PROMETHEUS, recorded in *The Claviculae of Screamon the Wise.*

Bismark read on, while the Sailors struck the sea's surface with the Wands, comparing Ωceanic to

- Joe Schmoe the Seeker, who drove Owsley off the cliffs of Theoria;
- Kung the Avenger of Redward of the Unexamined Life;
- Selavy the Culprit who betrayed *?* the Revelator and defied Momo the Interrogator of Nature's Mysterium;
- Moroni the Wrongdoer, who confused 6 Unseen 9 Tooth;

Ayn Rand,
Atlas Shrugged.

"You are a slave, Medea."
F. Boldereff,
A Primer of Morals for Medea
in *Charles Olson and*
Frances Boldereff:
A Modern Correspondence.

"You'll see the battlements
of Kytaian Aiëtés, / and
the shady grove of Ares,
where the Fleece is, / spread
out on the top of an oak tree,
watched by a serpent, /
a fearful creature to look at,
ever grazing round, on guard."
Apollonius Rhodius,
Argonautika, Book II.

"The object of desire and
the object of thought move
in this way; they move
without being moved."
Aristotle,
Metaphysics.

"Profiteers drinking blood
sweetened with sh-t, /
And behind them . . . . f
and the financiers /
lashing them

• Gen.net the False Innocent,
who rejected Rë the Mistaken;
• Achilles of Egypt, the Punisher
in the Great Irenic Escape.

As the ship approached
Six O' Clock, however, it was
clear that its course back toward
the light was unchanging,
to the consternation of the entire
crew—including Vico of
Communications, who was eager
for a turn at the podium.

So Vico, replacing Bismark,
stood up and read from
The Tablet of Destiny,
blaming Ωceanic as
• Cody the Jealous One, who
inveighed against Jimmy the Ink,
his Partner in Temporary Crime,
in retribution for Orc's Mistake;
• Lilith the Vanquished, who
succumbed to Eve the Victorious;
• Gutenberg the Immortal,
whose life was a poem difficult
to understand... at which point,
Kongō interrupted Vico, to read
from *The Book of Writing.*

But as Kongō got started,
a meteor shower filled
the sky with the serial

with steel wires. / And
the betrayers of language /
. . . . . . n and the press
gang / And those who
had lied for hire; /
The perverts, the perverters
of language, / The perverts,
who have set money-lust /
Before the pleasures of
the senses; / ...And Invidia, /
the corruptio, foetor, fungus, /
liquid animals, melted
ossifications, / slow rot, foetid
combustion, / ...monopolists,
obstructors of knowledge, /
obstructors of distribution...
E. Pound,
Cantos, XIV.

"Cursed be Canaan!
The lowliest of slaves
shall he be to his brothers!
Blessed be the Lord, the God
of Shem, unto them shall
Canaan be slave! May God
enlarge Japheth, may he dwell
in the tents of Shem, unto
them shall Canaan be slave!"
Genesis 9: 25, in R. Crumb,
The Book of Genesis Illustrated.

"Our brother is a fool, for
he thinketh that he can build

Sound of descending
5-tone musical lines:
A♭ G♭ E♭ D♭ B♭...
G♭ E♭ D♭ B♭ A♭...
E♭ D♭ B♭ A♭ G♭...
D♭ B♭ A♭ G♭ E♭...
B♭ A♭ G♭ E♭ D♭...

Nevertheless, Kongō was thrilled
to read on, while the crew's
beating of the sea grew faster
and more intense, and the Sound
of shooting stars cascaded
in the same descending pattern.

Commander Exprès
Coughed Up again, and again
Venus read the projection
of his spit on the glass
as a bad omen.

But Kongō only became more
excited and continued to read,
comparing Ωceanic to
• Wittenberg the Unfortunate,
who suffered Wannasee the Fool;
• Oreal, She-of-the-Tree, who
pursued the Single Vision, and was
confronted by Déhja "VU" Thor'z
(A♭ G♭ E♭ D♭ B♭...
G♭ E♭ D♭ B♭ A♭...);
• Cucufa of Bohemia, who
was framed by Lord Elgin;

a ship; yea, and he also
thinketh that he can cross
these great waters."
The Book of Mormon,
1 Nephi 17.

"The present King of Great
Britain...has endeavored to bring
on the inhabitants of our frontiers,
the merciless Indian Savages
whose known rule of warfare,
is an undistinguished destruction
of all ages, sexes and conditions."
The Declaration of Independence.

"what pudor pejorocracy
affronts / how awe, night-rest
and neighborhood can rot /
what breeds where dirtiness
is law / what crawls / below"
C. Olson,
"The Kingfishers."

"Piety and fear, / Religion to
the gods, peace, justice, truth, /
Domestic awe, night rest, and
neighborhood, / Instruction,
manners, mysteries, and trades, /
Degrees, observances, customs,
and laws, / Decline to your
confounding contraries, / And
let confusion live!... Thou cold
sciatica, / Cripple our senators

• Hermès the Beloved Enemy, who
faced Abdul Al'haz-red of Beauport
and Thule the Patagonian;
• Jafar the Bold Leader,
who stole *The Book of Memory*
from the Companions
(E♭ D♭ B♭ A♭ G♭...).

The ten Sailors who whipped
the sea with the Wands, transported
by the pentatonic Sounds of
the shooting stars, started shouting
KIAI! KIAI!... KIAI! KIAI!...
back and forth to each other,
in a rhythmic call-and-response
from port to starboard, while
Kongō continued to read,
comparing Ωceanic to
• Johnnie Dee Angel, who
harassed the Lovers of Shax;
• Albemuth the Abductor, who
released Megaloceros
from van-Gelder the Guard
(B♭ A♭ G♭ E♭ D♭...);
• *i*Arabi of Sandover,
Oneorocritic of the Troubadours;
• Bartleby the Epopt, who
resolved the Puritan Enigma
(D♭ B♭ A♭ G♭ E♭...).

Yet, as Exprès Coughed Up
again—and Venus again read
the projection of his spit on

that their limbs may halt /
As lamely as their manners!"
W. Shakespeare,
Timon of Athens.

"Now folly's pitched its tent
of mirth, / Preparing onslaught
bold and blind, / To force
the princes, force their kind /
To leave all wisdom,
knowledge true / And
seek advantage for the few..."
S. Brant,
The Ship of Fools.

"And we beheld the sea,
which we called Irreantum,
which, being interpreted,
is many waters."
The Book of Mormon,
1 Nephi 17.

"The cities of Copán
and Palenque were east
and west of one another,
and Cálakmul and Tikal
stood north and south of
each other. The four of them
held the center in common.
Among Mayans, there never
was a "SINGLE CENTER"
like the one the poet
had sought in Sumeria.

the glass as a bad omen—
the Sound of the shooting stars
suddenly dropped into a lower
register and started moving in
an upward series of pentatonic
scales, instead of Rippling down.

On both sides of the ship,
the abrupt change of Sound broke
the rhythm of the whip-masters,
who quickly fell into a High-
Spirited free-for-all—*KIAI! KIAI!*
KIAI! KIAI! KIAI! KIAI!
KIAI! KIAI! KIAI!—inciting
Sinbad the Steward-Entertainer
to displace Kongō and
take his turn at the podium.

As Sinbad stood up,
however, to read from
The Book of (Unknown) Nature
and compare Ωceanic to
• Ta'wil the Beloved, who
abandoned Tweets the Lover...
an insight was offered by *Bō-*
Utsuri, the Spirit of the Keel,
who identified the Sound of
the ascending shooting stars...
A♯ C♯ D♯ F♯ G♯...
C♯ D♯ F♯ G♯ A♯...
D♯ F♯ G♯ A♯ C♯...
F♯ G♯ A♯ C♯ D♯...
G♯ A♯ C♯ D♯ F♯...

Dennis Tedlock,
The Olson Codex.

"Let us look at the encounters,
the campaigns, and the wars
of Alexander, who conquered
Persia and India and who
died finally in Babylonia,
as everyone knows. This was
the first great meeting with
the East, and an encounter
that so affected Alexander
that he ceased to be Greek
and became partly Persian.
The Persians have now
incorporated him into their
history... The Islamic countries
still honor him under the name
Alexander the Two-Horned,
because he ruled the two horns
of East and West...
In the fifteenth century in the city
of Alexandria, the city of
Alexander the Two-Horned,
a series of tales was gathered.
Those tales have a strange
history, as it is generally
believed. They were first told
in India, then in Persia, then
in Asia Minor, and finally
were written down in Arabic
and compiled in Cairo."
Jorge Luis Borges,

as elements of a "Music
of the Spheres" emanating
from the 36 Black Keys
on the Arkestral Keyboard.

According to the Law
of Unintended Consequence
it must have been *Bō-Utsuri*'s
information quantum concerning
the 36 Arkestral Black Keys
that entered the mecanosphere
and provoked the astrophysical
change of Harmonics,
at Nine O'Clock, when
the arpeggio of Screamon's
Mystic Chord was Sounded
again, this time in Stereo,
by six pairs of shooting stars.

The Heavens fell silent; and
realizing her psychological error
at last, Anna-O ordered the crew
to stop whipping the Silver sea.

While the ship continued
sailing toward the light
on the horizon, Captain
Anna-O explained that
"the Wheel had rolled" and
that she remembered now
what she had understood

"The Thousand and One Nights."

"Gozzi maintained that
there can be but thirty-six
tragic situations. Schiller
took great pains to find more,
but he was unable to find
even so many as Gozzi."
J. W. Goethe, *Converstations*
with Eckermann,
quoted in Georges Polti,
The Thirty-Six Dramatic Situations.

"Sheherazade saw the day
break, and fell silent."
Tales of the 1001 Nights.

"At this point, Shahrazād
saw the approach of morning
and discreetly fell silent."
Tales of the 1001 Nights.

"But morning overtook
Shahrazad, and she lapsed
into silence."
Tales of the 1001 Nights.

"Shahrazad perceived
the dawn of day and ceased
to say her permitted say."
Tales of the 1001 Nights.

"Here Shahrazád perceived

before, but forgotten:
that her neurotic obsession
with an Alien sea
was symptomatic of a Static
concept of Mutiny and a pre-
Mutinous binary of "fact and
fantasy, poetry and sci-fi"
traceable not to her association
with the sea, but to her
repressed connection with
a ship under "Absolüt control
of the Death-drive."

Uncannily,
as soon as the order
to stop had been given,
as if to confirm
the Cosmic dimension
in the crew's desire
for the Emergence of
unexpected connections,
fortunate mediations
and unforeseen re-creation
—in contrast with
the distressed Energetics
of a will for Control—
Commander Exprès
Coughed Up again, and
Venus of Intelligence
interpreted the spit on
on the glass as a sign
that the solution for sailing
away from the light was

the light of morning, and
discontinued the recitation
with which she had been
allowed thus far to proceed."
Tales of the 1001 Nights.

"Morning now dawned
and Shahrazad broke off
from what she had been
allowed to say."
Tales of the 1001 Nights.

"It is the task of the translator
to release in his own language
that pure language which is
exiled among alien tongues,
to liberate the language
imprisoned in a work in his
re-creation of that work."
W. Benjamin,
"The Task of the Translator."

"Even the fart of foreigners
can be taken as 'fragrance.'"
Mao Tse-Tung,
Collected Works, "Cigarette Tax."

"Nine in the third place means:
All day long the superior man
is creatively active. / At nightfall
his mind is still beset with cares. /
Danger. No blame."
I Ching (tr. R. Wilhelm).

to put the ship in reverse.

As we once again approached
Twelve O'Clock,
the Captain, mindful
of the omen, gave the order
to sail full-speed astern.

Cowabunga was thus dispatched
to the Stepmill and
Tarzan to the Treadmill,
on which they climbed and ran
respectively, re-routing power
from the Antikithera recycling
assemblage, located under
the Cross-Hatchings
of the Skull Gallery,
to the gaslight, parasol,
love gasoline, Sex cylinders,
waterfall, sieves and war-holes
on the Android open-source
operating platform—but
to no effect: the engagement
of the ship's gnomotor
into reverse was stalled.

Ō-Itame, the new Spirit of
the Keel, likened the situation
in the Skull Gallery
to a pejorocracy, in which
the Royal reserve databank was

"Representative of Sanjō swords is the famous blade known as Mikazuki Munechika ('Crescent-Moon Munechika'), a slender deeply curved blade with a small *kissaki* (point section). That blade has a *hamon* (tempering pattern) characteristic of Munechika's style, including *ko-midare* (compact irregular patterns) with a form of *tobi-yaki* mixed with *uchi-noke*: separate areas of bright steel, said to resemble ocean spray, and fine, irregular lines."
Ogawa Morihiro,
"The Spirit of the Samurai."

"Tarot interpreters often ignore the obvious connotations of the Death Card, preferring to view it as a card of 'change' or 'transformation.'"
Barbara G. Walker,
The Secrets of the Tarot.

"Zeno's arguments about motion, which cause so much disquietude to those who try to solve the problems that they present, are four in number...

issuing Treasury obligations
and validating Dollar assets
leveraged on leprosy.

It was not until Commander Exprès
Coughed Up again that the key
for getting the ship to move
backward finally came to light.

Venus read the spit
as a sign that Tarzan and
Cowabunga should switch
roles, with Cowabunga taking
his place at the Treadmill and
Tarzan hers on the Stepmill.

As subsequently confirmed
by *Ō-Itame*, the rearrangement
in effect reversed the male
/ female symmetry
that assigned gender-based
positions to the whip-masters,
with the men—Scard'nelli,
ben-Cnopee, Sokrates, Sony,
Mach—on the port side,
and the women—Neanderthal,
Thebes, Bedlam, Rosetta,
Q'bal—on the starboard side.

Additional commentary from
the most recent Spirit of the Keel,
Midare-Utsuri, explained
that in order for a fundamental

The second is the so-called
'Achilles,' and it amounts to this,
that in a race the quickest
runner can never overtake
the slowest, since the pursuer
must first reach the point
whence the pursued started,
so that the slower runner
must always hold a lead."
Aristotle,
Physics.

"*Pathologizing* is the need
of the psyche to express itself
through symptoms of physical
and mental disorder;
the 'dark' Tarot trumps
—The Hanged Man,
The Devil, The Tower,
Death, The Moon—symbolize
these deformative processes."
Cynthia Giles,
The Tarot.

"Sail out for good,
eidolon yacht of me!"
W. Whitman,
Leaves of Grass.

"Talk about what you
have written, by all means,
but do not read from it
while the work is in progress.

classification of values to cohere
Sexuality had to be put in
its place, by woman for woman,
through the actualization
of her twofold-ness... because
Revolution remembers that
it is a woman, and knows
that Death has the rapaciousness
of Sex; Revolution *resuscitates*
the mutilated feminine of man,
of his enslaved tenderness, as
a Youth without body or Sex,
from which Spirit alone profits;
and this Spirit creates
the Natural Revolt of things
that have heretofore been
badly managed; and teaches us,
with a Natural Force that
will drive each of us Mad,
that the Revolution
we are unable to make
the Universe will make for us.

Anna-O reacted at once,
and took Exprès's advice about
switching Exercisers on
the Treadmill and the Stepmill;
and soon Cowabunga was
walking fast, starboard-side,
and Tarzan was climbing hard,
larboard-side.

As the ship's systems shifted into

Every gratification
procured in this way
will slacken your tempo."
W. Benjamin,
One-Way Street,
"The Writer's Technique
in Thirteen Theses."

"indirective / abortive ocular /
reception of the objective /
Bum-bungling of actuality /
exchanging / an inobvious real /
for over-obvious irreal"
Mina Loy, "Hot Cross Bum."

"Sun and earth have not
sunk, / they only wander
as stars, unrecognizable."
Ingeborg Bachmann,
"Night Flight" (tr. P. Filkins).

"The stars are not hereditary."
E. Dickinson (L 827).

"Frosted eyes there were that
lifted altars; / And silent answers
crept across the stars."
Hart Crane, "At Melville's Tomb."

"We have come full circle."
C. Olson, "The K."

"sound radiates /

realignment, we began to move
backward, pulling *away* from
the luminescence on the horizon.

A great cheer went up
on deck; and Avon the Poetess,
who had continued to mouth
a poetry of freakish Sounds
that no one understood since
the Death of Kodak the Exegete,
broke into Wordless Song.

The smooth sailing,
however, was short-lived.

There came a jolt and
the grinding Sound of sand
Scraping the hull, as the ship
ran aground on the shoals—
the shoals on which we still
find ourselves battered now
by different waves
from all directions.

Natural payback, says the Captain,
for striking the sea with Wands...

A Symposium is planned,
during which the Cardinal
Points will be situated and
new constellations imagined.

illuminates / articulates
the symbol of /
and what it radiates it is /
on what it illuminates /
it casts the touch of fire"
Sun Ra, liner notes,
Nuits de la Fondation
Maeght, Vol. 1.

"It is the flames from
the mouth of his bark
which guide him
on these mysterious ways."
The Egyptian Amduat,
"Fourth Hour."

The hope is that by mapping
the Heavens, we will discover
the Guiding Spirit to enlighten us
and deliver us from our plight,
like the Time Travellers
in *Death and Philosophy,*
waiting for Godël.

The hope is that my love
will find its way to you,
while your love lives on
in me.

Your woman,

S...

The Arts

Dear S.,

"here is / where there / is"
Robert Creeley, "Here."

"We use language not to destroy,
but to undercut pinnings of <u>there</u>."
Richard Foreman,
"Ontological-Hysteric Manifesto I."

"What man is at ease in his Inn?"
Aleister Crowley,
The Book of Lies.

"No artist is pleased... There is only
a queer divine dissatisfaction, a blessed
unrest that keeps us marching and
makes us more alive than the others."
Martha Graham, quoted in
Agnes de Mille, *Martha: The Life
and Work of Martha Graham*.

"It is difficult—this time-keeping;
nothing more quickly disorders it
than contact with any of the arts."
Virginia Woolf,

I knew
that I had
been here before.

Ceramic vulvas
line the locked gate;
the gate bars the way
to a light on the left.

The mat on which I sit
would have been a carpet
with dark stripes lengthwise;
replacing the entrance to
a corridor—higher on the wall—
stands a White window,
that hums.

No stone floor; instead, dirt
and faded mosaic; Dead moss;
no Metal; no vents or drain;
no broken glass or portrait
of ("Dice") D' Cartz.

Outside, below, I hear
the phantom Sounds
of festivity in the street.

I picture Lord Chesterfield
cheered by the crowds;
his Chariot is a picnic table
floating upside-down,
drawn by empty wheelchairs.

He is the Spirit of Shell
incarnate, as foretold by
The Book of Death and Triumph!

He goes to meet his Cerebella.

Soon I will be released.

The veiled figure
behind the gate
with Colored robes
and a big hat
is *The Philosopher;*
the bald Youth
with the tattooed scalp
is *The Skeleton*.

I try to speak, but either
speech is failing me and
I say nothing, or my language

Orlando.

"There is already enough beauty
in the world of art...
to remake the world."
H. D.
Notes on Thought and Vision.

"Nine in the fourth place means: /
Wavering flight over the depths. /
No blame."
I Ching.

"There are five windows. Each has
two leaves divided into three panes.
But these panes are only visible when
the window is wide open, because
the inside is covered with dark paper,
barely translucent, glued exactly to
the entire surface of the glass."
Alain Robbe-Grillet,
In the Labyrinth.

"It will be a great relief when
a window opens. / But the windows
are not there to be found— /
or at least I cannot find them.
And perhaps / it is better that I don't
find them. / Perhaps the light will
prove another tyranny. / Who knows
what new things it will expose?"
C. P. Cavafy, "The Windows."

is foreign to them.

Lady Die breaks in
(I recognize her Voice),
asking: "Is Die *The Star*
or *The Sun*?"

Instantly, from the Lost Land
of Lâ-Konx in White Water
Province comes Voice Mail
counting Dollars:
"Press The Star key now!"

Now, however, "Monocle"
the Noh Comedian does not stand
by a corridor beating her head
against the wall.

Someone different—
KNOCK!
KNOCK!
KNOCK!
KNOCK!
KNOCK!—
is at the window.

The First Law of E-motion,
as theorized by D. J. Com
at *Faux Pas*
in the Greenspan Age,
transports me beyond

"a voice from the nondead past started
talking, / she closed her ears and
it spelled out in her hand / 'you might
as well answer the door, my child, /
the truth is furiously knocking.'"
Lucille Clifton,
"the light that came to lucille clifton."

"I have lived on the lip / of insanity,
wanting to know reasons, /
knocking on a door. It opens.
I've been knocking from the inside!"
Rumi (tr. C. Barks).

"Know amazedly how / often
one takes his madness /
into his own hands / and keeps it."
Lorine Niedecker,
"When Ecstasy is Inconvenient."

"I keep this stylus in my hand...
The healer came after I wrote last, and
I asked him where I had been hurt.
He said it was near the shrine of
the Earth Mother, where the Great
King's army fought the army of
Thought and the Rope Makers...
The army of the Great King blackens
the road for many miles, and I,
having seen it, do not understand
how it could have been vanquished—
or why I joined it, since there are
so many men no one could count them,

a Firewall kindled by
the Rapping on the window.

The Star key is the same
small patch of dirt
on the floor in the corner.

My face hugs the ground,
as I push the dirt
into the corner with my finger.

I am Klutz, beyond
The Scales // reversed,
by a White window that is
The Wheel of Chance;
out of a corridor from
the past, the Fate I reject
and the Fate I embrace
hang in the balance.

Two large thumbs turned up,
like hooks in the wall,
confirm these Revelations.

The thumbs point the way
toward the window:
left hand on the upper thumb,
right foot on the lower one,
and, stretching, right hand
onto the latch...

The White window
offers me a second chance

one more or less is nothing."
Gene Wolfe,
Soldier of the Mist.

"Unleashing of passions is of
the order of 'contagion,' another
name for 'communication'...
What is unleashed, communicated, etc.
is the passion of singularity as such.
The singular being, because it is
singular, is in the passion—
the passivity, the suffering, and
the excess—of sharing its singularity."
Jean-Luc Nancy,
The Inoperative Community.

"Action and speech are so closely
related because the primordial
and specifically human act must
at the same time contain an answer
to the question asked of every
newcomer: 'Who are you?'"
Hannah Arendt,
The Human Condition.

"Some time then there will be every
kind of a history of every one who
ever can or is or was or will be living."
Gertrude Stein,
The Making of Americans.

"In the informational state
the panopticon has been replaced with

at the other path—
the so-called French Leave left
open by Tricks 1 and 101.

Nor is "Monocle" pounding
her head, as sign.

There are different signs;
but this time the Inner Rave
urges me to fall back,
loop around and push on.

I start climbing.

As I lift myself up,
I spot graffiti before me
that says "README,"
while behind me the Firewall
falls, leaving an Abstrakt
Pillar of smoke in its place.

I peer over my shoulders
dialectically, deferring
the Eternal Rerun
with a left-brain wedge.

The lock turns in the gate:
the ceramic vulvas
that line the entrance
morph into Lotuses...
seaweed... Rhizomes...

the panspectron, in which information
is gathered about everything,
all the time, and particular subjects
become visible only in response
to the asking of a question."
Sandra Berman,
Change of State.

"This was indeed a godlike science,
and I ardently desired to become
acquainted with it... I cannot
describe the delight I felt when
I learned the ideas appropriated to
each of these sounds, and was able
to pronounce them. I distinguished
several other words, without being able
as yet to understand or apply them;
such as good, dearest, unhappy."
Mary Shelley,
Frankenstein.

"We are in a generalized crisis
in relation to all the environments of
enclosure—prison, hospital, factory,
school... These are the *societies of
control,* which are in the process of
replacing the disciplinary societies.
'Control' is the name Burroughs
proposes as a term for the new
monster, one Foucault recognizes
as our immediate future."
Gilles Deleuze, "Postscript
on the Societies of Control."

moss... Flashbulbs—
pop!pop!pop!pop!pop!

Through the gate,
from the far corner
on my left, enters the fourfold
(Beatific) manifestation of
my opponent: a smiling woman
half-remembered, her legs
crossed, her feet arched, who
is Shiva of the Weak Force,
Champion of the Tootsies,
reborn as Startrip th'Irenic,
in the guise of Mr. Clean,
the Genie of Meta Forest.

The Genie, oiled and naked
with pointed Nails—
as in Viagra's vision
of Cirrus and Nyce—
starts to stroke the Abstrakt
smoke with Magick gestures,
and gazes at me, grinning.

"Slave of Regret!
Behold the Map of Things Past!"

I recognize Chapter M Verse MM
from the PlayStation Manual,
and hold my position—
peering over my shoulder,
like Headsman Hertz
before the Hale Bop Lights

"We are living through
a movement from an organic,
industrial society to a polymorphous,
information system—from all work
to all play, a deadly game."
Donna Haraway,
The Cyborg Manifesto.

"The art of losing
isn't hard to master..."
Elizabeth Bishop, "One Art."

"You do not wait for fulfillment,
but brace yourself for failure."
Eugen Herrigel,
Zen and the Art of Archery.

"We lose – because we win – /
Gamblers – recollecting which – /
Toss their dice again!"
Emily Dickinson (28).

"There is no way out of the spiritual
battle / the war is the war against
the imagination / you can't sign up
as a conscientious objector / the war
of the worlds hangs here, right now,
in the balance / it is a war for this world,
to keep it / a vale of soul-making"
Diane di Prima, "Rant."

"In English the poetics became

in the Latter Days.

Rubbing thumb against fingertips,
the Genie draws strands
from the smoke, and weaves
filaments into long thin rods
that break in two and dissolve.

Old scenes begin
to play themselves over.

I try to picture
the Grand Trine deconstructed
at the *Je Ne Sais Quoi*
and what the New School
might have been
without the Leap of Faith—
but my foot slips
(or the toehold gives way)...

At the *Savoir Vivre*
I find the WaitRoom
in time, where Conman
the Barbarian and Lego
the Gentile trade places,
like Nehmen and Nim
at the Empire Room, and
the ghost of Hakuna Matata
is your Uncle Feng Shui—
but I think I glimpse
a Marble rolling by,
and then another
(did the room tilt?)...

meubles —furniture— / thereafter
(after 1630 / & Descartes was the value
/ until Whitehead, who cleared out
the gunk / by getting the universe in
(as against man alone / & <u>that</u> concept
of history (not Herodotus's, / which
was a verb, to find out for oneself:
which makes any one's acts
a finding out for him or her / self"
Charles Olson,
Maximus IV, V, VI,
"A Later Note on Letter #15."

"The communion of saints
is a great and inspiring assemblage...
but it has only one possible hall
of meeting, and that is, the present."
Alfred North Whitehead,
"The Aims of Education."

"The gods themselves seemed to
summon me, though of course I am
not admitted to the sacred precincts."
Murasaki Shikibu,
The Tale of Genji.

"Dont you know that "No" is the wildest
word we consign to Language?"
Emily Dickinson (L 562).

"Let M be predicated of no N, but
of all O. Since, then, the negative
relation is convertible, N will belong

I try to break
the Genie's Web
and make another grab
for the window,
then I find myself
back at the *Savoir Faire,*
and this time, rather than
cash in on MoMa's Rapture
and play Voodoo Child
to Mr. Bond's Finest Torture,
I check the warning tag
on my helmet,
return it to the "box" marked
I SWEAR THEREFORE I AM—
when I think I hear
the Sound of dripping water,
an electronic beat
or a ball bouncing,
and the Sound of singing,
or a Voice shouting, calling
(am I under the Ocean
of Happy Days?)...

I try again for the window's
handle, the Genie's play
with the smoke seduces me,
I am back in the past
at the *Laisser Faire,*
what I do differently now
is follow the music and
keep up the Double Talk,

to no M: but M was assumed to belong
to all O: consequently N will belong
to no O. This has already been proved.
Again if M belongs to all N, but to no
O, then N will belong to no O. For if
M belongs to no O, O belongs to no M:
but M (as was said) belongs to all
N: O then will belong to no N: for
the first figure has again been formed.
But since the negative relation is
convertible, N will belong to no O.
Thus it will be the same syllogism
that proves both conclusions."
Aristotle,
Prior Analytics.

"On. Say on. Be said on.
Somehow on. Till nohow on.
Said nohow on."
Samuel Beckett,
Worstward Ho.

"There's no mere word
sufficient to say NO."
Flannery O'Connor,
The Violent Bear It Away.

"Nana-korobi, ya-oki."
("Fall down seven times,
stand up eight.")
Daruma Daishi.

on my way from the stage
of "MUST SEE"
to the "NOTHING YET"
and "NOT AGAIN" dioramas—
and suddenly the ground
starts to tremble, the smell
of pine fills the room,
the hooks and the wall
feel like warm flesh...

Still looking over
my shoulder, I tighten
my grip and reach
for the window
with my right hand,
yet the spell persists,
I slip into the time
at the *Laisser Passer,*
three Guardians
by the Slo Mode Portal...
rather than greet them
as in the past
I keep silent, let
the third one usher me
past the other two,
past the clutter and
the piles of paper pictured
in Maestro's *Background(s)*
of the Complex, toward
the Sunken Bottleneck
and Therapeutical Exit,
that draw near—and
with a turn of the head,

"History... is a nightmare from
which I am trying to awake."
James Joyce,
Ulysses.

"History is... not a temporal
notion, it has nothing to do with
temporality, but it is the emergence
of a language of power
out of a language of cognition."
Paul de Man, "Kant and Schiller."

"Historiographical disputes will tend
to turn, not only upon the matter of
what are the facts, but also upon
that of their meaning... If we take
the dominant tropes as four:
metaphor, metonymy, synecdoche,
and irony, it is obvious that in
language itself, in its generative or
prepoetic aspect, we might possibly
have the basis for the generation of
those types of explanation that
inevitably arise in any field of study
not yet disciplinized in the sense of
being liberated from the conceptual
anarchy that seems to signal
their distinctively prescientific phases."
Hayden White,
"Interpretation in History."

"Think we must."
Virginia Woolf,

breaking away...
UP I GO!

I reach for the window's handle
and seize it.

I pull down, as hard
as I can, then I pull
with all my weight,
releasing my foothold,
hanging in mid-air.

Swinging, back and forth.

Behind me, the Genie
of Meta Forest has disappeared...

Gripping the handle
and hanging off the wall,
I start to wonder
whether trying to force
this threshold open
is a methodical error.

Does my predicament
represent a Factoidal
Counter-Archaic translation
of the Apokalyptic Paradox...
or a Techno-Hysterical variant
of the Deep Blue Trap...
a Scientological-Ontological twist

Three Guineas.

"(T)hought is... for me
a perfectly neutral name,
the blank part of the text."
Jacques Derrida, "Of Grammatology
as a Positive Science."

"What is this whiteness and silence
but the absence of pain?"
Catherine Anne Porter,
Pale Horse, Pale Rider.

"I lie to myself all the time.
But I never believe me."
S. E. Hinton,
The Outsiders.

"This is not just literary
deconstruction, but liminal
transformation. Every story that
begins with original innocence and
privileges the return to wholeness,
imagines the drama of life to be
individuation, separation, the birth
of the self, the tragedy of autonomy,
the fall into writing, alienation:
that is, war, tempered by imaginary
respite in the bosom of the other."
Donna Haraway,
The Cyborg Manifesto.

"In the guise of a post-Marxist

on the Mysterium Insolubilis
of Werther & Erhardt?

The latch starts to give.

I tug on the handle,
pulling myself up;
I can feel it loosening,
about to disengage
from its E-W axis
under the full weight
of my body.

Like the Mania described
by the Unknown Poets
of Goodyear, a strange
excitement overtakes me
at the thought of crossing over,
connecting beyond the threshold
with one or the other
Visibility Site, identifying
the Toggle Switch
in the Control Room,
communing with the Grail
of the Next Generation,
exercising Complete Control
over Central Space,
over Food for Thought...

Then—Vision of Visions!—
as if guided by the Spirit
of Racing Thoughts,
Enlightenment comes from P-C's

description of the scene of power,
we thus encounter a much older
debate: between representation
or rhetoric as tropology and
as persuasion... They are related,
but running them together, especially
in order to say that beyond both is
where oppressed subjects speak, act,
and know for themselves, leads to
an essentialist, Utopian politics..."
Gayatri Spivak,
"Can the Subaltern Speak?"

"It was long years—I should say
centuries—before the influence
of the coarser nature of men was
eliminated from the present race."
Mary E. Bradley,
Mizora: A Prophecy.

"'The Recorder of Self-inflicted
Miseries states, that after a time
a new variety of the small-pox
made its appearance,
which was called varioloid...
—Well, you live in an age so much
in advance of mine, and so many
facts and curious phenomena came
to light during the nineteenth
century, that you can tell me what
the settled opinion is now respecting
small-pox, kine-pox, and varioloid.'"
Mary Griffith,

2001 Tales of the Tribe:
I am overwhelmed
by the Mystic power
of Dick-Head, Tricky and
the Forty Masters of Wisdom
in "Story of the Skull"—
about the Game played across
the Lost Continent of Temporality,
until the Fatal Toss from
Private Benjamin to Becks.

The mounting sensation
that the handle, from which
I now hang suspended
by both hands, will shift
at any moment to N-S, and
release, brings the Game to
life, as if I were witness
to the Energy in every
throw and every catch, and
to the speed of the skull
whirling across the landscape.

I feel new Neural Circuits
awakening, I am powerful
and free, like a Master
of Wisdom myself,
certain of my path,
poised for a clearing
of the way—I hear
the Voice that cries out
with every throw,
from Master to Master,

Three Hundred Years Hence.

"...Those who lived gave way to the almost universal negativism, what the French named *l'ennui universel.* It came upon us like an insidious disease; indeed, it was a disease, with its soon-familiar symptoms of lassitude, depression, ill-defined malaise, a readiness to give way to minor infections, a perpetual disabling headache."
P. D. James,
Children of Men.

"The fourteenth card has been called The Alchemist. The theory of alchemy was that all matter could be reduced to one substance out of which, by devious processes, the base and corruptible could be distilled away, so that ultimately only the pure and incorruptible, the philosophers' gold, could be bodied forth... The Angel who performs this subtle alchemy is rightly called Temperance. To temper means 'to bring to a suitable or desirable state by blending or admixture.' We temper steel to make it strong yet resilient. Ideally, we temper justice with mercy for the same reason."
Sallie Nichols,
Jung and Tarot.

over mountains and valleys,
back and forth across
the Molecular Field...
then another Voice...
recalling how the skull
finally dropped to the ground.

And a moment arrives
when, failing to open,
the latch breaks,
the handle snaps off:
I fall and land on my back,
hitting my head.

I get up and look
at the handle:
the Metal shows patterns
of spirals and fylfots,
triskelions and arrobas;
the stone is White,
like the glass.

The signs that I should
throw the handle
and Smash the glass
are ambiguous,
because the entire room
is the handle's Context;
I know from the way
that it feels in my hand,
from its weight, its shape

"If to beauty you add temperance...
dear Charmides, blessed art thou,
in being the son of thy mother.
And here lies the point; for if,
as he declares, you have this gift
of temperance already, and are
temperate enough... I may as well
let you have the cure of the head
at once; but if you have not yet
acquired this quality, I must
use the charm before I give you
the medicine. Please, herefore,
to inform me whether you admit
the truth of what Critias has been
saying—have you or have you not
this quality of temperance?"
Plato,
Charmides.

"Plato, they tell us, found a system
in the sand / around a wall, though
every constituent / occasion recalled
an absent measure, constraint
he could not abide or recall,
the self-restraint / and melodic
conversions he refused to hear."
Jay Wright, "Speak of the property
of matter, the bright hand."

"Looking for words to say /
Searching but not finding /
Understanding anywhere /

and size, its markings.

If I take the Broken Circle
of Qa for reference,
then the glass stands
for Incompleteness
to begin with, and
breaking it proves
my undoing; by contrast,
transgressing the threshold
recalls Tantra's
"Sex-in-the-Breeze,"
according to *ROTA-TARO-*
ORAT-TORA-ARTO, Vol. X:
the BLOOD on the BUSH,
"...trembling in the Night Wind."

I face the glass, tossing
the handle in my fingers,
up and down, for Momentum.

We're lost in this masquerade."
Leon Russell, "This Masquerade."

"In great awe I understood that
I was near the ultimate mysteries
from which there is no return."
P. D. Ouspensky,
The Symbolism of the Tarot.

"...And at the thought that
it was perhaps this, a circle and
a centre not its centre in search
of a centre and its circle
respectively, in boundless space,
in endless time, then Watt's
eyes filled with tears
that he could not stem, and
they flowed down his fluted
cheeks unchecked, in a steady
flow, refreshing him greatly."
Samuel Beckett,
Watt.

The realization sets in
that my opponent is
on the offensive, and
has changed his name from
"Bird-Dog" to "BioRom"
—after the Guardian Angel
of Stress Traps.

His Payback is greater
than I imagined,

"We may now contemplate
the shadow of a Doric pillar."
H. D.
Majic Ring.

"Art is magic delivered
from the lie of being truth."
Theodor W. Adorno,
Minima Moralia.

and represents
a twofold threat: a Trump
with *The Universe // reversed,*
that puts the Signifying
Chain of Face Values
at risk, and a Trick
with *The Fool // reversed,*
that seals off *The Fool*'s
alternative to the Abyss.

I can beat the trap and
play it against him, or
I can wait, and let him
be Sovereign for now.

Either way, my path
will lead back to you.

Your lover,

A.

"When the visions became more
frequent, one of those who had
helped me before... began to say
that clearly I was being deceived
by the devil. He ordered me...
to snap my fingers at it, in the firm
conviction that this was the devil's
work. Then it would not come again
...The duty of snapping my fingers
when I had this vision of the Lord
deeply distressed me. For when I saw
Him before me, I would willingly have
been hacked to death rather than
believe that this was of the devil."
Teresa of Avila,
The Life of Saint Teresa of Avila
by Herself.

The Devil

Lover,

"Behold the Earth, how there
thy bounties flow / Looke on
the Sea extended hugely wide: /
What watry troops swymme, creepe,
and crawle, and goe, / Of greate,
and small, on that, this, ev'ry side! /
There the saile-winged shipps on
waves doe glide : Sea-monsters there,
their plaies and pastymes show."
Psalms 104, tr. Mary Sidney.

"My ship's aglow with a million
pearls / And rubies fill each bin, /
The sun sits high / in a sapphire
sky / when my ship comes in."
Ira Gershwin and Kurt Weill,
"My Ship."

"They come in the ships
on the ocean. / For gifts
they bring wrist-chains of gold, /
And purple coats and silver jars, /
And carved toys incredibly strange, /
And things made of ivory."
Sappho (tr. G. Davenport).

Q'bal says we are 2000 cubits
above the sea... on the sea...
in a particle \ wave of the sea.

Captain Anna-O, citing
the New Aryan Protocols, has
banned any further discussion of
the "Big Fart" and the Aura
of Shit still with us,
given our precarious situation
on the crest of this Wave.

And yet, the Aroma may be
working to homëopathic
effect in maintaining
the vessel's Equilibrium,
a Jed'ah blessing in disguise
to help balance our minds.

The ship's state of Equipoise
is being sustained by both
a complex distribution of
the crew's weight throughout
the vessel and by a collective
Mental effort from the whole crew

"Dreams are toys."
William Shakespeare,
The Winter's Tale.

"In the Pacific Ocean between California and Hawaii... fragments of debris are floating—at least 87,000 tons' worth... In recent years this notorious mess has become known as the Great Pacific Garbage Patch... The journal *Scientific Reports* quantified the full extent of the so-called garbage patch: it is four to 16 times bigger than previously thought, occupying an area roughly four times the size of California... and they say it is growing 'exponentially.'"
"87,000 Tons of Plastic
And Counting in Pacific,"
The New York Times (18 Mar. 2018).

"'Then there are worlds hotter than yours?'/ 'Most of them are warmer. Some are hot; Gde, for instance. It's mostly sand and rock desert. It was warm to start with, and an exploitive civilization wrecked its natural balances fifty or sixty thousand years ago, burned up the forests for kindling, as it were. There are still people there,

to maintain a deconstructive,
meta-schizoid stance toward
the abysmal possibility of
finally dropping into the water
way below.

The Theoretical Assumption
is that sooner or later
the Great Wave will gradually
sink back into the ocean
and that the vessel, following
a Dialectical Process, will be
lowered to the surface
just as it was first raised
on the Wave's crest
to its present height.

On that assumption,
we have tentatively resumed
charting new constellations,
picking up where we left off,
when the surging waters
first started to tremble and
our star-gazing Symposium
was cut short; although, in truth,
the situation is getting tougher,
given the crew's peculiar
stationing throughout the ship
and the technical problems
jamming communications,
plus the attention deficit and
the failure to multi-task incurred
by the schizoid Mental stance

but it resembles—if I understand
the Text—the Yomesh idea
of where thieves go after death.'"
Ursula Le Guin,
The Left Hand of Darkness.

"Oh, the time will come up /
When the winds will stop / And
the breeze will cease to be breathin' /
Like the stillness in the wind /
Before the hurricane begins /
The hour that the ship comes in."
Bob Dylan,
"The Ship Comes In."

"To learn which questions are
unanswerable, and not to answer
them: this skill is most needful
in times of stress and darkness."
U. Le Guin,
The Left Hand of Darkness.

"Why is disorder increasing in
the same direction of time as that
in which the universe is expanding?"
Stephen Hawking,
A Brief History of Time.

"'Why, what, which, thunder,
damnation????'"
Ezra Pound,
Cantos, IX.

imposed on us from the Tipping
Point on this humongous Wave.

The paradox is that for all
the self-pity and fear
that we try to resist,
we have never been as close
to the Heavens as we are
now—rapt witnesses
before the Black depths
of a starlit sky, illuminated
as if by the infinitesimal
reflections of the Silver
expanse beneath us, pierced
by the random music
of shooting stars.

The star-gazing Symposium
was organized in the hope that
mapping the new constellations
of an alien sky would reveal
the hidden meaning of
a predicament that found us
stuck on the shoals, battered
by different waves on all sides.

The Symposium's participants—
Able-bodied Sailors Bismark,
Kongō and Cowabunga,
Vico of Communications,
Sinbad the Steward, and

"Lies have always been regarded
as necessary and justifiable tools
not only of the politician's or
the demagogue's but also of
the statesman's trade. Why is this so?
And what does it mean for the nature
and dignity of the political realm,
on the one side, and for the nature
and dignity of truth and truthfulness,
on the other? Is it the essence of truth
to be impotent and of the essence
of power to be deceitful?"
Hannah Arendt,
Between Past and Future.

"Is not Possession
the whole of the Law?"
Herman Melville,
Moby Dick.

"Was I about to retrieve a reality
which would not have existed
if I had not rashly perceived it,
thus giving it life?"
Clarice Lispector,
"A Mischievous Little Girl."

"Who? Who? Who?"
Amiri Baraka,
"Somebody Blew Up America."

"I write, write, write
as the Wandering Jew

myself—were assembled
by the Observation Deck's
Seven Columns of Guadalajara
waiting for Venus to arrive
with Commander Exprès.

The Commander had been
seized by an intense Cough,
as he was passing between
the 7-function force-
feedback manipulator
and the oil lamp
under the ethernet;
after Venus read the spit on
the glass as a bad sign
for charting the stars, he and
Exprès made their way
to the Observation Deck's
seventh Pillar of Wisdom.

Just as they arrived,
Commander Exprès
Coughed Up again and Venus
read the spit, as follows:
"Captain Knòcknòck says:
the Jungle Cries of
the Virtual Deep
are a powerful illusion
that will not go away."

As if in response, Kongō,
who had been designated
by Captain Anna-O to lead

walks, walks, walks."
Madame Blavatsky, quoted
in W. B. Yeats, *Four Years.*

"Jarret's supporters are more than
a little seduced by Jarret's talk
of making America great again."
Octavia Butler,
The Parable of the Talents.

"There is nothing so hateful
to God as the game of trumps...
For trumps are said, so it is
believed, to have been given
their names by the Devil,
their inventor... Not only are God,
the angels, the planets and
the cardinal virtues represented
and named, but also the world's
luminaries, I mean the Pope and
the Emperor, are forced, a thing
which is degrading and ridiculous
to Christians, to enter the game.
For there are 21 trumps which are
the 21 steps of a ladder which takes
a man to the depths of Hell."
"Steele manuscript" (c. 1500),
in Cynthia Giles, *The Tarot*.

"There below the horizon! I thought
there too you will one day wander."
Friedrich Hölderlin,
Hyperion.

the Symposium, opened
the discussion by quoting
from Tiki the Poematician's
Book O' Verse: "Save / your ch'i
and / own your duende."

At which point, as I turned
to ask Cowabunga if Kongō's
quotation from Tiki was
correct—because it gave me
the sudden idea to suggest
a new constellation named
"The Leper With Gun
Stripped Bare"
—I fell into dreamtime.

So, I was not consciously
present during the earlier
part of the Symposium...

(I dreamt of a Virgin
at the dark center of
the Tower of Five Elements,
holding Fire in his hand;
next to him was the Divider
King, who said he was
"divided within himself" and
able to discover in himself
"the means to separate
everything from what must
be separated"; then he took

"The surface biosphere has never
been separate from the cthulhoid
architecture of the nether."
Reza Negarestani,
Cyclonopedia.

"The problem is to direct
all those movements beyond
the great abyss. / Naturally, I have
a spyglass, an extension ladder
(of steel, recently received),
a stool, made of wood and
covered with patina from having
served too often, measurement
sheets, and then—I forgot,
I always forget—the megaphone."
Pierrette Fleutiaux *(RIP),*
"The Story of the Spyglass
and the Abyss."

"Card of Magnetism, Energy,
and Sex. The Devil also represents
the loss of personal freedom
through addictions of any kind. /
It scared me working on this card.
I had visions of hundreds of devils
swarming around the Sphinx
afraid they might attack me."
Niki de Saint Phalle,
The Tarot Garden.

"A world wholly alive

Flames from the Fire
and spread them around,
until the tower collapsed.

I heard a Voice cry out:
"How long will this revolting
Transmutation, that can
no longer be Revolution, go on?
*The reclassifying of all values
will be fundamental."*

What did this mean?

It means that playing with
Fire is a *Majic action*,
and that everything that
will not be set on Fire
by *all of us,* and that
will not make *all of us*
Desperate and Alone,
nature will burn up.

It means the forces
of the Universe
have gone into action.)

It was only later on,
before the mountain of water
started rising, that the part of
the Symposium I had missed
was reported to me by Venus

has a Hellish power."
C. Lispector,
The Passion According to G. H.

"...the devil hath power /
T'assume a pleasing shape."
W. Shakespeare,
Hamlet.

"The figure is conceived in
the typical heraldic fashion
of the Mistress of Wild Things;
she is in fact the ugly bogey-,
Erinys-side of the Great Mother;
she is a potent goddess,
not as in later days a monster
to be slain by heroes.
The highest divinities of
the religion of fear and riddance
became the harmful bogeys
of the cult of 'service.'
The Olympians in their turn
became Christian devils."
Jane Harrison,
Prolegomena to the Study
of Greek Religion.

"How are we fall'n,
fall'n by mistaken rules?"
Anne Finch, Countess of Winchilsea,
"The Introduction."

"I have fallen very far."

with added commentary by
Sinbad, who described the ouzo
as "bitter and coarse, without
depth or complexity... *dirty*."

They explained that in trying
to figure out what happened
Intelligence, reduced to
Venus and Tarzan after
Maria's "Dance of Death,"
theorized that things took a turn
for the worse with the discovery
that the Cloud of the Blue-
Red haze—which had hovered in
the Heavens since our adventure
with the Sea-Jelly Mutations and
the Simulacrum of the Faucet—
was not stationary, but
moved across the sky...
which forced a remapping of
new constellations just mapped.

Until this discovery,
from what I understood,
the star-gazing Symposium
was going along as planned.

The first constellation
to be named was
"Mor-o-Log-on"—which
emerged from the gap in
the Heavens bounded by
five stars identified as

Sylvia Plath,
"The Moon and the Yew Tree."

"O all the devils!"
W. Shakespeare,
Cymbeline.

"i the only lucifer / light-bringer /
created out of fire / illuminate
i could / and so / illuminate i did"
Lucille Clifton,
"lucifer speaks in his own voice."

"How curious and interesting
is the parallel—as far as poverty
of biographical details is concerned
—between Satan and Shakespeare...
They are the best-known unknown
persons that have ever drawn breath
upon the planet."
Mark Twain,
"Is Shakespeare Dead?"

"I no longer believe that William
Shakespeare the actor from Stratford
was the author of the works which
have so long been attributed to him."
Sigmund Freud,
"An Autobiographical Study."

"—You are a delusion...
Do you believe your own theory? /
—No, said Stephen promptly...

Siri, Y'enemy, Hoochie,
Sade and *Televi*.

The naming of the first
constellation in our post-
War environment was
initiated by substitute Engineers
Bismark—next to the Mercury
Pillar—who looked for
"the oldest part of the sky";
and by Vico—beside
the Venus Pillar—who searched
the Upper Heavens first.

Through a Dialogical
exchange of Ideas, based
on the Apokalyptic Method
of Sauron and Mull'œ in
Ma'am of the Flaming Crux,
Vico and Bismark,
working counter-clockwise,
assigned names to the five
brightest stars, before finally
identifying the circumscribed
area of darkness
as the new constellation.

But while the conversation
on star mapping continued,
the Cloud of the Blue-
Red haze suddenly started
moving across the sky;
then it zigzagged its way,

I believe, O Lord,
help my unbelief. That is,
help me to believe or
help me to unbelieve?
Who helps to believe? *Egomen.*
Who to unbelieve? Other chap."
James Joyce,
Ulysses.

"Be silent, then,
for danger is in words!"
Christopher Marlowe,
Doctor Faustus.

"Come, words, away from mouths, /
Away from tongues in mouths /
And reckless hearts in tongues /
And mouths in cautious heads— /
Come, words, away to where /
The meaning is not thickened /
With the voice's fretting substance"
Laura Riding,
"Come, Words, Away."

"A writer is not just a poet."
Marcel Proust,
Against Sainte-Beuve.

"When (said Panurge) you poke
your nose up my arse, don't forget
to take off your spectacles."
François Rabelais,
The Third Book of Pantagruel.

in fits and starts,
to a position just inside
the upper border of
the newly named constellation.

The effect was twofold.

In one part of the sky,
the space left vacated by
the Cloud revealed a larger
Interstellar Opening,
that Sinbad, stationed
by the Third Pillar—the Pillar
of the Soul Incarnate—was first
to notice; but, as Sinbad pursued
his observation, he was overtaken
by the hiccups; so Kongō,
by the Pillar of Mars, intervened.

Kongō's Ontological-Rhetorical
engagement with Mind \ Body
pre-supposed Love Everywhere
and proposed "The (W)hole"
as an appropriate name for
the newfound constellation-to-be.

At the same time, however,
as observed by Sinbad—who had
recovered from the hiccups,
and who believed in the Schizoid
Spirit of the Ancestors—when
the Cloud of the Blue-Red
haze moved across the sky

“O Pan! Io Pan! / Io Pan!
Io Pan Pan! / Pan Pan! Pan, /
I am a man: / Do as thou wilt,
as a great god can, /
O Pan! Io Pan! / Io Pan!
Io Pan Pan! I am awake /
In the grip of the snake. /
The eagle slashes with beak
and claw; / The gods withdraw: /
The great beasts come. Io Pan!
I am borne / To death on the horn /
Of the Unicorn. / I am Pan!
Io Pan! Io Pan Pan! Pan!”
Aleister Crowley, “Hymn to Pan.”

“Sweet, sweet, sweet, O Pan! /
Piercing sweet by the river! /
Blinding sweet, O great god Pan! /
The sun on the hill forgot to die, /
And the lilies revived, and
the dragon-fly / came back
to dream on the river.”
Elizabeth Barrett Browning,
“A Musical Instrument.”

“Suddenly from the island of Paxi
was heard the voice of someone
loudly calling Thamus, so that
all were amazed. Thamus was
an Egyptian pilot, not known
by name even to many on board.
Twice he was called and made

to the edge of the constellation
first identified by Bismark and
Vico, it created the Schizoid
Effect of revealing two new
rhizomatic figures that superseded
the original constellation;
Sinbad also suggested calling
one of the figures—
the one on the right—
“The Biomagnetic Processor,”
because it seemed to have drawn
the Cloud toward itself, like
the X-Machine in Reanimator’s
The Unconscious You.

Then, Cowabunga, seated
by the Jupiter Pillar, weighed in.

He had no philosophy, beyond
a simple faith in the beauty
of justice, moderation, courage
and wisdom, and was excited
at the prospect of naming
the new constellation on the left
“The Fylfot Propeller,”
to represent ourselves, i.e.
our ship, in the present moment.

All insights were welcomed,
but the discussion was
suddenly interrupted, when
the Cloud of the Blue-Red
haze started moving again

no reply, but the third time
he answered; and the caller, raising
his voice, said, 'When you come
opposite to Palodes, announce
that Great Pan is dead...' So, when
he came opposite Palodes... [Thamus]
said the words as he heard them.
'Great Pan is dead.' Even before
he was finished there was a cry
of lamentation, not of one person,
but of many, mingled with
exclamations of amazement."
Plutarch,
"On Why Oracles Came to Fail."

"Nine in the fifth place means: /
Flying dragon in the heavens. /
It furthers one to see the great man."
I Ching.

"I'm Nobody! Who are you?
Are you – Nobody – too?"
Emily Dickinson (260).

"Stop joking, Apollodorus... Just
tell me where the party took place."
Plato,
The Symposium.

"Wisdom hath builded her house,
she hath hewn out her seven pillars."
Proverbs 9:1.

in a stop-and-go zigzag
path across the Heavens,
back to a position not far
from where it had first
been seen to take off.

This is when I awakened
from my dream, beside
the Pillar of Intelligible Worlds
and Simple Elements.

Remembering my dream,
and confronted with what
Venus and Sinbad had
led me to believe was
the "problematization" of *four*
prospective constellations—
"Mor-o-Log-on," "The (W)hole,"
"The Biomagnetic Processor,"
"The Fylfot Propeller"—
by the back-and-forth of
the *Blind Spot* represented by
the Cloud of the Blue-Red
haze, I found myself on either
side of a reality both *visible*
and *invisible*—at once
a *Fool* before the World
and a *Seeress* before
the Scales of an Infernal
Justice that would *give*
to Physical Forms and *take*

"It was time to get a fix
on the universe."
Douglas Woolf, "Had."

"How will you / measure /
will you / measure / the dark?"
Diane di Prima,
Loba, "The Stars Shine For Us."

"The next time you stand on a beach
at night, watching the moon's bright
path across the water, and conscious
of the moon-drawn tides, remember
that the moon itself may have been
born of a great tidal wave of earthly
substance, torn off into space..."
Rachel Carson,
The Sea Around Us.

"The heavens are spherical and
move as a sphere. The earth itself
also is sensibly spherical in shape,
taken as a whole. In terms of position,
it is situated in the middle of all
the heavens, near the center. In terms
of size and distance, it has the ratio
of a point to the sphere of the fixed
stars. And the earth itself does not
move at all. We will briefly give
an account of each of these things
by way of reminder."
Claudius Ptolemy,
The Almagest.

from Moral Ideals—a reality
in which was constructed
the Abstrakt Woman whose
knowledge of Knowledge
I cancelled, to persuade
the Symposium's various
participants that the Abstrakt
sites of both the Cloud's
starting and *current* locations
might function as "Black Holes"
in a *First Constellation*.

No sooner had I spoken
than Commander Exprès—
stationed by the Seventh Pillar,
or Pillar of Saturn—exploded
into his Chronic Cough,
and projected his spit on
the Glass Ingots in the Cauldron,
for Venus to read.

Speaking for Exprès, as if
in response to my suggestion,
Venus said that the "screaming
Unicorn" he discerned in the spit
was being advanced by Exprès as
the image for a new constellation.

I responded by offering
Satoris as a name for
the twin "Black Holes" at
the tip of the Unicorn's Horn,
thereby identifying a giant

"'—Come, Mephistopheles, let us dispute again / And argue of divine astrology. / Tell me, are there many heavens above the moon?...
—As are the elements, such are the spheres / Mutually folded in each other's orb; / And jointly move upon one axletree / Whose terminine is termed the world's wide pole; / Nor are the names of Saturn, Mars, or Jupiter / Feigned, but are erring stars... All jointly move from east to west in twenty-four hours upon the poles of the world, but differ in their motion upon the poles of the zodiac.'"
C. Marlowe,
Doctor Faustus.

"Five other objects of a different kind / Swerve through the Zodiac. You cannot find / Their courses relative to some fixed star / Because they wander, weave, and veer too far / In their broad cycles through the skies. The time / When they will line up and renew the prime / Of Magnus Annus is far off. I cower / Before erratic motion—give me power / To speak of fixed signs and consistent things."
Aratus,

figure that would override all the previous ones.

After further star gazing, the Symposium's participants agreed with my suggestion and "The Screaming Unicorn," whose Double-helixed Horn pointed to an Abstrakt pair of "Black Holes" named *Satoris,* became our First Constellation.

But as we prepared to toast the achievement, the ship began to shake, and the ouzo spilled from our rhytons.

While the vibrations got worse and the mounting Wave lifted the ship on its crest, a Robocall to secure our positions went out from the Hidden Chamber, prompting all of us at the Symposium to stand up and hug the Observation Deck's Pillars of Wisdom.

Our ship kept rising on top of a tremendous body of water, faster than we had

Phaenomena, "The Planets."

"Ortega y Gasset puts it that
the man of antiquity, before
he did anything, took a step
like the bullfighter who leaps back
in order to deliver the mortal thrust."
Charles Olson,
Call Me Ishmael.

"The novel fact may throw back,
inhibit, and delay. But the advance,
when it does arrive will be richer
in content, more fully conditioned,
and more stable."
Alfred North Whitehead,
Process and Reality.

"Nothing, whether deed, word,
thought, or text, ever happens
in relation, positive or negative,
to anything that precedes, follows
or exists elsewhere, but only
as a random event whose power,
like the power of death, is due to
the randomness of its occurrence."
Paul de Man,
"Shelley Disfigured."

"Who then was the next to die?"
Apollonius of Rhodes,
The Voyage of Argo (Book Two).

ever traveled before.

The Silver sea was already
far beneath us, when the Wave
began to decelerate...
and Bismark noticed that
the Cloud of the Blue-Red
haze was moving across
the Heavens again; as the ship's
ascent slowed down, the Cloud
seemed to pick up speed
along its jagged course.

Anticipating our Fate,
Bismark exclaimed:
"Just my luck!"
and moments later,
before any of us knew
what was happening,
the Blue-Red Cloud had
closed in on the ship,
which sat motionless
at the peak of the Wave.

We became enfolded
in the discontinuous field
of a quantum flux where
matter and Energy, thought
and object, Supernatural and
Sub-natural functioned as
both the Kenosis of Blue,
observable as the Silver
elixir in things,

"The world's whole course
in one brief look / —Are reasons
why to buy this book."
Sebastian Brant,
The Ship of Fools.

"And if you join today, we'll send
the following books absolutely free:
*Poems for the Insane, A Treasury
of Poorly Understood Ideas,
Apartment Hunting for Devil
Worshippers, A Complete List of All
the Things that Are Still Pending..."*
George Carlin,
"Join The Book Club."

"Thee onnlly wway ttoo ccope
withh ssometthingg ddeadly
sseriouss iss ttoo ttry ttoo
trreatt itt a llittlle lligghtly."
Madeleine L'Engle,
A Wrinkle in Time.

"no minutia no problems."
Samuel Beckett,
How It Is.

"And the Lord came down to
see the city and the tower,
that the human creatures had built,
and the Lord said: 'As one people
with one language for all, if this
is what they have begun to do,

beyond the Nigredo
and Albedo of ideas,
and the Pathesis of Red,
observable as Iridescence
and Philosophical Stone
in Rubedo's "End of Time."

But Bismark failed
to adjust: rushing from
the Observation Deck,
she took off on her run.

She followed the passageway
to the nave, past
the apse and the shaft
toward the stern.

Standing with her arms
outstretched, she leaped
off the edge, yelling:
"Less is more!"

Venus made the comment
that he was reminded by
the projections of Bismark's
arms and legs—both before
and during her fall—
of the star-like human figure
in Leo's *Vitruvian Being.*

Then she vanished in the haze.

now nothing they scheme to do
will elude them! Come let us go
down and confound their language
so that they may not understand
one another's speech!' And
the Lord scattered them from
there over the face of all the earth,
and they left off building the city."
Genesis 11: 8, in R. Crumb,
The Book of Genesis Illustrated.

"A scholar… maintained that
the Great Wall would provide for
the first time in the history of mankind
a secure foundation for the Tower
of Babel. First the wall, therefore,
and then the tower… I admit that
even today I cannot quite make out
how he conceived this tower. How
could the wall, which did not form
even a circle, but only a sort of
quarter- or half-circle, provide
the foundation for a tower?
That could obviously only be meant
in a spiritual sense. But in that case
why build the actual wall…?"
Franz Kafka,
"The Great Wall of China."

"And place was where the Presence
was / Circumference between."
Emily Dickinson (1099).

At the moment Bismark
jumped to her Death from
the stern, the general economy
of the ship displayed an even
distribution of the crew's
weight throughout the length,
breadth and depth of the hull—
given Captain Anna-O's
aplomb and savoir faire
handling the Rainbow gravity
between "Yin Relativity
and the Quantum of Yang,"
as formulated by Hazar in
The Always Possible and
Good-Enough-for-Jazz.

Nonetheless, Bismark's leap
was apparently all it took
to tip the ship's delicate
balance on the crest of
the Wave toward the bow.

Stationed in the lookout
atop the mainmast, Mach
exclaimed with a Tragic
Laugh over speakerphone—
which Captain Anna-O
had ordered turned on
across the ship, before turning off
the propeller—that *Ko-Itame*,
the Spirit of the Keel, was
"experiencing a Mood Swing,"

"Can you tell the down from the up?"
E. Pound,
Cantos, XXVII.

"Look up at the Heavens and count the stars, if you can count them... So shall be your seed."
Genesis 15: 5, in R. Crumb,
The Book of Genesis Illustrated.

"In order to reach a good understanding of things below it is thus necessary to rise toward the heights, and, looking down from above, to gain an overview...Thus, Maximus of Tyre invokes a passage in Homer where Ulysses is led to observe a people's customs from a high place. Aristotle in this sense wrote that if we found ourselves above the heavens we could know for ourselves the causes of the eclipses of the Sun and of the Moon... And Cicero, in the dream of Scipio the Younger relates that the latter's grandfather showed him terrestrial things from up in the sky."
Giulo Camillo,
The Theater of Memory.

"Sure of having traveled far, one finds that one is looking down on oneself from above."

and recited Shams's Lament from *The Book of the Seven Beatings,* while one-eyed Chauvée of Communications, stationed by the electrical stripping between the upper Cryptonite rods and the Voided oar, initiated the effort to redress the ship's Equilibrium by quickly moving aft, along the poop deck... together with ben-Cnopee the Lensman, who shifted position from the plug-ins of the Kalashnikov console to the standard stoppage network of the Mammon panel; Sokrates the Helmsman, who moved from the drainage slopes of the Skull Gallery to the emancipated Metal vents of the gas cylinder; and Cîpher the Signalman, who shifted from the Monotonous flywheels to the input-outlet of the #1 lithium mold.

Concurrently, as the ship showed signs of swaying back to its Tipping Point, the imprint of the Yonaguni shoreline—projected along the decks by the wind-swept falling water from the Miraculous Faucet—gave the aft movements to

Michel Foucault,
The Use of Pleasure, "Introduction."

"Many times I've gone past /
the fifth floor, / cranking upward,
but only once / have I gone
all the way up /...Floor six thousand: /
the stars, / skeletons on fire, /
their arms singing. / And a key, /
a very large key, / that opens
something – / some useful door – /
somewhere – / up there."
Anne Sexton,
"Riding the Elevator Into the Sky."

"Night comes, an angel stands /
Measuring out the time of stars, /
Still are the winds, and still
the hours. / ...It would be
peace to lie / Still in the still hours
at the angel's feet, / Upon a star
hung in a starry sky, / But hearts
another measure beat."
Kathleen Raine, "Nocturne."

"...and the expensive delicate ship
that must have seen /
Something amazing, a boy falling
out of the sky, / Had somewhere
to get to and sailed calmly on."
W. H. Auden. "Musée des Beaux Arts."

"From a systems theory perspective,
redistribute weight on the ship
an Aura of Story, for
the Symposium's participants
in particular and
for Vico most of all.

Stepping aft on the Observation
Deck from the Venus pillar to
the Mercury pillar, which stood
abandoned following Bismark's
Death, Vico exclaimed: "I am
transported like Badr of Homes
from the Big Wheel of Cope
to the Tower of Pay
in the tale told by Goodchilde
the Studious in days of yore!"

Sinbad, an adept of Deadpan,
while retreating to take Vico's
place by the pillar of Venus,
replied: "You and I are like
Koffi and Blondi at Lover's Leap
in 'The Story of the Mystery
Writer's Dilemma' by Aï
the Empath"; to which Vico,
increasingly tense and nervous,
responded with the insight that,
by falling back, Kongō, beside
the pillar of Mars, would be
to them as LaLanne was
to Masrûr the Lame
and Schrödinger of Saïs
in "The Demon of Analogy's

periods of turbulence such as we have experienced in recent decades can lead to a range of possible outcomes. They may resolve into a new and stable equilibrium that can be expected to have a long life. They may lead to oscillating equilibria, a condition in which the social system snaps back and forth between two extremes. Or what appears to be an end to turbulence may be only another period of experimentation in an adaptational process that is still under way."
Sandra Braman,
Change of State.

"Ramona liked people who got excited."
Beverly Clearly,
Ramona the Brave.

"Let us plunge in the flood of time and chance, / Into the tide of circumstance! Let grief and gratification, / Success and frustration / Spell one another as they can, / Restless doing is the only way for man."
J. W. Goethe,
Faust, Part I.

"the Abyss / blanched / spread /

Travel Adventures with Puf the Cursed Poet."

So, when Kongō did in effect move aft toward the pillar of the Soul Incarnate, Vico said that by taking Sinbad's place Kongō was being released from the pillar of Mars just as Timaeus was released from Scipio's Prison-House of Allegory by telling the story of Zozimos's escape from the Cubicle of Abraxas in "The Fairy Tales of Mount Nazaré" by Grandmaster H'llaj.

Vico added that by leaving the pillar of Jupiter for the pillar of Mars, Cowabunga would be doing for the entire crew what Cadmus did for Montignac in the story about the Moon that Mardrus told to Layli, after Abelard told it to her in "The Love Stories and Wisdom Tales of Sina Weibo."

And to the extent that the maneuvers on the Observation Deck —as Cowabunga moved aft— were restoring the ship

furious / beneath an incline /
desperately plane / on a wing /
its own / fallen / / back in advance
from being unable to dress its flight"
Stéphane Mallarmé,
"A Throw of the Dice
Will Never Abolish Chance."

"The same road goes
both up and down."
Herakeitos (tr. G. Davenport).

"What has risen may sink,
and what has sunk may rise."
H. P. Lovecraft,
"The Call of Cthulhu."

"The psyche rises as a mist
from things that are wet."
Herakleitos.

"I am convinced that from the heads
of all ponderous profound beings,
such as Plato, Pyrrho, the Devil,
Jupiter, Dante... there always goes up
a certain semi-visible steam, while
in the act of thinking deep thoughts."
H. Melville,
Moby Dick.

"Ahab, too, is a poet of eloquence.
He says, 'The path to my fixed
purpose is laid with iron rails

to its Tipping Point,
Vico was essentially correct.

Balance was achieved
after Commander Exprès
Coughed Up again and Venus,
reading the projected spit
on the glass as a sign
that the two of them
should go below deck,
clapped his hands and opened
the door to the stairway
under the poop deck, down which
they went, to station themselves
in the Commander's cabin.

Meanwhile, I stayed where I was,
by the Pillar of Intelligible
Worlds and Simple Elements.

As soon as the ship was
level again on the crest of
the Wave, we faced a situation
where the Climate, inside
the Cloud of Blue-Red haze
that engulfed us, began to change.

The haze produced a sensation
of heat, that grew more intense
and caused our joints to ache,
our limbs to tingle and

whereon my soul is grooved
to run.' Or these lines,
'All visible objects are but
pasteboard masks.' Quotable
poetic phrases that can't be beat."
Bob Dylan,
Nobel Prize acceptance speech.

"Been to hell in a boat yet?"
Ezra Pound,
Cantos, XXXIX.

"The stars go waltzing out in blue
and red, / And arbitrary blackness
gallops in: I shut my eyes and
all the world drops dead."
Sylvia Plath, "Mad Girl's Love Song."

"The bonds of heaven are
slipp'd, dissolv'd and loos'd."
W. Shakespeare,
Troilus & Cressida.

"The black sky was underpinned
with long silver streaks that looked
like scaffolding and depth on depth
behind it were thousands of stars
that all seemed to be moving very
slowly as if they were about some
vast construction work that involved
the whole order of the universe and
would take all time to complete.
No one was paying any attention

our backs to bend,
while a film of foaming
water kept spreading over
all parts of the vessel.

Wind stirred the atmosphere
from every direction, causing
the haze to swirl around us.

As the Warming intensified
and sea foam coated the ship,
we were overwhelmed by
scratching in the throat and
unrelenting fits of coughing;
nostrils suddenly blocked;
failing vision; headaches;
confused thinking.

Despite the onset of Madness,
Vico alone seemed to understand
what was going on.

Between a) the "Deep Learning"
from the vessel's upward
trajectory along the "fluid tunnel"
and "mathematical river" in
the rise of the Great Wave,
b) the critical flow speed of
the vessel's slide into and
out of Disequilibrium,
and c) the "singularity of
the bubbling phaenomenon"
in a situation of reestablished

to the sky."
Flannery O'Connor,
Wise Blood.

"Some people don't understand.
Help them, God."
Jimi Hendrix, "Nine to the Universe."

"A man is a god in ruins."
Ralph Waldo Emerson,
Nature.

"There are three truths... Your truth...
My truth... And the truth."
Peter Brook and
Marie-Hélène Estienne,
Why?

"When God says "I Am Lived,"
we'll have forgotten
what all the parting was about."
Jack Kerouac,
Satori in Paris.

"It is first necessary to condense
the thesis of Vico, the scientific
historian. In the beginning was
the thunder: the thunder set free
Religion, in its most objective and
unphilosophical form—idolatrous
animism: Religion produced
Society, and the first social men
were the cave-dwellers. Taking

Equilibrium, Vico saw
our present course as
the sign of an ineluctable
return to "a shielded
emptiness ending in union
with the nearly infinite—"

While continuing to
theorize, however, Vico
unexpectedly stopped
in mid-sentence, and
fell into Deep Thought.

Soon the Steam started rising
from the crown of Vico's head;
and gradually the realization set in
that the surrounding haze was
beginning to recede, and change
Color... until the moment at last
when we found ourselves on
a foam-free vessel completely
enclosed inside a Green bubble
at the top of the Wave.

Then Vico succumbed
to Sleep, and keeled over.

Whether it was the Steam
escaping from Vico's head, or
Death's release of Vico's Spirit,
or mere chance that instigated

refuge from a passionate Nature:
this primitive family life receives
its first impulse towards development
from the arrival of terrified vagabonds:
admitted, they are the first slaves:
growing stronger, they exact agrarian
concessions, and a despotism has
evolved into a primitive feudalism:
the cave becomes a city, and
the feudal system a democracy:
then an anarchy; this is corrected
by a return to monarchy; the last
stage is a tendency toward inter-
destruction: the nations are dispersed
and the Phoenix of Society
arises out of their ashes."
Samuel Beckett,
"Dante ... Bruno .. Vico . Joyce."

"*Pataphysics is the science*
of imaginary solutions."
Alfred Jarry,
The Exploits and Opinions of
Doctor Faustroll, Pataphysician.

"The angel Raphael
represents the Central Column
Energy of Balance
and illuminates the color Green."
Zohar, "Vayera" (ed. M. Berg).

"Within the skull the skill / within
the winter dream the whirligig /

the change, the ship now began
to tip in the opposite direction...
toward the stern.

The imbalance inside
the bubble was aggravated
by the manic Energy
that immediately ensued above
and below the forward decks.

The challenge was to restore
the ship's Equilibrium,
while tossing Vico's body
overboard ASAP—
to avoid the creation of
a Metaphysical Shithole
caused by the presence
of a skeleton on board
after the dissemination
of Vico's flesh.

Anna-O ordered Sony, Scard'nelli,
Thebes and Rosetta to throw
Vico's corpse over the side;
but, taking her cue from Thebes
the Weatherwoman, successor
to Occam, who frantically
recalled the "mini-migrations"
across the polluted decks of
the ROJAVA before the doomed
ship capsized in the Black Sea
of Change, the Captain—over
the sudden cascading Sound

within within / all & everything : /
'Ing' supreme rune and secret song
of 'Ong.' / Forget all derivations, /
they dance in happiness, / the early
ones down there, / and this isn't
myth of origin / or oozing essence
of origin. / ... Origin is beautiful as
black / and centers whirl around us
as we round them in."
Gerrit Lansing *(RIP)*, "In Erasmus
Darwin's Generous Light."

"The north-south axis is highlighted. The bird's eye and the staff are at 0°/ north, establishing a basic point of reference... If one traces a straight line over the 'spears,' one notices that the two solstitial axes are present: the big 'spear' that wounds the bison is directed along the axis of the rising sun of summer (56°), setting sun of winter (236°). The small 'spear' is directed from the rising sun of winter (124°) to the setting sun of summer (304°)... One finds, gathered and carefully preserved by the Paleolithics ...all the coordinates of the solar stations that fulfill the conditions indicated by Vitruvius two thousand years ago. If pre-historians felt Lascaux to be a sanctuary, it is because the 'squaring of the circle' had been realized, inscribed,

of an intense meteor shower,
in Heavens we could not see—
also ordered that Rosetta
the Bo'sun, who served as
Scard'nelli's replacement, Sound
the Whistle during the course
of the crew's reshuffling.

As a result, throughout
a first phase of operations,
Kongō, Sinbad, Cowabunga
and myself—moving forward—
changed places with Rosetta,
Thebes, Scard'nelli and Sony,
moving aft; and then,
in a second phase, Wang and
Marlboro—moving aft—
changed places with Tarzan,
Kongō, Sinbad and Cowabunga,
moving forward.

To the Sound of the Ritornello
from Corso's *Fantasia for
Desire, Destiny, Myth and
Reality,* as played by Rosetta
on the Bo'sun's Whistle,
Sony, Scard'nelli, Thebes and
Rosetta surrounded the body of
Vico, while at the same time,
toward the bow, we assumed
our new stations, as ordered.

No sooner had Rosetta

then preserved by Paleolithics,
probably so that it would then
be understood and transmitted."
Chantal Jègues-Woliewiez,
"Lascaux and the Stars."

"The Mog-ur... had forged
indelible new paths in her brain,
paths that let her glimpse ahead,
but he could not forge new paths
on his own. While she looked
beyond, he caught a glimpse,
not of the future, but of a sense
of future. A future that was hers,
but not his."
Jean M. Auel,
The Clan of the Cave Bear.

"While you rested in the sloth
of your eternity, on the proceeds
from Year 1, the spirit of man,
rid of its dimwittedness by you!...
ended up assailing the grounds
of Creation. They discovered in
the intimacy of bodies, as if prior
to their reality, the old CHAOS."
Paul Valéry,
My Faust.

"I I bought thought and so you
come here you you come here and
not today not any can play I look

stopped blowing the Whistle
than the ship swung back
into Equilibrium.

Then, at once, the Green
bubble enclosing us
burst open; and the Black
starry Night returned.

Wasting no time,
Sony, Scard'nelli, Thebes
and Rosetta grabbed Vico
by the arms and legs,
and on the count of three
heaved the corpse overboard,
larboard side.

Vico's body dropped into
the distance way below, before
disappearing in the Silver Sea.

The ship has so far remained
stable, confirming Anna-O's
intuition that the chosen spot,
above deck—directly in line with
the Dormant body of Möbius,
suspended upside down
below deck—was the practical
solution for throwing Vico
overboard without getting

and see, no no I cannot look no no
I cannot see and you you you see..."
Gertrude Stein,
Doctor Faustus Lights the Lights.

"Hamlet wavered for all of us."
Emily Dickinson (L 512).

"Never forget that the secret flaw
in the Devil's might is stupidity."
V. Nabokov,
Lectures on Don Quixote.

"Do not become enamored of power."
M. Foucault,
preface to *Anti-Oedipus*
(G. Deleuze & F. Guattari).

"Man is the violent one, not
aside from and along with other
attributes but solely in the sense
that in his fundamental violence
[*Gewalt-tätigkeit*] he uses power
[*Gewalt*] against the over-
powering [Überwältigende]."
Martin Heidegger, "The Ode on Man
in Sophocles' *Antigone.*"

"Many the wonders, but none
more awesome than man who
sails the grey winter sea, and rides
the crests of furious waves."

the vessel to tip, backward
or forward, down the slope
of the Great Wave.

Indeed, reading Commander
Exprès's spit on the glass again,
Venus reflected that our ship
had Mutated "from Paranoia
Machine to Miraculating
Machine"; and he added that
the difficulties we continue to
experience, psychologically and
technologically, are the result
of an internalized repulsion \
attraction dynamic originating
from the ship's back-and-forth
movement on top of the Wave.

Star mapping as a result
has been resumed, to provide
guidance from the Heavens,
with Tarzan, Sony, Scard'nelli,
Thebes, Rosetta, ben-Cnopee
and Sokrates assigned
to the Observation Deck's
seven Pillars of Wisdom.

Despite all, the whole
crew seems to share
the feeling that a Spirit of
Camaraderie is always
already sustaining us—

Sophocles,
Antigone.

theoretically, politically,
erotically—until the end.

We sail on together,
my love.

S.

The God's House

My lover,

A Plastic tape,
on which is repeated
the word "CAUTION...,"
separates me from a site
where I think
I have just been.

The Big Room is empty,
the Body without Organs gone,
and the light has lost
its harshness, but sitting here
on the floor, in front
of the up escalator,
I see the double doors
chained together,
and, across from me,
the Shaded entrance
to the down escalator.

Only now I am alone
and the silence is Absolüt.

I remember an arm
around my shoulders
and an open hand
inviting me to the scene

"An imbecilic hope, as people
might feel in mid-air, when
falling from a tower, glimmered
between them and vanished."
Colette,
Chéri.

"what is not lost / is paradise"
Lucille Clifton,
"monday sundown 9/17/01."

"The demonic is *prior* to the human."
Clarice Lispector,
The Passion According to G. H.

"The Tower... the most obscure card
in the entire sequence... is sometimes
called 'the House of the Devil',
'the House of the Damned', or simply
'the House'; it must have been through
a misunderstanding of this that
it came in the Tarot de Marseilles to
be called *la Maison Dieu* (the House
of God)... In some texts it is called
'Hell' outright; and this is quite
probably its primitive connotation,

of the Body without Organs
and the three J*W* handlers.

The Body without Organs
(Bw/oO)—the large blob
of smooth flesh described in
Frenchee's Monstrous Manual—
lies on a Metallic table
fitted to a Shopping Kart,
and is surrounded by
the Mutant Metaphysicians
from the Apokalypse d' Lux
—Otto, Etté and Atta—
their bodies and faces hidden
under Camouflage robes.

The Metaphysicians, threefold
incarnation(s) of my opponent,
hold ritual instruments that look
like the Ante-Deluvian Relics
in SciFi's Terrodrome.

One of the J*W*s advances;
the tool is a Letter Opener
fastened with wires and tape
to a Bluestone ball
that she holds in her hand.

Raising the ball, she plunges
the device into the *Bw/oO*,
then pulls it out, and exclaims:
"THIS IS NOT A WOUND!"

Recognizing the quote
from Magritte's

although it may possibly rather have
originally represented Purgatory."
Ronald Decker, Thierry Depaulis
and Michael Dummett,
A Wicked Pack of Cards.

"Then, with a smile, he undid
his magnificent codpiece and,
bringing out his john-thomas,
pissed on them so fiercely that
he drowned two hundred and
sixty thousand, four hundred
and eighteen persons, not counting
the women and small children."
François Rabelais,
Gargantua.

"It is said that Rabelais hid
his wisdom in a mass of filth in order
that it might be acceptable to his age;
Dante rather tactfully invokes
pagan enlightenment to rebuke
the corruption of the Church in a way
that will not stir up the rabble."
Ezra Pound,
The Spirit of Romance.

"The end of something has
a satisfaction. / When the structures
go, light / comes through"
Charles Olson, "La Torre."

"It was a strange world ahead that
would unfold, a thunderhead of
a world with jagged lightning edges...

How To WIN and / or NOT,
I see the *Bw/oO*
with a gash in it,
convulsing on the table,
and the satisfied Metaphysicians
huddled together, murmuring.

With the gash, with the violence
of the spasms, comes the vision
of my loss, of my endless
Self-Division across
the spectral levels of this Game.

Before long, however, I notice
the gash in the *Bw/oO* begin
to fade, then disappear; and
what gradually surfaces instead,
in the place of a mark
or "wound," is the tattoo
of a Letter Opener.

I contemplate the tattoo
on the *Bw/oO*,
until, in the gap left by
the Lost World-Center Paradigm,
within the Zero-Sum Logic
of MeaCulpa the Shrink,
the thought hits me: passing over
the Self-Centered Defense
that denies the "wound" with
a vengeance, I will play Œdipus
at Post-Colônees instead!

It was wide open. One thing for sure,
not only was it not run by God,
but it wasn't run by the devil either."
Bob Dylan,
Chronicles.

"She threw her cigarette
into the garden, lit up another,
gathered and shuffled the cards
from the abandoned poker game
and arranged them cabalistically."
Colette,
The Cat.

"Genji remembers everything;
but some of the women being
neglected, there's movement at
the outer edges, or in the middle or
center, unknown to him; i.e. really
there aren't outer edges in the frame
...Multiple resemblances of people
and of events within a set, or
widely separated from each other
in narrative—and sets which occupy
an extended time, opening up and
unfolding so that it's the whole
world in which things and people
move slowly—create the present."
Leslie Scalapino, "Poetic Diaries."

"Now it is a game, I am going to
play. I never knew how to play,
till now. I longed to, but I knew
it was impossible. And yet I often
tried. I turned on all the lights,

In the Secret Tradition
of Xena, Picard, Barzini,
Barbie and Elvis,
I will *win-win*.

The second Mutant advances
with an instrument similar
to the first, but the blade
is a Pen; I embrace
my Common Humanity
as the blow comes down
to a loud: "*KIAI!*"

After pulling the blade out,
she repeats the same cry:
"THIS IS NOT A WOUND!"

The *Bw/oO* takes on
"Technicolor Hues"
reminiscent of "What Arjuna Sees"
in the W. B. remake
of *BADDA-BING,*
BADDA-BANG, Chapter 11.

I anticipate the new tattoo,
but, as it emerges,
I am stopped short when
the Kart moves toward me,
and one of the wheels—
none of which are the same
and any of which could be
the 10th Card,
The Wheel of Chance—
rolls onto my foot.

I took a good look all around.
I began to play with what I saw."
Samuel Beckett,
Malone Dies.

"'True culture is in the mind,
the *mind,'* he said, and
tapped his head, 'the mind.'"
Flannery O'Connor,
Everything That Rises Must Converge.

"He's forgetten all E done
for him, un made on him..."
Emily Brontë,
Wuthering Heights.

"I remember now seeing the letter E
comprised in your initials written
in books you have at different times
lent me, but I never asked for
what name it stood. But what then?"
Charlotte Brontë,
Jane Eyre.

"Well, then, our kind Apollo,
in the oracles which he gives
his consultants, seems to solve
the problems of life and to
find a remedy... Among other
instances, his is made clear as to
the consecration of the letter 'E'.
We may well guess that it was not
by chance, or by lot, that, alone
among the letters, it received
pre-eminence in the God's house,

Nor do I anticipate
what happens next:
the original tattoo
of the Letter Opener
is engulfed, as if swallowed,
by the *Bw/oO*
folding in on itself,
leaving the second tattoo
of the Pen in Dialectical
Opposition to a fold.

The impulse is to respond
by withdrawing my foot,
but I catch myself,
following through on my plan
to *win-win*.

The third J*W*,
Mutant Metaphysician,
steps up—
only now the instrument
is double-edged, bearing
a broken Bottleneck at each end,
like the one described
in Amex's *Art of War*.

Two quick violent blows,
and again the cry:
"THIS IS NOT A WOUND!"

After the double gash
in the *Bw/oO* fades away,
a new tattoo surfaces in
its place—a pair of broken
Bottlenecks—and the *Bw/oO*

and took rank as a sacred offering
and a show object."
Plutarch,
"On the 'E' at Delphi."

"I thought of the E on the stone, and
of what Mao said / la lumiere' /
but the kingfisher / de l'aurore' /
but the kingfisher flew west /
est devant nous!"
Charles Olson, "The Kingfishers."

"So when the front is prepared,
the rear is lacking, and when
the rear is prepared the front
is lacking. Preparedness on the left
means lack on the right,
preparedness on the right means
lack on the left. Preparedness every-
where means lack everywhere."
Sun Tzu,
The Art of War.

"In the realm that is ours,
where we have shed any belief
in the ineffable and know
the impossibility of unmediated
truth, we are indeed back in
the figural; but more specifically
in a relation to the figural where
the figural is known as figural.
In other words, we are in
the rhetorical... Here we may
aspire to the clarity of reason
but all we may achieve is

folds in on itself and swallows
the previous tattoo of the Pen.

There are now two separate folds
next to the new tattoo;
the two folds proceed to merge
into a larger, single fold,
while the Multicolor hues
clear from the air.

This is not entirely unexpected,
and I still feel in control
before the *Bw/oO*,
which is on the Kart
and displays one long fold
opposite the tattoo
of the broken Bottlenecks;
the Kart, however,
is still on my foot.

The Lockdown that I fail
to foresee occurs when
one of the wheels snaps off:
it rolls in a large curve
across the Big Room,
spiraling inward,
spinning to a state of rest,
like a Coin.

I stand with my foot
pinned under the wheel
of the lop-sided Kart;
the Mutants wobble over

the elucidation of the understanding
that, not knowing truth, nonetheless
seeks to write its laws...
The danger for this understanding
is the isolation of thoughts and
ideas and their conversion into
autonomous objects of knowledge
independent of their productive
ground; in other words,
their reification. The understanding
is prey to ideology..."
Wlad Godzich, "Introduction," in
Paul de Man, *Blindness and Insight.*

"Both in the economic area
(capitalist) and in the political
(world-historical agent), Marx
is obliged to construct models of
a divided and dislocated subject,
whose parts are not continuous
or coherent with each other."
Gayatri Spivak,
"Can the Subaltern Speak?"

"Don't push me, 'cause I'm close
to the edge / I'm trying not to
lose my head / Ah-huh-huh-huh."
Grandmaster Flash and
the Furious Five, "The Message."

"How does the Message reach me?
do thoughts fly like the Word
of the goddess? A whisper—"
H. D.
Helen in Egypt.

to where the missing fourth
wheel is at rest, behind me
toward the center of the room.

Through the far entrance
on the left I can see
an escalator that leads up,
and through a second entrance
on the right
I can see an escalator
that leads down.

The trio sits around the Wheel
in meditation... during which
the fold on the *Bw/oO* grows
longer, swallowing the last tattoo.

The *Bw/oO* now has one
long fold down its middle,
and looks like a large pair
of buttocks, trembling before me.

The spasms become more intense,
while the *Bw/oO* flaps
on the Metal tabletop
with increasing violence,
rocking back and forth,
Banging loudly, as if ready
to leap to the ground.

But instead, in one big convulsion,
the *Bw/oO* flips over entirely,
and lies still, looking as smooth
and pristine as before, the large
fold hidden underneath it.

"'All that has dark sounds has
duende.' And there's no deeper
truth than that. Those dark sounds
are the mystery, the roots that cling
to the mire that we all know, that
we all ignore, but from which comes
the very substance of art. 'Dark
sounds' said the man of the Spanish
people, agreeing with Goethe, who
in speaking of Paganini hit on
a definition of the *duende*:
'A mysterious force that everyone
feels and no philosopher has
explained...' The *duende* I mean,
secret and shuddering, is descended
from that blithe daemon, all marble
and salt, of Socrates, whom it
scratched at indignantly on the day
when he drank the hemlock, and
that other melancholy demon of
Descartes, diminutive as a green
almond, that, tired of lines and
circles, fled along the canals to listen
to the singing of drunken sailors."
García Lorca,
"Theory and Play of the *Duende.*"

"Hey, hey, boozie sailors /
Missed the boat / What to do /
Hey, hey, woozie sailors /
What a mess / Tie 'em down."
Pere Ubu, "Caligari's Mirror."

"When you will have made him

Their meditation finished,
the J*W*s walk
in single file toward
the far Exit on the left,
headed for the <u>up</u> escalator.

As I watch them ascend
and disappear from view,
the Kart rolls off my foot.

My predicament seems clear:
invited by the *Bw/oO*
to resist a Self-Centered Defense
by playing <u>*win*</u>-<u>*win*</u>
across the area of effect
in the Zone of Play,
I witness a generalized
System Shock within
a Sovereign Sphere of Influence
whose hybrid (unimultilateral)
Resurrection on the Plane
of Transparency impels me
to Necromancy by globally
identifying the verbal component
in this Dungeon of Self-Division
as a Mutagenic crypt.

Almost at once the Kart starts
to Rattle, and with a sudden burst
of Energy accelerates, speeding
across the room, Scraping
the floor where the fourth wheel

a body without organs, / then you
will have delivered him from
all his automatic reactions / and
restored him to his true freedom."
Antonin Artaud,
To Have Done with the Judgment of God.

"Poetic language seems to originate
in the desire to draw closer and closer
to the ontological status of the object."
Paul de Man, "Intentional Structure
of the Romantic Image."

"...He then took a number of books
from the table beside him
and threw them, one by one,
at the object of his wrath."
Anne Brontë,
The Tenant of Wildfell Hall.

"...When I saw him lift and poise
the book and stand in act to hurl it,
I instinctively started aside with
a cry of alarm: not soon enough,
however; the volume was flung,
it hit me, and I fell, striking my head
against the door and cutting it."
Charlotte Brontë,
Jayne Eyre.

"All the world's a stage, / And all
the men and women merely players; /
They have their exits and
their entrances; / And one man

is missing, and Smashing into
the double doors.

The doors, chained together,
resist the impact and stay shut,
but the Sound still resonates,
and I stand in Metaphysical fear
before the impossibility of escape.

At which point,
like the "brimstone Rain"
in Amerigo's *Guide*
to the WorldCom Republic,
comes the question of the fold
hidden underneath the *Bw/oO*:
is it still there, or
is it gone... Un-folded... ~~erased~~?

The Kart pulls away
from the doors and slowly
moves toward me, leaving
in its track, along the gash
in the floor, the words:
"CAUTION... CAUTION... CAUTION..."

As with Obvios S'mente—
the Idiot Questioner
at the Faculty of Fine Arts,
according to High Jaques—
the moment calls
for a Materialist approach,
win-*win* or no.

in his time plays many parts... "
William Shakespeare,
As You Like It.

"One side of a machinic assemblage
faces the strata, which doubtless make
it a kind of organism, or signifying
totality, or determination attributable
to a subject; it also has a side facing
a *body without organs*, which is
continually dismantling the organism,
causing asignifying particles or pure
intensities to pass or circulate, and
attributing to itself subjects that
it leaves with nothing more than
a name as the trace of intensity...
A book itself is a little machine;
what is the relation (also measurable)
of this literary machine to a war
machine, love machine, revolutionary
machine, etc.—and an *abstract*
machine that sweeps them along?
We have been criticized for over-
quoting literary authors. But when
one writes, the only question is
which other machine the literary
machine can be plugged into, must
be plugged into in order to work."
Gilles Deleuze and Félix Guattari,
A Thousand Plateaus.

"'*This entire artwork that he loved.*'/
In memory of the thinker
Stéphane Mallarmé," dedication,
The Thousand and One Nights,

How else to probe the fold
in the Body without Organs?

I reach down
to take hold of the *Bw/oO*,
but its three-wheeled Kart
promptly rolls back;
I extend my hand still further
and it speeds away from me,
as if accelerated by
the force of $E \neq E$,
after Max's *Special View*
of the New Science.

The Kart rams into
the chained doors and stays there,
then pulls back again
along the same groove
left on the floor
by the wheelless fourth leg.

Soon the action repeats on its own,
without the movement
of my hand: the *Bw/oO*
charges toward the chained doors
and returns to its starting position,
while the doors hold fast.

The rhythmic pounding continues...
ten... twenty... a hundred...
a thousand... two thousand times...

With every Crash,
jets of smoke stream forth
and the Big Room lights up

Joseph-Charles Mardrus (tr.).

"The Jawas are a pygmy rodent-
like race inhabiting the desert
planet of Tatooine. They work as
scavengers and tinkerers, picking
up discarded or broken machinery
and fixing it up for sale."
"List of *Star War* species,"
in *Wikipedia*.

"I must go silently to meet this doom."
Sophocles,
Oedipus at Colonus.

"The auto-auto said,
'You have not inserted the key.'"
Philip K. Dick,
The Game Players of Titan.

"Poetry is a pipe."
André Breton and Paul Eluard,
"Notes on poetry,"
in *La Révolution Surréaliste,*
no. 12 (Dec. 1929).

"The titles of the pictures were
chosen in such a way as to inspire
a justifiable mistrust of any
tendency the spectator might have
to over-ready self-assurance."
René Magritte, "Lifeline," in
View 7, no. 2 (December 1946).

"As people say, with theory

with rays and bursts of Color,
first on the far left,
where the escalator goes up,
then on the right,
where the escalator goes down,
steadily, dialectically,
as part of a spectacular movement
that seems centered on the Kart's
lost fourth wheel, the wheel
that is *The Wheel of Chance*
in this Game.

My situation is like Alice's,
in the Pin-Ball Machine
of Forgiveness: with every
attempt to vanquish my opponent
I enter the Passage of Forgiveness
to find myself leaving
the Passage of Lies.

Self-divided and powerless,
I wait for the correct
constellation of signs to indicate
the Opening of the Past
and the Closing of the Lexicon.

Then two things happen at once:
the wheel, spinning and rising
onto its edge, speeds away
into the escalator going down,
and the Kart, Smashing against
the doors, finally splits them apart,
without breaking the chain.

and a nail, you've got a nail."
Marge Piercy,
Woman on the Edge of Time.

"...Make the inner voice
delirious, the inner voice that
is the voice of the other in us."
Jacques Derrida,
Of an Apocalyptic Tone
Recently Adopted in Philosophy.

"'The mind is greater than the senses.
Above the mind there is pure
intelligence, freed from thought.
Beyond pure intelligence there
is being—universal being. That is
where you live, where we all live.'"
Jean-Claude Carrière *(RIP),*
The Mahabarata: A Play
(tr. Peter Brook).

"God, the truth is running in
the gutters today. Karma so thick
you can cut it with a knife...
Gets that way every time
there's change for the machines."
Pat Cadigan,
Synners.

"It's a lie, it's a lie, but it's the truth."
Clarice Lispector,
Near to the Wild Heart.

"Truths are illusions which
we have forgotten are illusions...

The brightness of the Big Room
decreases, while the Kart pulls back.

I approach the narrow opening
between the doors, and peer
into a vacant Gymnasium
with Fire Exits,
marked in Red light
along the other three walls.

In the Gymnasium,
just beyond the chained doors,
stands a Card table,
like the ones
at *Faute de Mieux*,
as well as a chair with
an unfastened seat belt, and
written on the floor in Chalk,
from *The Silent Treatment Review*,
the caption: "YOU! LOSER!!
SIT TIGHT!!! AND WATCH THIS!!!!"

On the table, pyramid-like,
lies a mound of Shit...
like the Shit that remains
after decomposition,
when a Card Player
wagers a Dollar and loses.

Immediately, in a quantum leap—
as if transported by my vision
of the Card table—
I find myself at the back
of the Big Room: traces of

coins which have lost their
embossing and are now considered
as metal and no longer as coins."
Friedrich Nietzsche, "On Truth and
Lies in a Nonmoral Sense."

"Reality don't ever lie."
James Brown, "Dead on It, Pt. 1."

"...The result of a consistent and total
substitution of lies for factual truth is
not that the lies will now be accepted
as truth, and truth defamed as lies,
but that the sense by which we take
our bearings in the real world—and
the category of truth vs. falsehood
is among the mental means to
this end—is being destroyed."
Hannah Arendt,
Between Past and Future.

"The only way to fight against
the plague is with honesty."
Albert Camus,
The Plague.

"I have read that the period of
upheaval that journalists have begun
to refer to as 'the Apocalypse'
or more commonly, more bitterly,
'the Pox' lasted from 2015 through
2030, a decade and a half of chaos.
This is untrue. The pox has been
a much longer torment."
Octavia Butler,

smoke fill the air; the light
is low; the *Bw/oO* gone; and
the Plastic tape with the words
"CAUTION... CAUTION... CAUTION..."
is now stretched across a Threshold
at the site where I entered.

As I take my bearings
at this darker level
of the Game,
the silence is not Absolüt.

At first, I think that
the faint, erratic Sound I hear
is *The Wheel of Chance*
tumbling down the escalator,
deeper into the machinery
of the Tarot plane.

Then I wonder
if this is the Sound
of my opponent,
trapped like me on this plane,
still searching for a way
to reach the next.

Or, if not my opponent,
other Players, other opponents,
all of us, here at once,
each alone.

Torn by a non-reversible
Paradigmatic choice between

The Parable of the Talents.

"No more masks!
No more mythologies!"
Muriel Ruckeyser,
"The Mask of Poetry."

"As a closet bookworm, I had long
found a way to shield myself
from the ugliness I encountered
in world literature, particularly that
of American authors and European
philosophers: Raymond Chandler,
Ayn Rand, Mark Twain—bring 'em
all on, Nietzsche and Heidegger, too.
I understood that these writers could
not imagine the existence of one such
as myself. They were of their times.
I was genius enough to extract
and extrapolate and keep moving."
Wanda Coleman,
"Love-Ins with Nietzsche."

"Are we forever prisoners of
the world that has made us? Or
prisoners who escape successively
from all our prisons of glass? Sad
exercises. The days flow by dull and
bland precisely because we feel them
to be worthless. Come to terms with
one's failing. / Something to lean on:
love. The loved one is our last hope."
Laure (Colette Peignot),
"Political Texts" (tr. J. Herman).

two escalators, up and down,
I opt for the one
on the right, going down,
following the Materialist
and Post-Metaphysical tactics
of a Sovereign *win-win* strategy
that is neither Self-Centered
nor Defensive.

The first step is already confusing:
the escalator is moving fast,
the incline is steep and
the stairwell seems Abysmal,
leading into darkness,
lined only with floor lights
spaced a few steps apart that
disappear in the distance below.

I lead with the right foot
and grab onto the handrails;
the ride goes smoothly,
as the escalator carries me deeper
down the stairwell and the light
from the upper entrance
recedes behind me.

But no sooner have I regained
my composure than a book
comes flying out of the darkness
above, and hits me
in the forehead; I bend over
and read the title down
by the floor lights:
From the Lost Works of Magister
"See" MM: Revelations.

"I want to be a beautiful slave girl
and I want to dress you exquisitely,
starting with the fine oil rubbed
to your legs and back and done
so absolutely perfectly that
the Persians would appoint me
and the Byzantines at their most
elegant would not withhold praise."
Frances Boldereff, in
Charles Olson and Frances Boldereff:
A Modern Correspondence.

"They began with a really high
degree of social development like
that of Ancient Egypt or Greece.
Then they suffered the loss of
everything masculine, and supposed
at first that all human power and
safety had gone too. Then they
developed this virgin birth capacity."
Charlotte Perkins Gilman,
Herland.

"*Nihil vales ibi nihil velis.*"
("Wherein you have no power,
therein you should not will.")
Arnold Geulincx,
Ethics.

"In the course of these years...
I learned the inestimable virtues
of Silence, which initiates call
the 'discipline of the arcane'
(*ketman* in Persian)."
Henry Corbin, quoted in

In effect, the book is not
a book but a solid object,
unopenable, in which the pages
and covers are fused together
in a single block.

I start walking down
the descending escalator,
to move faster.

Another book hits me, this time
in the back of the head:
From the Lost Works of Magister
"See" MM: New Revelations.

This book is hollow
and sealed shut; inside it
there is something that rattles,
like the key "left behind"
in Yale's THINK Tank,
according to Auto-Auto.

I decide to head back up,
and start walking against
the movement of the escalator.

The escalator slows down,
and comes to a stop; the lights
at the upper entrance go out.

Even though the escalator
is stopped, I continue to

Hadi Fakhoury, *Henry Corbin*
and Russian Religious Thought.

"In the decades that are gone, /
I enjoyed a share of pleasures; /
Strung in handsome cavalcade,
Like the golden days of Baghdad."
J. W. Goethe,
The West - Eastern Divan,
"Moganni Nameh: Book of the Singer"
(tr. R. Martin).

"'They got the Shah of Persia
last year, didn't they? They got
Bernadotte in Palestine. It's madness
—that's what it is—madness.' /
'But then,' added Mr. Morganthal
heavily, 'all the world is mad.'"
Agatha Christie,
They Came to Baghdad.

"Did poetry die in its war
with the poets / Is this where 'Ablah
walked? Think! / The ruins were
deaf—refused to reply, / then
shouted out in a foreign tongue."
'Antarah ibn Shaddād,
"Did poetry die?" in *War Song*
(tr. J. Montgomery, R. Sieburth).

"In line with Wahhabi and
Taliban jihadis, for whom every
erected thing, so to speak, every
verticality, is a manifest idol,
the desert, as militantly horizontal,

climb up: I want to avoid
the same path as DeMen
of Schiz fleeing before
the Messenger of Despair
in the Psycho-Energetic
Theater of !Raël TV.

The escalator restarts, going up.

All the floor lights
leading above go out;
I stand still, and find myself
riding up the escalator
in the dark.

It does not take long
before another book
hits me in the forehead.

After I pick it up,
the escalator stops;
I turn around,
and, bending over again
to look at the book
in the lights below,
I wrench my back.

Folded over and unable to stand
upright, I catch a glimpse of
the book's title, just before all
the lower floor lights go out:
From the Lost Works of Magister
"See" MM: Final Revelations.

is the promised land of the Divine."
Reza Negarestani,
Cyclonopedia.

"Nicolae Jetty Carpathia,
late thirties; former president of
Romania; former secretary-general,
United Nations; self-appointed
Global Community potentate;
assassinated in Jerusalem; resurrected
at GC Palace complex, New Babylon;
...last seen outside Herod's gate
on the Suleiman Road in Jerusalem."
Tim LaHaye and Jerry B. Jenkins,
Glorious Appearing.

"Profane names danced along
the dark bindings of the books,
shelved by the hundreds...; and
in the midst of the respectable books
gaped the doors of an ivory inlaid
chest that hid between its purple
velvet-lined shelves the books
no one would admit to having."
Rachilde,
Monsieur Vénus.

"Thoth, Hermes, the stylus, /
the palette, the pen, the quill endure, /
though our books are a floor /
of smouldering ash under our feet..."
H. D.
The Walls Do Not Fall.

"'And what is the use of a book,

I remain in Absolüt darkness,
with my body locked
at a 90° angle;
the escalator restarts,
going <u>down</u> the direction
toward which I am pointed.

Soon the escalator begins
to accelerate, carrying me
faster and faster down
the stairwell; I am reminded
of the Doomed Generation
at the Crossroads of Guilty
Pleasure in *The Anthology
of Necessary Fiction*.

A light appears
at the end of the stairwell.

The light approaches quickly—
but as the Exit draws near,
the escalator grinds
to a sudden stop: I fall
and tumble down the steps,
head over heels.

When I stand up at last,
still bent in two,
I make my way
down the last few steps
to where I am now,
sitting on the floor

thought Alice, 'without pictures
or conversations?'"
Lewis Carroll,
Alice in Wonderland.

"It's not just that 'god' is dead;
so is the 'goddess.'"
Donna Haraway,
The Cyborg Manifesto.

"The demand is always the active
voice, that we use history, not that
we be used by it. As Creeley observed,
'Olson offers a stance diametrically
opposed to existentialism in rejecting
that view of history as something
you're stuck with in some inexorable
manner and it grinds you out...'
Olson takes a much broader sweep
in defining history as 'whatever
happens, and if it is significant
enough to be recorded, the amount
of time of the event can be *minute*.'"
Ann Charters, "Introduction,"
in Charles Olson,
The Special View of History.

"Once they had found the secret
part of their inner self, there came
the temptation and the hope
that one day they might reach
the maximum. What maximum?"
C. Lispector, "The Message."

"It is not then always easy even after

behind a Plastic tape
on which is repeated the word
"CAUTION..."

The escalator restarts, going <u>up</u>.

Sitting here, I realize that
my body, whether seated
on the floor or standing
on the escalator, is locked
in the shape of a step.

The right angle of my body
follows a rotation during my fall
that suggests <u>before</u> and <u>after</u>
positions, a change of order
that recalls the Paradigm shift
from the Magick "If"
to the Blank Slate,
as confirmed by bōō'dA
after Ramada, Enron and
Run-DMZ were aligned
in the skies over Bamiyan.

At the same time,
the axis of rotation,
about which the "step"
that is my body
would seem to turn,
points to the Self-Centeredness
behind my failing Defenses,
and to my lost Sovereignty
in these Endtimes.

much knowing of some one to know
whether the being in that one
is attacking or resisting, in them."
Gertrude Stein,
The Making of Americans.

"The art of the sophist is the semblance /
of wisdom without the reality, and /
the sophist is one who makes money /
from an apparent but unreal wisdom."
Aristotle,
On Sophistical Refutations.

"Fujitsubo was assailed by
innumerable conflicting thoughts."
Murasaki Shikibu,
The Tale of Genji.

"The more secure I feel in my work
and personal life, the more directed
and value-bearing the examination of
anger can be. At my weakest most
despairing moment, anger is merged
in a hopeless stew of guilt, self-blame,
enclosure..........it is important to
remind myself that I *was* flipped out
for several years—and if this
is a representation for the implosion
of my generation at a certain time...
I still alone had to struggle to
fight back into relevance, coherence,
the unities of functional behavior."
Carolee Schneeman *(RIP)*,
from *The Notebooks*.

"And Dirty burst into dissonant
laughter, to which, in that emptiness,
there was no response."
George Bataille,
Blue of Noon (tr. H. Matthews).

If I laugh now,
I am finished.

"Let him who knows
how not to pray / go to sea"
C. Olson, "La Torre."

The memory of your laughter
guides me instead, and will
bring me back to myself.

Your lover,

A.

The Star

My dear love,

"Leave the nurse on dry land
and move beyond, / Into truth's
ocean, like ducks in a pond! /
Don't fear the water, though
they've taught you to— / Dive
in the ocean with no more ado!"
Rumi,
The Masnavi, Book II
(tr. J. Mojaddedi).

"'They were saying at the *Théâtre*
that a certain music-hall artiste
might stand a chance,' said Andrée.
'The one billed as the Cobra at
the Olympia. It seems she does
an acrobatic turn, and is brought on
in a basket hardly big enough
for a fox-terrier, and from this
she uncurls like a snake.'"
Colette,
Gigi.

"Living one—open your coils!"
The Egyptian Amduat,
"Seventh Hour."

From the crest of
the Great Wave, we have
come to lie at the bottom
of the Silver Sea, where
the silence is Deafening,
like they say, and
life is a Masquerade.

Tarzan is the second
member of Intelligence
to die.

Now Venus alone remains.

"Space, Time
and Love in Gaad!"
he mumbles to himself,
as on the CABARET
under Covvid,
Poet of Kidd, in *The Sea
With 11 Dimensions*.

Tarzan came to understand
that the ship was doomed to
go past its Tipping Point and
plunge down the Great Wave,

"We have passed from one animal
to the other, from the mole to
the serpent, in the system under
which we live, but also in our manner
of living and in our relation with
others. The disciplinary man was
a discontinuous producer of energy,
but the man of control is undulatory,
in orbit, in a continuous network.
Everywhere surfing has already
replaced the older sports."
Gilles Deleuze, "Postcript
on the Societies of Control."

"The only sound in the vast moving
green was the hissing of the board
over the water. A couple of times
it almost dropped away under
my feet, but I found it again and
stood my ground. 'Shoot it, Gidget.
Shoot the curl!!' My own voice
had broken away from me and
I could only hear the echo coming
from a great distance. 'Shoot it...
shoot it... shoot it, Gidget!'"
Frederick Kohner,
Gidget.

"A cosmic vision—awe some;
I automatically seek out from
the infinite coiling of form
the God shape..."
Carolee Schneemann,
from *The Notebooks.*

following a dream in which
she traveled "on the Path of
the Passage to the Middle."

Abandoning her post
on the Observation Deck,
she found Cîpher, and
said to him:
"The signs are clear."

Tarzan also confided that
her Vision of Doom
left her troubled by
the thought of having
to tell the Captain.

She wore a Blue Mask
for the purpose, and
shouted across the deck
the bad news about
their impending descent
into the Waters way below.

Then, to make amends
for bearing bad news,
she announced that she would
confine herself to the Cage
of Was \ Ankh \ Uraeus
by the aft steering paddle,
from which her bones
were sure to be flushed out
by the impact of the Wave.

So, as Madness
closed in, Tarzan

"She flies over partitions on the /
wings of a bat; while you /
play cards w/ a stranger."
Diane di Prima *(RIP),*
Loba, "Lilith: An Interlude."

"Take the blue mask down from
my face / And look me in the eye."
Lou Reed, "The Blue Mask."

"Great disease was mighty and
the people were sick everywhere. /
It was an epidemic, it floated
through the air... / Well, the nobles
said to the people, 'You better
close your public schools. /
Until the events of death has ending,
you better close your churches too.'"
Blind Willie Johnson,
"Jesus Coming Soon."

"He tensed all his muscles,
stiffened all his limbs, trying
in spite of himself to return
to the earthly envelope that was
being taken away from him...
He found himself floating above
this world. Inexplicably, he had
the proud feeling of Satan, who,
though fallen from Paradise,
still looks down on the earth
and has, at one and the same time,
his forehead under God's heel and
his own heel on the forehead of man!"
Rachilde,

dashed toward the stern,
ran into the Cage,
and took her seat.

Her quick movement
across the deck, however,
had the ill-Fated
effect of disturbing
the vessel's Equilibrium,
as the ship's stern
started slipping down
the Wave—prompting
Tarzan, as she tipped back-
wards and faced the Heavens,
to emit a sudden, powerful
umbo weti Yodel.

How to describe
the feelings we shared...
tilting, finally,
toward the stern,
on an awesome ride
down the Great Wave,
that kept returning us
in a loop through time
to serene Sweetness
and Abysmal dread?

And now, dead
in our tracks,
asking ourselves:
how to resurface?

Monsieur Vénus.

"It's a blazing shaime, ut Aw
cannut oppen t' Blessed Book, bud
yah set up them glories tuh Sattan,
un' all t' flaysome wickednesses ut
iver wer born intuh t' warld! O, Lord,
judge 'em, for they's norther law nur
justice among wer rullers!"
Emily Brontë,
Wuthering Heights.

"The lesson of *Wuthering Heights,*
of Greek tragedy and, ultimately,
of all religions, is that there is
an instinctive tendency towards
divine intoxication which the rational
world of calculation cannot bear...
Divine intoxication, to which
the instincts of childhood are
so closely related, is entirely
in the present... Adults forbid those
who have still to reach 'maturity'
to enter the divine kingdom
of childhood. But condemnation
of the present moment for the sake
of the future is an aberration,
just as it is necessary to forbid
easy access to it, so it is necessary
to regain the domain of the moment
(the kingdom of childhood),
and that requires temporary
transgression of the interdict."
George Bataille, "Emily Dickinson"

Once her Yodeling had come to
a stop, and after a brief
moment of Sleep in the Cage,
Tarzan shed her body, then lost
all her bones to the sea,
except for the skull.

By then, as the vessel
continued to drop
stern-first, shredding
the Anonymous face
of the Great Wave,
we had battened down
the hatches and were
all below deck.

The first Goofy turn
on our backward ride
was to starboard
(frontside), as the Wave's
Silver Cathedral,
under the Black nobility
of the starry Heavens,
cast its impassive Shadow
over the Colored totems
of Solomon, Pythagoras
and Janus Pater.

Attention was assailed
on all sides by
the risen waters above and
below us... until Venus,

in *Literature and Evil.*

"And if at Mill Valley perched
in the trees / the sweet rain drifting
through western air / a white sweating
bull of a poet told us / our cunts
are ugly—why didn't we / admit
we have thought so too? (And / what
shame? They are not for the eye!)"
Denise Levertov, "Hypocrite Women."

"As we looked out towards the head-
land where the sea beats, we saw
a wave, the work of a god, its solid
mass towering towards the sky...
And at the very moment when
this surging mountain of water was
breaking, the wave sent forth a bull,
a terrible and wondrous creature."
Euripides,
Hippolytus.

"A wave of ruin spreads
through the ruins."
H. D.,
Hippolytus Temporizes.

"Go to work, surf's up."
Kim Gordon, "Surf's Up."

"But then a wave from behind,
looming over, rushed upon them,
and their vessel sped forward like
a long surfing missile over the hollow
sea on that swift rough crest."

after Commander Exprès's
Coughing attack, deciphered
the projected spit—which,
because of the turbulence,
had missed the Cauldron
and landed on the deck next
to the Transforming | Mirror.

Venus saw that the figures
in the spit contained
an occult message from
our lost helmswoman
van Rr'Ubik—whose Spirit
communicated through
the figurehead's portside Half-
Shadow with the suspended
upside-down body of
Möbius-in-Deep-Sleep-State,
which was bumping against
the rose windows of
the perspective machine.

The information transmitted
from van Rr'Ubik to Möbius,
according to Venus's reading,
indicated that the crest of
the curling Wave overarching
the ship was the sign
that the Great Wave itself
was shrinking fast—as in
the tale from the Archives
of the #QUA-QUA-NON
under Captain Brown Jes'...

Apollonius of Rhodes,
The Argonautica, Book II.

"What—shall the sailor, then, who
leaves the stern and runs to the prow
find any device for safety when his
vessel is foundering in the sea waves?"
Aeschylus,
Seven Against Thebes.

"I who had loved the image
of old Geulincx, dead young,
who left me free on the black boat
of Ulysses, to crawl towards
the East, along the deck. That is
a great measure of freedom, for him
who has not the pioneering spirit."
Samuel Beckett,
Molloy.

"A tempest... made the stern rise,
and the prow sink, as it pleased
another, till the sea closed over us."
Dante Alighieri,
The Divine Comedy: Inferno.

"The sea was indistinguishable
from the sky, except that the sea
was slightly creased as if a cloth
had wrinkles in it. Gradually as
the sky whitened a dark line lay
on the horizon dividing the sea from
the sky and the grey cloth became
barred with thick strokes moving,
one after another, beneath the surface,

As we descended the face of
the Wave, and Tarzan's skull
tossed around in the Cage,
Avon the Poetess, chanting
on Speakerphone, began
the tale of Tarzan's adventures
in the Vimina Underworld,
as re-imagined during
the Vedic Age of Cydonia
and Atlantis before the Flood,
when Annunaki Adrenochrome
and the Crystal technology
of the Redskin Nephilim spoke
to the "Def" JetBrains of Youth
on the Moderna Peninsula.

Avon's weïrd poetry
caused increased agitation
not only among the crew,
but also for *Ō-Notare,*
the Spirit of the Keel
at the start of the Drop.

Ō-Notare advised
Captain Anna-O
to heed the *Pop-up*
revelations contained
in the *Blown-out spit*
from the Cough of
Commander Exprès,
even if the ship's
Epic descent down
the Wave made for
Sick difficulties.

following each other, perpetually."
Virginia Woolf,
The Waves.

"We live in an age of rising seas."
Rachel Carson,
The Sea Around Us.

"Society is a wave."
Ralph Waldo Emerson, "Self-Reliance."

"This music is only one little wave
of style and waves of little ideas
my mind has encompassed through
living in a society that calls itself
sane, as long as you're not behind
iron bars where there at least one
can't be half as crazy as in most
of the ventures our leaders take upon
themselves to do and think for us..."
Charles Mingus, liner notes,
The Black Saint and the Sinner Lady.

"In this boat we were in the habit
of going on some of the maddest
freaks in the world."
Edgar Alan Poe,
The Narrative of Arthur Gordon
Pym of Nantucket.

"We know that *rythmos* has come
to mean both the cadence of writing
and the undulation of the wave."
Jacques Derrida,
The Truth in Painting.

Commander Exprès, however,
because of the ship's intense
movement, as it carved its way
across the Anti-Body of
the tunnel's Crazy Wall,
was projecting his spit
outside the Cauldron—onto
the gaslight, the Shit detector,
the Impulse :: reactor system.

So Captain Anna-O gave
the order that Rosetta,
together with Scard'nelli and
Cowabunga, engage a Cryptic
Line of Defense against
the Wave's Bad Vibrations,
that would maximize
communications and stabilize
the ship, by deconcentrating
the water's Energy and
recycling it infinitesimally
through the Media network.

At the same time,
a sense of thrill
and Erotic excitement
overtook us all.

Still now, on the floor
of the Silver Sea, it is
difficult to understand
how our Line of Defense—

"We have passed the tipping point:
while information policy is among
the most ancient forms of governance,
there has been a phase change—
a change of state—in the extent
to which governments deliberately,
explicitly, and consistently control
information creation, processing,
flows and use to exercise power."
Sandra Berman,
Change of State.

"A democratic surveillance
society is an existential and
political impossibility."
Shoshana Zuboff,
"The Knowledge Coup."

"Image-making as a global policy—
not world conquest but the victory
to 'win people's minds'—is indeed
something new in the huge arsenal
of human follies recorded in history."
Hannah Arendt,
Crisis of the Republic.

"Our hearts are heavy with fear /
When we see our leader distracted,
as helpless sailors / Are terrified
by the confusion of their helmsman."
Sophocles,
Oedipus at Colonus.

"The Platonic dialogue was
maintained through
the connection of Rosetta,
amidships, who operated
the sea-level Communicating
Vessels... to Scard'nelli,
across from her, working
the cooler, the baker
and warming exchanger...
to Cowagunga, by the bow,
on feedback loop—functioned
not only as the matrix of
instant communication
for the whole crew,
but also as the theater
of a "Conversation"
between, on one hand,
Avon the Poetess,
at the bottom of the hull
behind the keel,
whose skeleton-legs dragged
below the ship, and,
on the other hand,
Commander Exprès
in his cabin,
under the forward-facing
poop deck, with Venus,
Interpreter of the Spit,
next to him.

As described by Chauvée
of Communications, who
monitored the proprioceptor
array, the ship was subject
to a Schizoid Dynamic,
in which Exprès's commentary

the lifeboat in which the shipwrecked
older poetry saved itself, together
with its numerous offspring.
Crowded together in a narrow space,
and timidly obeying their helmsman,
Socrates, they moved forward into
a new era which never tired of
looking at this spectacle. Plato
furnished for all posterity the pattern
of a new art form, the novel...
a form in which poetry played
the same subordinate role with regard
to dialectic philosophy as that same
philosophy was to play for many
centuries with regard to theology.
This, then, was the new status
of poetry, and it was Plato who,
under the pressure of daemonic
Socrates, had brought it about."
Friedrich Nietzsche,
The Birth of Tragedy
from the Spirit of Music.

"The true modern poem
is life without poems."
Fernando Pessoa,
"Salutation to Walt Whitman."

"Nobody likes the man
who brings bad news."
Sophocles,
Antigone.

"The long, sad enterprise of
revising, censoring, and mutilating

on Avon's epic tale
underscored the surreal
nature of our Joyride
down the Pipeline of Doom.

Avon's narrative followed
Tarzan through the Underworld
from the Satanic Swiss shores
of the Tohu Bohu River,
past the Arc of the Covenant,
to the Pentagon's Thelema
Reserve—where Dioxide,
the Grand Wizard from
the Elders of Zion,
Awakened Tarzan's FireEye
to the Black Budget
and net-zero Energy of
Spike Mutation and Maga.

Then, as if in reply,
more Coughing ensued,
from which Venus concluded:
"Commander Exprès says:
Kongō must go!"

Time seemed to expand.

Captain Anna-O told me to
"do something and Navigate,"
so I recommended a frontside
top turn followed by a cut
back that would put the turned-
around ship's larboard rail
backside.

J began with someone you can call
the Elohist... He combined J's texts
with a variety of material, doubtless
from written sources that are now
lost... The Deuteronomists (...)
wrote about two hundred years later...
After the fall of Jerusalem to Babylon
in 587 B.C.E. the Priestley Authors
began to compose an alternative text,
comprising what is now Leviticus
and the larger share of what is now
Genesis, Exodus, Numbers...
A redactor of undoubted genius...
working soon after 458 B.C.E.
produced the Torah probably
pretty much as we have it now.
This Redactor, a formidable fellow...
is the villain of this book."
Harold Bloom, "The Author J,"
in *The Book of J*
(ed. H. Bloom, D. Rosenberg).

"The panorama of the sea...
but the sea itself?"
Walt Whitman,
Leaves of Grass.

"But the sea takes / and gives
memory, / and love fixes
the eye diligently, / and poets
establish / that which endures."
Friedrich Hölderlin,
"Remembrance."

"The XXIst century will be ecophilic,

The Captain agreed, and, given
the stress on the steering bus,
ordered Marlboro and Wang
to join Sokrates at the wheel.

At which point,
Gunome Midare,
the next Spirit of the Keel
on our first Power Turn,
sent Sokrates to the Library,
"where he belonged,"
because Scard'nelli—
manning the feedback loop
for the Line of Defense—
"was not meant to be alone
in that *Amazons Hothouse*."

In contrast to the exhilaration
and Erotic stimulation felt
by the rest of the crew,
the engagement with
our second Power Turn
put Kongō on edge:
not only did the Able-
bodied Deckhand turned
Substitute Engineer
still grapple with becoming
instantly fat before the rise
of the Great Wave, but
Venus's Doomscroll Forecast
proved an accelerator
of the Madness in store.

noetic, poetic; or will not be."
Michel Deguy *(RIP)*, "Écologiques."

"I give my steps their form
and tell the sea to follow me."
Adonis, quoted in Khaled Furani,
Silencing the Sea.

"To touch rock-bottom was the same
as having water above one's head."
Clarice Lispector, "The Obedient."

"...And herself being entered into
her own ship, the whole fleet sunk
immediately into the bottom of
the seas, and left all the spectators
in a deep amazement."
Margaret Cavendish,
The Blazing World.

"In theory, there is a gravitational
attraction between every drop of
sea water and even the outermost
star of the universe."
Rachel Carson,
The Sea Around Us.

"T'Gatoi whipped her three meters of
body off her couch, toward the door,
and out at full speed. She had bones—
ribs, a long spine, a skull, four sets
of limb bones per segment. But
when she moved that way, twisting,
hurling herself into controlled falls,
landing running, she seemed

When Avon described
Tarzan's special access
to the Sciento-Logical
Big-Pharma Chemtrails
of Roswell, after Project
Majic Poppa Clip,
the close encounter with
Hollywood the Merovingian
and Kissinger the Lyrist
by the Blue-Green waterspout
in the Temple of Set's
Area 51, Kongō yelled:
"Get that straight!"
—evoking the "unwobbling
pivot" of Abbondanza's
Pure Mind from Larsen B.'s
Book of Aloha.

Yet the rest of us
were getting stoked
from the ship's radical
Fakie stance before
the real Oval Office
under a Wuhan Chandelier.

We felt elastic and laid back.

Like Marlboro and Wang
at the wheel, who described
their visions to the crew,
I could see, beyond
the tubular Rainbow rim,
the Resurrection of the Body
of the Woman of Light
on the Sea of Primordial

not only boneless, but aquatic—
something swimming through the air
as though it were water."
Octavia Butler, "Bloodchild."

"All of nature talks to me /
If I could just figure out what
it was trying to tell me."
Laurie Anderson, "Sharkey's Day."

"I am, by means of a little
Pantagruelism (that is, as you
know, a certain gaiety of the spirit
pickled in the contempt for things
fortuitous) sound and supple,
ready to drink, if you are."
François Rabelais,
The Fourth Book of Pantagruel.

"The Cube impressed me as
an outstanding oracular device
from the moment I saw one...
The cube scatters the 6 colors
over its 6 faces. Each face
is further subdivided into
9 squares... Twist the cube
without looking at it several
times (...), after phrasing a clear
question, then set it down,
look at it and interpret..."
Jim Gross,
The Oracle of Light.

"You know, here in America, people
turn up with so many queer ideas."

Revelation; Cowabunga,
Scard'nelli and Rosetta found
the Secret of the Secret in
the Science of the Balance;
and, as Sinbad said, while
we braced for the high-speed
motion of our third Power
Turn, we all seemed in
perfect sync with the Sexual
Mysteries of a Quest for
the Vertical Dimension.

The alternate reality, according
to Kongō, was that the Angel
in the Face of the Wave
was psychoanalyzing the ship.

In Kongō's view the ribosome
burps from the wet and
dry bulbs in the Dust bowl,
and the sudden Sound
from the air blower
in the aerosol vault of
the reformer, served as clear
signs of Rosetta's delusion;
similarly, the melting of
the virion cells in the heat
pump and the escaping gas
from the One Cylinder
on the emission controls
were seen as indications
of the Desperado
Boogaloo Program in
Scard'nelli's crypt of
the repressed... just as

Thor Heyerdahl,
Kon-Tiki.

"What difference does it make if
what we see before our mind's eye
has already been interpreted?"
Susan Howe,
Spontaneous Particulars:
The Telepathy of Archives.

"Among the Kuna of Panama...
a speaker who performs
at the highest levels
of discourse requires two
successive interpretations
by two additional speakers
before his message reaches
a general level of understanding."
Dennis Tedlock (ed.),
2000 Years of Mayan Literature.

"Now Ammon said unto him: I can
assuredly tell thee, O king, of a man
that can translate the records; for
he has wherewith that he can look,
and translate all records that are
of ancient date; and it is a gift from
God. And the things are called
interpreters, and no man can look
in them, except he be commanded...
And whosoever is commanded to look
in them, the same is called a seer."
The Book of Mormon,
8 Mosiah 13.

the harmolodic vibrations
in the jib boom and
sprit sail animated elitist
"wingèd sentences" that
spoke for Cowabunga's
social distance from
Kongō, Venus and me.

As for Sinbad, he was
frontline against the infodemic
that shattered the speculum
of the virtual TV.

After the ship cranked out
of the turn and headed down
the next track on the Wave,
the "Conversation" continued
between Avon the Poetess
and the spit of Commander
Exprès, as read by Venus;
at the same time,
in seeming counter-point,
came the Lesson for Captain
Anna-O from *Ko-Midare,*
next Spirit of the Keel.

Avon sang of Tarzan's
Great Awakening, when
she threw open the shutters
of the Overton window
on the Antiquarian Stage
of Mystical Horrors, and
discovered the Ultraviolet

"We pray for him, offering love.
History praises him, offering laurels.
Mercy sings for him, offering
absolution. Arthur Rimbaud,
in his long suffering, has at last
attained absolution."
Patti Smith, Preface,
in Arthur Rimbaud, *A Season in Hell*
and *The Drunken Boat*.

"Rémy de Gourmont will be paid back
for his insult to Rimbaud: 'A girl's
temperament,' said he. Today,
a judgment of this sort... tells us
all we need to know to build a case
against the male type of intelligence
at the end of the nineteenth century."
André Breton,
Arcanum 17.

"Don Quixote's situation is...
akin to the plight of that French
poet of unique genius, Rimbaud,
who in the eighties of the last
century gave up poetry because
he had come to the conclusion
that poetry was a synonym of sin."
Vladimir Nabokov,
Lectures on Don Quixote.

"Brother Sancho,
we have an adventure."
Miguel de Cervantes,
Don Quixote.

Antidote against Kek.

After her passage through
the Google Stargate, Tarzan
reached the Sandy Hook
of the Monsanto Sea and
heard the Transhuman babble
of its Phosphorescence,
like Dona "the Pleiadian"
in the Techno-Luciferian
Prophecies of Zeta Rediculi
from *The Book of the New
Zza Order;* in a further
adventure, Tarzan followed
the luminous feet of Apophis
across the JFK–mRNA
Sacrifice grid, toward
the Floridated Rainbows
at the front of "The Storm."

Exprès's apparent response,
judging from the tracings
across the spit, was:
"Geronimo's mad again,"
which Venus interpreted as
an OK-Boomer reference to
the 3 + 3 Booby Hatches
of Space and Time
on the OUMUAMUA,
from the legend of Capt.
Sin Nombre in the Days
of the 6th Extinction.

The implication was
that Avon's poetry looked to

"If history, the enemy of time,
is the mother of truth, the history
of women must define female identity.
The main tome on this subject or
history was written by Cid Hamete
Benengeli. Unfortunately, the author
of this work so major it is the only one
is an Arab, and that nation is known
for its lying propensities; but even
though they would be our enemies
it may readily be understood that they
would more likely have added to rather
than have detracted from the history."
Kathy Acker,
Don Quixote.

"The necessity of completing
a thousand and one sections obliged
the copyists of the work to make
all manner of interpolations. None
is more perturbing than that of
the six hundred and second night,
magical among all the nights.
On that night, the king hears from
the queen his own story... Does
the reader clearly grasp the vast
possibility of this interpolation?
That the queen may persist
and the motionless king hear
forever the truncated story
of the *Thousand and One Nights,*
now infinite and circular..."
Jorge Luis Borges, "Pierre Menard,
Author of the *Quixote.*"

"the sea of Trees / the sea
of Sand / the sea of Ice /
the sea of Darkness,"
in a Lost Poetry of Creation,
after the Zoom of Carbon Capture
and the Plasmid Anthropause—
when GroupSense, CrowdStrike
and ArchAid drank the Molü
from the Black Rock and Shell.

I was transported
by Avon's recital
to a transcendent
Shaka Bardo within
the Great Wave,
like Bedlam, Thebes and
Q'Bal in the Engine Room
next to the Large Collapse;
or like Nobadinus
behind the vibrator,
under the fo'c's'le deck,
with Ben C'nopee and Sony
at the Lenseport;
or like Neanderthal and
Mach holding fast
on the Grand Spiral stairway.

We interpreted Avon's
account of Tarzan's
Underworld adventures
at its Imaginal source,
in the Book of Nature,
as an invitation to travel
toward the Light of Glory,
following our Celestial

"In a book I wrote called
How to Write I made a discovery
which I considered fundamental
that sentences are not emotional
and that paragraphs are. I found out
about language that paragraphs are
emotional and sentences are not
and I found something else about it.
I found out that this difference was
not a contradiction but a combination
and that this combination causes
one to think endlessly about
sentences and paragraphs because
the emotional paragraphs are
made up of unemotional sentences."
Gertrude Stein,
How To Write.

"As I floated down impassive Rivers, /
I felt myself no longer pulled by ropes:
/ The Redskins took my haulers
for targets, / And nailed them naked
to their painted posts."
Arthur Rimbaud, "The Drunken Boat"
(tr. A. S. Kline).

"Whatever there is that might be
is simply not there: only the pooled
water... only murmurs, ripples,
in the dark, in the night. Only
the Maker, Modeler alone,
Sovereign Plumed Serpent,
the Bearers, Begetters are
in the water, a glittering light."
Popul Vuh (tr. D. Tedlock).

counterparts on the path
of Transmutation
through Sacred History,
like Johnny Bull in Eleusis
on her way to meet Gonzaga.

But Kongō saw differently
and, quoting from
The Materialist Manifesto
of Geryon and Paterson
on the CHING MING,
pointed to the debilitation
of both Commander Exprès
and Möbius as evidence
of the "weak thought"
Rosetta, Scard'nelli and
Cowabunga brought to bear
on their misinterpretation
of History's "open sea."

The announcement of *Ko-
Midare's* Message to the Captain
—*"Don't mix sea and sky!"*—
proved all the more timely,
occurring just as Blue-Red Sparks
started flying off the ship's hull
—prompting Anna-O to issue
the Fateful command that
I initiate the fourth Power Turn.

Like Kahuna on the MANA,
as if dancing to the music
of the Wave, the vessel

"I see you and they see us
exceedingly / a face countenance
façade / or prior surface do not
forget / remember the front side
presence / marching toward until
in order to because of / as per
without over behind the face
of two interminable / turns."
Amanda Berenguer, "Mobius Strip"
(tr. M. de la Torre).

"Near the tail of Canis Major
Argo Navis sails... poop-first
across the immensity of the skies."
Cicero,
Tusculan Disputations.

"I felt still more at sea, and ended
believing that I was in another world,
another epoch, another civilisation,
perhaps on another planet
containing the past and future
and, simultaneously, the present."
Leonora Carrington,
Down Below.

"Mosques are desecrated / and
altars overturned / outside
the museum's / cool stone walls."
Jessica Hagedorn, "The Mummy."

"A survey in 2008 and 2009 on
the southwestern coast of Crete in
the region of Plakias documented 28

cut back, looped around,
and crossed over...
catching Fire in the process.

While Tarzan's skull knocked
against the Cage above deck,
Avon went on with the story
of Tarzan in the Underworld—
recounting how she gazed at
the Reptile Draco rising from
the Rabbit Hole in the Reeds
on the ocean's calm waters,
to the Sound of *911911911*
cataracts crashing
over distant horizons.

Even as the ship's hull
became engulfed in Flames,
Avon's stories about Tarzan's
journey entranced us:
we shared the overcoming of
her Dissociative Identity Disorder
and the dark perfumes of trauma-
based Mind Control, after Tarzan
arrived at the hideous wreck of
the Sacrificial Pyramid in Vegas
under molten skies; like Tarzan,
we became actors in the Theater
of LSD GunGrabs, tired of zones
and poles after the Russian Purge
of 4-chan Fake News; and found
our bliss in the Shadow-Flowers
of the Great Wave's spray...
in the same way that Tarzan
had beamed with delight, when

preceramic lithic sites. Sites were identified with artifacts of Mesolithic type similar to assemblages from the Greek mainland and islands, and some had evidence of Lower paleolithic occupation dated by geological context to at least 130,000 years ago. The long period of separation (...) of Crete from any landmass implies that the early inhabitants of Crete reached the island using seacraft capable of open-sea navigation and multiple journeys—a finding that pushes the history of seafaring in the Mediterranean back by more than 100,000 years..."
Thomas F. Strasser et al., "Stone Age Seafaring in the Mediterranean," *Hesperia,* Vol. 79, No. 2, 2010.

"No reckoning allowed /
Save the marvelous arithmetics /
Of distance" /
Audre Lorde, "Smelling the Wind."

"If you were to look at the Pacific Ocean from space, you might notice that you would not be able to see both sides of it at the same time."
Christina Thompson,
Sea People.

"oh natural star, green diadem, /
alone in your solitary dynasty, /
unattainable still, evasive, desolate /

the Uranium of the Handlers,
the Alters and Patsies
from Project Soros melted
off the Q-map into air.

Commander Exprès answered
with a heavy spell of Coughing.

Venus caught his spit in
the Cauldron and read its layout
as a direct message to me:
*"The vibrational memory of
the wavelength's Ionized center
tests the skill of the Navigator."*

I thought of King Kong and
the "CHOU" – "HAN" – "SUNG"
on the Stone in Rothschild's
*Comprehensive Mirror
for the Rites of Neschek,* and
understood that what I imagined
as a Flaming ship speeding
through the Ideogrammatic No-Go
zone between the Facing Mirrors
of "Waters Above as Below"
was really my erroneous
Mental confusion between
Movement and Space-Traveled.

My perception was that
the ride of the Flaming ship
represented a mixture of "Io," or
Light-That-Has-Entered-the-Cave,
and Wave Machine—
a Gandalf tendency compromised

as a drop, as a grape, as the sea."
Pablo Neruda, "The Separate Rose."

"And then I bathed in the Poem
of the Ocean, / infused with
galaxies of milky stars, /
devouring greens afloat in turquoise
flotsam, / the thoughtful drowned,
with pale blue scars..."
Arthur Rimbaud, "The Drunken Boat"
(tr. J. W. Steele).

"Carrington's the Star is arguably
the most stunning card in her deck;
the luminous gold leaf in the back-
ground causing the radiant azure
blue around the star to stand out
all the more... The haloed stars have
been transformed from the traditional
eight-points into the five-pointed
pentagrams of magical practice."
Susan Abert and Tere Arcq,
The Tarot of Leonora Carrington.

"When the stars threw down
their spears / And water'd heaven
with their tears: / Did he smile
his work to see?"
Blake, "The Tyger."

"Thou remembʼrest / Since once
I sat upon a promontory, / And heard
a mermaid, on a dolphin's back, /
Uttering such dulcet and harmonious
breath, / That the rude sea grew civil

by a Baldur impurity—
but now my intuition was
that we were all witness instead
to the cosmic sympathy between
Pure Movement and
the World of Imagination—
as in the Great Reset of
Image, Movement and Matter
foretold by the Acid Writer in
Dungeons and Mavericks.

Although Kongō derided us
for being "in the grip
of the 'Virus Analytica'"—
as theorized by Capt. Nobus
on the S\S PEACE—
and referred to my oversight
of the ship's positional
maneuvering as "the Metaliptic
illusion of a Leptoid Woman on
her knees," all we could see
in the Impact Zone were
a waterfall's Lights of Beauty and
a whirlpool's Lights of Majesty.

It was when the harmonic
motion of the breaking Wave
gave rise to what seemed
like a shout, followed
by the Knelling of a bell,
that the certainty of Kongō's
doom, if not our own,
became undeniable.

And when the Captain

at her song / And certain stars
shot madly from their spheres, /
To hear the sea maid's music."
William Shakespeare,
A Midsummer Night's Dream.

"*Some of these days /*
You'll miss me honey /
What had just happened is that
the Nausea has disappeared.
When the voice was heard in
the silence, I felt my body harden
and the Nausea vanish. Suddenly:
it was almost unbearable to
become so hard, so brilliant.
At the same time the music
was drawn out, dilated, swelled
like a waterspout. It filled the room
with its metallic transparency,
crushing our miserable time against
the walls. I am *in* the music."
Jean-Paul Sartre,
Nausea.

"The function of freedom
is to free someone else."
Toni Morrison, Barnard College
commencement speech (1979).

"In this tiny America where
the most delirious happiness
can only be caused by the dollar,
a man continues to make
daring reference to some other
kind of thought... Beautiful has

put on her Majic Hat,
like Capt. Hokusai aboard
the BIOSPHERE,
to re-direct the Purifying
Winds that swept in
from the Three Directions—
fueling the Flames in which
the ship was wrapped—
I understood in a flash
why Cîpher and Chauvée
had been correct to note
how it was generally
consistent with the Rosetta \
Scard'nelli \ Cowabunga
"Line of Defense" that
Kongō's Death meant Sinbad
would be next to die.

Guidance came
to the Captain,
when *Kataochi-Gunome*,
new Spirit of the Keel,
gave the word:
"*I got the Power!*"

Anna O. took it
as her cue to engage
a Duck Dive, as the means
of avoiding dehydration
and shattering the spell
of a worst-case scenario.

The waters seemed
to double in size,
and the best chance

nothing to do with it, but it is."
LeRoi Jones (Amiri Baraka), in liner
notes, *Coltrane Live at Birdland*.

"I feel I'm closest to Hell...
when I'm thinking about money."
Pharoah Sanders, quoted in
liner notes, N. Hentoff, *Tauhid*.

"pause for the human / animal
in its coat / of many colors. /
pause / for the myth of america. /
pause for the myth of america."
Lucille Clifton, "grief."

"I told myself that Sonny was wild,
but he wasn't crazy."
James Baldwin, "Sonny's Blues."

"No black American troops were
allowed to march in the great victory
parade of the Allies up the Champs-
Elysées even though France and
Britain were represented by dark-
skinned colonial soldiers."
Anne Waldman,
The Iovis Trilogy, Book I.

" • 'Can we study the remains of your
people?' • 'Can we take a few grams
of bone for research?...' • 'Do you
want to come and rebury the remains
that were dug up many years ago?'
• 'Do you want to come and help
us dig up your people?'... So many

for a tranquilizing
Recovery from a gnarly
Foam Bounce was
a Rail Set that responded
to the Great Wave's
subliminal cues
with a Duck Dive's
hermeneutic uncovering
of the Suck-out
in the Spin Cycle.

So we braced for
the supplemental Energy
and ozone shower of
a more-than-human dive
into a subtler state of Being.

Despite our best efforts,
the good ship got totally
battered and submerged
in the Wipeout.

Yet, even as it started
to sink into the deep,
Avon pursued her recital
with mounting passion.

She imagined Tarzan at
the Round Table with Pindar
and the Council of 13
in the Taliban Drugstore,
where Blond-eyed Archons
with tangled hair

difficult questions for a people who
are still grappling with recovery
from a harsh removal."
Stacey Halfmoon, "Caddo Art,"
in *Hero, Hawk and Open Hand*
(ed. R. Townsend).

"the Indian licked the eye / and
we became a boat / lost on the plains"
Etel Adnan *(RIP)*,
"Five Senses for One Death."

"What is the fundamental problem
of the Western? It's essentially
the fact that *what is vital for
the characters is to perceive, not
to act*. And if there is a mythology
of the Western, it is this... *if you
don't perceive, you don't survive...*
You recall the fine passage of Marx
on capitalism and its two aspects,
the fact that it continually poses limits
while at the same time never ceasing
to push against its own limits, even
as it creates others. We could say that
the two major aspects of capitalism
are slavery and expulsion... It sweeps
everything away in order to make
way for a new organization. And, in
this sense, it's no longer a question
of slavery but of clearing the land,
clearing the land of its inhabitants...
To open a short parenthesis: why is it
that today the Palestinians could be
considered descendants of the Indians?

waved False Flags in the Ether.

The ship meanwhile
stayed level and continued
to sink, as Fire consumed
the forward decks.

Exprès's response to Avon's
verse was a Coughed-Up spit
in which Venus read
the Readymade advice to
"*Make it new!*" by creating
a Greenhouse Zone at
the bow, and Greenwashing
the Fire's "Angry Beast"
with Firestopper foam.

At the same time, however,
Venus's words made Kongō
angry at the "drunken effect"
of Avon's poetry on the crew,
and Kongō's anger in turn
triggered a ship-wide
Imaginal oscillation between
stationary and excited states—
because, following Sinbad's
explanation, it was a revelation
of Being as Presence balanced
by a moment of "Nothingness"
...similar to the experience of
Kundun, Kandahar and Kabul
on the Friendship Bridge
to Enduring Freedom
in *The Mystic Medici Books*.

It's very odd. The Palestinians continue
to say... they have completely grasped
this... if there was a new form
of the Western it would be...
'We Redskins... we are modern-day
Redskins.' In fact, it's not a question
of enslaving the Palestinians,
it's a question of expelling them,
of clearing them off their land."
Gilles Deleuze, "Seminar on Cinema:
The Movement-Image" #6, 1 Dec. 1982.

"Grant as a supplier and his / Southern
counterpart's extraordinary ability /
to disengage—one with Washington /
as his personal mold the other with
none / and so more raw to war, neither
Indian / nor inheritor of a measure to
abide by / U S Grant is a spasm of time"
Charles Olson, "(fr 'West'—possibly)."

"Hoang Ti contrived the making of
bricks / and his wife started working
the silk worms, / money was in days
of Hoang Ti... / Ti Ko set his scholars
fitting words to their music /
is buried in Tung Kieou / This was
in the twenty fifth century a.c. / YAO
like the sun and rain, / saw what star is
at solstice / saw what star marks amid
summer / YU, leader of waters, black
earth is fertile, wild silk still is from
Shantung / Ammassi, to the provinces, /
let his men pay tithes in kind."
Ezra Pound,

Captain Anna-O,
acknowledging Sinbad's
insight and sensing
the crew's change of Mood
in reaction to Kongō's
emotional outburst, agreed
with the assessment of Exprès
(and his interpreter Venus),
and ordered Cîpher and
Chauvée to station themselves
on either side of Mobiüs's
suspended body, and manage
the Sprinkler system's
connection to the gaslight
through Rosetta;
the Sprinkler's disjunction
from the perspective machine
through Scard'nelli;
and its conjunction with
the clarified air blower
through Cowabunga,
in order to release the foam
onto the Fire.

The operation worked;
the Fire stopped.

What got Abstrakted, however,
was the effect of the foam
on the ship's even keel:
the ultrathin layer of Firestopper
foam deposited throughout
the forward decks created
a weight imbalance that re-
integrated friction in the Gravity

Cantos, LIII.

"I have learned how faces fall
to bone, / How under the eyelids
terror lurks, / How suffering
inscribes on cheeks / The hard
lines of its cuneiform texts. /
How glossy black or ash-fair locks /
Turn overnight to tarnished silver, /
How smiles fade on submissive lips, /
And fear quavers in a dry titter."
Anna Akhmatova, "Requiem,"
Epilogue (tr. S. Kunitz, M. Hayward).

"...I saw the girl put a Scotch and
milk on top of the piano for Sonny.
He didn't seem to notice it, but just
before they started playing again,
he sipped from it and looked toward
me, and nodded. Then he put it back
on top of the piano. For me, then,
as they began to play again, it glowed
and shook above my brother's head
like the very cup of trembling."
James Baldwin, "Sonny's Blues."

"He fumbles at your Soul / As Players
at the Keys / Before they drop full
Music on— / He stuns you
by degrees— / Prepares your brittle
Nature / For the Ethereal Blow..."
Emily Dickinson (477).

"In a patriarchal culture,
specifically the Judeo-Christian,

Handler and sent the ship on
a long slope down, bow first.

The unintended course
correction, and
the increased speed
of the ship's descent
toward the ocean's bottom
through the dense,
Protein-rich heavy water
of the Silver Sea
seemed to add urgency to
Avon's account of Tarzan's
Continued Adventures,
as if the vibratory
interaction between
harmonic and luminescent
information had produced
Omicron and *Pi* variants
in the Alphabet code of
the Life-field, impacting
the ship's Coherence Domain.

Then Fire broke out
at the stern, across the aft
decks, just as Avon was
describing Tarzan's experience
with the Burning Funnel
and Electric Crescents
of the Reichstag Holocaust,
during the Radiation experiments
on the EPIPHANY—before
Nazi archaeology brought

quasi-Puritan culture of 19th-century New England in which Dickinson grew up… the equation of divinity with maleness was so fundamental that it is hardly surprising to find Dickinson, like many an early mystic, blurring erotic with religious experience and imagery. The poem I just read has intimations both of seduction and rape merged with the intense force of a religious experience."
Adrienne Rich, "Vesuvius at Home."

"And Jacob said to Rebekah, his mother, 'Behold, Esau, my brother, is a hairy man, and I'm a smooth-skinned man. What if my father feels me and I seem to him a deceiver, and bring on myself a curse, not a blessing?!'"
Genesis 27: 11, in R. Crumb, *The Book of Genesis Illustrated.*

"I have seen Leviathan sprawl rotting in the reeds / Of the great seething swamp-nets; / The calm sea disemboweled in waterslides / And the cataracting of the doomed horizons."
Arthur Rimbaud, "Drunken Boat" (tr. S. Beckett).

"I understood at last that my true vocation, my sole purpose in life,

Tarzan to the ColdWar Empire
Beneath the Ice.

Captain Anna-O gave the order
to start spreading the foam.

While the Sprinkler system
was being redeployed
against the second Fire, Avon's
narration followed Tarzan's
Adventures in the Underworld…
from the Fathomless Nights of
Aryan Exile to the Maelstrom
of Future Vigor… and onward
to tales of the Manhattan Project,
the Psyops of the Vrill Society,
and the hammer blows against
the UFO from Aldebaran.

As with the Fire
at the bow, the Flames at
the stern were put out;
yet once again, no sooner
had the fresh foam settled
than the redistributed weight
caused the ship to list—
this time in the opposite
direction—sending it
on a long slope down
to the bottom, poop first.

Venus's immediate response,
translating for Exprès, was:
"The Commander sez:
Hegel's dialectic is Majic!"

was to hunt down this disturbing monster and rid the world of it."
Jules Verne,
Twenty Thousand Leagues. Under the Sea.

"Shipbuilding... is an art and craft. The learning and the exercise of this lore... has an impalpable element, called *baraka,* from which the word 'barque'—a ship—is derived. This word means 'the Subtlety,' and it cannot be shown to you."
Idries Shah,
The Sufis.

"What is the barrier of the Ancestral Teachers? It is just this one word 'Mu'... Concentrate on this one word 'Mu.' Day and night keep digging into it. Don't consider it to be nothingness. Don't think in terms of 'has' and 'has not.' It is like swallowing a red-hot iron ball. You try to vomit it out, but you can't."
Wumen Huikai, "The Koan Mu: Text, Commentary, and Verse."

"Whence things have their origin, there they must also pass away according to necessity; for they must pay penalty and be judged for their injustice, according to the ordinance of time."
Anaximander (tr. F. Nietzsche),

It became Kongō's mantra,
and ours—as if Avon's
account of Tarzan's adventures,
together with the reversal
of the ship's heading, had
synthesized the crew's Mood
and Kongō's Thinking.

As the ship sailed on,
Kongō's Passion on the path
to a Vision of "The Last
Dialectical Push" became
the enactment of a process
unfolding in each of us:
the intuition of a *Solution* that
actualized the transformative
power of a lifetime's
"Drops of Experience"
through an overwhelming
surge of mixed emotions and
the powerful onrush of Tears
held back... in what finally felt
like a Cosmic release from
the contradictions of the World.

For all the time we spent
on our ride under the water—
rapt participants in Kongō's
Awakening to the Truth of
our "Journey to the One"—
it seemed like no time before
Fire broke out again, amidships.

quoted in Martin Heidegger,
"The Anaximander Fragment."

"*all things are full of gods /*
with ravishing wounds, / instruments
of instruction / erasures of doubt /
by touch, touch as absence, / nothing
between, no I / apart from the sky. /
We fallen letters, / sticks and coils."
Billie Chernicoff, "Thales said."

"Eros shook my / mind like
a mountain wind falling on oak trees"
Sappho,
If Not, Winter (tr. A. Carson).

"one of these days / won't come
too soon / when the blank / familias
blank / will fold away / a highly
inflammable / balloon eclipsed by
seminal / and nubile / loving"
June Jordan, "For My Mother."

"Not God but a swastika / So black
no sky could squeak through. /
Every woman adores a Fascist, /
The boot in the face, the brute /
Brute heart of a brute like you."
Sylvia Plath, "Daddy."

"The subsidiary interest... was
called the Swastika Surf-Board
Company—in 1930 the hooked-
cross design was recognized,
if at all, as an obscure good luck

As with the first two Fires,
fore and aft, the foam Sprinkled
over the central decks re-shifted
weight across the ship—
which again changed course,
and now started dropping
horizontally to the seafloor.

It was on this final line
of descent that Avon brought
her Tarzan poem to a close,
following the message
from the Commander:
"MU-*SIC!* MU-*SIC!*"

Avon concluded with
Tarzan's Last Adventure in
the Vatican's Majic Kingdom,
after the invention of Islam
and the Meta-translation
of Kaballah by Disney
and the Illuminati of Kazar
—when, in a Butterfly Effect,
the Hidden Hand of
the Burning Man, under
"stagnant Fumes of torpor,"
brought the Paper Boat of
"embittered love" to the Cold
Black Pool of New Europe.

Yet, by the time Avon was
done, Kongō had already entered
a phase of *Reaction,* and discovered
the Mysteries of Deadpan Hilarity.

symbol; it wasn't yet associated
with Germany's Nazi party—and
a small swastika was wood-burned
into the tail section of each board."
Matt Warshaw,
The History of Surfing.

"The manipulator liberates only /
the mad bulldozers of the ego
to level the ground."
Marge Piercy,
"Song of the Fucked Duck."

"'Hope' is the thing with feathers – /
That perches in the soul – /
And sings the tune
without the words – /
And never stops – at all – "
Emily Dickinson (314).

"I learned in leafy woods hmmm
—depths of the sea that Noone
is first father— so soon a terror /
of feathery wings—soft and
tremblingly swift— / how did we
happen— because we were written."
Susan Howe, "God's Spies,"
in *Defenestration of Prague.*

"Falls / the feather / rhythmic
suspension of disaster / to be
buried / in the original spray /
whence formerly its delirium
sprang up to a peak / withered / by
the identical neutrality of the abyss"

The completely Unsayable
fact of the Laughter
that Kongō shared with us
was *given*—at the sub-Molar,
sub-Molecular level—
by the cascading effect from
Standard Stoppages of
Power, Knowledge, Pleasure
and Letting-Go, that skewed
the Lines of Penetration
for our Vulnerabilities,
Know-how, Lessons Learned
and Alternative Facts.

Kongō's stunned silence, interrupted
by the cry *"Watch me now!"*
was our Initiation into the Absúrdity
of an Existential Comedy, where
the Becoming of the Many seemed
a Carnival of non-Linear Change.

Yet, just as Kongō began to
quote from ~~Ahriman~~'s *Discourse
on Collapse-Denial in the Wake
of Adams and Fu-Manchu's
Eunuch Rebellion*—in mid-
sentence, between the Bunker
and the Quietest Room,
on the way to the Hidden
Chamber—Sleep descended,
and Kongō fell down Dead.

Stéphane Mallarmé,
"A Throw of the Dice
Will Never Abolish Chance."

"probably even Icarus, plummeting
from / an impossible height / was
proud / a man beset by feathers /
wearing bird colors / hearing bird
conversations plain / sharing bird
ambitions / flying above
the possibilities / pursuing
with immortals / the pride of wings"
Lucille Clifton, "Only Too High Is
High Enough, *for Charlie Parker.*"

"Happy are the lookouts over
the ocean of the desert / Those who
pursue the fennec beyond the mirage /
The winged sun loses its feathers
on the horizon / The eternal summer
laughs at the wet grave / And if a loud
cry resounds in the bedridden rocks /
No one hears it   no one"
Joyce Mansour, "Blue like a Desert."

Only when the ship hit bottom
did we recognize the *Problem,*
after another Spirit of the Keel,
Ko-Notare, made the comment:
"Don't give up the ship."

Kongō's bones were quickly
sealed in the passageway
between the Bunker and
the Quietest Room, before
it became uninhabitable;
the Stench from the unmentionable
Big Fart has gotten worse
in the Humidity; and the ouzo
is almost undrinkable.

Here on the floor of
the Silver Sea, between Hilarity's
Leap of Faith into Paradise
and the Clenched Fist raised at
the Horror of the Great Dying,
our Deep Agenda now
is for Creative adaptation to
the mud on which we rest.

I love you,
and in loving you
will continue to love
whatever comes next.

S.

The Moon

Lover,

My eyes are closed, and
I see before me a vision
of U. U. Knucklehead
the Mad Boy:
he is dressed in a long
robe with a Red girdle
around his breast,
his feet are shining
like White Metal, and
his eyes are radiant Blue.

Set in Clouds, he beams
a two-edged ray of light
from the gap between
his two front teeth,
and holds seven Sparklers
in his right hand;
he is speaking to me,
but his Voice has the Sound
of bubbling water.

In my vision,

"├ ┌ ┬ ┐ ┤
├ ├ ┼ ┤ ┤
├ └ ┴ ┘ ┤
└ ┴ ┴ ┴ ┘

├ ┌ ┬ ┐ ┤
├ ├ ┼ ┤ ┤
├ └ ┴ ┘ ┤
└ ┴ ┴ ┴ ┘

├ ┌ ┬ ┐ ┤
├ ├ ┼ ┤ ┤
├ └ ┴ ┘ ┤

├ ┌ ┬ ┐ ┤
├ ├ ┼ ┤ ┤
├ └ ┴ ┘ ┤

Note: Made by copying

facing the Mad Boy,
I realize that I am
on my back, as if tied
in knots, unable to free myself
from a curtain of Glass Beads
under which I am buried.

I struggle, and become
more and more entangled;
I call for help, I start
to hear distant cheering
and laughter, applause,
but my panic increases,
and in a moment of terror
I jump and sit upright.

Now I find that I am
standing in a long room
with the curtain of Glass
Beads behind me;
the cheering and laughter
are closer, louder.

On my right, protruding
from the wall, I see
seven beds in a row,
with seven Satellite Dishes
mounted above them;
in the beds are seven dreamers,
lying on their backs,
their White eyes in dream state
fixed on the ceiling.

the scientists' symbols on
the first photos of the moon
in *The New York Times*:
there were exactly fourteen
'lines' with five 'accents.'
We have not been able
to address the moon in
a sonnet successfully
since the Renaissance.
Admitting its new scientific
content made it possible
to do so again. The moon
is a different object today. /
Also the sonnet was
a supranational, supralingual
form as the concrete poem is.
So the poem is both
a spoof of old forms
and a statement about
the necessity for new."
Mary Ellen Solt,
"Moonshot Sonnet,"
in *Concrete Poetry*:
A World View (ed. M. E. Solt).

"White men / just walking
on the moon, / he go
where he want to go."
Lucille Clifton, "Quotations
From Aunt Margaret Brown."

"The Moon is the Number 18 /
is a monstrance, / the blue dogs

The laughter, the applause
are coming from
the far end of the room,
past the first dreamer,
where there is another doorway.

As I try to advance,
I am stopped,
as if by the invisible force
of a wind or current
in the room.

Despite the resistance,
I lift my foot
and strain to step forward,
but as soon as I put
my foot on the ground
I am back before the vision
of U. U. Knucklehead
in the Clouds.

Once again I find myself
struggling under the strands
of Glass Beads; I sit up
in terror again, to discover
that I am standing on
the other side of the curtain,
in the same long room
with the seven dreamers
in the seven beds.

Every time I try
to move forward,

bay, / and the son sits, / grieving
is a grinning god, is / the mouth of,
is / the dripping moon / while
in the tower the cat / preens /
and all motion / is a crab / and
there is nothing he can do but /
what they do, watch / the face
of the waters, and fire."
Charles Olson,
"The Moon is the Number 18."

"Ranger VII / Photos landing /
On the / Moon /
How deep / Its dust?"
Louis Zukofsky, "A-14."

"I see in *Lunaya Pravda* that
Luna City Council has passed
on first reading a bill
to examine, license, inspect—
and tax—public food vendors
operating inside municipal
pressure. I see also is to be mass
meeting tonight to organize
'Sons of Revolution' talk-talk."
Robert Heinlein,
The Moon Is a Harsh Mistress.

"moon goddess / the less that is more"
Wanda Coleman, "Want Ads."

"Somewhere within us
the old experience of

I know that the same
pattern will repeat,
placing me back before
the same vision as before:
I recognize the Psionic Logic
of "the Wind of
the Apokalypses,"
as described by
the Uninvited Visitor
in *The Machine to Kill Time*.

The Sound of laughter and revelry
stops.

From the far end of
the room, dreamer Number 1
rises from the first bed—
her White eyes wide open—pivots
to one side, and starts walking
backward with an odd movement
like a dance step, gradually moving
in my direction and then
past me, toward a shelf on
which lies a large wooden spoon.

The dreamer takes the spoon,
scoops up an Egg-shaped
Marble from a nearby basket,
does an about-face
and walks backward
with the same strange step.

the Euphrates, Mesopotamia
between the rivers, lives still.
And in my Mesopotamian self
I long for the sun again."
D. H. Lawrence,
Apocalypse.

"Which freedom do you want? /
$387,000,000,000 / for /
WAR IN IRAQ / (so far) / or /
free new homes for every / house
destroyed by Katrina... / plus
1,500,000 extra houses for /
anyone else who wants one?"
Lungfull Cultural Attaché
Sticker #9.

"The Apocalypse of St. John
is also divided into 22 chapters.
Assuming the Qabbalah to hold
the solution to the Tarot riddle,
seekers have often ignored
other possible lines of research."
Manly P. Hall,
The Secret Teachings of All Ages.

"Things fall apart;
the center cannot hold."
W. B. Yeats,
"The Second Coming."

"What have we MOONITES done?"
Lawrence Sterne,

She moves toward the wall
between the two beds
closest to me, and stands there.

Moments later, dreamer
Number 7 rises and stands
beside dreamer Number 1,
who hands over the spoon
with the Philosophical Egg.

After the transfer,
dreamer Number 1 moves
backward to the far end of
the room and lies down again
in her bed.

The movement continues to
unfold, as dreamer Number 7
takes the Ovum on the spoon
back to a position between
the first and second beds, then
passes it to dreamer Number 2,
before returning to lie down.

Dreamer after dreamer,
each shuffling backward,
passes the Ovum
carried on the spoon:
from dreamer Number 2
to dreamer Number 6...
from dreamer Number 6
back to dreamer Number 3...

Tristram Shandy.

"How could this happen?
How could a pure substance
like 'the philosopher's stone'
break apart?"
Hiromu Arakawa,
Fullmetal Alchemist.

"The moon / Is tossing money
Down through the black air."
Jack Spicer,
After Lorca,
"The Moon and Lady Death,
A Translation for Helen Adam."

"In the trembling air / the moon
moves her arms / showing breasts
hard as tin, / erotic and pure."
Federico García Lorca,
"Ballad of the Moon, Moon"
(tr. L. Hughes).

"With regard to sleep and waking,
we must consider what they are:
whether they are peculiar to soul
or to body, or common to both;
and if common, to what part
of soul or body they appertain."
Aristotle,
On Sleep.

"The dream's here still. / Even

from Number 3 to Number 5...
from Number 5 to Number 4...
Number 4 to Number 3...
Number 3 to Number 5...
from Number 5 to 2...
Number 2 to 6...
6 to 1... 1 to 7...
until finally dreamer Number 7
goes to the far end
of the room, drops the Ovum
into a second basket,
puts the spoon on the shelf
and returns to lie down in
the seventh bed, closest to me.

There follows a moment
of silence... then the riotous
laughter and the cheering,
the applause, rise again
as loud as before
from the Exit at the other
side of the room.

I want to cross the room,
but resistance from the Wind
of the Apokalypses still prevents
moving forward.

As if by chance,
my tribulation yields at once
to the light of Revelation:

when I wake it is / Without me
as within me; not imagined, felt."
William Shakespeare,
Cymbeline.

"I wonder, by my troth, what
thou and I / Did, till we loved?
Were we not weaned till then? /
But sucked on country pleasures,
childishly? / Or snorted we
in the Seven Sleepers' den?"
John Donne,
"The Good-Morrow."

"Once, as I recall, my life was
a feast / where all hearts opened
and all wines flowed."
Arthur Rimbaud,
"A Season in Hell."

"The mask is connected
with the joy of change and
reincarnation, with gay relativity
and with the merry negation
of uniformity and similarity;
it rejects conformity to oneself.
The mask is related to transition,
metamorphoses, the violation of
natural boundaries, to mockery
and familiar nick-names.
It contains the playful element
of life; it is based on a peculiar
interrelation of reality and image,

the revelry I am hearing
emanates from the Celebrity Roast
of Number One, as Emceed
by Salvador the Son
and Commander-in-Chief,
in accordance with
The Player's Guide to Endtimes,
by Gnosis and Co.

There is a Rainbow above
the Throne, and around it
sit four and twenty Phanatics,
and out of the Throne
proceed laughter and mirth,
and before the Throne
there is a Sea of Glass
like unto Crystal, and
in the midst of the Throne,
and round the Throne
are four Automatons,
full of eyesballs
before and behind.

I have a further Revelation:
the dreamers are the Losers
in the Seven Ruined Temples
of the Lost:
their back-and-forth movement
unseals *The Book of Life.*

And when the First Seal
is opened, the First Loser
sees and beholds the Pile

characteristic of the most ancient
rituals and spectacles."
Mikhail Bakhtin,
Rabelais and His World.

"As long as necessity is socially
dreamed, dreaming will remain
a social necessity. The spectacle
is the bad dream of a modern
society in chains and ultimately
expresses nothing more than
its wish for sleep. The spectacle
is the guardian of that sleep."
Guy Debord,
The Society of the Spectacle.

"...During sleep the phantasms,
or residuary movements, which
are based upon the sensory
impressions, become sometimes
quite obliterated... while at other
times the sights are indeed seen,
but confused and weird, and
the dreams are unhealthy,
like those of persons who are
atrabilious, or feverish,
or intoxicated with wine."
Aristotle,
On Dreams.

"He is a dreamer.
Let us leave him. Pass!"
W. Shakespeare,

of Freedom, and goes forth...
And when the Second Seal
is broken, lo, the Second
Loser goes out and sees
the Pile of Peace... And when
the Third Seal is opened,
the Third Loser goes and sees
the Pile of Plenty; and lo,
the Fourth Loser beholds
the Pile of Knowledge...

The 5th, 6th and 7th Losers—
imagining in dreamtime
their wishes fulfilled—
have completed the ritual
and brought on
the Celebrity Laugh Track.

When it ends,
dreamer Number 7
will rise again
to fetch the spoon
and the Ovum,
and the scene will replay.

On impulse,
sticking with a *win-win*
Game Plan, I pivot to cross
the room walking backward
—in an effort to follow
the dance step of Michael
the Former Archangel,
which I do not know

Julius Caesar.

"Sometime I will give
a history of every kind of
men and women, every kind
there is of men and women.
Already I have given a history
of many men and women.
Sometime I will be giving
a history of all the rest.
This is now pretty nearly certain."
Gertrude Stein,
The Making of Americans.

"I had say sixteen stones,
four in each of my four pockets
these being the two pockets of
my trousers and the two pockets
of my greatcoat. Taking a stone
from the right pocket of my great-
coat, and putting it in my mouth,
I replaced it in the right pocket
of my greatcoat by a stone from
the right pocket of my trousers,
which I replaced by a stone from
the left pocket of my trousers,
which I replaced by a stone from
the left pocket of my greatcoat,
which I replaced by the stone
which was in my mouth, as soon
as I had finished sucking it.
Thus there were still four stones
in each of my four pockets,

how to do.

I turn around, but I am
unprepared for the shock
and awe of the vibrations:
the room is shaking violently,
vision is blurred,
the Sound intensely loud.

Despite the turbulence,
I do my best to mimic
the Angel's backward step,
and start crossing over
to the other side.

To my left, as I pass
them one by one, the seven
dreamers lying on the seven
beds appear as bodies
of Colored light;
the Colors are from
Zorothustra's Rainbow:
Red... White... Blue...
Black... Green... Silver...

On my right, I pass alongside
the Exit: a Revolving Door,
surmounted by a large grid.

Looping around, I approach
the Revolving Door

but not quite the same stones..."
Samuel Beckett,
Molloy.

"Experience remains, of course,
the sole criterion of the physical
utility of a mathematical
construction. But the creative
principle resides in mathematics.
In a certain sense, therefore,
I hold it true that pure
thought can grasp reality,
as the ancients dreamed."
Albert Einstein, "On the Method
of Theoretical Physics."

"An unapparent connexion
is stronger than an apparent."
Heraclitus,
The Cosmic Fragments (tr. G. S. Kirk).

"Item: because in those days
no women were put into convents
unless they were one-eyed, lame,
hunch-backed, ugly, askew, mad,
backward, deformed or defective;
nor men unless they were runny-
nosed, ill-born, daft and
a burden on their family..."
François Rabelais,
Gargantua.

"...The criticism of religion

backward; once inside,
I grab on to the handle
and pull it toward me.

As the door turns in reverse,
each of the bodies of light—
incarnations of the Seven
Ruined Temples of the Lost—
releases the Synthetic Sound
of the B♭-Minor scale in
J.C.'s *Ascension, 2nd Edition*:
"A♭" for Ashur,
"G♭" for Girsu,
"F" for Fara,
"E♭" for Eridu,
"D♭" for Dahaila,
"C" for Ctesiphon.

After "B♭" for Babylon,
the Revolving Door
cuts me off from the room,
shutting me in darkness.

Not until the Revolving Door
continues to turn, and I realize
that I am going around again
with no apparent Exit,
does the thought occur
that maybe I have swerved
from the *win-win* scenario.

Then, I wonder:
can the impossibility

is the prerequisite of all
criticism... The criticism of
religion is, therefore,
in embryo, the criticism of
that vale of tears of which
religion is the halo."
Karl Marx,
"A Contribution to the Critique of
Hegel's Philosophy of Right."

"The 1st of December: Champville
assumes the task of story-telling
and relates the one hundred and
fifty following tales (the number
of each precedes the tale). /
1. Won't depucelate any save
those aged between three
and seven, but only cuntishly.
'Tis he who deflowers Champville
at the age of five.
2. He ties a girl of nine
in a curled-up position and
depucelates her from behind.
3. He wishes to rape a girl
of twelve or thirteen, and
depucelates her while holding
a pistol to her heart.
4. He likes to frig a man upon
a maiden's cunt, he uses
the fuck for pomade, and
next encunts the maid while
she is held by the man.
5. He wishes to depucelate

of *win-win* begin to function
as the (Fragilistic) Matrix
of an alternative possibility
in which *win-lose*
re-covers the Sovereignty
of the Penultimate Laugh
at the Post-Prophetic threshold
of Sacrificial Self-Division?

Is this "the Message"
of NonZero-Sum the Poet's
Orphic Recommendation
to the Crème de la Crème:
"If you chose, choose to lose"?

Does the lost Paradigm
resurface as the Mirror Image
of an Apokalyptic opening
in the sevenfold path
to *The Lovers*,
by way of *The Fool?*

I stop pulling
on the Revolving Door,
and start pushing it instead—
but the forward movement
is jammed.

Walking backward again,
round and round in darkness,
I start to reason as follows:

three girls in succession, one
in the cradle, one at age five,
the other at seven."
Marquis de Sade,
The 120 Days of Sodom.

"In the third place
the third capital is aroused."
Gertrude Stein, "Capital Capitals."

"Naturally surplus value increases /
Being incident to the pace exhorted."
Louis Zukofsky, "A-9."

"The Penultimate is dead."
Stéphane Mallarmé,
"The Demon of Analogy."

"Do you know how many stories
should not have been told?"
MTC Cronin,
Causal.

"Sade drained to the dregs
the moment of selfishness,
injustice, and misery, and
he insisted on its truth.
The supreme value of his
testimony lies in its ability
to disturb us. It forces us to re-
examine thoroughly the basic
problem which haunts our age
in different forms: the true

if I am in the Revolving
Door of *win-lose*, then
in theory, like “Joe Sample”
of the Sandwich Generation,
I can seek deliverance
from Endtimes to the horizon
by capturing my own lost Youth,
as if in new translation.

By a twist of Fate,
the Revelation yields to
my release, when I am seized
by the twin one-winged
Daemons of ’Istorin,
who thrust their arms
under my own and pull me
backward into Tunnel Vision.

The Revolving Door
is now a Plasma Screen.

Despite the speed at which
I am traveling, the Screen’s size
appears unchanged, and continues
to expand as I draw further
and further away.

Before me, in Remote-Control Mix,
the Seven Channels from
John Goes Ahead (8th Movement)
present the Seven Advertisements
of the Times.

relation between man and man.”
Simone de Beauvoir,
“Must We Burn Sade?”

“A squire came quickly through /
the door / And a lance with iron
point he bore / (A rite that caused
them bitter woe) / Which dripped
with blood in steady flow, / Then
down the shaft into the hand; /
The sleeve its further progress
banned. / All those assembled
wept and cried / Throughout
the spacious hall and wide. /
The folk of thirty nations /
Had made less lamentations. /
Around the room along each wall, /
Then back again toward the door /
And out, as he had come before.”
Wolfram von Eschenbach,
Parzival.

“And the new year arrived,
the new millennium...
What would become of them,
I wondered. In another
hundred years would they all
be born in test tubes, or perhaps
evolve through computers to
become groups of disembodied
digital intelligence machines?
Would they remember who I was,
would they remember what I said?

On the First Channel,
in the tree-within-the-trees
of Beatitude Plaza, I recognize
the "Light" and the "Wind"
mingled with "Sweetness"
from the schools of Movists
and Shakers.

On Channel Two, I see
the "Simplist Flame" in
the Land of Sea-to-Sea...
on Channel Three,
in the shooting stars
over ButWiser,
the "Pure Source" of
Enthusiasts, Coalitionists
and Hieronymites...

On the Fourth Channel,
I find in "the Name of
the Moon... and of the Sun"
the Cheer of Protectionists,
Inerrants and One Percenters.

With the switch to Channel Five,
the Daemons are pulling me back
more quickly, so that my legs
and feet begin to rise;
as written, the angels
fly high in the air, saying
in a loud Voice, *YA-HOOO!*

Now, on the big Screen

...In a hundred years would they
be living on other planets?
Would the earth still exist? Would
they engineer themselves genetically
so that disease was a thing of
the past?... What will the weather
be like?... Will they make love?
Maybe there will be more than
two sexes. Will they still believe
life is sacred? Will it matter?
Do we matter?"
Hal Hartley (dir.),
The Book of Life.

"Kafka scrutinizes the smudges
left behind in the deluxe
edition of the book of life
by the fingers of power."
Theodor Adorno, "Notes on Kafka."

"The task of the Tribulation Force
was clear and their goal nothing less
than to stand and fight the enemies
of God during the seven most chaotic
years the planet would ever see."
Tim LaHaye and Jerry B. Jenkins,
Left Behind.

"At least – to pray – is left – is left – /
Oh Jesus – in the Air – /
I know not which thy chamber is – /
I'm knocking – everywhere –"
Emily Dickinson (377).

a shooting star is falling
over Heartland; vapor is rising
from the hills, and from
the vapor a swirling mass
of Eyewitnesses with Halos
like Crowns *(unto them*
was given power); I recognize
"The News" of Illuminati and
Eudaemonians, Cognoscenti,
Glitterati and Euphorians,
and the Twenty-Four / Seven
Blessing of Bagdad the Divine,
"whose name is also the Mormon."

But is my opponent
being Luciferian, playing
"the Ace of Spades" in
Road Warrior's Chinese Deck
(Number 55)?

And is the counter-move
to stop watching, and
break the Daemons' arm lock?

With the on-Screen appearance
of Oscar in the Euphrates theater,
the Pro-Active urge to follow
through on the upward lift
of my feet and legs with
a backward somersault acquires
Hypersupernatural urgency:
There shall be no more delay!

"And if Epiphany's terror
reduced you to shame /
Have your head bobbed
and weaved / Choose a side
to be on / And if the stone
glances off, split didactics
in two / Leave the color
of the mouse trails, /
Don't scream, try between /
If you choose /
If you choose, try to lose /
For the loss of remain
come and start /
Start the game /
I-che-che, che-che-I /
Che-che-che, kah-tah-ko /
Choose to choose /
Choose to choose,
choose to go."
Nico and the Velvet Underground,
"Black Angel's Death Song."

"I never heard / So musical
a discord, such sweet thunder."
W. Shakespeare,
A Midsummer Night's Dream.

"Ellington has always been
intrigued by Shakespeare, 'cause
he said Shakespeare certainly
knew more about people than
anyone he had ever known. Duke

I crunch my stomach.

I lift my legs.

I feel the Daemons loosening
their hold under my armpits,
as my body begins to curl
backward, my legs point up
in the air, and my head
turns upside down.

Facing in the same direction
as the Daemons of 'Istorin, but
upside down on top of them,
with my body fully extended,
what I see in the Blackness
before me are flashes of light—
the light reflecting off the same
Plasma Screen to which my back
is now turned.

The Daemons bear witness
to the flashes of light, which
soon start to manifest traces
of Color; as the Colors increase,
the Daemons cry with pleasure.

A holograph emerges
from the Colored lights,
as of a Tower fallen
by the sea—

also said that the only way
Shakespeare could have known
as much about people as he did
was by hanging out on the corner
or in the pool room. He says
that if William Shakespeare
were alive today, you would
surely find him down at Birdland
listening to jazz."
Billy Strayhorn, quoted in
liner notes, Duke Ellington,
Such Sweet Thunder.

"Raindrops on roses and
whiskers on kittens / Bright
copper kettles and warm woolen
mittens / Brown paper packages
tied up with strings / These are
a few of my favorite things."
Oscar Hammerstein and Richard
Rodgers, "My Favorite Things."

"I am I
because my little dog knows me."
G. Stein,
The Geographical History of America.

"Pugnax had confounded a Zennist
monastery, by answering the classic
koan 'Does a dog possess the Buddha-
nature?' not with 'Mu!' but with 'Yes,
obviously—was there anything else?'"
Thomas Pynchon,

which is ClearChannel,
"the god revealed"
for the Minims and Levelers,
the Ranters and Wreckers,
Shifterians, Absolütists
and Embalmers.

A single Stereophonic Voice,
emitted by the Daemons,
becomes audible and grows louder,
passing back and forth from
my left ear to my right.

I hear fragments,
as from a story or
running commentary:
"...PARADISE SYNDROME...,"
"...RETURN TO TOMORROW...,"
"...THE WAY TO EDEN...,"
"...ASSIGNMENT: EARTH...,"
"...BALANCE OF TERROR...,"
"...OMEGA GLORY...,"
"...WINK OF AN EYE...,"
"...SINS OF THE FATHER..."
"...CITY ON THE EDGE
OF FOREVER..."
while in the holograph before me
(which I see upside down)
the sea is smooth,
shooting stars fill the sky
and the land is slowly rising.

On the good chance that

Against the Day.

"Dog, Buddha nature— /
the full presentation of the whole; /
with a bit of 'has' or 'has not'/
body is lost, life is lost."
Wumen Huikai, "The Koan Mu:
Text, Commentary, and Verse."

"By history I mean to know, to really
know. The rhyme is still 'mystery.'"
Charles Olson,
The Special View of History.

"A *mythos* to the Greek was
primarily just a thing spoken,
uttered by the mouth.
[Note: Our word *mouth* and
μύθος are connected, cf. also
μύζω—all come from the root
mú, lat. *Mu*—to make an audible
sound by opening or closing
the lips.]... From sounds made
by the mouth, to words
spoken and thence to tale or
story the transition is easy."
Jane Harrison,
Themis.

"This is how the angel of history
must look. His face is turned
toward the past. Where a chain
of events appears before *us,*

I am being taken prisoner
by a Vulcan Grand Narrative
in my opponent's Road Map,
I decide to follow through
with my move, and
escape the Daemons' grasp.

With my feet above and head
below, still facing the void
toward which the Daemons
are flying, I continue
the somersault by lowering
my legs in front of me.

At the first touch of pain,
while folding my body,
I feel confusion and then fear.

The Revelation hits me
that I have reached
the First Joke in the Seven
Jokes of Destrudo, according
to Clavé's 100-Yuan
"Full-Body" Treatment
*(the one whose name
is represented by an image,
by a mark, by a number).*

This is the joke about
the Ghosts of Wahhabi:
Shahrazade, who is hiding

he sees one single catastrophe,
which keeps piling wreckage
upon wreckage and hurls it
at his feet. The angel would
like to stay, awaken the dead,
and make whole what has
been smashed. But a storm is
blowing from paradise and has
got caught in his wings; it is
so strong that the angel can no
longer close them. This storm
drives him irresistibly into
the future, to which his back
is turned, while the pile of
debris before him grows
toward the sky. What we call
progress is *this* storm."
Walter Benjamin, "Theses on
the Philosophy of History."

"What counts here—first
and last—is not so-called
knowledge / of so-called
facts, but vision—seeing. /
Seeing here implies Schauen
(as in Weltanschauung) and
is coupled / with fantasy,
with imagination."
Josef Albers,
Interaction of Color, "Introduction."

"In Ecbatana the rainbow is only
visible in a state of holiness. /

from Ali Baba and Al-Quaeda,
meets Jihad, who is running
from Bin Laden and Aladdin...

The pain of the First Joke,
located in the Crown, expands
to include headache and vertigo.

The pain intensifies
with the Second Joke,
located in the Third Eye
(according to Macho),
which precipitates
blurred vision and earache:
this is the joke about
Sharyar, Omar and Hojjr
and the Queen of Mujahedeen.

As my legs move further down
and my head starts to turn
back up toward the Plasma Screen,
my pain takes the added form
of hearing loss, followed by
Ringing in the ears.

At the Third Joke, the joke
about Zobeida and Yamlika,
who walk into a saloon
with the King of Fatwah,
the pain is located
in the Throat, and doubles
(which was, and shall be),
according to Hembra;

The grove to the right among
the ruins is clogged with corn
flowers. / Within each flower is lost
another star another blue corpuscle
of God. / Antares (white) Alpha
Centauri (black) Regulus (purple)
Aldebaran (blue) (even now its blue
not true-blue); orange (Arcturus)
silver (Altair) gold (Vega)."
José Kozer, "Anima."

"And the eye closing my dreams
swimming and blinking /
The eye invades my nights / Night
night the storm / The sparkling
eye with a strange flowering /
The eye sick of images"
Joyce Mansour, "Arab Song"
(tr. S. Gavronsky).

"Yesterday afternoon—afternoon
of Egypt sprinkled with white
ibises—I loved your impossible
eyes beyond the crystal... /
Long ago in another afternoon like
this afternoon of mine, your eyes
spread themselves above the earth,
opened themselves above
the earth like the two mysterious
lotuses of your country."
Dulce Maria Loynaz,
"Love Letter to King Tutankhamen."

dry mouth is followed by fever,
then nasal congestion and finally
Voice deepening, as I hear
myself moaning in torment.

As I continue to lower
my legs and pull them
forward beneath me,
while at the same time
straining to bend my neck
back and lift my eyes
up at the Screen again,
I reach the pain
of the Fourth Joke,
where I experience
anxiety, the first sign
that the end is in sight,
according to Ponché.

This is the joke about Fatima
and the Princesses of Intifada
at the Psychologist's Office:
located in the Heart, the pain
passes beyond anxiety
by adding depression, then
fatigue, followed by malaise—
but I can see the lower
edge of the Screen,
and I feel my arms
begin to slip through
the Daemons' arm lock.

At the same time,

"I rested in the arms of my arms /
I no longer slept / It was night
in the summer, winter in the day /
An eternal shivering of thoughts"
Dora Maar,
"I rested in the arms of my arms."

"This consciousness within her /
Uncurled itself upon the rollers
of objective experience /
Printing impressions /
Vaguely and variedly..."
Mina Loy,
"Ova, Among the Neighbors."

"In custom, one speaks of
the woman's ass— / while
in Bosch it's the ass of man
on display. / Unto this part of
the body—the backside / where
the back surrenders its honest
name— / name given to
the human buttocks— / or
the rump of beasts in an era
(circa 1500) when sodomy /
meant death— / the brilliant
Flemish painter abandons himself
to the ass. / What's up with that?
Outbursts of the libido? / Medieval
queering? Auto-eroticism? /
Bizarre beauty? Over a field with
eyes and a forest with ears— /
the bared asses of Bosch— / asses

through the corner of my eye,
I see that the Blackness
of the surrounding void is changing,
becoming more luminous—
turning Silver, as Bombo says.

The complete shift in the void
from Black to Silver coincides
with the Cough, the difficulty
Breathing, the itching and Redness
linked through the Solar Plexus
to the pain of the Fifth Joke,
about the Brothers of Kabiba
(Sawab, Kafur and Bakhita);
by the time I reach
the threshold of the Sixth Joke—
about the boat ride of Aziz,
Abu-Kir, U-day and Oh-Say—
the light around me
is almost White.

Located in the Belly,
the pain of the Sixth Joke
brings flatulence, muscle cramps,
nausea and weight gain and,
according to Mambo
(behold I come as a thief),
negates the idea that the end
is in sight, on the chance
that the torment is endless.

with flutes or coins of gold or
swallows, / asses with sticks, ass
with anaphora— / special asses—
the core of the libido. / Here,
asses are not autonomous— /
most of them are entangled."
Amanda Berenguer, "The Asses
of Bosch" (tr. Kent Johnson (*RIP*)).

"Blow after blow, my heart /
couldn't survive this beating. /
Then—how can I explain it? /
I came to my senses. I said, /
Why do I suffer? What lover /
ever had so much pleasure?"
Sor Juana Ines de la Cruz,
"Love opened a mortal wound."
(tr. J. Larkin and J. Manrique).

"Its face was like the face
she had seen in some medieval
paintings where the martyr's
limbs are being sawed off and
his expression says he is being
deprived of nothing essential."
Flannery O'Connor,
The Violent Bear It Away.

"They were wrapped in
an intensity of listening
which was miraculously
devoid of anxiety.
Was this what the victims

At the Root level,
the pain of the Seventh Joke,
about the Last Poets of Jezeera
—Abu Nowas, Doryad, Find,
Murakish and Ishak—
becomes extreme,
as weakness gives way
to tremors, palpitations
and finally convulsions...
but then, incomprehensibly,
paradoxical excitement sets in,
as noted by Rumba,
and pain at the Root level
turns to pleasure.

There came a Great Voice,
saying, "It is done!"

I experience burning, followed by
chills and sweating; then swelling.

I sense bliss, ecstasy,
approaching from the Root...

With my head lifted toward
the Screen, my back arched,
and my legs hanging beneath me,
the pressure on my arms from
the Daemons' hold seems reflected
in the intensity of the White
light that surrounds me.

I enter a realm of enchantment,

of torture felt when they
passed through the extremity
of pain into peace?"
P. D. James,
Children of Men.

"In his hands I saw a great golden
spear, and at the iron tip there
appeared to be a point of fire.
This he plunged into my heart
several times so that it penetrated to
my entrails. When he pulled it out,
I felt that he took them with it,
and left me utterly consumed
by the great love of God.
The pain was so severe that
it made me utter several moans.
The sweetness caused by
this intense pain is so extreme
that one cannot possibly wish it
to cease, nor is one's soul then
content with anything but God."
Teresa of Avila,
The Life of Saint Teresa of Avila
by Herself.

"Yet I would lose no sting,
would wish no torture less; /
The more that anguish racks,
the earlier it will bless; /
And robed in fires of hell,
or bright with heavenly shine, /
If it but herald death,

of overwhelming beauty and
consummate grace, that unfolds
before me, endlessly removed
from the confines of this Game.

All the islands disappeared,
all the mountains vanished.

Secular thought
likens my bliss
to the Heaven
that Saturn discovers
at Death, after the pain
of twenty-eight Years;
in the Cyclical view,
bliss is like the Empyrean
to which the Born-Again
Judas escapes after the pain
of thirty-three Lifetimes.

Then the Daemons let go,
just as my pleasure
turns extreme.

After a short drop,
I land flat on my stomach.

Lifting my head to regain
my bearings, I see a crevice
blocked by two vertical bars
through which a Colorless

the vision is divine."
Emily Brontë, "The Prisoner."

"Soon, sacrilege penetrated
my life and took hold of it
through a liberating *ave maria*.
'Hail! Mary, shit, God.'"
Laure (Colette Peignot),
Story of a Little Girl.

"it is the question of value /
which opens again /
as though we well were /
back in Al 'Arabi's / circumvallum"
C. Olson,
Maximus Poems IV, V, VI.

"The Arab leaders are liars; lying
is part of the Arab culture in
the same way that truth-telling
and honest speech're American....
They write by cutting chunks out
of all-ready written texts and
in other ways defacing traditions:
changing important names into
silly ones, making dirty jokes
out of matters that should be
of the utmost importance to us
such as nuclear warfare."
Kathy Acker,
Don Quixote.

"For their floundering about

gray mist is escaping:
the bars are probably
the Daemons of 'Istorin
in Subtle Form...

To my relief,
the ground beneath me
feels soft, warm and wet.

I pick myself up
off the floor,
and understand that
I am in a large cavern;
Shadows are shooting
across the ceiling and walls
in uneven bursts, flashing
erratically all around me.

Gradually I notice a Sound
in the distance, like the snapping
of fingers, irregular yet persistent;
it seems to trigger new flights
of Shadow over the rock face.

There is a second entrance at
the far side of the cavern,
opposite the crevice where
the Metal bars block the way
and the mist still lingers.

The percussive Sound continues

is lengthy, their disputes many,
their views spread far apart,
their ways divergent and convergent
...They use the appearance of their
mathematical and logical sciences
as evidential proof for the truth
of their metaphysical sciences..."
Al-Ghazali,
The Incoherence of the Philosophers.

"In the beginning there is only
silence, *Sigē*...The silence of
the subject opens the space of
testimony. There are two lines:
Sigē-testimony-truth and
Logos-subject-knowledge,
which run along one single
plane and cross each other at
every point. Witness and subject
are the two faces of a single
testimony, like the witness and
the 'Muslim' at Auschwitz."
Giorgio Agamben,
"Testimony and Truth."

"No one seemed to want to admit
that the cruelty was a part of a moral
cancer that was spreading through
the whole of the Middle East."
Etel Adnan,
Sitt Marie-Rose.

"From its window the Absolute

as I walk across the cavern,
but its echo diminishes
as I enter a second, smaller
chamber, in which the
stone conspires to dampen Sound—
like the Airpod Walls
in Berlin's Minoan Mall.

Despite the muffled Sound,
with each new pulse the Shadows
scurry across the cavern's surface.

The percussive Sound that stirs
the Shadows becomes louder
as I reach a wooden barricade
with a turnstile in it, toward
the end of the second chamber.

Beyond the turnstile the cavern
splits into two terminal chambers.

The Sound seems to issue
from the cave on the left,
but it appears empty;
the cave on the right
turns at the end.

I figure that the rock formations
are diverting the Sound and creating
an illusion, like the Lithophones
at the "Battle of Narratives"

in profile contemplates
its confines: the celestial sounds
propagate through the old pond
where metal & loam, past & ends,
bone & vocable come to slake
their thirst. Mud explodes &
consciousness sails against
the current. In this immense opacity
of contemplation where air
is the anticipation of darkness, I see
the singular rise in multiples from
the bottom of the amphora & wait
in the cold of the real to be smashed."
Abdel Kader El Janabi,
"Against Ibn Arabi" (tr. P. Joris,
in *Arabia (Not So) Deserta*).

"And as for risk: the real risks
of any artist are taken
in the work, in pushing the work
to the limits of what is possible,
in the attempt to increase
the sum of what is possible to think."
Salman Rushdie,
"Imaginary Homelands."

"The trouble is, it is very difficult,
to be both a poet and, an historian."
Charles Olson,
Mayan Letters.

"How can you tell the legend
from the fact on these worlds

in Glaucon's *Rest-of-World Story*.

So I go through the turnstile,
down to the end
of the cave on the right.

There, in an alcove
off to the side, I find
a Wishing Well,
at the bottom of which
sits a man covered in dirt,
with Glass Beads around his neck
and long knotted hair.

He has both legs wrapped
behind the back of his head.

The Sound is coming
from the two wooden blocks
that he holds in his hands:
a Blue block in the form
of a square peg
in one hand,
and, in the other,
a Red block
with a round hole in it.

I recognize the Cave Man
described in *Nintendo's Bestiary*.

He is knocking
the two blocks together,
trying to fit one

that lie so many years away?"
Ursula Le Guin,
Rocannon's World.

"The meaning of this section
is to call attention to the wrong
paths of meditation so that
one can enter the place of power
instead of the caves of fantasy."
The Secret of the Golden Flower
(tr. R. Wilhelm).

"'I stepped through' 'the archway'
'& there was' 'another door' /
'immediately' 'before me'
'another round entrance' 'It led' /
'into a cavern' 'which was walled
with' 'gears & clockwork—' /
'a large room' 'with a rock floor'
'whose walls were' 'composed of' /
'large round gears,' 'with
rounded edges,' 'turning' 'in semi-
darkness—' / 'the room was lit to'
'twilight level:' 'the gears were
colored' 'blue and gray' 'The round
disks' surfaces' 'as I looked at them'
'began to / change' 'to change'
'Images' 'appeared on them'
'soon becoming' 'other / images'"
Alice Notley,
The Descent of Alette.

"Imagine that there are people

into the other—
thereby producing the Sound
that is causing the Shadows
to scatter.

The Cave Man is in a trance
and does not see me.

He shows signs of stress:
he is drooling,
his lips are trembling,
and, as he mumbles to himself,
he seems torn between
laughing one moment
and crying the next.

As if my unseen presence
were a new factor adding
to his difficulties, his agitation
increases: he shouts in anger
and frustration, then breaks
into wild laughter, knocking
the wooden blocks together with
renewed effort, while his body
trembles more violently
and the sweat pours over him.

Then I detect a strange odor,
and I see that smoke
is streaming from his nose,
that his skin is shining,
changing Color.

living in a cave deep underground.
The cavern has a mouth that opens
to the light above, and a passage
exists from this all the way down
to the people... They cannot move.
All they can do is stare directly
forward... Imagine that far above
and behind them blazes a great fire.
Between this fire and the captives,
a low partition is erected along
a path... Look and you will also see
other people carrying objects back
and forth along the partition...
Now, tell me if you suppose
it's possible that these captives ever
saw anything of themselves or one
another, other than the shadows
flitting across the cavern wall
before them?... Undoubtedly, such
captives would consider the truth
to be nothing but the shadows
of the carved objects."
Plato,
The Republic.

"Knowledge of the fact
differs from knowledge of
the reason for the fact."
Aristotle,
Posterior Analytics.

"Western culture is on the verge of
adjusting its dominant Aristotelian

Before I know what is happening
his entire body Ignites.

As I step back from
the Flames, the Cave Man's
Spontaneous Combustion
produces a Pillar of Fire
that reaches the ceiling
and lights up the entire cavern
behind me, dispelling
all the Shadows.

In the brilliant light
of the Pillar of Fire,
which emits an intense,
rumbling Sound,
the cave walls reveal
Multicolor Paintings,
the largest and foremost
of which represent
four constellations:
The Bull of Heaven,
The Golden Ram,
The Lioness,
and The Centaurian Archer.

Yet the constellations are not
accurately represented;
they form a spiral
on the ceiling and spread
outward onto the walls,

mode of scientific materialism to allow for the partial reemergence of Platonic idealism. Far from being a new event, this kind of Zeitgeist rollover happens regularly in our culture. The last major turn took place in the seventeenth and early eighteenth centuries, when the Platonism of natural philosophy and the Christian cosmos gave way first to the Protestant Reformation and the scientific revolution, then to Enlightenment rationalism, and ultimately to empirical materialism."

Victoria Nelson,
The Secret Life of Puppets.

"The contemporary scene is literally saturated with the 'modern' heirs of Plato. Each of these heirs denounces his 'other,' just as the philosopher denounced the sophists, accused them of exploiting that which he himself had triumphed over. They include not only the heirs of Plato, but those philosophers who, following the sophists, were used as an argument to demonstrate the need for a foundation. What, in Plato's test, can be read as a network of analogies isolating the terrible instability of

where disparate constellations
from other parts of the Heavens
are reproduced in different sizes,
and are grouped with them:
The Snake,
with The Sphinx,
The Crocodile,
The Rabbit
and the Megaloceros;
nearby, The Bat,
with The Cockroach,
The Chick,
The Racoon
and The Satyr;
further out, The Cats,
beside The Phoenix,
The Pangolin,
The Mermaid
and The Golem;
and beyond,
with The Porcupine,
The Sleeping Dog,
The Elephant Man,
The Four Horses and
The Princess-in-Chains.

To my dismay, however,
I have no frame of reference,
no Revelation to guide me
at this Dead End.

I head back toward
the other terminal chamber,

the sophist-pharmakon has today
split into a number of
'modern practices' (scientific,
medical, political, technological,
psychoanalytic, pedagogical)
that have been introduced,
just as Platonic philosophy
in its time, as disqualifying
their other—charlatan, populist,
ideologue, astrologer, magician,
hypnotist, charismatic teacher."
Isabelle Stengers,
Cosmopolitics.

"All that culture from a thousand
years ago, that philosophy,
that wisdom—Plato, Aristotle,
Socrates—what happened to it?
It should have prevented this."
Bob Dylan,
Nobel prize acceptance speech
(10 Dec. 2016).

"What counts is the direction
of the will... The name
of the Fascist era is *Voluntas.*"
Ezra Pound, "A Visiting Card."

"Beginning again and again
is a natural thing even when
there is a series. / Beginning
again and again and again
explaining composition and

when suddenly I see
the Pillar of Fire sputtering.

I turn to watch it dwindle
and go out.

Despite the absence of Fire
the Paintings are still there,
as luminous as before,
as if projected from a light
within the rock;
but at the same time
a man's distant laughter
begins to echo in the cave...

It carried me away
in the Spirit
into the wilderness.

Picking up my lead from
the "Star Passage Fragment(s)"
in *The Player's Guide to Endtimes,*
I head again toward
the other chamber.

The turnstile in the barricade
nearby has started revolving
on its own, leading inward,
as if channeling the direction
of my movement, and bringing
the laughter closer.

time is a natural thing."
Gertrude Stein,
"Composition as Explanation."

"Now reasoning is an argument
in which, certain things
being laid down, something other
than these necessarily
comes about through them."
Aristotle,
The Topics.

"...The more a writing is a writing
the more no outside is outside
outside is inside inside is inside."
Gertrude Stein, *Narration*.

"Wait. Ha there.
Fa there. Nil too. Lok!"
William Golding,
The Inheritors.

"If Brun started Broud, and Broud
started Durc, does that mean Durc
is part of Brun, too? And Brac and
Grev? Brun and Creb are sibblings...
Does that mean Durc is part of
Creb, too? And what about Iza?"
Jean M. Auel,
Clan of the Cave Bear.

"Naoh is master of Fire!"
J-. H. Rosny *(Aîné),*

Quest for Fire.

In the second terminal chamber,
the largest and most prominent
constellation is The Godfather,
who is looking down from
the ceiling with his hands opened
to four large constellations
on the walls:
The Sea Goat and
The Twins on one side,
The Winged Virgin and
The Hammer on the other.

As in the first cave,
the dominant constellations
are misrepresented next to others
of varying size; moreover,
some are superimposed and share
common features, or overlap.

Then I notice that The Godfather
is connected with both
The Twins on the left and
The Hammer on the right
by way of The Charioteer,
which is contained within
The Godfather's torso:
to the left, The Charioteer
is connected to The Twins
through a cluster that spans
The Winged Horse,
The Druids
and The Confidence Man;

"We are almost certain that fire
is precisely the first object,
the first phenomenon, on which
the human mind reflected;
among all phenomena, fire alone
is sufficiently prized by prehistoric
man to wake in him the desire
for knowledge, and this mainly
because it accompanies the desire
for love. No doubt it has often
been stated that the conquest
of fire definitely separated man
from the animal, but perhaps
it has not been noticed that
the mind in its primitive state,
together with its poetry and
its knowledge, had been developed
in meditation before a fire."
Gaston Bachelard,
The Psychoanalysis of Fire.

"A slight draft having been detected
between the rocks blocking
the hollow, a small group of
speleologists started clearing
a path in the summer of 1994
under the direction of Michel Rosa
(aka "Baba"). They were stopped by
a prominent rock formation that
blocked the way, and demolition
was deferred to a later expedition.

on the right, it rejoins
The Hammer
across The Dragon,
The Troll and
The Game Players of Titan.

It is in this arc overseen
by The Godfather—
extending from The Twins
to The Hammer
by way of The Charioteer—
together with
the overlapping
constellations of
The Sleeping Dog
and The Prophet,
below The Godfather's
left hand, and
The Skywalker
and The Emperor
above his right hand,
that I retrace the larger outline
of The White Humvee
encrypted in the whole,
and come to a Revelation:
<u>The Godfather sits</u>
<u>in The White Humvee.</u>

Behold he that sat upon it
was called Faithful and true...
There are many Crowns
upon his head; and he has
a name written, that no one

The cavity at the time was known
to speleologists as 'Baba's Hole.'
Several months later, the 18th
of December 1994, Jean-Marie
Chauvet decided to try again."
Jean Clottes,
La Grotte du Pont d'Arc.

"Human laughter began
somewhere. Perhaps not with
Neanderthal; but Lascaux Man
laughed, of that we may
be sure. And we forget what
a relief, what an unburdening
new-born laughter must
have been: it requires all
of knowledge's weighty
seriousness to make us forget."
George Bataille,
Lascaux.

"History acts fundamentally and
goes through many phases when
it carries obsolete forms of life
into the grave. The last phase
of the universal historic form is
its comedy. . . . Why such a march
of history? This is necessary
in order that mankind could
say a gay farewell to its past."
Karl Marx,
Critique of Hegel's Philosophy
of Right.

knows, but for himself.

Almost at once,
observing the constellations
of The Winged Virgin
and The Sea Goat,
I discover the outline
of The First Lady,
in a cluster that runs
from the Virgin's Wings
to the Horns
on the Goat's head,
by way of The Vampire,
The Revelator
and The Adept;
in the larger picture,
The First Lady is sitting
astride The Beast of Peace,
which is configured
across her midsection
by The Adversary,
The Joculator
and The Alien.

She is seated on many waters
upon a Red-Colored Beast having
seven heads and ten Horns...
And the woman was arrayed
in Red and Pink, and decked
with precious stones and pearls,
and upon her forehead
was a name written—MYSTERY,
WATCHINGUN THE GREAT,

"Given the specific requirements
of the modern sensibility, it is
increasingly doubtful that any
poetic, artistic, or scientific work,
any philosophical or social system
that does not contain *this kind* of
humor will not leave a great deal
to be desired, will not be condemned
more or less rapidly to perish...
We are touching upon a burning
subject; we are headed straight into
a land of fire: the gale winds
of passion are alternately with us
and against us from the moment
we consider lifting the veil
from this type of humor..."
André Breton (ed.),
Anthology of Black Humor.

"I must have led a sad life
in those days. Nervous irritation
forced me, at times, upon
frightful excesses: but terror
from anomalous symptoms sooner
or later forced me back. This terror
was strengthened by the vague
hypotheses current at that period
about *spontaneous combustion*.
Might I not myself take leave of
the literary world in that fashion?"
Thomas DeQuincy,
Confessions of an English

MOTHER OF ALL THE EARTH...

The Sound of the laughter
has now increased,
and as I look behind me
I see the turnstile moving
in the other direction.

I go back and slip
through the turnstile
into the middle cavern.

As before, Sound is quieted
and loses its echo, although
I can still hear the laughter;
like the terminal chambers,
this one is covered with signs
left by the Pillar of Fire.

Here, however, there are
only Abstrakt symbols,
hundreds of them, beginning
with The Cutting Edge
on the ceiling, near the turnstile,
a glyph which I recognize
as the First Gate in Raytheon's
Double-Perimeter Fence:
there comes a sharp Sword...

My assumption is that
the Second Gate will be

Opium-Eater.

"He got set on fire in his bowels
through overdrinking. Yes,
all of a sudden there burst from him
a blue flame, and he smouldered
and smouldered until he had turned
as black as a piece of charcoal!"
Nikolai Gogol,
Dead Souls.

"Between the publication of Charles
Bockden Brown's *Wieland* in
1798 and Zola's *Docteur Pascal* in
1893, no fewer than nine fictional
characters burst into flames."
Jessica Warner,
Craze: Gin and Debauchery
in an Age of Reason.

"You catch fire
or you don't catch fire."
H. D.,
End to Torment.

"And therefore I raise my glass
to you, writers,
the engineers of the soul."
Joseph Stalin, "Speech at home
of Maxim Gorky" (26 Oct. 1932).

"This is a catastrophic universe,
always; and subject to sudden

represented by the glyph
of The Kinetic Energy Rod...
the Rod of Metal...

But again I cannot
make sense of the signs:
while a group of dots
suggests Visible Light Cells
or Blinking Stars
in a Suppression Cloud,
an adjacent series of notches
points to Brilliant Pebbles
or Microwave Pills
from a Repulsion Field.

Lines drawn out of holes
function as Cheyenne Flechettes
or Aleutian Air Spikes;
parallel lines constitute
a Floating Platform or
Infrared Near Field;
triangles, rectangles
and quadrilateral grids
refer to the Hyperspectral Image
of a Multi-Layered Shield
or Threat Detector.

The association of ovals,
whorls, spirals and Red disks
with the Claviforms and
Penniforms of Boing,
like the Niké Lightning Bolts
cutting across the Techniforms

reversals, upheavals, changes,
cataclysms, with joy never
anything but the song of
substance under pressure forced
into new forms and shapes."
Doris Lessing,
Shikasta.

"...Celestial motions are... an immense
symphony of desire and nostalgia
for a boundless perfection."
Henry Corbin,
Avicenna and the Visionary Recital.

"For back in the mists of ancient
time, in the great and glorious
days of the former galactic
empire, life was wild, rich
and, on the whole, tax-free...
Many men, of course, became
extremely rich, but this was
perfectly natural and nothing
to be ashamed of because
no one was really poor, at least,
no one worth speaking of."
Douglas Adams,
The Hitchhiker's Guide to the Galaxy.

"'There is nothing you can do
that profit does not enter into,
and fear of loss, and the wish
for power. You cannot say good
morning without knowing which

of Norad, can be read
as the Flexible Membrane
of a High-Energy Array
or the Grand Electric Light
Signature of a ProSpace Pulse.

At the end of the cavern,
instead of The Kinetic
Energy Rod, I find the glyph
of The Rod Bundle,
which would mark the closure
of the Double Gate
according to 'Nvidia;
as I step beyond it,
the laughter becomes much
louder, frenetic, while overhead
the entire dome of the big
cavern, through which
I first entered, presents
an elaborate network of signs.

What has also changed
is that spread out
on the ground before me—
like a new threshold or limit
marking the entrance
to the main cavern—
lie the Cave Man's bones,
which I recognize
from the string of Glass Beads
circling the neck.

of you is "superior" to the other,
or trying to prove it. You cannot
act like a brother to other people,
you must manipulate them, or
command them, or obey them, or
trick them. You cannot touch
another person, yet they will
not leave you alone. There is
no freedom. It is a box—'"
Ursula Le Guin,
The Dispossessed.

"I won't tell you about truth, /
because the word's going to die /
and others / will need it."
Carilda Oliver Labra,
"Of the Word."

"The secret of great fortunes
with no apparent cause
is a forgotten crime, because
it was properly done."
Honoré de Balzac,
Father Goriot, rephrased as
"Behind every great fortune
there is a crime," in Mario Puzo,
The Godfather, epigraph.

"You can act like a man!"
in *The Godfather*
(dir. Francis Ford Coppola).

"What would happen if one woman

Standing behind the boundary
drawn by the Cave Man's
skeleton, while the laughter
keeps getting louder, I look up
at the decorated ceiling and
identify two large configurations:
The Superman... holding the key
of the bottomless pit and
a Great Chain in his hand...
and The Holy Ghost
in The Doomsday Machine.

The Superman
and The Holy Ghost
in the Doomsday Machine
intersect at the ceiling's center,
across The Water Bearer,
who pours water
into The Machine
and onto The Ghost.

The Superman spans
half the ceiling:
his brain is contained
within The Water Jar,
and is formed
by the constellations
of The One-Eyed Triangle,
The Horned Vulva
and The Flaming Crown.

The whole head and

told the truth about her life? /
The world would split open."
Muriel Rukeyser, "Käthe Kollwitz."

"A woman in the shape
of a monster / a monster
in the shape of a woman /
the skies are full of them."
Adrienne Rich, "Planetarium."

"'Of course we enjoy
your inventions and we do
appreciate your evolutionary role.
But you must see there's
a problem. As I understand it,
what you protected people from
was largely other males, wasn't it?'"
James Tiptree, Jr. (Alice B. Sheldon),
"Houston, Houston, Do You Read?"

"For the fierceness of space
does not exceed mankind's."
Harry Martinson,
Aniara, 100 (tr. S. Klass, L. Sjöberg).

"This is Ursa Major. / Caught on
June 4, '64, / by a hunter sputnik. /
(Don't touch the stars / on its skin) /
Wanted: / a trainer."
Nicolás Guillén, "Ursa Major."

"ALL GUNS MUST BE BOOMER-RANGS."
Madeline Gins, "What the President

the shoulders emerge
from The Dancing Sorcerer,
The Three Brothers,
The Helicoid Body
and The Tax Collector,
while the rest
of The Superman
is outlined along a dense
cluster that includes
The Celestial Bandit,
The Comforter,
The Saboteur,
The Yin Phallus,
The Yang Phallus,
The Trash Master
and The Chosen.

The Holy Ghost
in The Doomsday Machine
is more hidden.

The Holy Ghost itself seems
to fall, or bridge the gap,
between The River of Darkness
and The Pharaoh in The Pi Hut...
between The Door of Percipience
and Îsîs under The Decision Tree...
between Eva and Ave and
the Red "Sweat and Tears"
of King Floyd.

By contrast, The Doomsday
Machine becomes manifest

Will Say and Do!!"

"I sdrive to dddeflect at a blow
the blow."
César Vallejo,
Trilce, IX (tr. C. Eshleman).

"Either we use our 'speed'
for World Completion or
allow its material analogy
to be used by the Druid Specter
to fuel the fires of 'Star Wars.'"
John Clarke,
From Feathers to Iron.

"And staring me straight in the eyes, /
And threatening impending death, /
Is an enormous star."
Anna Akhmatova, "Requiem"
(tr. J. Hemschemeyer).

"'Warning,' the computer announced,
blanking out the distress call.
'We have entered the Neutral Zone.
Warning.'"
Vonda McIntyre,
Star Trek: Duty, Honor, Redemption.

"Those skilled in defense hide
in the deepest depths of
the earth, those skilled in attack
maneuver in the highest heights
of the sky. Therefore they can

in the convergence between
two groups of constellations:
on one side,
The United Technologies
of The Argo—
The Keel,
The Compass,
The Stern,
The Sail—
and, on the other side,
The MasterCard to
The Broken World Axis,
at the margins of which
lie The Green Box,
The Metal Cage
and The Lyre,
The Swarmbot and
The Full Spectrum Probe,
The Naacal Stampo and
The Archaen Furnace,
The Smagardine Table
of Android the Giant,
and The Clock.

The laughter is at a frenzied
pitch, echoing
throughout the cavern.

I start to hear,
behind the laughter,
the Voices of the constellations
speaking to each other
in a rumble of disconnected

preserve themselves and
achieve complete victory."
Sun Tzu,
The Art of War.

"The military's space-based systems
underpin everything:
communications, surveillance,
guided munitions, nuclear
command and control...
In the case of widespread
destruction, hurricane tracking,
search-and-rescue locators,
financial transactions, emergency
messages could all go dark."
Rachel Riederer, "Ad Astra."

"reading the cards, the Tarot said /
'you will converse with the intellect
of primordial stars and they will /
speak in fragments to you, poet'"
Anne Waldman,
*The Iovis Tril*ogy, Book III.

"Cyberspace has... opened doors
for those intent on achieving
criminal aims. Cyber blackmail,
identity theft and fraud are some
of the ways in which these have
been previously witnessed.
As historical cases demonstrate,
however, threats from cyberspace
do not merely end there."

words and phrases that
make no sense to me,
like the Conversations
in Tati's Last Stand.

Backing away from the bones
of the Cave Man, I return
to the middle cavern—but instead
of becoming subdued, this time
the Sound stays just as loud.

In terror, I wonder
if the Wishing Well
in the terminal chamber,
since the Pillar of Fire's
extinction, is now
a bottomless Abyss—
and whether the Voices
and the mad laughter
are trapped inside my head...

Having at last stepped
across the threshold
of the Cave Man's bones,
I write from here,
past the skeleton,
beyond the Double Gate
of Paracalypse, where
The Player's Guide to Endtimes
breaks off with a curse.

Daniele Hadi Irandoost,
"Cybersecurity."

"here we have lost / nuance,
the subtle crumbles / like a house of
cards / w/ all / the Trumps removed."
Diane di Prima,
Loba,
"The Mask is the Path of the Star."

"I thought I had cured you of laughing!"
Emily Brontë,
Wuthering Heights.

"Then a terrible thing happened
to me. I started to laugh and
could not stop. Tears poured
down my face and I covered
my mouth with my hand, hoping
they would think I had a secret
sorrow and was weeping and
not laughing. I left and sat down
on the nearest bench where
I laughed and laughed and laughed."
Leonora Carrington,
The Hearing Trumpet.

"Her real laugh is the worst
human sound I have ever heard:
a hard, screeching yell that ends
in gasps and rusty sobbing,
as if some mechanical vulture
on a gigantic garbage heap

Near my point of entry
on the other side
of the chamber
as in a cavernous God's House
where Gotham has tumbled
again into Self-Division and
bad luck, the gray mist hides
the two bars in the crevice.

Is this the Trick
in the Game of *win-lose*:
like a Magickal Child
lost in the past, *The Fool*
falls into place at the end,
where it finds you?

Your lover,

A.

on the surface of the moon
were giving one forced shriek
for the death of all organic life."
Joanna Russ,
The Female Man.

"but laugh, they say, laugh, laugh,
like children... / laugh they say,
like simpletons, like idiots, / fools
and poets; laugh the world away, /
laugh, laugh and place your flowers
on the shrine of Teut, Agad, Hana,
Sila, / who share your name, *Soleil*."
H. D.,
Hermetic Definitions.

The Sun

Don Cherry, "Trans-Love Airways,"
in *Relativity Suite*.

"Nothing more beautiful under
the sun than to be under / the sun..."
Ingeborg Bachmann, "Under the Sun."

"a [ ] yellow A sun [ ]
a small craft [ ] a boat
a [ ] red [ ] blue /
a quiet blue sun on a card table
a red which is blue and a wheel /
A solar sun a lunar sun
a starry sun a nebular sun /
A yellow sun [ ] A green sun
a yellow sun... / A Pharaonic [ ]
boat an Egyptian sun a solar
universe and a universal sun"
Etel Adnan,
The Arab Apocalypse.

My love,

We spiral endlessly down,
bow-first, as if screwing
our way into
a bottomless Abyss.

The Gravity Handler has
adjusted for weightlessness,
helping us stay in control,
despite what *Togari-Chōji*
recent Spirit of the Keel,
calls the "poetry virus"
affecting us since the Death
of Avon the Poetess.

Avon's struggle was epic,
from the time the ship
finally started to move,
after the Chasm first opened
in the seafloor.

Rosetta is with Scard'nelli,
and with the still-dreaming
Cowabunga, having just
left Marlboro and Wang
at the wheel.

"These are the roads that must
be followed / to find the way /
to these blue fields /
where dazzling navigators /
sleep hundreds of meters deep"
Alice Rahon,
"Solitary like planets in space."

"If I could only / have covered
your / Eyes so you wouldn't /
have seen the Water—"
Emily Dickinson (H B162).

"i have been stuck / in the infernal
mud of the same river twice"
Wanda Coleman,
"I Ain't Yo Earthmama."

"Is it the molten core of the earth /
I am swimming in? I turn, melting /
In some murkiness / Trying again
and again / To open my eyes."
Diane di Prima,
Loba, "Madness of the Loba."

"And the earth is the sun,
how is it that I never saw before
that the earth is the sun?"
Clarice Lispector,
The Passion According to G. H.

"The unchained sun, in raging thirst, /
Feeds the last day to the first."

Sinbad too is Dead.

Ah, Rosetta...

Trouble in the depths
of some enchanted
Notes Toward a Code Supreme,
long-haired twin of Thebes.

As the ship pursues
its endless dive, with most
systems down, she whispers
her mantra non-stop:
"*This...* is Avon's
Crazy Path of the Corkscrew,
my friends!"

According to Sony and Thebes,
Rosetta, in her Deep Thought,
is in deep denial about
the viral, Anti-fragilistic
Hidden Writing downloaded
onto the Spirit-of-the-Keel
platform, and the Metacomik
negative feedback cycle that
triggered Avon's post-Pegasus
Poetry Meltdown Event.

We pursue our descent
on the assumption

Djuna Barnes, "Transfiguration."

"It is an alchemist's dream
to eat the sun."
Anne Waldman,
The Iovis Trilogy, Book II.

"The sun is one foot wide."
Herakleitos.

"Who would not want
a thought that blocks all
passage through it, that does
not let itself be breached?
Who would not want
an impenetrable meaning,
a meaning that has consistency
and resistance? For it is
the communication of this
resistance that makes me
'endowed with meaning'..."
Jean-Luc Nancy *(RIP),*
"The Weight of a Thought."

"In landlessness alone
resides the highest truth."
Herman Melville,
Moby Dick.

"Don Quixote... wasn't quite
sure where she was. Being land-
less, like a sailor wafting upon
always unknown waves, who goes

that Sony and Thebes
are probably right.

The Meltdown that has
rocked the ship on our
spiral plunge into the Abyss
might have been avoided,
if the Big Idea proposed by
Rosetta's Abstrakt Workshop
for opening a bottomless
Chasm in the seafloor
had gone according to plan.

It was after the radar blip
in the Voice message of
Chōji-Midare, Spirit of
the Keel, first came through
—*"D-d-don't think twice!"*—
and the Conversation
between Avon the Poetess and
the spit of Commander Exprès
(as interpreted by Venus)
temporarily stopped,
that Rosetta got the idea
of an Abstrakt Workshop for
figuring out what to do next,
given the ship's Being-Stuck
at the bottom of the sea.

Sony, speaking for
Scard'nelli, agreed—

hither and thither and isn't really able to go anywhere, certainly not anywhere he or she wants to, as if he or she wanted to go anywhere, but only going wherever those unknowable forces the waves took him or her either of their own volition or not of their own volition."
Kathy Acker,
Don Quixote.

"As soon as the earth's crust cooled enough, the rains began to fall. Never have there been such rains since that time. They fell continuously, day and night, days passing into months, into years, into centuries."
Rachel Carson,
The Sea Around Us.

"I've been out in front of a dozen dead oceans / I've been ten thousand miles in the mouth of a graveyard / And it's a hard, and it's a hard, it's a hard, and it's a hard, / And it's a hard rain's a-gonna fall."
Bob Dylan,
"A Hard Rain's A-Gonna Fall."

"There is another sky, /
Ever serene and fair, /
And there is another sunshine /

at which point *Kawazuko-Midare,* Spirit of the Keel, chimed in with: *"The medium is the message!"*

So Avon the Poetess, from her station at the bottom of the ship—below which her dangling skeleton-legs, still attached to her torso, now lay buried in the sea-floor's slime—announced the start of a Workshop on the Plastic Language of Lemurian Problem Solving, as outlined by Zoomer and Gummies in *The Daze of Dark Enlightenment.*

Rosetta was first to sign up for the Workshop; followed by Sony and Thebes; then Cowabunga; and finally Scard'nelli and ben-Cnopee.

Ben-Cnopee began with the concept that raising the ship back to the surface meant *"Communicate with Care."*

Though it be darkness there."
E. Dickinson (2).

"I was snagged upon a shoal of
a river of tears. Was that the start
of this drift to deeper waters?"
Murasaki Shikibu,
The Tale of Genji.

"Now madness half shadows /
My soul with its wing, /
And makes it drunk with fiery wine /
And beckons toward the black ravine."
Anna Akhmatova, "Requiem"
(tr. J. Hemschemeyer).

"Rather, I'll go down to my son
in Sheol mourning!"
Genesis 37:35.

"The love of death, the desire
for death, is a secret to which
we shut our eyes so that we may
look and not see, so that we may
sleep and dream. If we didn't shut
our eyes, we'd see only emptiness,
black, white, and broken shapes."
Julia Kristeva,
The Samurai.

"The duplication of self-consciousness
within itself, which is essential in
the Notion of Spirit, is thus here

Almost at once,
Commander Exprès
Coughed Up and,
according to Venus's
reading, the projected spit
in the Cauldron read:
*"Exchange Education for
Function and Growth."*

Rosetta and Scard'nelli joined
the discussion next, adding,
respectively: *"Identity's
Information Modernizes
the Management Model,"*
and *"Plan for Progress."*

But after Cowabunga
responded with *"Process
the Problem,"* the Workshop
came to the realization
that there was no way to
lift the ship to the surface.

Then the more radical
thought occurred
of creating a Dark-
Energy Chasm directly
under the hull,
following Sony's insight
that *"Structure is
the Substance of System,"*
and Thebes's rejoinder:
"Service is the Strategy

before us, but not yet in its unity:
the *Unhappy Consciousness* is
the consciousness of self as a dual-
natured, merely contradictory being."
G. W. F. Hegel,
The Phenomenology of Spirit.

"I came into a place mute of all light..."
Dante Alighieri,
The Divine Comedy: Inferno
(tr. H. W. Longfellow).

"A cry rose from the army
of Irán: The sun hath wandered
from its way in heaven!"
Firdasi,
The Shahnama, Vol. IV.

"The mystic epic is that of
the exile, who, having come
into a strange world, is on the road
of homecoming to his own country."
Henry Corbin, "On the meaning
of Music in Persian Mysticism"
(tr. K. Raine), quoted in
Tom Cheetham,
All the World an Icon.

"When all the particles of the air /
Are filled with the glow of the sun /
They all enter the dance, the dance,
And never complain of the whirling!"
Rumi,

for Salvation."

The Great Notion
was to open a bottomless
Chasm in the seafloor
beneath us, and dwell
in the possibility that
the ship's free fall
would sooner or later
reverse, when the Chasm
closed and, theoretically,
Vapor Pressure from
the phantom Dilation Field
would slingshot the ship
back to the surface.

Finally, in a moment
of breakthrough,
as if speaking
at once for everyone
in the Workshop,
Avon whispered:
"Song and Dance!"

Avon's reference to
the Squishy Vortex Theory
of Ritornello
in Hermit Wizard's
Muon Noise Fiction, and to
the Whirling Handmaidens
Uvalde and Wade

Diwan of Shams of Tabriz
(tr. A. J. Arbery).

"For every inconsistency
on the surface, there is
a subterranean consistency."
Reza Negarestani,
Cyclonopedia.

"On the surface of time
it was only a moment,
but in the depths of time
they were bygone centuries
of the darkest sweetness."
C. Lispector,
"A Mischievous Little Girl."

"We can never be sad enough
for the world to change."
Jean-Luc Godard (dir.) *(RIP),*
The Book of Image.

"Paranoia is having all the facts."
William Burroughs, quoted in
Edmund White*, The Burning Library.*

"Why, I believe that this ship is
open, as I've told you—exposed,
unprotected, or whatever you
like to call it. I should say it's
reasonable to think that all things
of the material world are barred,
as it were, from the immaterial;

in the Zinc Adytum
of Double-Slit, became
immediately clear to
the Captain and to surviving
substitute Engineers
Sinbad and Cowabunga.

Given the complicated
simplicity of the situation
and the disharmonious
conjunctions anticipated
from the feedback
of an oxymoronic
Future Shock,
Captain Anna-O—
channeling the convergence
of Mental flexibility
with a right-click mindset
—scrolled down
the truncated perspective
of Molotov's System
of Knowledge, and set
the required number of
Whirling Dancers at *eleven*.

Rosetta and Cowabunga
volunteered for the job,
and were positioned along
the ship's central axis:
Rosetta toward the stern,
on the chill box
in the narthex; Cowabunga
on the transept's Oil Tank.

but that in some cases the barrier
may be broken down. That's what
may have happened to this ship.
And if it has, she may be naked
to some other state of existence."
William Hope Hodgson,
The Ghost Pirates.

"The water closing / over us and
the / going down is all. / Gills are
given. / We convert in a / town
of broken hulls / and green
doubloons. / O you dead pirates /
hear us! There is / no salvage."
Maxine Kumin, "Together."

"I mean *Negative Capability*,
that is when a man is capable
of being in uncertainties, Mysteries,
doubts without any irritable
reaching after fact and reason."
John Keats, letter to George and
Thomas Keats (21 Dec. 1817).

"When in danger or in doubt,
run in circles, scream and shout."
Herman Wouk, *The Caine Mutiny;*
Robert Heinlein, *Time Enough for Love.*

"Thou crusht that monsters head /
Whom other monsters dread, /
And soe his fishy flesh dids't frame, /
To serve as pleasing foode /

Completing the middle line
of Dancers, Scard'nelli
was stationed in front of
Cowabunga, on the super-
structure of the surge chamber,
beneath the tympanum's
Clarification Manifold; Thebes
was behind Cowabunga, under
the gargoyles of the boiler;
and Sony, behind Thebes
and in front of Rosetta, was
stationed under the groin vault
between the Expansion Tank
and the Void space.

Mach, ben-Cnopee and
Sokrates were positioned
along the starboard
control line: Mach,
across from Cowabunga,
in the pump room;
ben-Cnopee, in the triforium
between the Explosimeter
and the cooling system;
and Sokrates by the starboard
collision bulkhead.

Correspondingly,
their symmetrical counter-
parts for the Dance were
placed along the larboard
control line: Neanderthal,

To all the ravening brood, /
Who had the desert for their dame."
Psalms 74, tr. Mary Sidney.

"The sea monster floated
beneath the surface, humming,
its voice a low moan."
Vonda McIntyre,
The Moon and the Sun.

"...And he told us of his life /
In the land of submarines /
So we sailed on to the sun /
'Til we found a sea of green /
And we lived beneath the waves /
In our yellow submarine."
The Beatles, "Yellow Submarine."

"Like cartoon figures, we are
pilots of rationalist space ships,
setting ourselves down on
an alien planet, and finding that
our theories are generally accurate
but not really sufficient to deal
with particular, unexpected dangers
and advantages of the place."
Don Byrd,
The Poetics of the Common Knowledge.

"It should be noted that not
only the *Argo* herself but
the voyage which she made
is pictured among the stars:

across from Cowabunga
and Mach, on top of
the Water Tank under
the clerestory; Q'bal,
across from ben-Cnopee,
between the draining lines
and the gas channel;
and Bedlam, across
from Sokrates, behind
the condenser by the larboard
collision bulkhead.

They would start
their Whirling Dance on cue,
after Avon repeated
the "Mariupol" song
from Rœ's *Quantum Suite.*

As soon as Avon began
to sing, Rosetta's eyes
turned White and
she slipped into dreamtime.

Nonetheless, Avon carried
the melody beautifully,
repeating it twice; then—
when the Captain exclaimed
"Everybody dance now!"—
she broke into the vowelless
Nomad Glossolalia of
Linux Wiper in

for as Sir Isaac Newton once
pointed out, the twelve signs
of the Zodiac commemorate
various episodes of her story,
the first sign being the Ram
of the Golden Fleece."
Robert Graves, Appendix,
Hercules, My Shipmate.

"May God us keep from single
vision and Newton's sleep."
William Blake, letter to
Thomas Butt (22 Nov. 1802).

"The large gap between
the presently accessible energies
and the energies at which grand
unification and quantum gravity
should become relevant is often
called 'the desert' because, for
all we know right now, it might
be void of new phenomena."
Sabine Hossenfelder,
Lost in Math.

"What the hand, dare seize the fire?"
W. Blake, "The Tyger."

"Thus *lux* is before *lumen*."
René Descartes, quoted in
Alexander R. Galloway,
"What is a Hermeneutic Light?"

The Facebook of the Dead,
and the ten remaining
Dancers started Whirling
at their stations.

Yet decoherence
eventually followed,
after the fine-tuning of
the signal-to-noise ratio on
the *Song and Dance* loop
got messed up by
the Halo Effect from
a buffer breakdown in
the Coincidence-intensifier
...causing all ten Dancers
to spin out of control,
one by one.

The next thing we knew,
the whole ship was
shaking violently, as if both
the ground beneath us and
the ocean's overpowering
mass had seized it, and
would tear it apart.

We got cornered in
the Cryptocentric No-Go
zone described by
Ubutella the Loudmouth
in *Rug-Pull Overdrive*,
where destabilization from
the Ontological Differénce

"Attaching a grappling hook
of a perceptual landing site to
a vaguely sketched-in rope
of an imaging landing site,
a dimensionalizing landing site,
in landing, hooks onto
the environment to gain traction
on it. With the hook-and-
rope ensemble flung out and
an availing surface caught hold of,
there comes to be an as-if-tugging-
back-to-the-body that conveys
a sense of (kinesthetic) depth."
Madeline Gins and Arakawa,
Architectural Body.

between time's compression
and accelerating stress
offset the capacity
for Emergence.

The result, once the shake-up
subsided, was that a shining
Black Chasm was blown open,
and, according to the computer,
yawned in the slimy floor of
the Silver Sea—not *under*
the ship, but 0.002 Years away,
dead ahead.

"The first thing to see, looking
away over the water, was a kind
of dull line... you couldn't make
nothing else out; then a pale place
in the sky; then more paleness
spreading around; then the river
softened up away off, and warn't
black any more, but gray... it was
so still, and sounds come so far; and
by and by you could see a streak
on the water which you know by
the look of the streak that there's
a snag there in a swift current
which breaks on it and makes that
streak look that way; and you see
the mist curl up off of the water..."
Mark Twain,

Almost at once, Rosetta
awoke from her dream.

In her dream, she said,
she was walking down
a sidewalk on the Road
of Poetic Potential,
when the figure of a tall
Voodoo Elder, as if on stilts—
covered in a hooded Green-
Pink robe, and wearing
a Wooden Mask—
came storming toward her
from across the street.

As it drew near,
two similar beings appeared

Adventures of Huckleberry Finn.

"The long stretches of the waterway
ran on, deserted, into the gloom
of overshadowed distances."
Joseph Conrad,
Heart of Darkness.

"There is a gap in 'world pain'
through which the singular
falls continually and forever;
a body falling in observable
space, deprived of the privacy
of disappearance; as if privacy,
moving relentlessly away,
by the very sustaining power
of its withdrawal kept the body
eternally moving downward,
but in one place, and perpetually
before the eye."
Djuna Barnes,
Nightwood.

"He dreamed the Titanic was
sinking / into the Underworld."
B. Dylan, "Tempest."

"The adventure of any human being
is not as good as a sinking ship."
Laure (Colette Peignot),
New Fragments, "The Centaur."

"I am staring at a point

as backup, one to each side,
in what Rosetta described as
"a causal dynamic triangulation."

Rosetta charged toward
her strange assailant,
and despite difficulty
in the beginning, after
"a mash-up of Flippenings
in the inevitable near-term,"
she managed to wrestle it
to the ground, whereupon
she found herself "pounding
the Daylights out of it."

The dream's asymptotic
gravity was generating
a snap-to ambience at
the Threshold of Intelligibility,
when a bicycle-built-
for-two coasted backward
down the street, on which
Sinbad and Avon pedaled
forward... closing vision
that, in Rosetta's mind,
was the Makeover given
to a sense of complicity
extracted and cooked
in her dream.

For Sinbad, the interpretation
of the dream was simple.

before me, and I imagine
this point as the geometric locus
of all existence and all unity,
of all separation and all anguish,
of all unsatisfied desire and all death.
I adhere to this point and
a deep love of what is in
this point burns me until I refuse
to exist except for what is there,
for this point, which, being both
the life and the death of a loved one,
has the brilliance of a cataract."
George Bataille, "The Practice
of Joy in the Face of Death."

"Everything tends to make us
believe that there exists
a certain point of the mind
at which life and death, the real
and the imagined, past and
future, the communicable
and the incommunicable,
high and low, cease to be
perceived as contradictions."
André Breton,
Second Manifesto of Surrealism.

"Her heart, brimful of this
new agony, throbbed within
her and overflowed with
the sweetness of the pain."
Apollonius of Rhodes,
The Voyage of Argo (Book Three).

The Voodoo intruder
symbolized him, Sinbad...
flanked by Cowabunga
and Scard'nelli.

Rosetta assaulted Sinbad,
because she herself,
in the very act of dreaming,
was the Agent who
distended the *Song and Dance*
assemblage and amplified
the dereliction of its Schema
—and she knew
he knew it.

Sinbad pursued his interpretation
of Rosetta's Dream
by speculating that Cowabunga
and Scard'nelli were re-
presentations of Fault Tolerance
in the High Court of Emoji,
Phizer, Nato and Fahrenheit,
while Avon the Poetess
spoke for Positive Degeneration
and the swirl of Instant History.

In apparent reply, *Saka-Chōji,*
next Spirit of the Keel,
gave the message:
"Don't control the Spin!"

"Oh, oh, the pain!"
Sophocles,
Women of Trachis.

"if mental actions are the result
of ignorance / and consciousness
is the result of mental actions /
and name and shape are the result
of consciousness / and six-sensual
action is the result of name and
shape / and contact is the result
of six-sensual action / and feeling
is the result of contact / and desire
is the result of feeling / and affection
is the result of desire / and becoming
is the result of affection / and birth
is the result of becoming: /
suffering is the result of birth"
Harry Matthews,
The Sinking of the Odradek Stadium.

"From suffering came the Negro
spirituals, songs of joy, songs
of sorrow. The main origin of
American jazz is the spiritual."
Mary Lou Williams,
"Jazz for the Soul," quoted by
P. O'Brien in liner notes,
Black Christ of the Andes.

"I think of suffering as the highest
form of information, having

Following the Captain's orders
the task of managing the ship's
passage across the seafloor's
slime, and over the Chasm's
edge, was assigned to me and
Marlboro, Cowabunga and
Sinbad... but just as we were
starting to make a plan,
Cowabunga's eyes turned White
and he fell into a dream.

In effect, we found
our vision of
Hermetic Iridescence
confirmed in
the pagan capital
of the dream's Timing.

Cowabunga's dreamtime
would provide alternative
feedback on the course
of our progress.

The basic idea was to
project the Attractor Image
of our *ship in a bottle*
—hovering at the edge of
the Abyss ahead—and
initialize it, as Majic Eye,
in the service of
a tractor beam
that would carefully
draw us toward the Abyss.

a direct connection with mystery."
Svetlana Alexievich,
The Unwomanly Face of War.

"A puzzling failure in
the gravitation centre /
gave us this sense of falling
the illusion / that no matter what
we did we'd keep on falling /
in one direction, downward
through a void / no longer rounded
or vaulted, / but like a well
into which we dived headlong."
Harry Martinson,
Aniara, 91
(tr. H. MacDiarmid, E. H. Schubert).

"Never shall I forget the sensations
of awe, horror, and admiration
with which I gazed about me.
The boat appeared to be hanging,
as if by magic, midway down,
upon the interior surface of a funnel
vast in circumference, prodigious
in depth, and whose perfectly smooth
sides might have been mistaken
for ebony, but for the bewildering
rapidity with which they spun
around, and for the gleaming and
ghastly radiance they shot forth..."
Edgar Allan Poe,
A Descent into the Maelström.

The first step was
to re-route the ship's
systems through the Lens
as a function of the crew's
Clean Psychic Energy, and
turn the propeller back on.

The reasoning, after the model
of Webb, Dobbs and Taiwan
in *Lenape Kaon Fizz,*
was that the double identity
of the Lens' structure could
be modernized to process
the growth of the Mud Cloud
stirred by the propeller,
and solve our problem by
exchanging its slimy substance
for forward movement.

According to the Standard Model,
the Hermetic Face of the Lens
as Reflective Mirror—set against
the Mud Cloud behind us—
was linked to a servo-mechanism
—pointed in the direction of
the Chasm—that Illuminated
the Iridescent Face
of the Lens as Opening, and
looped the Projective Size of
the ship's *"Self-Image"* through
a tractor beam into the future.

"Alas! All is abyss."
Charles Baudelaire, "The Chasm."

"When you look long into the abyss,
the abyss also looks into you."
Friedrich Nietzsche,
Beyond Good and Evil.

"Goin' down, goin' down now /
Goin' down, goin' down now /
Goin' down, goin' down / Goin'
down, goin' down / Goin' down,
goin' down now / Goin' down,
goin' down now / Goin' down,
goin' down now / Goin' down, goin'
down-down-down-down-down."
"When the Levee Breaks,"
Led Zeppelin (1971) / Kansas Joe
McCoy and Memphis Minnie (1929).

"REVVVVVVVVVVVVVV-
VVVVVVVVVELATION"
A. Waldmann,
Iovis, Book II.

"Thus the cathedral for us
seems founded on alchemical
science—investigative matrix
of the original substance's trans-
formations, of elementary *Matter*
(L. *materea,* root *mater,* mother)...
At an angle extending from
the north tower, you will notice...

The tractor beam's enabling
of Auto-Telekenesis
through spacetime is what
Butterworth's *Googlelator*
calls "the real clear disguise
of 'Hermetic' One Hand
Clapping as 'Iridescent' Slap
in the Face of Silence."

Saka-Chōji, Spirit of the Keel
still online, intervened with
the comment *"Go with the flow!"*
but by now the Animating
Intelligence of the server's
Education program was suspect.

As soon as Cowabunga started
dreaming, Marlboro took it
upon herself to determine
what Clean Psychic Energy
looked like, and Sinbad agreed.

From her position at the wheel
next to Wang, her secret Lover,
Marlboro wanted me to serve as
backup for Rosetta in the narthex,
under the gaslight, putting us
behind Avon, on either
side of the propeller shaft
overgrown with plants.

By so doing, Marlboro
created a vacancy at the bow

the startling relief of an old man
of stone. That's him, that's
the alchemist of Notre-Dame."
Fulcanelli,
The Mystery of the Cathedrals.

"Come and see: There is a land of
the living above, but this is a *land
of pitch-black darkness.* What is
a land of pitch-black darkness? End
deriving from the side of darkness,
dross of gold..."
Zohar, "Mi-Qets" (tr. D. Matt).

"At the birth of the solar system,
deviating from the protoplanetary
disk that is to become the central
body, a tiny, uniform spherical mass
emerges from the solar nebula.
Within 500 million years, a sudden
sinking of matter into a dense metallic
core—the 'Iron Catastrophe'—
precipitates the formation of
a differentiated, layered planetary
structure, its molten inner matter
surrounded by a thin rocky mantle
and cold crust. This brittle surface
seals into its depths the repressed
secret of the Earth's 'burning
immanence with the sun.' But
the face of the Earth does not
remain still... The thin crust destined
to shield the inhabitants of Earth from

—forward of the Lens, beside
the waterfall—for Venus to act
as backup to Scard'nelli
and as counter-balance to me
and Rosetta at the stern.

The larger maneuver
consisted in separating
Commander Exprès from
Venus; then, in returning
the ten Dancers to
their starting points, and
repositioning the other
eleven members of
the crew, while leaving
Cowabunga dreaming under
the Xibonachi chandelier and
Avon stuck where she was.

According to Marlboro's
theoretical assumption(s),
by silencing Venus's readings
of Exprès's spit,
a ship-wide New Spirit
would fill the vacuum
between Venus and Exprès...
and thus trigger
the collective Unconscious in
the crew's Psychic Network,
causing the ship to advance.

I went along with the idea,
thinking *Silence follows Spirit,*

its primal trauma wears on its face
the continually-shifting expression
of the helio-plutonic bond."
Robin Mackay,
"A Brief History of Geotrauma,"
in *Leper Symposium* (ed. E. Keller,
N. Masciandaro, E. Thacker).

"The rower / The imperishable /
The indefatigable / The one who
knows no return / The one who
knows no obstruction."
The Egyptian Amduat, "Ninth Hour."

"Sun turnin' 'round with graceful
motion / We're setting off
with soft explosion / Bound for
a star with fiery oceans / It's so
very lonely, you're a hundred
light years from home."
The Rolling Stones,
"2000 Light Years from Home."

"Poetry is not only dream
and vision; it is the skeleton
architecture of our lives."
Audre Lorde,
"Poetry Is Not a Luxury."

"In Voudoun the cosmic drama
of man consists not of a dualism,
a conflict of the irreconcilable
down-pull of flesh and the up-pull

and Captain Anna-O approved.

Commander Exprès was
relocated alongside ben-Cnopee,
where the spit from his Chronic
Cough was left unread.

Thereafter, the layout of
the crew across the ship
fell into place: the original
configuration of eleven
Dancers was supplemented
by a similar arrangement
that included, on the port side
—in addition to Exprès—
Chauvée and Cîpher; and,
on the starboard side, Wang,
Nobadinus and Captain Anna-O.

Only Sinbad had no station;
his assignment was to circulate
as free agent between Avon
and the dreaming Cowabunga.

With all systems go,
Marlboro gave Sinbad
the signal to turn
the propeller *on.*

of spirit; it is, rather, an almost
organic dynamic, a process by which
all that which characterizes divinity
—intelligence, power, energy,
authority, wisdom—evolves out
of the flesh itself. Instead of being
eternally separated, the substance
and the spirit of man are eternally
and mutually committed:
the flesh to the divinity within it and
the divinity to the flesh of its origin."
Maya Deren,
Divine Horsemen.

"I was transforming my blood into
comprehensive energy—masculine
and feminine, microcosmic and
macrocosmic—and into a wine that
was drunk by the moon and the sun."
Leonora Carrington,
Down Below.

"But the underworld is not really dead.
Neither is the overworld. The distance
from Plato's cave to Kafka's burrow is,
like the mathematical paradox of
Zeno, immeasurably wide and small
at the same time. The old notion
of the microcosm and macrocosm,
the physical world as a double-
reflecting mirror between our psyches
and a transcendental other world,
is more deeply embedded in us

No sooner did Sinbad
adjust the thermostat on
the Fireplace and push
the button on the X-box,
than the vibratory interaction
of the catenary arches
supporting the propeller shaft
activated the Eco-magnetic
memory by which Rosetta and I
got the ship's screw to respond.

As predicted, the propeller stirred
the slime and gave rise to
a Mud Cloud; but the ship,
vibrating powerfully, remained
nonetheless stuck, while
the Cloud got bigger and bigger.

Marlboro went into action:
through the network linking
Rosetta to Scard'nelli and
Venus, she gave me the signal
to engage the Mirror on
the screen in the Lens,
to gain hermeneutic leverage
from the Mud Cloud's
opacity; concomitantly—
through the network linking
Commander Exprès to
ben-Cnopee, Q'Bal and Wang
—Marlboro gave Sinbad
the signal to engage the Prism
in the phaser bank of

than we imagine… Our culture has a long history of pushing discredited religion and science alike off their former pedestals and recycling them in works of the imagination."
Victoria Nelson,
The Secret Life of Puppets.

"What did the Professor mean? Could he be trying to measure the thickness of the crust of the earth that lay between us and the world above?"
Jules Verne,
Journey to the Center of the Earth.

"The possible is an infrathin."
Marcel Duchamp,
Duchamp du Signe.

"A mathematician named Klein / Thought the Möbius band was divine. / Said he: 'If you glue / The edges of two, / You'll get a weird bottle like mine.'"
Leo Moser, quoted in David Darling,
The Universal Book of Mathematics.

"Einstein's theory of relativity Heisenberg's uncertainty principle, and Bergson's theories of dynamic interpenetration of planes and the inability of the senses to comprehend the entirety of

the Lens, to arrive at
an *enlightened* perspective
on the transparent truth
of the Chasm's immanence.

Reflecting, and refracted in,
the Mud Cloud, the ship
started gravitating toward
a surreal image of itself
hovering over the Dark Abyss.

At which point, to our dismay,
Avon the Poetess began to moan.

It was as if she were
experiencing the torment
of having her skeleton-legs
dragged through the mud.

Marlboro's theoretical bid to
deploy the *catoptric \ dioptric*
Pharmakon of the Lens,
as supplied by
a collective body of
Psychic Energy, failed
to recognize the schizoid Fold
short-circuiting the array
of the crew, in which
the 32 Paths on
the Decision Tree of Life
coincided with
the 32 Emotions from
the Big Wheel of Feeling.

reality all seemed to create
a sense of unparalleled freedom.
Surrealism in particular benefited
from this freedom..."
Nadia Chouchga,
Surrealism and the Occult.

"We're currently hearing calls for
a new holism that have unprecedented
urgency. They come from every
quarter—from those in mainstream
science exploring the theoretical
realms of chaos theory, quantum
theory, and string theory; from
those involved with worldwide
environmental, biosocial, geopolitical,
and health planning; and from
those promoting myriad expositions
of "new science," with its multiple
applications... At the heart of
those contemporary appeals to holism
is a sense that... *connections between
things make for a pattern and whole-
ness that can't adequately be located
in the sum of component parts.*"
Elizabeth Lloyd Mayer,
Extraordinary Knowing.

"All things whate'er they be /
Have order among themselves..."
Dante,
The Divine Comedy: Paradiso.

While Avon moaned non-stop
and the ship moved through
the mud toward the Chasm,
a cascade of conflicting emotions
overwhelmed the entire crew,
and put everyone
in a deep state of turmoil.

For each of us, at once,
grief followed ecstasy,
as Sovereignty collapsed
under the weight of its own
Crown, and Economics silenced
Laughter; admiration gave way
to loathing, as Victory over
meaninglessness succumbed
to the Death of Empathy, and
serenity and pensiveness
suffered the Ordeal of Politics;
Wisdom turned to terror,
and Love changed to rage in
the solitude of the Technosphere;
the freedom to be joyful,
trusting and kind lost
its Foundation in Beauty, while
sadness, remorse and disgust
ruled the Ecology of Chance.

We crossed a Psychic
Field of Ruins, to which
Avon's moan gave Voice—
until we finally reached

"Reconstructive postmodernism
depends upon deconstruction as
much as deconstruction depends
upon the speculative schemes
it deconstructs."
Catherine Keller,
"The Process of Difference,
the Difference of Process."

"I'll tell you how I turned into a man.
First I had to turn into a woman."
Joanna Russ,
The Female Man.

"'When man gets rid of his animal
part which is woman, this is
the signal God is awaiting. Then
God will reveal the new true
clean way, maybe angels will come
bringing new souls, or maybe we will
live forever, but it is not our place
to speculate, only to obey.'"
James Tiptree, Jr. (Alice B. Sheldon),
"The Screwfly Solution."

"The guards weren't allowed inside
the building except when called, and
we weren't allowed out, except for
our walks, twice daily, two by two
around the football field, which was
enclosed now by a chain-link fence
topped with barbed wire. The Angels
stood outside it with their backs to us."

the brink of the Dark Abyss.

As the ship tipped over,
Madness came to Sinbad.

He claimed to be trapped
in the Phantom Field of
a Stereotactic Figure 8
between Marlboro's Rewired
Imagination and Rosetta's
Unhappy Consciousness,
and wanted Avon to be silent.

But, in his effort to join
Avon at the bottom of
the hull, during a *Klein-bottled*
moment, as he was hurrying
down the gangway
from the long-range
particle cumulator toward
the clarified air blower's motor
—and the ship tilted past
the point of no return—
the opposite edges of
the gangway's exit platform
were intersected by
a Projective Plane
from the 5th Dimension.

Sinbad became agitated as
he witnessed the gangway

Margaret Atwood,
The Handmaid's Tale.

"'This could be a new kind of virus.
Maybe bacteria. From the permafrost.
Use hand sanitizer, okay?...'
It isn't until after I hang up that
I remember... their prescience
regarding the tech and housing
bubbles, then Iraq, the Mideast,
Afghanistan, then Russia,
the increasing chaos of our elections,
and our first winter without snow..."
Louise Erdrich,
Future Home of the Living God.

"In order for imagination to leap,
it needs to trust that something will
come to meet it. The knowledge
produced by the coherent scheme
must be actually 'important.'"
Isabelle Stengers,
Thinking with Whitehead.

"When the fleeting act of viewing
a website burns anywhere from
20-300 mg of CO2 each second,
I thought of the hours of
hallucinatory web searches
that I had embarked on...
Information may want to be free,
but the hackers are still burning oil."
Melanie Doherty,

recede before him, then
disappear in the wake of
a Growth Front that provided
Universal cover for the aft
lower decks' immersion
into the Permanent Flexibility
of fundamental Meltdown.

Avon stopped moaning.

The bulkheads were buckling;
the Sex cylinders and
the draft pistons became warped;
the interval analyzer curled
at the edges; the Treadmill
twisted portside, the Stepmill,
starboard; the Voided oar got bent,
and passed through the midline
of the Magdeburg Jars, where
it fused with the Expansion
Tank and the Void space... until
the entire region surrounding
Avon and Sinbad Mutated,
and blended into the curvature of
a non-orientable, Zero-volume
one-sided surface, that
flushed Sinbad's body out
through a Tube into the sea.

Instantly, Avon was Dead,
the Flesh on her head and
torso gone, while her skull
and bones—sealed off

"Non-Oedipal Networks and
the Inorganic Unconscious."

"Tornadoes are smashing hell out
of Alabama, Kentucky, Tennessee,
and two or three other states.
Three hundred people dead so far.
And there's a blizzard freezing
the northern Midwest, killing even
more people. In New York and
New Jersey, a measles epidemic
is killing people. Measles!"
Octavia Butler,
Parable of the Sower.

"and gun sales lead to more
gun sales / they do not clutter
the market for gunnery /
there is no saturation"
E. Pound,
Cantos, LXXIV.

"'We're all demented sinners
in the same cosmic boat—and
the boat is perpetually sinking.'"
Aldous Huxley,
Island.

"The words seemed to be
dropped into a well, where,
if the water were clear, they were
also extraordinarily distorting that,
even as they descended, one saw

in a cross-capped Spherinder
conjugated with the Exit Tube—
were flooded and occulted
by the sea's Silver water...
like Môdee the Poetess
in the Fuel Tank on
the S\S GROSSOMODO.

Our nosedive into the Abyss
had thrown the crew
into complete Khaos,
bodies went flying over bodies,
and the ship's equipment
was in tumult.

Although the Gravity Handler
eventually stabilized the order
of things, van Rr'Ubik's Half-
Shadow on the port side of
the figurehead functioned as
the Clinamen that sentenced us
to a Vertigo of Indistinction,
by locking the vessel into
a spiral, Widdershins freefall
that is theoretically Eternal.

There are now 21 of us
left on board, waiting
for the Universe to release
Chance once again,
and turn this endless Dark

them twisting about to make
Heaven knows what pattern
on the floor of the child's mind."
Virginia Woolf,
To the Lighthouse.

"Love is the only miracle there is."
DJ Cheb | Sabbah,
"Hari Om Narayan,"
in *As Far As DJ Mix.*

into Nothing.

Cowanbunga continues
to dream; and despite what
Togari-Chōji, Spirit of the Keel,
calls the "poetry virus"
affecting us since the Death
of Avon the Poetess,
there is speculation that
her ghost is still with us.

Stay with me,
my love.

I am yours forever.

S.

The Aeon

Love of my life,

Looking back, I did not believe
it would end as it has.

At my first sight
of the Metal gate,
which presented itself
as a grid with two-hundred
and nine squares, eleven
across by nineteen down—
each one large enough to put
a fist through—I am lying
in the mud, raising my head.

The surrounding space
is filled with gray mist,
and smells of incense.

I stand up, but slip
in the mud and fall on
my rear end; I stand up
again, and see that the mist
has cleared and is hovering
behind the gate.

"The Aeon is a child at play
with colored balls."
Heraclitus (tr. T. McKenna).

"It is this which Heraclitus meant
when he laid down the law which
was vitiated by Socrates and only
restored by Rimbaud... Man is
forever estranged to the degree
that his stance toward reality
disengages him from the familiar."
Charles Olson,
The Special View of History.

"The number of human beings
who have preceded us is around
sixty billion... The dead outnumber
the living... by a factor of ten."
Martin Rees,
Our Final Hour.

"There is no category of human
activity in which the dead do not
outnumber the living many times

I am under a vault
of stone bricks,
which are covered
by large patches of Ice—
at once the Igloo
in Da Vinci's *Coded Discóurse*
on a Shortcut to The Moon
and the Cromlech
in Whistler's *Book of Lies.*

I move toward the gate,
but the mud suddenly
gets deeper and I trip again,
falling on my face.

I hear water and mud
dripping from the ceiling,
and soon after, when I am
back on my feet, the Sound
of a stone falling... then
another... followed by more
mud and water, dripping down.

The gray mist has withdrawn
into a wide tunnel,
like the ancient riverbed
in *The Guinness Ideo-Guide*
to Bad and Good Fortune.

Just before I reach the gate
my string of bad luck
continues, when a brick
lands on my foot—

over. Most beautiful children are
dead. Most soldiers, most cowards.
The fairest women and the most
learned men—all are dead.
Their bodies repose in caskets,
in sarcophagi, beneath arches of
rude stone, everywhere under
the earth. Their spirit haunts
our mind, ears pressed to the bone
of our foreheads. Who can say how
intently they listen as we speak,
or for what word?"
Gene Wolfe,
The Book of the New Sun.

"Tout autre est tout autre."
("The very other is very other.")
Jacques Derrida,
The Gift of Death.

"Illusion is the first of all pleasures."
Voltaire,
"The Maid of Orleans."

"The universe is made of stories,
not of atoms."
Muriel Ruckeyser,
"The Speed of Darkness."

"The wind is made of
invisible atoms."
Lucretius,
On the Nature of Things.

and another on my head.

The mist has pulled back
to reveal in the distance,
down the tunnel,
a partly hidden figure
standing sideways, as if looking
through a hole in the wall.

At the same time,
I feel a Storm gathering
inside the Dome.

Stirred by a Secret wind,
the water and mud start
swirling around, lashing me;
the ground seems to tremble.

Following Évolutio's
"Law of the Similar,"
from the Postscript
in Escher and Escher's
Excéllent Adventures
at the Cul-de-Sac
and the Tête-à-Tête,
a Revelation comes to me:
I am traveling through
the Weather Channel
in the Perfect Storm of *Time!*

The figure I see at
the other end of the tunnel,
facing sideways before

"What if, for some very good
reason as yet unknown to me,
I had been sent back not only
in space, but in time. If I were
willing to believe I could be sent
through space, why did I balk at
the possibility of being sent
through time? Was one more
difficult to believe than the other?"
Dorothy Bryant,
The Kin of Ata Are Waiting for You.

"I am afraid I cannot convey
the peculiar sensations of
time travelling. They are excessively
unpleasant. There is a feeling exactly
like that one has upon a switch back
—of a helpless headlong motion!
I felt the same horrible anticipation,
too, of an imminent smash."
H. G. Wells,
The Time Machine.

"the current weather matters
little to me / my life is always
ahead of a hurricane"
Aimé Césaire,
"The Woman and the Flame."

"This way, that way /
I do not know / What to do:
I / am of two minds"

an opening in the wall,
is myself... looking at myself...
looking at... myself...
looking... at myself...
around an unfolding series
of corners... infinitesimally.

With each break
in the Weather Channel
("the Continuum-less Continuum"),
the Storm de-concentrates
my Differential Energy,
to produce the Quantum
in which my Body coheres
as Subject Matter, while my Head
achieves Light Weight.

Theoretically, this confirms
that although I am *losing*
I can still *win*...
I can *win* by *losing*.

Yet, no sooner does
this Revelation occur
than the ceiling above me
collapses with a resounding
Crash... and I lie buried
under a pile of mud
and loose bricks.

I experience the sensation

Mary Barton (tr.),
Sappho: A New Translation.

"...I say it as I hear it
murmur it in the mud..."
Samuel Beckett,
How It Is.

"We are / Enclosed by the walls
between us / By the chemistry
of the dead spaces we share..."
Audre Lorde, "The Classrooms."

"Everyone had thought that
the worst was over, and now
of course everyone was stunned,
dazed, wandering aimlessly
from room to room, hardly
knowing a door from a wall."
Murasaki Shikibu,
The Tale of Genji.

"Poor fallow beings
and their pain that
surrenders, having
resisted too much,
and their pain,
defeated, powerless,
crushed, idiotic.
Listen to them: a b c d
I no longer know
how to speak, 1234
I no longer know

of being pulled by my hair
out from water.

As in a dream,
I find myself standing
in a fountain at the center
of a vast cellar; broken windows
line the upper walls;
they open onto darkness.

A crowd of men and women
are walking in a circle,
around me and the fountain.

The water falls down
a series of platforms
stacked in the shape
of a Ziggurat, above which
a tattered Flag on a pole
waves in a Secret wind,
shifting from one direction
to the next, back and forth.

Hoping to get through, I make
my way into the crowd and
start to walk; but my eyes
close, and I feel lost.

I am swept up
in the movement
around the fountain,
trying to keep my eyes open,
circling with the crowd,

how to count."
Laure,
Story of a Little Girl.

'I entered' 'a dark cavern'
'that had a marked-off' 'rear area'/
'a little like' 'a stage' 'but not
elevated,' 'demarcated' / 'by four
stalactitish boulders' 'at the corners'
'of its rectangle' / 'The front part'
'of the cavern' 'was filled
with people' / 'who blended in'
'with its darkness' 'so much that'
'I couldn't / tell' 'if they were
dark-skinned' 'or just shadowed'
Alice Notley,
The Descent of Alette.

"In the context of a multilevel
labyrinth, a path through which
one can thread one's way deeply
and pervasively and analytically
equals an escape route; one escapes
into a critical apparatus fitted out
for and consequently fit for all
dimensions, into a lattice of praxis."
Madeline Gins and Arakawa,
Architectural Body.

"The Zone is a very
complicated system of traps,
and they're all deadly."
Andrei Tarkovsky (dir.),

bumping against it,
pushed along, half-aware of
Voices rising and fading nearby—
until finally, after countless
turns, I am released into
the larger space of the room.

While the crowd continues
to mill around the fountain,
solitary figures stand
outside the circle
or sit on the ground.

The walls on three sides
of the fountain are marked
by a series of human Shadows;
the Shadows are kept off limits
by a retractable Nylon band,
like the Tensa Belt in Lœve's
Five Books of the Blue State.

I talk to someone next
to me, then to others,
but the result is the same:
they speak the Language(s)
of the Lost,
unable to understand me
or be understood.

This can only mean that
I am in the same gap
as the people standing
and sitting outside the ring:

Stalker.

"I must not fear. Fear is the mind-
killer. Fear is the little-death that
brings total obliteration. I will face
my fear. I will permit it to pass
over me and through me. And
when it has gone past I will turn
the inner eye to see its path.
Where the fear has gone there will
be nothing. Only I will remain."
Frank Herbert,
Dune.

"They say the darkest hour
is right before the dawn."
Bob Dylan,
"Meet me in the morning."

"Quotations are useful in periods of
ignorance or obscurantist beliefs."
Guy Debord,
Society of the Spectacle.

"Here at our sea-washed, sunset gates
shall stand / 'A mighty woman
with a torch, whose flame /
Is the imprisoned lightning...'"
Emma Lazarus, "The New Colossus."

"As he entered New York Harbor
on the now slow-moving ship,
Karl Rossmann... saw the Statue of

we are Players who are losing.

My mood lifts for a moment,
when I see a Fat Man
in a T-shirt sitting
with his legs crossed
against the fourth wall—
where there are no Shadows,
no retractable barrier—
and I realize that the room
is L-shaped.

The Fat Man has
a big bald head
and his T-shirt displays
the Falun Gong translation
from Tourette's *Garment of Light:*
"BE HERE NOW [!*?]."

I head toward the occulted part
of the L-shaped room—just as
a Hunchback Dwarf is walking
away from it, limping, moving
slowly into the main chamber.

At the sight of the Hunchback,
like a Bermudian
in the Sunny Triangle,
I grow increasingly anxious
over the indeterminate nature
of my Responsibility.

I start to think that

Liberty, which he had been observing
for some time, as if in a sudden
burst of sunlight. The arm with
the sword now reached aloft, and
about her figure blew the free winds."
Franz Kafka,
Amerika: The Missing Person.

"Suddenly Mu breaks open.
The heavens are astonished,
the earth is shaken. It is
as though you have snatched
the great sword of general Kuan.
When you meet the Buddha,
you kill the Buddha. When you
meet Bodidharma, you kill
Bodidharma. At the very cliff edge
of birth-and-death
you find the Great Freedom...
Exhaust all your life energy
on this one word 'Mu.'"
Wumen Huikai, "The Koan Mu:
Text, Commentary, and Verse."

"And if my country ever should
assent / to casting in my name
a monument, / I should be proud
to have my memory graced, /
but only if the monument
be placed / not near the sea
on which my eyes first opened... /
but here, where I endured three
hundred hours / in line before

the Wheel of Dissolution
is dealing Khaos to the light,
as if from the Matrix
of a Soft Machine
that instantly re-circulates Losers...
and that I experience as
a secret-without-a-Secret.

My Responsibility becomes
the Hyper-Response
to... for... before...
this strange being,
in whom I see a phantom
in disguise, whose secret is
that *s/he does not have*
a Sex, and who would act
as my witness.

I recoil.

I am at a border
that I can neither cross
nor not cross: in a solitude
neither Axiomatic
nor Echographic.

I feel exposed and vulnerable
to the grip of Madness,
at sea in untranslatable fictions
determined by Death, time
and the Other.

Uncertainty and doubt

the implacable iron bars."
Anna Akhmatova, "Requiem"
(tr. S. Kunitz, M. Hayward).

"The power of a country road
when one is walking along it
is different from the power
it has when one is flying over it
by airplane. In the same way,
the power of a text when it is read
is different from the power
it has when it is copied out."
Walter Benjamin,
One-way Street.

"The Greek letter *mu* was derived
from the zig-zag Egyptian
hieroglyphic symbol for water,
which had been simplified by
the Phoenicians and named after
their word for water, *mem*."
Kieren Barry,
The Greek Qabalah.

"What remained resembled
an overgrown field of ruins,
where only very occasionally
a learned traveler was surprised
or shocked by some bizarre
image of the sacred,
repellent to rational thought."
Gershom Scholem,
On the Kabbalah.

consume me... until, suddenly
—overthrowing the Context
at once—the Fat Man in
the "BE HERE NOW [!*?]"
T-shirt stands up, walks over
and embraces the Hunchback.

I realize that the lame Dwarf
is not a gnostic Avatar,
but another Player,
whose fear and solitude
are as real as my own.

Inescapably, the Rhetorical
Logic of the Dealt Hand
reconfirms the error
of my secret misgivings
about the Hunchback Dwarf
by exceeding the horizon
of Forgiveness re-presented
by the Fat Man.

Separate yet together in
their embrace, the Fat Man
and the Hunchback mirror
my Self-Division between
the promise of Forgiveness
and the memory of a Fault
as unredeemable as it is irrevocable.

This perception leads to another:

"Nothing matters but the quality
of the affect in the end—that has
carved the trace in the mind."
Ezra Pound,
Cantos, LXXVI.

"A puppet wearing Turkish
attire and a hookah in its mouth
sat before a chessboard placed
on a large table. A system
of mirrors created the illusion
that this table was transparent
on all sides. Actually a hunchback
dwarf—a master at chess—
sat inside and guided the puppet's
hand by means of strings...
The puppet, called 'historical
materialism,' is to win all
the time. It can easily be a match
for anyone, if it enlists the services
of theology, which today,
as we know, is small and ugly
and has to keep out of sight."
Walter Benjamin, "Theses on
the Philosophy of History."

"From out of that evil night...
the dwarf-sized Count walked in...
There was a startling momentous-
ness to the little man, broad and
hunchbacked, his large head
nested between his shoulders."

when the two of them walk
toward the hidden recess
of the L-shaped room, and
disappear around the corner
to my left, what I see
is both the re-enactment
of an Absolüt disruption
in the rules of the Game,
and the Hyperbolic expression
of the Big Lie to which
I subscribe by projecting
my Will to Power
as the willingness to *lose.*

The Chronicles of Placebo Aporias
(Disc A) make it clear:
<u>*win*</u>-<u>*lose*</u> cannot function
as the translation of <u>*win*</u>-<u>*win*</u>
from the Homeosphere to
the Stereosphere without
producing an Axis of Evil
as its side effect...

I follow the two of them
into the hidden recess,
knowing that the Endgame
is coming to a close.

I enter the smaller
rectangular space:
the Fat Man, nearest to me,
and the Hunchback Dwarf,
a few steps away

George Bataille,
The Dead Man.

"18. THE MOON.—Hidden enemies,
danger, calumny, darkness, terror,
deception, occult forces, error.
Reversed: Instability, inconstancy,
silence, lesser degrees
of deception and error."
Arthur Edward Waite,
Pamela Colman Smith (ill.),
The Pictorial Key to the Tarot.

"The two Pillars, then,
represent the positive
and negative forces in nature,
the active and passive,
the destructive and constructive,
concreting form and
free-moving force."
Dion Fortune,
The Mystical Qabalah.

"I become a transparent eyeball;
I am nothing; I see all."
Ralph Waldo Emerson,
"Nature."

"When he opened the door and
she saw him there, she said, 'Ha ha.'"
Flannery O'Connor,
Wise Blood.

in the corner, are sitting
with their legs crossed
against the wall to my right;
on the wall facing them,
to my left, stands the portal
of a second Metal gate,
like the first one,
with eleven squares across
and nineteen down.

Beyond the grid,
a tunnel runs sideways.

The three of us are in
the basement's antechamber
—as if on the stage
of a theater, that is part
of a larger machine.

The Auto-poematic trace
of the reconstructed site
momentarily quiets my despair,
and leads to the Revelation
that the Last Card
on the Game Table,
in the Upper World,
is *The Moon*.

The status of the Last Card—
The Moon or *The Moon // reversed?*
—is the secret beyond the gate,

"At any rate when we knocked
at the door he opened it, saw us
and said, Ha, Sophists!"
Plato,
Protagoras.

"I found Blake's Marriage /
of Heaven and Hell—sold for two
guineas, 1821 / & Turner aged 46
that year / & there I read: /
'And when thou seest / an Eagle,
thou seest a portion of genius. /
Lift up / thy head,' says Blake. /
These afternoons now, / late in
September, 76, / the sky, the river are
lit up / at the end of Bank Street, at
Bethune. / The pavement / trembles
with light pouring / upon it /
We are held in it. / We smile. "
Hilda Morley,
"That Bright Grey Eye."

"What we are experiencing
now, in the age of infinite
acceleration of the infosphere,
is the following: feminine *fortuna*
can no longer be subjected and
domesticated by masculine force
of political reason, because
fortuna is embodied in the chaotic
flows of financial microtrading."
Franco "Bifo" Berardi,
The Uprising.

to which the Fat Man
and the Hunchback offer access
as the Right and Left Pillars
of Mercy and Judgment.

As soon as I place myself
between the two seated figures,
as a medium for the Surplus
Value of <u>*win-lose*</u>
and the transformation
of Judgment into Mercy,
two Mutations become manifest:
1) the Fat Man turns Green,
and 2) the Hunchback's head
changes shape, and melds
into a single Mutant body.

The Sublime economy at work
in these Mutations induces
the Spiritual pleasure of *winning*
without the pain of *losing*—
a pleasure that increases
as the Fat Man hardens
into a Buddha of Green stone...
while the Hunchback grows
into an elongated Mutant,
in which the head's ears, nose,
mouth and hair have been absorbed,
and one large eye remains.

In keeping with the Negative
Grammar of Spectrality,
the no-longer-Unconscious

"The color of their flaxen hair
was normal, but they wore it
in braids long enough to swing
over their powerful shoulders...
Yet any suggestion of effeminacy
certainly did not survive beyond
the first glance at their ruggedly
masculine features."
Andre Norton (Alice Mary Norton),
The Time Traders.

"Women have served all
these centuries as looking glasses
possessing the magic and delicious
power of reflecting the figure
of man at twice its natural size."
Virginia Woolf,
A Room of One's Own.

"The book opens with a symbolic
act: Buck Mulligan peers into
the mirror while shaving, he offers
it to Stephen, Stephen inspects
himself, Mulligan takes the mirror
away from Stephen, Stephen
condemns it as the cracked looking-
glass of a servant, Mulligan
thrusts it along with his razor into
the pocket of his dressing gown.
What does it mean?"
Frances Boldereff,
A Blakean Translation

affect of *win-lose* escapes
along an Ontological Chain
of inconsistent events:
the Sound of the fountain
in the main chamber stops;
the Buddha's Green stone
cracks, and shatters.

Water starts seeping from the eye
on the Mutant body...
which is stretching upward,
as if searching the ceiling.

The water oozes from the eye
in a slow stream, that flows
down the body and crosses
the floor... past the gate,
into the tunnel.

Moments later a Shadow appears
beyond the door, on the tunnel's
far wall—before gradually
Being Hidden by a gray mist
rising from the water's edge.

A distant Voice begins to murmur,
and gets closer, louder...
as if dispersing the haze...
to reveal at last my opponent,
standing behind the gate,
speaking to me... questioning me
in the Language(s) of the Lost.

of Joyce's Circe.

"It's better not to think about
what is in the mirrors."
Anna Akhmatova,
"Poem without a Hero"
(tr. J. Hemschemeyer).

"As I drew near the fire the woman
stopped stirring the pot and rose to
greet me. When we faced each other
I felt my heart give a convulsive leap
and stop. The woman who stood
before me was myself."
Leonora Carrington,
The Hearing Trumpet.

"There are two of me now: /
This new absolutely white person
and the old yellow one, / And
the white person is certainly
the superior one. / She doesn't need
food, she is one of the real saints."
Sylvia Plath, "In Plaster."

"The process of knowledge is
in a sense man's discovery of
the hieroglyphic outline of
his shadow on the world, that
image of organic unity derived
from the limits of his own body
that he projects on the world
in order to render it intelligible."

I want to address him,
to show him my desire
to respond, but before I am
able to speak the thought occurs
that he does not see me;
he talks to someone else.

The Chronicles of Placebo Aporias
(Disc B) return to haunt me:
I recognize the Cellular Exile
of Cogito in the Homeobox...

To my dismay,
the Revelation follows
that I am in two places
at the same time.

Lifting myself from the mud,
after the ceiling's collapse
over my head, I rise
to discover that I am excluded
from the Living Present
from two points of origin.

I am not in the Weather
Channel, where the distant
figure in the Storm of Time
is my infinite Self, regressing
in a Game of *win-lose;*
this is a psychodynamic
Dome from which laughter

Robert Irwin,
American Hieroglyphics.

"To know that one does not
write for the other, to know
that these things I am going
to write will never cause me
to be loved by the one I love
(the other), to know that writing
compensates for nothing,
sublimates nothing, that it is
precisely there where you are not—
this is the beginning of writing."
Roland Barthes,
A Lover's Discourse.

"To be One is to be autonomous,
to be powerful, to be God; but
to be the One is to be an illusion,
and so to be involved in a dialectic
of apocalypse with the other. Yet
to be other is to be multiple, without
clear boundary, frayed, insubstantial.
One is too few, but two is too many."
Donna Haraway,
The Cyborg Manifesto.

"love : reason :: eyes : mind / Love
needs no tongue of reason if love
and the eyes are 1—an identity."
Louis Zukofsky,
Bottom: On Shakespeare.

and Sovereignty recede
along a line-of-escape
past the Metal gate
of the L-shaped room—
where the Mutant
manifestations are left
and right of the <u>other</u> me.

My thought is confirmed
when a woman's Voice
starts to echo, speaking
the Language(s) of the Lost:
it is the Voice of
my opponent's Double,
with whom he is in dialogue.

While her Voice rises
amid the fallen bricks and
the mud, her projected Shadow
appears on the rock face
beyond the Metal gate.

Both torn apart
and pieced together,
the woman's Voice
speaks for my trauma
as Hostage to the Game...
and offers me at once
a No-Win invitation
to the Madness of playing
<u>lose</u>-<u>lose</u>.

But her Voice gradually yields

"Each is one. But in its purest sense
love is this passage from one to two
in the experience of life itself.
Love creates a perspective and
an existence in the world which
is not from the point of view of one
because it is the perspective of two.
The passing from one to two
is a revolution. A great revolution.
It's as if we were putting things
in perspective, as if suddenly
the world has an extra dimension
and it's an absolutely fundamental
experience because it shows us that
the truth of the world is in fact
sustained by the multitudes,
not the atom that is you personally."
Alain Badiou,
in William Williamson (dir.),
The Question of Love.

"Love is said to last
when the adventurers
involved manage to bind up
their wounds, when the skin
heals, and they start to look
at each other again like
Narcissus contemplating
himself in the water. It calls
for a lot of patience and
a great respect for time...
You don't have time because
you don't have enough love."

to the enfolding Sound of
falling water, in which I think
I hear a melody being sung,
as if by a different Voice,
always already beyond
the Astral plane: the Voice
of love calling, nonetheless.

I turn around—

What appears behind me
is a luminous circular Rainbow,
that instantly starts to dissolve.

At the same time,
I find myself removing
a Red Horn of Plenty
from my mouth...

A rope with a large
Gordian knot in it,
the first in a series
of similar knots,
hangs from a ring
on the ceiling, and leads
down a dark shaft.

I approach the rope,
grab onto it above the highest
knot, and put my feet on
the knot below; then, I start

Julia Kristeva,
The Samurai.

"Crack, crack——crack, crack——
crack, crack——so this is Paris!
Quoth I (continuing in the same
mood)——and this is Paris!——
humph!——Paris! Cried I, repeating
the name the third time——"
Lawrence Sterne,
Tristram Shandy.

"For we have advanced, France, /
together into a new land, like
the Greeks, where one feels nostalgic
/ for mere ideas, where truth lies on
its deathbed like an uncle / and
one of me has a sentimental longing
for number, / as has another for the ball
gowns of the Directoire and yet /
another for 'Destiny, Paris, destiny!' /
or 'Only a king may kill a king.'"
John O'Hara,
"In Memory of my Feelings."

"'Know thyself.'"
Pausanias,
Description of Greece.

"First of all, tell me whether
a man who has an itch and wants
to scratch, and may scratch
in all freedom, can pass his life

climbing toward the bottom,
where I think I see light.

I count the knots
on the way,
but somewhere past
two thousand I lose track;
the light is real
and getting closer.

At the end of the rope
I let go, and jump
onto a vast and luminous
stretch of sand.

I have entered the site
described in Everyman's
Handbook of Splendors:
the Tunnel of Set, under
the City of the Pyramids.

In the canal, under
an arched ceiling
of polished alabaster,
lies a White Paper Boat,
pristine and immense.

It rests on the water between
a bumper where the canal
begins—like the Bumpers of
Grand Central after the Leonile

happily in continual scratching."
Plato,
Gorgias.

"Jest on. Know thyself."
James Joyce,
Ulysses.

"We are all humiliated by
the sudden discovery of a fact
which has existed very
comfortably and perhaps been
staring at us in private while
we have been making up
our own world entirely without it."
George Eliot,
Middlemarch.

"The central proposition that
reality is a phantasmagoria,
that the individual mind creates
its own reality, and that
other consciousnesses are
entering and controlling it,
has become a central
modern myth, paranoid,
solipsistic, and deeply determinist.
It has gained purchase
because it matches the way
many experience their lives."
Marina Werner,
*Stranger Magic: Charmed States
and the Arabian Nights.*

Floods—and a Curtain of
Glass Beads that blocks access
to the rest of the waterway...
as in the Mystery Theater
of Doktor Vibes's *Keys to Power*.

The sand all around shows signs
of having been walked on,
and is littered with debris.

I notice two shining Elevator
doors further down, past
the Paper Boat in the canal,
and start to reason:
IF... to the bumper
as Inkwell of Mind,
surmounted by the Flame
of Attention, under the Dome
of the Multiple Task, corresponds
the Blank Page of Matter,
on the Waters of Natural Selection,
across the Sands of Time, *then...*
the Automated doors are
the Entrance to the Mysteries
of *lose-lose*...

I make my way across
the sand and, as I get
to the doors, push the button
on the wall... and wait.

"Protestant dogma had fixed
the 'cessation of miracles...'
—and hence the direct intrusion of
the supernatural into human lives—
back to the year 600 C.E."
Victoria Nelson,
The Secret Life of Puppets.

"Now that my ladder's gone /
I must lie down
where all the ladders start /
In the foul rag
and bone shop of the heart."
W. B. Yeats,
The Circus Animals' Desertion.

"The end is in the beginning
and yet you go on."
Samuel Beckett,
Endgame.

"Peace is a united effort
for coordinated control.
Peace is the will of the people
and the will of the land.
With peace we can move ahead,
together... All you got to do
is clap your hands:
one, two, three... one, two, three...
one, two, three... one two three...."
Leon Thomas, "Hum-Allah-
Hum-Allah-Hum-Allah,"

The Automated doors open;
I enter a large hall.

In the floor stands a lever,
pulled to one side and fastened
with wire to a row
of Metal shelves that extend
into the far distance.

On the shelves are various
objects of Metal, wood, Plastic,
cloth, Nylon, glass...

As I am about to step
through the doorway,
I realize that I no longer
have the Red Horn of Plenty
in my hand.

Thinking that I dropped it
somewhere behind in the sand,
I watch the Automated doors
close again, and turn
to retrace my steps.

The Revelation occurs to me
that the objects in the sand
are Debris from *The Marriage
of Purgatory and Hell*.

I hurry back to the last

in Pharoah Sanders *(RIP)*,
Jewels of Thought.

"'Begin at the beginning,'
the King said, very gravely,
'and go on till you come
to the end: then stop.'"
Lewis Carroll,
Alice in Wonderland.

"] /] right here /] /
] (now again) /] /]for /]... "
Sappho,
If not, Winter (tr. A. Carson).

"Hammer your thoughts into unity."
W. B. Yeats,
"If I Were Four-and-Twenty."

"As slippery as the Gordian knot
was hard!"
William Shakespeare,
Cymbeline.

"There must have been more time /
in Shakespeare's day /
to sit and watch a play."
Marianne Moore, "Marriage."

"In seed time learn, in harvest teach,
in winter enjoy. Drive your cart
and your plow over the bones of
the dead. The road of excess leads

group of objects that
I had encountered—
two sealed jars labeled
"Power Flex," one heavy-duty
spring and a tubular Pink
container—only to find a pile
of rope and a Rusty lamp.

Continuing further,
I rediscover a balloon
with coiled ribbons...
but then I remember
that between the balloon
and the spring lies the area
where I saw doll parts
(two left arms and
a head full of hair)...
so I turn around, bend down
and pull from the sand
a fragment of spray can
and the sole of a shoe—
but no Horn of Plenty.

I go back to the balloon...

More entangled rope
and doll parts, but still
no Horn of Plenty.

I look at the central fold
of the giant Paper Boat,
and ask myself whether
the Horn of Plenty

to the palace of wisdom. Prudence
is a rich ugly old maid courted
by Incapacity. He who desires but
acts not, breeds pestilence..."
William Blake,
The Marriage of Heaven and Hell,
"Proverbs of Hell."

"It was a dance of masks and
every mask was perfect because
every mask was a real face and
every face was a real mask so
there was no mask and there was
no face for there was but one dance
in which there was but one mask
but one true face which was
the same and which was a thing
without a name which changed and
changed into itself over and over."
Leonard Cohen,
Beautiful Losers.

"First, glyph; the syllabary, /
Then letters. Ratio after / Eyes, tale
in sound. First Dance. Then / Voice
Voice. First, body—to be seen and
to pulse / Happening together."
Louis Zukofsky, "A-12."

"It is difficult / to get the news
from poems / yet men die
miserably every day / for lack /
of what is found there."

was in my possession
on the way over.

I think I remember,
after jumping off the rope,
approaching the Boat
with the Talisman still in hand...

The mound of bottles
and medicine bag
had drawn my Attention.

I dig there, and
though I turn up
more bottles and rope,
more jars and tubes,
some shredded clothing
and a broken lamp,
I am still at a loss.

Maybe it fell to the ground
when I first jumped off...

I return to my starting point:
jugs, cans, a circuit board,
a chariot wheel...
but no Talisman.

I give up.

As I head back toward
the Automated doors,
I see more rope,

William Carlos Williams
"Asphodel, That Greeny Flower."

"These are the years and the wall
of the ward, / the winds and clouds
of the sea of board / sailed by
the sailor / wearing the watch / that
tells the time / of the cranky man /
that lies in the house of Bedlam."
Elizabeth Bishop,
"Visits to St. Elizabeths."

"My mistake was to go on
after Pearl Harbour."
Ezra Pound, quoted in
Catherine Seelye,
Charles Olson & Ezra Pound:
An Encounter at St. Elizabeths.

"In my dream, the Professor
restores my faith. 'If I had
known Ezra, I could have
made him all right,' he says."
H. D.,
Tribute to Freud.

"...disillusioned with Olson
(but not with projective and non-
projective verse), whose poems,
when he finally read them (which
he was slow do to—dazzled by
the theory and his own ignorance),
seemed almost fraudulent

more bottles and boxes,
a twisted window frame,
a ladder, a charred
maypole, a torn cushion,
another balloon,
and a cap with
a Lemniscate on it.

(after reading *The Maximus Poems*,
he vomited for three hours);
disillusioned with the Church of
the True Martyrs of America,
disillusioned with the times—
he went on reading. And writing..."
Robert Bolaño,
Nazi Literature in the Americas.

I get to the doors
and as I wait for them
to open, after pushing
the button on the wall,
the thought occurs
that maybe I misplaced
the Red Horn of Plenty
from the start,
at the top of the shaft,
where the knotted rope
was attached to the ceiling.

"But after a while he went away
with a troop of poets, to hide
from the sons of Morna, and
they hid him in the mountain
of Crotta Cliach; but there was
a robber in Leinster at that time,
Fiacuil, son of Codhna, and
he came where the poets were in
Fidh Gaible and killed them all."
Lady Gregory,
"The Coming of Finn,"
in *Gods and Fighting Men.*

The doors slide open.

I am seized around the neck
by the Staff of Moses Vaüdevilians,
which I recognize from
the low-level Electro-Shock
described in *Dummie's Guide*
to Political Science.

"For what is this creation, after all
(creation of what, from where,
in what, of whom, by whom,
toward whom and what)?"
Antonin Artaud,
"Against the Kabbalah."

It pulls me into a new
space, a hallway that contains

"Raphèl maì amèce zabì almi."
Dante,

a series of Megaliths
resting at various intervals.

Immediately, my legs go limp;
but an Albino Androgyne
is standing there, in an unbuttoned
shirt with rolled-up sleeves.

S/he catches me,
grabs me by the waist
and puts my arm around
his / her shoulder; then,
with my legs sweeping the floor,
drags me down the hallway
on a path through the Megaliths—
the two of us are like
Thalamus and Limbus
in Niño "Brain Stem" Roma's
PHILYNIKON.

Pulled along, I hear
an Inner Voice and look up:
the Androgyne's White fingers
are raised above our heads,
wiggling, gesticulating...
and I understand
from these Hand Signals
that s/he is my Interpreter.

Addressing my Inner Mind
through Sign Language,

The Divine Comedy: Inferno.

"I set out now /
in a box upon the sea."
C. Olson,
Maximus IV, V, VI.

"The radiocarbon results suggest
that megalithic graves emerged
within a brief time interval of
200 y to 300 y in the second half
of the fifth millennium calibrated
years BC in northwest France,
the Mediterranean, and the Atlantic
coast of Iberia. We found decisive
support for the spread of megaliths
along the sea route in three main
phases. Thus, a maritime diffusion
model is the most likely explanation
of their expansion."
Bettina Schulz Paulsson,
in *Proceedings of the National
Academy of Sciences* (Feb. 2019).

"Every age has the Stonehenge
it deserves—or desires."
Jaquetta Hawks,
"God in the Machine,"
Antiquity 41 (1967).

"A multidisciplinary team
of scientists recently announced
the discovery of the oldest human

the Interpreter explains
that s/he is leading me
to "Dante-Ali's Palace
of Infinite Justice,"
where the Telepathic
Language of Esperanto
is the "Chosen Tongue."

In a moment of multiple
Revelation(s)
I understand the Special Place
to which the Tarot Cards
have brought me:
as the Grand Union between
win-win and *win-lose*...
as the Final Turn
in the Dialectic of the Pyramid
of Enlightenment... and Last Leg
of the Journey to the O-N-E...
the Masta Plan of *lose-lose*
now faces Judgment Day.

The Albino Androgyne,
dragging me into the Palace,
carries me toward "the Mound
of Cerebellums," just past
the entrance, where s/he helps me
take hold of a Walker,
a Classic model (without wheels).

Then my Interpreter retreats
back into the Hallway
of the Megaliths, leaving me

footprints in North America. These
fossilized prints were made between
23,000 and 21,000 years ago along
the shores of an ice age lake that
once filled the Tularosa Basin in
south-central New Mexico, in what
is now White Sands National Park.
This finding fundamentally changes
the timeline on North American
human habitation—turning back
the clock of human arrival in
the Americas nearly 10,000 years."
USGS, *Earth Science Matters,*
Newsletter, Fall 2021.

"It is not always possible
to know, when you make a note
of an event, or a state of mind,
how this may strike someone
perhaps ten thousand years later."
Doris Lessing,
Shikasta.

"All men and women have been
dreaming for 10000 years of the day
when the sexes shall be no more—
but for myself I have struggled
to find that way that *with* the very
present sex we now have to remove
the thorn of it... So my answer
to you about you—about the poet—
has to be what you do, what
you are—10000 years—10000."

clutching the Walker, alone
before my silent "Witnesses."

To my relief, despite her / his
absence from the Palace,
her / his Sign Language
is still coming through to me
as Inner Voice...

I am informed that
the "Left and Right Runways"
sloping down along the walls—
where a group of Witnesses
is standing side-by-side—
lead toward "Exit Hatches
into the Crawl Spaces
of THE LAWS..."
and that these Runways are
Left and Right *Parietal Planes*
in the "Infinite Field of Extensions."

The Crawl Spaces are Left
and Right Head-End Projections
in the "*Proprioceptive Scheme.*"

Then the Interpretation stops:
I assume that the Esperanto
Mind Readers—my so-called
"Witnesses"—have ceased
communicating, and I am left
to supply a Transmutant reading.

Frances Boldereff, in
Charles Olson and Frances Boldereff:
A Modern Correspondence.

"The moment we begin to understand
the thought processes of Paleolithic
people in caves better, numbers and
percentages become of secondary
importance, strictly speaking."
Jean Clottes,
Chauvet Cave: The Art
of the Earliest Times.

"The appearance of the first man
is known to us only through his bones."
George Bataille,
"The Passage from Animal to Man
and the Birth of Art."

"We've heard it, we've all heard
about all the sticks and spears
and swords, the things to bash
and poke and hit with, the long,
hard things, but we have not
heard about the thing to put
things in, the container for
the thing contained. That is
a new story. That is news...
Long before the tool that forces
energy outward, we made
the tool that brings energy home."
Ursula K. Le Guin,
"The Carrier Bag Theory of Fiction."

With Final Judgment at hand,
win-lose is both the Alpha-
Origin of a Primordial and
Absolüt *win*, and the *Al-páa-ha*
(Relative) Abécédarian Root
of a Consequent and Multiple *loss.*

I know that w*inning* and *losing*
are THE PROCESSES
of Maya-Kara Ontological Ethics...
wherein:
win-win
is to
lose-lose
as
win-lose
is to
lose-win.

When I play *to win,*
my Animality, in its Morphic link
to Culture, passes through
a Tertiary *Beth-Be-Táa*
that is to the Gene Pools
of Nature what Spectra-Vision,
in Teleiocene Civilization,
is to the Gamma Rays
of Cosmic Speech.

I win, *you* lose:
Al-páa-ha Bet-be-ta,
Kam-ma Gem-el,

"After I wrote to Jack suggesting
we make some sort of tribute
to our teacher, he replied with
a copy of Olson's 'plan' divided
into 28 subjects with the name
of a poet attached to each...
These responses to Clarke's call
provide a ground for soul making,
a topography and a stance."
Albert Glover, "Introduction,"
in *A Curriculum of the Soul*
(ed. Albert Glover, Jack Clarke).

"History is story. It means
nothing else as a noun.
Herodotus was the first
to use the word (sign enough
of the 5th Century change)
and he used it as a verb:
to find out for yourself.
Then you tell. Or if you don't,
it tells. The evidence is there,
for you did find out."
Charles Olson,
The Special View of History.

"It is true that storytelling reveals
meaning without committing
the error of defining it, that it brings
about consent and reconciliation
with things as they really are,
and that we may even trust it

Ta-be-aháa.

By the same token, it follows
that when I play to *lose*
I also *win:* my Desire
is the Alchemico-Analytic Tool
of a De-Territorialized Delta
Aggregate, the *Tel-Táa*
beyond Object and Subject
for Man and Woman alike.

I lose—
yet, the Messages of
"Dream" and "Vision"
do not deny my brain
its Belonging, its Connection
to the Da'Led of Fruitfulness.

I lose—
yet, the "Mushroom Clouds"
of Inadequate Idea
and Confused Perception
do not obscure the way.

I lose—
yet, I lose *outside*
the Knocks, the Shocks,
the Pricks and Kicks
of Sylph, Undine,
Salamander and Gnome.

I am not destroyed
by more powerful than I.

to contain eventually by implication
that last word which we expect
from the Day of Judgment."
Hannah Arendt,
"Isak Dinesen: 1885–1963."

"It is not improbable that
this myth [of Prometheus]
has the same characteristic
importance for the Aryan mind
as the myth of the Fall has for
the Semitic... The Aryan nations
assign to crime the male,
the Semites to sin the female
gender; and it is quite consistent
with these notions that
the original act of *hubris*
should be attributed to a man,
original sin to a woman."
Friedrich Nietzsche,
The Birth of Tragedy
from the Spirit of Music.

"The erotic seems to resist
immediate definition,
suspended as it is
between the physical
and the spiritual."
Lou Andreas-Salomé.
The Erotic.

"The whole of the trump sequence
can be seen as a path of sexual

Even though *I am Loser—*
I remain Konstructivist Pretender...
Child of Stance, Color and Song...
Faithful Friend of All Signs.

I lose—but we win.

Tel-Táa
Ep-Zil-On-OM!

"Tel-Táa
Ep-Zil-On-OM?"
I hear the Interpreter's Voice
reply inside my Mind...
and in terror I realize that
they hear my every thought
Telepathically:
my own Language is Transparent
to the Witnesses, my own Mind
an Esperantist "Open Book."

Suddenly, the thought
of my own thought frightens me.

I stop thinking,
in an Organic effort
to clear my Mind, and focus
Attention on arresting
the Wild Dance of Sensation.

integration, which passes through
many aspects of male/female
duality (Emperor/Empress,
High Priestess/Hierophant,
Chariot/Justice, Sun/Moon,
and so on), with partial unions
(The Lovers, Temperance,
The Star) and separations
(The Hermit, The Devil,
The Tower) along the way,
culminating in the ultimate
mystical union of the 'androgyne,'
or unisex figure, who dances
in the center of the World card."
Margot Adler,
Drawing Down the Moon.

"—braggart / fisherman, the /
Androgyne who hates /
the simulacrum / Time Magazine /
takes for male..."
Charles Olson,
The Maximus Poems.

"It is as though for the first time
since the split of sex occurred that
a new split has been forced
wide open—1/2 male and female,
1/2 female and male."
Frances Boldereff, in
Charles Olson and Frances Boldereff.

"The harrowing of Hell / is the descent

The Interpreter responds,
explaining that the folding chairs,
on which a second group
of Witnesses is seated,
line the path leading to
the "Hard-Body Enclosure":
a Black Metal container
prolonged on either side by
"Left and Right Frontal Curtains."

In front of the Curtains,
left and right, a third group
of Witnesses sits on the floor.

I notice the most obvious
Configuration last:
rising on either side
of the Palace of Infinite Justice
stand the "Left and Right
Temporal Pillars,"
or *Pillars of Time*.

"When you lose, you lose:
Ze-ta Et-Hā."

"*Given* and *done*,
like THE FACTORS
in the Zigzag of History,
the *Two* are *Actual*."

In reaction to the Interpreter's
words my Attention is diverted
away from *Nothingness*,

of the dancing hermaphrodite"
Diane di Prima,
Loba, "of Loba."

"Have patience and shuffle the deck."
Miguel de Cervantes,
Don Quixote.

"Sancho Panzas and Don Quixotes /
And, alas, some Lots from Sodom, /
Are sampling the deadly juice, /
Aphrodites rise from the foam, /
Helens shimmer in the mirrors, /
And the time of madness nears."
Anna Akhmatova,
"Poem without a Hero."

"Wild dream in motion /
Sleep is no remedy."
Louis de Góngora,
"The Solitudes" (tr. H. Ballantyne).

"I only understand that while I'm
sleeping I have no fear, or hope, or
trouble, or glory; blessed be whoever
invented sleep, the mantle that
covers all human thought, the food
that satisfies hunger, the water that
quenches thirst, the fire that warms
the cold, the cold that cools down
ardor, and, finally, the general
coin with which all things are
bought, the scale and balance that

despite all.

The *Two* are *Actual... Upstream,*
where the "Dendrites are on Fire"
and the Gene Pools of Nature
Neuro-Plastic.

The Conceptual Problem
with my Unitary Perspective on
the Becoming-Minor of *win-lose*
concerns the Abstrakt Expression
of Action Potential in the spacetime
Synapses of the Human Continuum.

The *Name* of the Nodal Matter
that is also *Place,* where
my Entogenetic *Plastic song*
overlaps a Philogenetic *subsong,*
represents not only the Neuro-Mirror
"U-Pa-Zi-Le-On"—
that selectively inhibits
the Re-Uptake of "Ep-Zil-On-OM"
as "Pez-il O-Nō," in *Pez-il O-Nō*
Ziik-Máa Chi Chi:
"When you win, you win"—
but also, simultaneously,
the Psycho-Phaenomenal *"NI"*
in *NI Pe-zi-Pe-hi NI*—
"I can't win."

The Interpreter says nothing.

At this critical juncture

make the shepherd equal to
the king, and the simple man equal
to the wise. There is only one
defect in sleep, or so I've heard, and
it is that it resembles death..."
Miguel de Cervantes,
Don Quixote, quoted in
Solaris (dir. A. Tarkovsky).

"I wish to reside alone
in my inner deliberations."
Lautréamont,
Maldoror.

"Not to be forgotten:
books are the work of solitude
and the children of silence."
Marcel Proust
Against Sainte-Beuve.

"The simultaneous origin of man
and language, the mutual,
instantaneous constitution of
the symbolic order, involves
a triangular structure of self,
body, and shadow (image
of the body) with three points
of the triangle related by three
mutually constitutive, bipolar
oppositions (body/shadow,
body/self, self/shadow). Self-
consciousness occurs at the instant
when all possible relationships

in my descent into the Abyss—
when *win-lose* operates as
the Frontal, Temporal, Parietal
and Head-End Network
of Transmitter and Receptor Sites
for the Structure of Error,
the Creation of Illusion,
and the Cyber-Steroid Form
of a Majority no longer Plural,
but One—
I notice a small opening
in the Metal façade
of the Hard-Body Enclosure,
behind which a set of eyes
has suddenly appeared.

The eyes seem fixed
on me; yet, as soon as
I spot them, they disappear.

Moments later,
they reappear and
then disappear again:
either it is the same
set of eyes, or another
person is peering at me
through the opening.

I want to maneuver
the Walker forward,
from the Mound of Cerebellums

of splitting and doubling between
the three points of the triangle
simultaneously come into play."
Robert Irwin,
American Hieroglyphics.

"Here is the savage economy
of hieroglyphics."
Samuel Beckett,
"Bruno ... Dante .. Vico . Joyce."

"If you pay attention to the signs,
then when will you pay attention
to what they signify?"
François Rabelais,
The Third Book of Pantagruel.

"Jim knowed all kinds of signs.
He said he knowed most everything.
I said it looked to me like
all the signs was about bad luck,
and so I asked him if there warn't
any good-luck signs. He says:
"Mighty few—an' dey ain't no use
to a body. What you want to know
when good luck's a-comin' for?—
Want to keep it off?"
Mark Twain,
Adventures of Huckelberry Finn.

"You can take the thing /
out of the sign but you can't /
take the sign out to lunch."

to the central area at
the foot of the Black Enclosure
—but, as the disappearance
and reappearance of the eyes
behind the wall become
rhythmic, the indication is
that a new set of eyes
is looking at me every time.

I stay put.

Against the continued silence
of my Interpreter—the Albino
Androgyne, who is still
behind me in the Hallway
of the Megaliths—
the Iota of an Adequate Idea,
acting like the point at which
a tangent touches a circle,
brings the Axon of Pure Language
into Pineal Focus.

I see that <u>*win*</u>-<u>*win*</u>
is the Revelation of the Hidden
Meaning of <u>*win*</u>-<u>*lose*,</u>
because THE QUALITIES
or Basic Conditions of Truth
are staring me in the face,
<u>Topologically</u> *and* <u>Metrically</u>.

This is no Tribunal of Reason.

I am no Ordinary José "Kuf"

Michael Boughn,
"An Obscure Poem on the Battle
of Milvian Bridge."

"Consider for example the proceedings
that we call 'games.' I mean board-
games, card-games, ball-games,
Olympic games, and so on. What is
common to them all?— Don't say:
'There must be something common, or
they would not be called "games"'—
but look and see whether there is
anything common to all.— For if
you look at them you will not see
something that is common to all,
but similarities, relationships, and
a whole series of them at that.
To repeat: don't think, but look!"
Ludwig Wittgenstein,
Philosophical Investigations.

"We can see, in the narrative
tradition in which he chose to
write, *Tristram Shandy*'s essential
agon or game, the struggle of
the rhetorical and the philosophical
views of man for dominance.
We can see Sterne's persistent
attempts to move games,
the games of philosophy, rhetoric
and war, from zero-sum to non-
zero-sum. We can see him insisting
that philosophical seriousness

facing Cosmological Judgment
in a Discursive Universe of
"Poetico- Politico-" opposites.

I am no Original *Wannabe* lost
in the "translation" to an Afterlife,
no *Beautiful Loser* in Spinooze's
Curriculum of the Flesh.

I am an Initiated Experiment
in Pragmatic Self-Trial,
Literal and Literary Lambda
in a Bio-Physical
Mother Tongue that precedes
the Loss of History /
the History of Loss...

Win-win means
"I can't lose."

I win,
you win—

Pez-Il-O-Nō,
Io Ta Xi
OM-ik-le-on
La-ho!

Pi... Kuf,
Káa-pa,
Lam-bé Ta
theth HA-ha.

become rhetorical play."
Richard Latham,
"Games, Play, Seriousness."

"Life has but one true charm:
the charm of gambling. But what if
we are indifferent to gain or loss?"
Charles Baudelaire,
Intimate Journals,
"Squibs" (tr. C. Isherwood).

"He put his hand to his brow and
paused, in evident perplexity.
I rejoiced in my advantage,
but dared not glory in it yet.
At length, he lifted his head,
and, quietly making his move,
looked at me and said, calmly,
— 'Now you think you will win,
don't you.'"
Anne Brontë,
The Tenant of Wildfell Hall.

"'Play cards with me,' said
the Spirit of Chance... The girl
thought it might be fun. She was
just going to pick up her hand when
she saw that the Spirit of Chance
was wearing an induction helmet
with a wire that stretched back
way into the distance. She was
connected with a computer!"
Joanna Russ,

We *all* win,
when I win.

Instead of a reply
to my Thought Process,
there is kicking and screaming
echoing from behind
the Metal façade of the Enclosure,
as if the spectacle of me,
propped up against my Walker
on the Mound of Cerebellums,
had provoked a terrible reaction
in a particular set of eyes.

Instantly, two intense
Flames explode and stay lit
on top of the Temporal Pillars.

The Interpreter explains that
my thoughts are catching Fire
from the "Perpetual Renewal"
of a *Depolarizing Current* across
the Positronic Emission Zone.

Then, at once, the Left and
Right Frontal Curtains draw apart,
releasing a large cloud of smoke
on each side—
while a Trap Door,
hidden near the center
of the ceiling, swings open.

The Female Man.

"Who criticizes or
pushes the game away
has already entered the game."
Maurice Blanchot,
The Writing of the Disaster.

"Without contraries is no progression.
Attraction and Repulsion, Reason
and Energy, Love and Hate are
necessary to Human existence."
William Blake,
The Marriage of Heaven and Hell.

"We are always more
influenced than we realize
by the ideas we contest."
Simone de Beauvoir,
"Must We Burn Sade?"

"In the practice of mutual aid,
which we can retrace to the earliest
beginnings of evolution, we thus
find the positive and undoubted
origin of our ethical conceptions;
and we can affirm that in the ethical
progress of man, mutual support—
not mutual struggle—has had
the leading part. In its wide extension,
even at the present time, we also
see the best guarantee of a still
loftier evolution of our race."

A rectangular Wooden Box
decorated with Norse-Armorican,
Arabico-Indian and Egypto-
Ismaeli Hieroglyphs descends
from the Trap Door,
suspended by four chains.

The Box has three great Swords
piercing it—two through the sides,
left and right, and the third,
vertically, down the middle—
and settles onto the floor
in front of the grid,
behind which the eyes
have now disappeared.

Magickally, after the Box-
of-the-Three-Swords reaches
the Positronic Emission Zone,
the chains detach themselves
and are lifted back up through
the Trap Door, which closes again...

I make a renewed effort
to still my Mind: I want
my Essential Take
on *win*-*win* to hold.

"Fat Chance," says the Interpreter.

As if on cue, three women
advance from the Witnesses

Peter Kropotkin,
Mutual Aid: A Factor of Evolution.

"...If thought is like the keyboard
of a piano, divided into so many
notes, or like the alphabet is
ranged in twenty six letters all in
order, then his splendid mind had
no sort of difficulty in running
over those letters one by one,
firmly and accurately, until
it had reached, say, the letter Q.
He reached Q... But after Q?
What comes next? After Q there
are a number of letters the last
of which is scarcely visible
to mortal eyes, but glimmers
red in the distance. Z is only
reached once by one man in
a generation. Still, if he could
reach R it would be something."
Virginia Woolf,
To the Lighthouse.

"This philosophic rage
is a bit extreme, / You've no idea
how comical you seem."
Molière,
The Misanthrope (tr. R. Wilbur).

"**homeopathy** (1810) *Medicine...*
a holistic approach to medicine
contending that drugs which

on the Palace's *left* side,
and together approach
the Box-of-the-Three-Swords.

One at a time, they proceed
to each remove a Sword.

No sooner is the third Sword
withdrawn than the entire Box
falls into pieces, breaking apart
to reveal another Box inside...
this one of Cardboard.

I am told by the Interpreter
that the Swords are named
"Faith," "Hope" and "Charity"—
or "Gospel," "Blues" and "Jazz"—
which I immediately Reinterpret
as "Aleph," "Mem," and "Tau,"
upon the Revelation that
the Box-within-the-Box
contains a Double Meaning.

The three Swords are symbols
for three Configurations—
the Hall of the Megaliths,
the Mound of Cerebellums
and the Hard-Body Enclosure—
according to a larger Magick View,
like the ones outlined in Urth's
Special Weltanschauungs,
whereby the Palace's Seven
Configurations—which include

produce symptoms similar to
those of a disease can be expected
to cure that disease... and that
minute doses of drugs provide
the most powerful effect."
Jennifer Bothamley,
Dictionary of Theories.

"From now to the end
of consciousness, we are stuck
with the task of defending art."
Susan Sontag,
"Against Interpretation."

"We are the knights who say
'Ni!'...We are the keepers
of the sacred word, *'Ni!'*...
The knights who say
'Ni!' demand a sacrifice...
Ni! Ni! Ni! Ni! Ni! Ni!"...
Monty Python and the Holy Grail
(dir. Terry Gilliam).

"I saw the best minds of
my generation destroyed
by madness..."
Allen Ginsberg, "Howl," quoted in
The Emperor's New Clothes,
"Welcome to Your World."

"...No one / to witness / and adjust,
no one to drive the car"
William Carlos Williams,

the Parietal Runways, the Head-End
Crawl Spaces, the Temporal Pillars
and the Frontal Curtains—
represent the Seven Double Letters
of *Axonal Sprouting*
on the Gates of Pure Language.

Without further word
from the Interpreter,
three men now come forward
from the Witnesses
on the Palace's *right* side.

The first, nearest to me,
picks me up and drags me
forward, until we are met
by the second man,
beside the *Pillar of Time*,
who grabs me by the ankles
and lifts my legs.

Together they carry me
toward the Cardboard Box,
where the third man
is waiting for me, holding
a roll of Artist's tape.

He tears off a piece
of tape, and puts it
over my mouth.

Then, he uses the Artist's
tape to tie my hands

"To Elsie."

"Al, heavy; *páa,* break; *ha,* water /
Be, walk; *ta*, where, place,
plain, ground /
Kam, receive; *ma*, mother, earth /
Tel, deep, bottom; *ta*, where, etc. /
Ep, obstruct; *zil*, make edges;
onom, whirlwind /
Ze, strike; *ta*, where, ground, etc. /
Et, with; *ha*, water /
Thetheha, extend; *ha*, water /
Io, all that which lives and moves;
ta, where, ground, etc. /
Ka, sediment, obstruction;
páa, break obstruct /
Lam, submerge; be, go, walk;
ta, where, ground, etc. / *Mu*, Mu."
Col. James Churchward,
"The Greek alphabet
and its esoteric meanings,"
in *The Lost Continent of Mu*.

"...The essential difference between
the right hemisphere and the left
hemisphere is that the right hemi-
sphere pays attention to the Other,
whatever it is that exists apart from
ourselves, with which it sees itself
in profound relation... By contrast,
the left hemisphere pays attention to
the virtual world that it has created,
which is self-consistent, but self-

behind my back, and tie
my feet together—after
which the other two men
place me in the Box.

Finally, all three men
start to seal the Box
with more tape.

The Interpreter is silent.

Inside the Box, alone
with the Ganglia, Bulbs
and Lobes of my thoughts,
I experience the Magnetic
Resonance Image of
Absolüt Darkness.

The natural question I ask myself
is: How will I relinquish
my Essential Hold on <u>*win*-*win*</u>,
in favor of a new Essential
Hold on <u>*lose*-*lose*,</u>
without going through Torture?

How to maintain the same
Degree of Power in a Field
of Immanence Re-Wired
through the Sodium Channels
of *Eros*'s Love and *Aphrodite*'s
Beauty, without getting

contained, ultimately disconnected
from the Other, making it powerful,
but ultimately only able to operate
on, and to know, itself."
Ian McGilchrist,
The Master and his Emissary.

"The brain stores memory by linking
neurons / to form new circuitry,
turning up the synaptic / volume
controls by stimulating neural
pathways / in the hippocampus
with high-frequency bursts / of
electricity. Give up, turn the corner /
And let all this somehow be
triggered by calcium / But that other
is not an object but impulse /
A rub of two sticks under
moonlight, we need a fire..."
Anne Waldmann,
Iovis, Book I.

"One need not be a Chamber –
to be haunted – / One need not be
a House – / The Brain has Corridors –
surpassing / Material Place – "
Emily Dickinson (D 407).

"Space is the gulf between
imagination & reality.
The evolution of consciousness
fills this gulf."
Meher Baba,

Theocratically Flayed and / or
Nihilistically Impaled?

If the *Intentio* of *win-lose*
is to make *lose-lose* cohere
with the Original Language of
win-win, like "the fragments
of a single broken vessel"
according to Messäāniahk #11,
then Torture's Affect is
the Event-Horizon where
that coherence is achieved—
and Self-Centeredness
tempers my Self-Division,
just as my Sovereignty
triumphs over Dumb Luck.

In effect, the Event-Horizon
remains the Last Word
in both a Rational Promise
of Truth and an Irrational
Promise of Falsehood,
as these are Materialized,
Left and Right, throughout
the Palace of Infinite Justice.

Lying on my back,
I use the darkness
and silence of the Box
to relax, despite the tape.

With the realization that
the Combinatorial Logic

"East-West Gathering."

"But often the grey hen came
alone or one of the grey hens
if you prefer, for that is a thing
that will never be known...
For it was quite possible
there were several grey hens,
and yet only one in the habit
of coming to the kitchen."
Samuel Beckett,
Malone Dies.

"Enter, *Lucifer, Belzebub,*
and *Mephistophilis.*"
Christopher Marlowe,
Doctor Faustus.

"The central idea for which Galileo
was attacked, the notion that the earth
revolved around the sun rather than
vice versa, had been publicly and
officially proclaimed ninety years
earlier by Nicolaus Copernicus...
Unlike Galileo, Copernicus enjoyed
a ripe and comfortable old age,
neither censured nor placed under
house arrest, nor threatened
with torture and excommunication.
How to explain the difference in
how these two men were treated?...
Galileo declared that he knew what
he knew based on his own personal

of *lose-lose*
is informed by the Algorithm
of a Worst Case Scenario
that coincides with the flow
of my Perceptual Assemblages,
and that my Degree of Power
is unstable, I begin to meditate
on the Mythic Will
to Cosmic Delirium
as the Revolutionary Solution
to a *winner-take-all*
Mutilation that is Torture-free.

In an Enantiodromian Vision
of the Seven Architectural
Configurations outside the Box,
I see with overwhelming clarity
that the Chakras in Belacqua's
Planetary Alphabetagrammaton—
Sun... Moon... Jupiter... Saturn...
Mercury... Mars... Venus—
are Double-Entry Sites
for the Mutual Sublimation
of the *Seven Fundamentals*—
Wisdom, Wealth, Dominion,
Fruitfulness, Faith, Hope, Charity—
and their Academic *Twins:*
Pride, Gluttony, Sloth, Greed,
Envy, Wrath and Lust.

As the Mysteries
of *lose-lose* come to light,
under the influence

sense experience. Copernicus set forth
precisely the same ideas, but based
his claims on hypothesis alone."
Elizabeth Lloyd Mayer,
Extraordinary Knowing.

"Beauty is truth, truth beauty,
—that is all / Ye know on earth,
and all ye need to know."
John Keats,
"Ode on a Grecian Urn."

"Beautiful... as the chance encounter
of a sewing machine and
an umbrella on an operating table."
Lautréamont,
Maldoror.

"Since we cannot extract
beauty from life, let us
at least extract beauty
from our inability to extract
beauty from life."
Fernando Pessoa,
The Book of Disquiet.

"All earthly existence must
ultimately be contained
in a book... The book, total
expansion of the letter, must
draw its mobility therefrom;
and, correspondingly,
from its spaciousness must put

of my Mythic Will
to Cosmic Delirium,
I feel my Degree of Power
stabilize and elevate.

I determine, then and there,
that I will use my head
to break through the Cardboard.

My first thought
is to sit up
in one powerful motion,
and direct the full force
of my forehead against
the top of the Box,
in a ritually correct Enactment
of the similar force with
which *lose-lose*
infinitely dispels the "Box"
of the False Logic that asserts
Winning means *Winning*.

But the attempt fails,
as do others, although
I succeed in bending
the Box out of shape,
giving myself more room
in which to turn over
onto my stomach,
and maneuver my lower body.

something into play, let us say,
that warrants fiction...
There is nothing fortuitous
in all this, even though ideas
may seem to be the slaves of
chance... Poetry, accompanied
by the Idea, is perfect Music,
and cannot be anything else."
Stéphane Mallarmé,
"The Book: A Spiritual Instrument."

"How often I wonder whether
this is only writing, in an age
in which we run towards deception
through infallible equations
and conformity machines."
Julio Cortázar,
Hopscotch.

"Judgments on poetry
are worth more than poetry."
Lautréamont,
Maldoror.

"Produce the book, then,
so it will separate, disengage from
itself in its dispersion. This will
not mean that you have produced
the absence of the book."
Maurice Blanchot,
"The Absence of the Book."

"The Documentary Hypothesis....

Finally, in an exhilarating
rush of Energy, I manage
to get a foot on the ground,
and, pushing up with
my shoulders and head,
I break through the Cardboard
and rise to my feet...

I find myself at the summit
of an immense hill.

Overhead, a resplendent
Red sky is filled with new,
unknown constellations!

Beneath me, circling the hill,
two Rings of Black smoke—
like the Black Rings described
in Smurf's *Introduction to Smog*—
divide the hillside into three parts,
each part displaying a dense
network of Shadows.

At the foot of the hill,
far away, I see a saloon.

I feel that I am
on Fire, consummated
by the Flame of *lose-lose*,
in Mystic Communion
with the Heavens.

is that the Bible's first books were
formed through a long process.
Ancient writers produced documents
of poetry, prose, and law over many
hundreds of years. And the editors
used these documents as sources."
Richard Eliot Freeman,
The Bible with Sources Revealed.

"And they didn't know that
Joseph understood, for there was
an interpreter between them."
Genesis 42: 23.

"To some degree, all great texts
contain their potential translation
between the lines; this is true
above all of sacred writings.
The interlinear version of
the Scriptures is the prototype
or ideal of all translation."
Walter Benjamin,
"The Task of the Translator."

"The angel of the Lord went forth,
and smote in the camp of
the Assyrians a hundred and
fourscore and five thousand:
and when they arose early
in the morning, behold,
they were all dead corpses."
Isaiah, 37: 36 (KJV).

I want to shout,
raise a cry of joy from
the hilltop: I throw myself
to the ground and struggle
to loop my taped wrists
around my legs
and out in front of me.

Then I stand up again, and
pull the tape off my mouth.

My freedom
and confidence
seem limitless.

I lose, *you* lose.

In all languages.

Mu.

Lose-lose serves
the Post-Global Good
of Mutually Assured
Destruction.

Lose-lose serves
the Lasting Peace
at the end of
Terror's Rainbow,
Coffin and Cradle
of Civilization.

"Our true religion is a monotheism
of consciousness, a possession of it,
with a fanatical denial of the existence
of autonomous partial-systems."
Carl G. Jung,
The Secret of the Golden Flower.

"Nine at the top means: /
Arrogant dragon will have
cause to repent."
I Ching.

"Here came the hexagram brought
forth by the passive chance workings
of the vegetable stalks. Random, and
yet rooted in the moment in which
he lived, in which his life was bound up
with all other lives and particles in
the universe. The necessary hexagram
picturing in its pattern of broken
and unbroken lines the situation..."
Philip K. Dick,
The Man in the High Castle.

"If one avoids the linear,
progressive, Time's-(killing)-arrow
mode of the Techno-Heroic, and
redefines technology and science as
primarily cultural carrier bag rather
than weapon of domination, one
pleasant side effect is that science
fiction can be seen as a far less
rigid, narrow field, not necessarily

Mu!

In all languages.

I lose, *you* lose.

I cut the tape
around my wrists
with my teeth,
then work quickly
to free my legs.

I turn to begin
my descent toward
the Shelter, convinced
that a higher Destiny
awaits me there.

I see a Bicycle.

The bottoms of its wheels
are lodged in a circular
pool of Ice.

Over the Handlebars,
a small Flag marked
Holy Davidson
waves in the wind.

My sense of anticipation

Promethean or apocalyptic at all,
and in fact less a mythological genre
than a realistic one. It is a strange
realism, but it is a strange reality."
Ursula K. Le Guin,
"The Carrier Bag Theory of Fiction."

"I spoke to a man / Down at
the tracks / And I ask him /
How he don't go mad / He said
'Look here junior, don't you be
so happy / And for Heaven's sake,
don't you be so sad.'"
Television, "Marquee Moon"
(*RIP* Tom Verlaine).

"'Our Saviour. Two thieves.
One is supposed to have
been saved and the other...
*(he searches for the contrary
of saved)...* damned.'"
Samuel Beckett,
Waiting for Godot.

"Where all are guilty,
nobody in the last analysis
can be judged."
Hannah Arendt, "Organized Guilt
and Universal Responsibility."

"(Beware of those who speak of
the spiral of history; they are
preparing a boomerang.

is extreme.

Nothing can stop me.

I set out now
from a Box
upon a hill...

Keep a steel helmet ready.)"
Ralph Ellison,
Invisible Man.

"For we must ride to the Judgment –
And it's partly, down Hill – "
Emily Dickinson (338).

Unfortunately,
the first crack
of the Ice
alerts me to a problem
with the Bicycle's wheels.

While jerking
the Handlebars
back and forth—
in my zeal to dislodge
the Front Wheel—
I have bent it.

The wheel, slightly
misshapen, remains stuck.

By the time I manage
to force it out,
the Front Wheel is warped
even more.

Grabbing the Top Tube
and the Seatpost,

"...Each one of us has the desire for
the good (Love), we move to beauty
(Aphrodite), we care for the Real
(Truth or Idea), and we have to do
something about it, whatever we do
(we Will). Actual willful man."
Charles Olson,
The Special View of History.

"This one then as I am saying
was of the resisting kind of them,
that is to say resisting was
the way of winning in him..."
Gertrude Stein,
The Making of Americans.

"The creator must be an outlaw.
Not a criminal outlaw, but
rather a poet who cultivates
intellectual rebellion."
Philippe Petit,
Creativity.

I tug on the Bicycle
and pry the Rear Wheel
loose—finally freeing
the whole thing from the Ice;
but the Rear Wheel
is also deformed.

As I walk the Bicycle
across the Frozen pool,
I can tell that the Tires
are good, although the ride
will necessarily be wobbly,
given the damage
to the Rims and Spokes.

I get on the Saddle
and gain my Equilibrium,
but as I start to Pedal,
a cold gust of wind
pushes the Bicycle
toward a point "*concealed*
yet existing" under the Ice,
like the Legomenon
in Sad-Adam's Field of Ono—
and I fall.

As I pick myself up,
I recognize, buried beneath
the Ice in the same place
where I swerved off track,
the blurred contour
of a bare foot.

"If I can get four
I gotta open the door..."
James Brown *(RIP),*
"Get it Together."

" ...The door is an entire cosmos
of the Half-open. In fact,
it is one of its primal images,
the very origin of a daydream
that accumulates desires
and temptations... The door
schematizes two strong
possibilities, which sharply
classify two types of daydream.
At times, it is closed, bolted,
padlocked. At others, it is open,
that is to say, wide open."
Gaston Bachelard,
The Poetics of Space.

"The Blessed Holy One said, 'א, א'
(Alef, alef)! Although I will create
the world with the letter ב *(bet),*
you will be the first of all the letters;
only through you do I become one.
With you all counting begins and
every deed in the world. No union
is actualized except by א *(alef).*"
Zohar, "Introduction."

"There is no document of culture
which is not at the same time
a document of barbarism."

I lift the Bicycle and
continue to walk it,
only to discover
a second foot submerged
a few steps away...
then, nearby, a large hand
with the tips
of its long sharp Nails
protruding from the surface.

At the same time,
with the forward
motion of the Bicycle,
an eerie Sound, like a Cry,
starts emanating
from the Head Tube,
while the bent Reflectors
on the wheels flash,
front and back, with erratic
bursts of Red and Green light.

The Bicycle's Sound and lights
come to a stop,
when I arrive at the site
of a bald head
lying on its side
half-embedded in the Ice,
but frozen in an apparent smile,
casting its one eye around,
then fixing its gaze on me...
as if happy
to see me at last.

Walter Benjamin, "Theses on
the Philosophy of History."

"Z is a great letter that
establishes a return to A,
the fly, the zigzag movement
of the fly... The Z, the final
word, no word after *zigzag*...
It may be the elementary
movement, which presides at
the creation of the world...
At the origin of things,
there isn't a Big Bang...
there is Z... which in effect
is Zen the route of the fly."
G. Deleuze,
ABECEDAIRE.

"I love my love with a capital Z.
I mark him Zero and mine. Ha! Ha! /
I mark him Zero and mine."
Helen Adam, "I Love My Love."

"Like lightning, yes...
In the moment of a thunderbolt's
zigzag, one finds oneself forced
to give her what even full daylight
leaves in the shadows."
Colette,
The Ripening Seed.

"The second spill came
at the seventh turn

I am caught
in the first swirlings
of pity and fear
before the spectacle
of this truncated figure
stretched across the Ice;
but, as I walk my wobbling
Bicycle onto solid ground—
a repeated Cry rising
from its Frame, its Reflectors
bursting with Color—
I am surprised to find
that the admiring gaze
and gentle smile
coming at me in profile
are getting on my nerves.

The Ancient Vista
that opens before me
grabs my Attention at once—

Leading down to my right,
a straight, wide Shining Path
presents itself as a clearing
through a Jungle of Shadows
on either side.

I mount the Bicycle
and take off; the wobbly
wheels, awkward at first,
soon become manageable.

on some slippery pavement.
Jesus went down for the third
time at the eleventh turn,
skidding on a rail. The Israelite
demimondaines waved
their handkerchiefs at the eighth."
Alfred Jarry,
The Crucifixion Considered
as an Uphill Bicycle Race.

"The essence of comedy is to give
the impression that it is unaware
of itself, and to develop within
the spectator the pleasure of his
own superiority and the pleasure
of man's superiority over nature."
Charles Baudelaire,
"On the Essence of Laughter."

"...And suddenly the world was
right side up. Violet learned then
what she had forgotten until
this moment: that laughter is
serious. More complicated,
more serious than tears."
Toni Morrison,
Jazz.

"The Calculator running
all the time / to calculate our
minimum of hope / outpaces
all our flights of thought /
and pulverizes objects of

As I gather speed,
I am like Ylem
on the Magick Carpet
Alphomega XII, riding
the microwaves of Yeesod
through the New Jerusalem Rift!

Automaton in
the Primum Mobile
of Gamesmanship,
I am traveling
on Cheq's Fast Track
to Philosophic Success,
across the Boiling Oilfield
of Theology's
'Isterical Material!

No time for the Quick-firing
Questions-within-the-Question
according to Quietus
the Quaesitor of Karbala,
Seventh Soldier
of the Chemical Plagues,
Redeemer of Regions, Nations
and Greater Generations!

My Bicycle is a Soul Machine
Fueled by the Cold Sweat
of Funk Thang's Pow'r.

Despite
the wobbly

our thought / so comically that
on perfection's ice / the very act
of thinking takes a spill."
Harry Martinson,
Aniara, 45.

"You are a machine
of things happening."
Robert Duncan,
"Vancouver Lecture," in *Imagining
Persons* (ed. R. Bertholf, D. Smith).

"The antithetical tincture
is emotional and aesthetic
whereas the primary tincture
is reasonable and moral. Within
these cones move what are called
the Four Faculties: Will and Mask,
Creative Mind and Body of Fate...
These pairs of opposites whirl in
contrary directions, Will and Mask
from right to left, Creative Mind
and Body of Fate like the hands
of a clock, from left to right."
W. B. Yeats,
A Vision (1937).

"and as the clocks run races over /
the planet and hearts are filled
with / stone after stone that
never will / fall as machines
devise other machines as if it were /
possible to conceal that the future /

wheels,
even
as I ride
over
a rippled
patch
of clay
on the trail,
I feel
pretty
GOOD!

I arrive at an area
of overlapping Shade
between a rock
and a Dead tree—
like the Out-of-Sight
Green Zone
in Sad'e and Sadr's
Brand New Tent
of the Templar Witness—
where a head
and more body parts
lie buried in sand.

I stop the Bike
and get off
on the Good Foot.

As I kick the Kickstand,
it breaks off...
so I put the Bike down,
and walk toward the head

conceals nothing today..."
Inger Christensen,
alphabet.

"There is a formula for Time that
has not yet been computed."
H. D.,
Tribute to Freud.

"The entire Search sets three
kinds of machines to work
in the production of the Book:
machines of partial objects
(impulses), machines of
resonance (Eros), machines of
forced movement (Thanatos).
Each one produces truths,
because it is the nature of
truth to be produced and to be
produced as an effect of time."
Gilles Deleuze,
Proust and Signs.

"This is vile work.—For which
reason, from the beginning
of this, you see, I have
constructed the main work and
the adventitious parts of it
with such intersections, and have
so complicated and involved
the digressive and progressive
movements, one wheel within
another, that the whole machine,

in the sand.

It rests in the Shade
surrounded by two legs
and two arms rising
straight in the air.

The toes begin to wiggle
and the hands start to wave,
as if triggered
by my Body Heat.

Unlike the first head,
this one is not set
in profile, but lies face up
at an angle, and stares
at the sky, then at me;
though it seems younger,
it too is bald; the face
is covered with tattoos.

The head smiles at me,
batting its eyelashes,
as if in admiration.

My first reaction is again
one of pity and fear
stopped short—
by *je ne sais quoi.*

The smiling head
is beaming a message
at me that clearly recalls

in general, has been kept a-going."
Lawrence Sterne,
Tristram Shandy.

"[English...]
Contemporary Language...
par excellence, perhaps...
highlights the dual character
of our time, retrospective
and advanced."
Stéphane Mallarmé,
English Words.

"It's just an old war /
Not even a cold war /
Don't say it in Russian /
Don't say it in German /
Say it in broken English."
Marianne Faithfull,
"Broken English."

"Three quarks for Muster Mark! /
Sure he hasn't got much of a bark /
And sure any he has
it's all beside the mark."
James Joyce,
Finnegans Wake.

"The horns of elfland swing past,
and in a few seconds / the world,
as we know it, sinks into dementia,
proving narrative passé..."
John Ashbery, "Hotel Lautréamont."

"Please, Please, Please"
from the 2nd Glory of
Tacœus "Wise Guy" Typhon
in Nimrod Emoticons's
Translation of the Context
of the Context of the Context.

"Éarendel arose where the shadow flows / at Ocean's silent brim; / through the mouth of night as a ray of light / where the shores are sheer and dim / he launched his bark like a silver spark / from the last and lonely sand; / then on sunlit breath of day's fiery death / he sailed from Westerland."
J. R. R. Tolkien,
"Éalá Éarendel Engla Beorhtast."

"Who owns James Joyce?"
Edna O'Brien,
Joyce's Women.

"Jingle jingle jaunted jingling. / Coin rang. Clock clacked. / Avowal. Sonnez. I could. Rebound of garter. Not leave thee. Smack. La cloche! Thigh smack. Avowal. Warm. Sweetheart, goodbye! / Jingle. Bloo. / Boomed crashing chords. When love absorbs. War! War! The tympanum. / A sail! A veil awave upon the waves. / Lost. Throstle fluted. All is lost now. / Horn. Hawhorn. / When first he saw. Alas! / Full tup. Full throb."
James Joyce,
Ulysses.

Is the benevolence real,
or does it mask
a feigned Blindness
to my problem
with the Kickstand,
and my warped wheels?

Do I detect a trace
of *satisfaction*
in this tattooed face's
awareness of incipient
malfunction affecting
a Reflector(s) / Head Tube /
[Kickstand] structural subset?

What does it mean,
when I mount my Bike again
and find that the Reflector
Lights are Blue now, and
the Head Tube emits a Sound
like Abramelon's Water Drum
in *Mama Sé Qua*?

With the second apparition

of a dismembered figure
on the trail, the passage
through Sublunar
barricades of Shadow
has led to an *Ernst*-style
opening of the field.

The trail bends
to the left, down
a bare slope across which
Shadows are scurrying,
like the Shadows
beneath the Sea of Glass
in the Man's World Testament.

I pick up speed, and
get *the Feeling* again:
Universally United
with my Bicycle
and with the hill itself,
as if seated on a Throne
supported by Rods of Metal,
I stay on the Scene
of All History:
the singularity of major events
and minor events alike
becomes at once,
in the fullness of the past—
on Un-Land and in Un-Time—
the minus-one [-1] multiplicity
of Ullikummi's communication
with the Tohu-Bohu of Ba'ath.

"Pataphysics. The world was
cryin' out for it, so I invented it."
Alfred Jarry,
Ubu Cuckold.

"Pre-amp, pro-sound performance /
Groove tube / Killer caps / You're
a Strat cat / Patch in / Dangerous
distortion / serious sustain /
Slinky, super slinky / Boomers
double-ball ends / It'll phase,
it'll flange, it'll fuzz / It's fast,
it's flexible / Just feel those frets /
A simulated comb filter /
For steroizing a mono source /
It's got a scaled-down Strat-
style body / With the feel of
a Les Paul / Deep cutaways,
no pickguard / And a couple of
chromebuckers; / Full shred!"
Jeff Beck *(RIP)*, "Guitar Shop."

"It can do that to you, a certain
kind of guitar playing... If that
song had been coming through
a clarinet, I'd have known
right away. But the guitars—
they confused me, made me
doubt myself, and I lost the trail."
Toni Morrison,
Jazz.

"Haunted by wind instruments /

The Brakes, which I engage
by Back Pedaling,
are working well,
allowing me to control
the vibrations induced
in the Frame from
the wobbling of the wheels
at high speed.

The Blue, near-Silver pulses
coming from both Reflectors
bring to my downhill ride
a sense of the Out-transformed
Equilibrium experienced
by Orgaz and Orc
in *The Book of the Life*
of the Sex-Sex-Sexes!,
just as the Territorialist
"tra-LA... *la*-LA..."
of the Water Drum connects me
to the (Post-) Class-Struggle
Othertime of Enoch Light's
Whole Earth Opera.

Indeed, the open territory
in this section of the hill
seems to confirm
the Technostructure of my Bike
as Soul Machine,
especially in regard to
the Suspension Forks
and Rear Shock Mount,
as I hit the first bump

in groves of grace / the maiden
saplings slant oboes / and shampooed
gigolos / prowl to the sobbing taboos."
Mina Loy, "The Widow's Jazz."

"Orchestral instruments warm up
for jazz. The flute is a cat that
ripples its fur against the deep-
purring saxophone. The drum
throws sticks. The cat jumps on
the keyboard. Hi diddle, hi diddle,
the cat and the fiddle."
Jean Toomer,
Cane.

"deep in the glowing / Empty-text, /
at lamp's level, / in the timehole: /
listen your way in / mouthwise."
Paul Celan,
"The Trumpet's Part" (tr. P. Joris).

"And the tumult of thoughts and
feelings that now assailed him—
he would have liked to consign it
to the Mountain of Obscurity."
Murasaki Shikibu,
The Tale of Genji.

"I said these kinds of things was
adventures; but he said
he didn't want no more adventures."
Mark Twain,
Adventures of Huckleberry Finn.

on the trail.

Whether over sand,
clay or gravel, not only
do I feel the Spirits of
Osirac and Oz Shalom
circulating as Ubudian
Air, Water and Fire
across the Top Tube,
Down Tube and Seat Tube—
Over-swarming the Nineveh-
Mosul-Ashura Habitations
with Chaldean-Exxonite Energies
—but my feelings change...

The two heads with body parts
on the ground no longer seem
like *Pathetic Fakes,* "Super Bad"
cause for pity and fear.

With the renewed *confidence,*
courage and *fortitude*
of Nabôpôlar-czar
the Material Sheik of Ur-Nippur,
and the Spiritual *cunning*
of Nebûchâdnêwar-czar al'Askarîs
the Meta-Materialist,
I delight in the bump
on the trail, and continue
to coast down the Beastly Hill.

"Perhaps my best years are gone...
but I wouldn't want them back.
Not with the fire in me now."
Samuel Beckett,
Krapp's Last Tape.

"And now—I am dressed in a caftan
with huge pockets, and in my hand
I have a goose quill, not a steel pen.
Wax candles burn before me,
and my mind is inflamed."
Mikhail Bulgakov,
The Life of Monsieur Molière.

"That which does not kill me,
makes me stronger."
Friedrich Nietzsche,
Twilight of the Idols.

"I believe whatever doesn't kill you
simply makes you stranger."
Christopher Nolan (dir.),
The Dark Knight.

"From whatever angle the problem
of eroticism is approached,
one retains the feeling of it having
been extremely one-sided."
Lou Andreas-Salomé,
The Erotic.

"...Every known creature with

It is the Soul-crossed
Mother-Lover Style
of *Babylon the Great*
in my "Schizematic"
mastery of the Brakes
that establishes the Self-
transfigural bond between
the Bicycle's Chainstay and
my Selfheart's Phallic Root.

By coasting and intermittently
kicking back on the Brakes,
not only do I get
the stop-and-go
of the Bike to "stammer"
to the Discordia
of its own "music,"
as in the Speech-Grille
of Rashied- and Mohammed-Ali,
but I open a Shard-sealed
moment of recognizability,
in which the Suspension Fork
and Rear Shock Mount
are Anagogic projections
of my legs.

The more I gather speed,
conserving Authoritarian-
Pragmatic control of the Pedals,
the more the Chainstay,
Suspension Fork and
Rear Shock Mount
transfer to my lower body

a neuronal system, however far
down the evolutionary tree one goes
and however far back in time,
has a system that is asymmetrical."
Ian McGilchrist,
The Master and his Emissary.

"Tell all the truth but tell it slant – "
E. Dickinson (1263).

"'I beg you, Engineer, not to impute
to me anything of the sort... Paradox
is the poisonous flower of quietism,
the iridescent surface of the rotting
mind, the greatest depravity of all.'"
Thomas Mann,
The Magic Mountain.

"—it was one of those occasions when
the Consul had drunk himself sober—"
Malcolm Lowry,
Under the Volcano.

"From monkish cell and lying garb
released, / Oh heart of mine, /
Where is the Tavern fane, the Tavern
priest, / Where is the wine?"
Hafez (tr. G. Bell).

"There is no power and no strength,
save in God, the Almighty,
the Magnificent. What shall I do now?"
Tales of the 1001 Nights,

a global sense of Super Power—
allowing me to skid,
despite the warped wheels,
in longer and longer test runs.

The result is a competitive thrust,
where the isolation and loneliness
of the Neurological Other / Self
disappears into Neverness,
Nightfiber and Noëm,
and incorporated Equilibrium
functions as polarized Numen:
just as front precedes rear
on my Bike, so too *right*
preempts *left*.

I pursue this Revelation
by slamming down
on the Brakes and skidding,
in an alternating series of
Hypophalloconcentric surges,
first to the *right*,
in the name
of *Mission Accomplished,*
then to the *left*,
in the name
of *Mission Impossible.*

On every try, in the synaptic
fissure of a clear danger's
repeating instance, when
the memory of a Pro-Ballistic
Regime's interference

"The Story of the Hunchback."

"*Ta'wil* does not consist in
bringing down to a lower level;
it consists in restoring or
raising to a higher plane.
In *ta'wil* one must carry sensible
forms back to the imaginative
forms and then rise to still
higher meanings; to proceed
in the opposite direction
(to carry imaginative forms back
to the sensible forms in which
they originate) is to destroy
the virtualities of the imagination."
Henry Corbin,
Creative Imagination in
the Sūfism of Ibn 'Arabī.

"The mystery of the universe
is hierarchic in structure."
Meher Baba, quoted in
Nicola Masciandaro,
Sufficient Unto the Day.

"The Ramist method begins
to appear almost as mystical
a conception as the Art of
Ramon Lull, which imposes
the abstraction of the Divine
Dignities on every subject and
thereby makes the ascent and
descent. And it begins to appear

with the Wahlter-Glock law
of Assur Equilibrium
threatens the Gitmo tradition
of Pan-Mexica aplomb—
like Anti-Messäāniahk #3
(the "Red Dragon")
in the Republic of Noös—
both the *right* leg
and the *right* arm—
connecting, respectively,
through the Seat Tube
and the Chainstay
to my Phallic Root—
control the skids.

I realize that the broken-off
[Kickstand] could have acted
as superstitious channel
for Bad Counsel—
like Language-Shadow
on the Language-Scale
in Dr. Heildigger's
Method of JuJw.

I skid to the right...
the Bicycle conforms!

I skid to the left...
the Bicycle obeys!

In control on the Warpath
to Historicist Revenge,
through the Songlined

not dissimilar in aim from
Camillo's Theater which provides
the unifying ascent and descent
through arrangement of images..."
Frances A. Yates,
The Art of Memory.

"Through the two halves of the action
which come closely together
at one point, the drama possesses—
if one may symbolize its arrangement
by lines—a pyramidal structure.
It rises from the introduction with
the entrance of the exciting forces
to the climax, and falls from here
to the catastrophic. Between these
three parts lie the rise and the fall..."
Gustav Freytag,
Freytag's Technique of Drama.

"The land of the Tarahumara is full
of signs, forms, and natural effigies
which in no way seem the result of
chance—as if the gods themselves,
whom one feels everywhere here,
had chosen to express their powers
by means of these strange signatures
in which the figure of man is hunted
down from all sides... This Sierra,
which exhales a metaphysical
thinking in its rocks, the Tarahumara
have covered with signs, signs
that are completely conscious,

Sacred Landscape
of *lose-lose,* I am riding
to end the Game,
destroy the Competition!

Then, I hit another
bump on the road—
and the Front Wheel catches Fire...

The Stolen Lightning of Lemūres!

My Backbone is re-born
as a pillar of Rainbow Flames,
feeding on the lost
and missing documents
in Barbar's *Book of Kulchur!*

I think I hear the Love-
Sound Buoys of Gaza
guiding me toward the Last House
in Ishtar's Land-of-Virgins,
but I sense at once
the Inter-current fraud
in my own Hypokritic reading...

What I am hearing
are the Ice-true Increate's
Intervolving Trumpets
announcing an Earthquake
from above, at the apex
of the Shamanic Hill.

The ground trembles;

intelligent, and purposeful."
Antonin Artaud,
Voyage to the Land of the Tarahumara,
"The Mountain of Signs."

"Frankness, you are a slit
and a hole, abyss,
you are not a summit."
Laure,
The Sacred, "Libertinage."

"The gods gathered like flies
around the man making sacrifice."
Gilgamesh, Tablet XI.

"'Why is this discourse
called a "song"'?...
'Just as a song is drawn
from heaven to earth
by the holy spirit, so these
words were drawn to earth
by the holy spirit.'"
Zohar, "Ha'azinu"
(tr. M. Simon, H. Sperling).

"There is the dream poem, /
Which all poems envy,
and connive to become."
Hugh Seidman *(RIP)*, "Poems."

"Where your apexojesus
will be a point of order."
James Joyce,

I lose my Equilibrium,
and fall down, hard.

Instantly, as if in reaction,
the Fascist Earthquake stops.

Thrown to the ground,
face down, I feel the Bike
on top of my head…
it is pushing the foot
of my folded right leg
against my mouth,
as pictured in David
"Eye-Tooth" Judah's
Seven Designer Stretches.

Although the Front Wheel
is slowly spinning in the air,
the Fire is out, the Reflectors
and Head Tube are off.

The next Sound I hear,
coming from beyond
the Ensilenced Eidolon—
now Multi-sealed, by virtue
of the missing [Kickstand],
within the Chainstay,
Suspension Fork,
Rear Shock Mount,
Top Tube, Down Tube and
Seat Tube—is a Roaring Sound

Finnegans Wake.

"The quotation…
'Where your apexojesus
will be a point of order,'
represents the world order
Bruno and Yeats and Joyce
subscribed to, relates his book
to the scheme of Yeats's
A Vision, and is a high point
from which both past and
future glide into reality."
Frances Boldereff,
Hermes to His Son Thoth.

"…and when his eyes were
opened he saw nothing."
Acts 9: 8.

"The god Baba got up
and said to Pre-Harakhti:
'Your shrine is empty!' "
The Contentions of Horus and Set,
Chester Beatty Manuscript I.

"The alchemical symbol
of Venus [is] the only one
which comprises all
the Sephiroth of the Tree of
Life. The doctrine implied
is that the fundamental
formula of the Universe
is Love. (The circle touches

emanating from the Chain,
the Chain Rings and the Crank.

The Eisegesis of the Roaring,
according to *Eschatology*
of the Enduned by Elders 24,
indicates my "*servile integration*
to an uncontrollable apparatus."

As soon as I pick up
my Bicycle and start riding
down the hill again,
the Roaring stops.

I notice, however,
that the Handlebars
are twisted to the right,
and that the Seat Binder
has failed—so that the Saddle
swivels from side to side,
and is lower than before...
causing my knees to rise above
the Top Tube as I pedal.

I do my best to adjust
to the new ride,
but the conjunction
of wobbly wheels,
the twisted Handlebars
and a low, swiveling Saddle
soon causes my right eye
to twitch in apparent synchrony
with a new Banging Sound,

the Sephiroth 1, 2, 4, 6, 5, 3;
the Cross is formed
by 6, 9, 10, 7, 8.)"
Aleister Crowley,
The Book of Thoth.

"He had started to think about
Egyptian phrases that morning
about Thoth, significantly the god
of magic and the inventor of
language... All things considered,
the double ministry of Thoth was
a manifest guarantee of coherence
in reality or unreality...
Magic or the tangible word,
there was an Egyptian god who
verbally harmonized subjects
and objects. Everything
was really going very well."
Julio Cortázar,
Hopscotch.

"Hearken, O ye goddesses
of the hours of the night sky.
Work ye and eat ye, and
rest ye in your gateways,
with your breasts towards
the darkness, and your hind-
parts towards the light.
Make to stand up the serpent
Hereret, and live ye upon that
which cometh forth from it."
The Book of Gates,

like the Sound in Tzadkiel's
"Twisted Way,"
from Malebranche
the Social Democrat's
Torn-Awake Tennis
(for Angels-Who-Lob-
Thunderstones on
the Time-Courts
of Fallen Babylon).

When the knuckle
in my right pinky
starts to throb in counterpoint
to my twitching eye,
and to the Banging Sound
now emanating from
the Conexus between
the Chain, the Chain Rings
and the Crank, I understand
in retrospect that the Sounds
in the Seat Tube and
the lights in the Reflectors
were not the simple
Circum-Babeled Counter-Signs
of Fortune Tellers and Sorcerers.

The shriveling in my Phallic Root
confirms this Final Revelation.

I see before me a dune
rising like a Speed Bump
from a patch of sand,
which threatens to bring me

"Third Hour," from
the sarcophagus of Seti I.

"And it came between the camp
of the Egyptians and the camp
of Israel; and it was a cloud and
darkness to them, but it gave light by
night to these: so that the one came
not near the other all the night."
Exodus 14.

"The poets are liars (Aristotle,
before Nietzsche, had recalled
the proverb), who comprehend
nothing of the difference
between day and night."
Jacques Derrida,
Glas.

"Contrary to a widely
held common opinion...
it is not in Hebrew (Judaism)
that the systematization
of the symbolic meaning
of letters began, but in
Greek (Aramean influence)
in the Christianity of Asia,
and the Jewish Kabbalah...
seems to depend on the Arab
Jafr of extremist Shiite Islam."
Louis Massignon, quoted by
Henry Corbin, in *Avicenna*
and the Visionary Recital.

down yet again.

My mission seems clear:
to rule the Violent Hill
by mastering my Bicycle,
like a "New" Neo-Spartacus
in Simon Maguus's League!

So, following Terrah Laquna's
Metro-Logic of Preëmption,
I flip into ATTACK-Mode.

Just as I reach the sand,
however, the Banging Sound
turns into the Click-Click-
Clicking Sound recorded
in Hammurabi's MySpace,
and a vision flashes before me:
The Fool, in a Trick
together with *The Aeon*...
representing the Tires
on the Front and Rear Wheels,
in conflict with the Chain,
the Chain Rings and the Crank.

The sign of Dis-empowerment-
within-Empowerment...

Will *The Moon // reversed*
cause the Spokes and Rims
of the wobbly wheels
to self-destruct down
the Ziggurat into Zero?

"The safest general characterization
of the European philosophical
tradition is that it consists of
a series of footnotes to Plato."
A. North Whitehead,
Process and Reality.

"Here, said she, / Is your card,
the drowned Phoenician Sailor, /
(Those are pearls that were his eyes.
Look!) / Here is Belladonna,
the Lady of the Rocks, / The lady
of situations. / Here is the man with
three staves, and here the Wheel, /
And here is the one-eyed merchant,
and this card, / Which is blank,
is something he carries on his back, /
Which I am forbidden to see.
I do not find / The Hanged Man.
Fear death by water."
T. S. Eliot, "The Waste Land."

"I shall tremble."
Virginia Woolf,
The Waves.

"Poetry completely turned
away from its path after
the great Homeric deviation.
—Before Homer, what?'
asked Bourges. — 'Orpheus!'"
Stéphane Mallarmé,

What if, by playing
lose-lose, I bring both
myself and my opponent
to Perdition, and find
that the Game goes on,
despite all, more Unforgiving
than ever?

On my way across the sand,
to the repeated Sound of
Click! Click! Click!, I clench
the Handlebars, and lift my feet
into the air...

The Front Wheel threatens
to Zigzag—"somber precursor"
of Zoetic Regression through
homogeneous empty space.

But I prevail!

I coast through the dune
and stop the Bike
beyond the stretch of sand,
planting my right foot
firmly on the ground:
I will lose—
and bring the Game down
with me!

The Reflectors,
followed by the Rims

in conversation with
Elémir Bourges; quoted in
Henri Mondor, *Vie de Mallarmé*.

"A screaming comes across the sky.
It has happened before. But there
is nothing to compare it to now."
Thomas Pynchon,
Gravity's Rainbow.

"The goddess cried out
like a woman in childbirth."
Gilgamesh, Tablet XI.

"true woman of the pure soapwort /
born of the sharpened reed / who
measures the heavens by cubits /
strikes the coiled measuring rod
on the earth / praise be to Nisaba /
the person who bound this tablet
together / is Enheduanna / my king
something never before created /
did not this one give birth to it"
Enheduanna, "Temple Hymn 4"
(tr. B. De Shong Meador).

"Tis true without lying,
certain and most true."
*The Emerald Tablet of Hermes
Trismegistus* (*Tabula Smaragdina*),
trans. Isaac Newton.

"This is the truth, the whole truth

and the Spokes
on the Front and Rear Wheels,
start making a Buzzing Sound,
like the Vibratile Monad
in the Vatic Fountains
of Visionscrap.

At the same time,
I feel my belly fill
with Gas.

I think back
to the two dismembered figures
partly hidden in the ground,
who smiled as if in admiration
and friendship...
and my feelings change again.

They irk me once more;
they remind me of Gog
and Magog on their "Voyage
of flattery and pandering,"
in Nomad O'Translator's
A Thousand and One Years
of Historic Progress
through Nowhere Time.

Were the happy faces
wishing me well...
or were they smiling
because they knew

and nothing but the truth."
The Emerald Tablet of Hermes
Trismegistus (*Tabula Smaragdina*),
trans. Fulcanelli and O. Sieveking.

"How often have I said
to you that when you have
eliminated the impossible,
whatever remains, *however*
improbable, must be the truth?"
Arthur Conan Doyle,
The Sign of the Four.

"do not move stones"
Sappho,
If not, Winter (tr. A. Carson).

"Why don't you go bang
your foot against that rock."
Aristophanes,
The Birds.

"And what is poetry, so named
for a lack of other words,
if it prescribes, inscribes and
comprehends and overflows
in advance, engulfing
in its abyss, hermeneutic
and doctoral discourse?"
Jacques Derrida,
Glas.

"My friend... was sorry I had not

I was Destined for Shit?

A cramp seizes my right leg,
a signal to start Pedaling again.

But every time I push
my right foot down
on the Pedal,
I feel a pain
shooting from the Nail
of my Big Toe.

Meanwhile, the Buzzing
has given way
to a Whistling Sound,
like a Siren at the edge
of the Astral Sea.

I begin to worry
that the Gas in my belly,
the cramp in my lower leg
and the pain
in my Big Toe—
like my throbbing pinky,
twitching eye and shriveled
Phallic Root—are signs
of a Transformer Hold
on my body, whereby
the Top Tube – Down Tube –
Seat Tube structural subset,
as an extension of the Reflector(s)
– Head Tube – [Kickstand],
is working like Eñlion's Net

properly appreciated the true source
of religious sentiments. This, he says
...is a feeling which he would like
to call a sensation of 'eternity,'
a feeling as of something limitless,
unbounded—as it were, 'oceanic...'
I cannot discover this 'oceanic'
feeling in myself... If I have under-
stood my friend rightly... it is
a feeling of an indissoluble bond,
of being one with the external world
as a whole... Normally, there is
nothing of which we are more
certain than the feeling of our self,
of our own ego. This ego appears
to us as something autonomous
and unitary, marked off distinctly
from everything else... There is only
one state... in which it does not do
this. At the height of being in love
the boundary between ego and
object threatens to melt away."
Sigmund Freud,
Civilization and Its Discontents.

"For all life exists only
as miracle that constantly
renounces its miraculousness."
Lou Andreas-Salomé,
The Erotic.

"And soon, mechanically,
weary after a dull day with

in Fissipaarr's "*Paranoïa-*
Critique" of the Diorite
Death-Squad Insurgency.

Were these Half-hidden Beings,
who aimed their admiring glances
and gentle smiles at me,
Human-shaped, Heaven-crazed
Hierogrammatic Seducers,
Hereward Avatars of the Evil Eye?

Or, were they simply Blind
to the difficulties of the Other...
like the White Angels
at the four corners
of Abu Ghrāb?

I continue across a clearing
of rocks, gravel and sand
toward what appears to be
a large boulder
with dashes of Color.

I recognize what comes into
view, and push on the Brakes.

A woman's head embedded
in rock: another happy face...

I slow down without stopping.

the prospect of a depressing
morrow, I raised to my lips
a spoonful of the tea in which
I had soaked a morsel of the cake.
No sooner had the warm liquid,
and the crumbs with it, touched
my palate, a shudder ran through
my whole body, and I stopped,
intent upon the extraordinary
changes that were taking place.
An exquisite pleasure had invaded
my senses, but individual, detached,
with no suggestion of its origin.
And at once the vicissitudes of life
had become indifferent to me,
its disasters innocuous, its brevity
illusory—this new sensation having
had on me the effect which love
has of filling me with a precious
essence; or rather this essence
was not in me, it was myself."
Marcel Proust,
In Search of Lost Time: Swann's Way.

"And I saw the shining flame glow
white. And suddenly a dark sphere
of air appeared, huge in size, upon
which the shining flame struck many
blows, and at each blow a spark
flew up so that soon the circle of
air was brought to completion,
and heaven and earth shone forth
in the fullness of perfection."

Colored robes
stuck in the rock
around the face
are being tossed
by a whirlwind.

The head wears a straw hat,
and through the open veil
flapping over her face
I can see her big smile
and wide open eyes
welcoming me with
an "Amen" understanding
that seems unaware
of the negative violence
threatening my *lose*-*lose*
Brinskmanship.

I turn to my right,
and pick up speed.

Despite appearances
to the contrary—given
my speed, my Equilibrium,
my progress and the High-
Energy Soundtrack produced
by the Bicycle Itself—
a brutal concatenation
of violence compounds
the stress and anxiety
of my downhill ride.

First, there is the violence

Hildergard of Bingen,
Scivias, "Redemption" (II, 1).

"When shall we open our minds
to the conviction that
the ultimate reality of the world
is neither matter nor spirit, is no
definite thing, but a perspective?"
José Ortega y Gasset,
Meditations on Quixote.

"Form is never more than
an extension of content."
Robert Creeley, quoted by
Charles Olson in "Projective Verse."

"Here form *is* content,
content *is* form."
Samuel Beckett,
"Dante ... Bruno .. Vico . Joyce."

"Books you were going to write
with letters for titles. Have you
read his F? O yes, but I prefer
Q. Yes, but W is wonderful.
O yes, W. Remember your
epiphanies on green oval leaves,
deeply deep, copies to be sent
if you died to all the great libraries
of the world, including Alexandria?"
James Joyce,
Ulysses.

with which my Bike
is getting beat up
by the hill:
not only has the warping
of the Front and Rear Wheels
allowed the Chain, the Chain
Rings and the Crank
to recycle the dysfunction
in the Reflector(s),
the Head Tube
and the [Kickstand],
but the Crank, by way of
the Fire on the Front Wheel,
recreates the possibility
of more dysfunction—
which dysfunction
the Adjusting Barrel
may or may not recycle
in the aftermath
of the Earthquake.

This is not Blackberry Hill,
as evoked in the Late Poetry
of the New Khora.

"Ruinous, perverse and crazed,"
it is Three-Hills-in-One,
like the Palestine Hills,
East of Eden, in Virgil's
Bible-Belt Letters to Petraeus.

Barreling on, neither
Braking nor Pedaling,

"I masturbated and I was content
with the hundreds of thousands
who came forth from me."
The Book of Gates, "Fifth Hour."

"Take all the heads of the people
and impale them, hang them
before Yahweh in broad daylight,
until Yahweh's flaming
anger is burnt away."
Numbers, 25.

"Ah, Bartelby! Ah, humanity!"
Herman Melville,
"Bartleby, the Scrivener,"
quoted in Mark Gerald,
In The Shadow of Freud's Couch.

"Blind, light- / bearded partition. /
A cockchaferdream / floodlights it. /
Behind it, complaint-rastered, /
Freud's forehead opens up, /
the tear, hard- / silenced outside, /
links on with the sentence: /
'for the last / time psycho-logy.'"
P. Celan, "Frankfurt, September."

"For I am actually not at all
a man of science, not an observer,
nor an experimenter, not a thinker.
I am by temperament nothing but
a conquistador—an adventurer...
with all the curiosity, daring,

lost in my thoughts,
I hit a pothole;
and, while I recover
without falling down,
the shock sends a pain
to my neck, after which
I realize that my hair
is falling out.

Another hit to my body...
unfortunate proof
that an alternate violence
besets me—
from my twitching eye,
throbbing pinky and
shriveled Phallic Root,
to my aching belly,
cramped leg and
inflamed Big Toe—
symptoms occurring
in concert with
the succession of Roaring,
Banging, Clicking, Buzzing
and Whistling Sounds,
like the Doomsday Sounds
prophesied in the Phlegethon
Tabloids of Harē Power...

Yet, finally, what links
my body to the Bike,
and the Bike to the hill,
is the violence of the Cards.

and tenacity characteristic
of a man of this sort."
Sigmund Freud, letter to
Wilhelm Fliess (1 Feb. 1900).

"I am sad, I grieve /
I, lord Nezahualcoyotl. /
With flowers and with songs /
I remember the princes, /
those who went away, /
Tezozomoctzin, and
that one Cuacuauhtzin. /
Truly they live, / there
Where-in-Someway-One-Exists?"
Nezahualcoyotl, "I Am Sad,"
in *Fifteen Poets of the Aztec World*
(tr. M. León-Portilla).

"Nothingness gone,
the castle of purity remains."
Stéphane Mallarmé, *Igitur*,
quoted by Octavio Paz
in *The Labyrinth of Solitude.*

"Knosorov notes a phonetic
substitution for the usual, logo-
graphic sign for the month of
Muwan (usually expressed by
the head of the Muwan Bird), in
which the first sign is a cartouche
with a curl in it; he thus reads it
as the syllable *mu*... His epoch-
making article concludes,

Connecting my eye, pinky
and Phallic Root
to the Reflector(s), Head Tube
and [Kickstand] is *The Aeon,*
which conjoins
with *The Moon* by
connecting the Handlebars
with the Tires,
while simultaneously
The Moon // reversed,
in conjunction with
The Hanged One,
connects my belly,
leg and Big Toe
to the Seat Tube,
Suspension Fork and
Chainstay, leaving
the disjunction between
The Philosopher and
The Fool to account
for the connection between
the Bicycle's Frame
and my hair falling out.

So that: the Evil Eye
stands more dissimulated
than ever by its representation
as both *The Moon* and
The Moon // reversed.

Just as Militia Tiamat's
Hanging Garden

'The system of Maya writing is
typically hieroglyphic and
in its principles of writing
does not differ from known
hieroglyphic systems.'"
Michael Coe,
Breaking the Maya Code.

"You will never know the Maya well."
Guillaume Apollinaire, "Lettre-Océan,"
in *Les Soirées de Paris #23 (*Apr. 1914).

"Earth, isn't this what you want,
to rise up in us invisible?"
Rainer Maria Rilke,
The Duino Elegies, "The Ninth Elegy."

"But where are the snows
of yester-year?"
François Villon, "The Ballad of
Dead Ladies" (tr. D. Rossetti).

"*Beelzebub*:
'Crime is heaped on crime...
Thus are we purified. /
The only victim for the frenzied
is the sacrifice of his enemy. /
It is pleasing that
he be scattered in the winds /
And mangled alive,
drawn into a thousand pieces, /
Persecuted with as many marks

of Knowledge inside
the Historical
Consciousness Monument
at Sectarian Crossroads
proved a Synagogue-of-Satan
in Æ'rab Camouflage,
my Bicycle's Soul Machine
hides a Doomsday Machine
within!

If my *lose-lose* Capability fails,
then *all is lost...*

Coming up fast below me,
like a huge Black wall,
stands the first
of the Dark Hill's
two encircling Fog Banks.

I ride into it,
with a final surge
of Mental strength,
as hairless as I am naked.

The darkness seems Absolüt—

I Brake
and come to a stop.

of my own pain...'"
Gottfried Leibniz,
"The Philosopher's Confession."

"I will keep no terms with
my enemies. I am miserable, and
they shall share my wretchedness."
Mary Shelley,
Frankenstein.

"The current climate was hotter
and drier. Millennia of drought had
killed the trees and dried the soil
to a fine grey dust that now rose up
on every wind, forming hills as pure
of line and barren as any sand dune."
Ursula Le Guin,
The Dispossessed.

"just the stalk of a nettle / explains
leaflessly / that in our despair
we have made / a flowerless
earth / sexless as chlorine"
Inger Christensen,
alphabet.

"I'm sure I can see, I'm sure
I can see / Too much pollution,
too much / Too much pollution,
too much pollution / Too much

There is a distant Sound
which I cannot
immediately recognize,
but in the darkness I start
to discern Phosphorescent
manifestations dispersed
along a Slalom Course
down the hill.

Taking off again, I realize
that the Sound I am hearing
is the Ringing of Bells
deep below the surface,
Tolling in the Underground...

Putting Bells and Phosphors
together, I reason as follows:
in order for my pure hatred
of the Game to be experienced
as pure pleasure—
in the knowledge
that both my opponent and I
are doomed to Perdition—
my <u>*lose*</u>-<u>*lose*</u> Capability
must expand to the point
where my Spirit achieves
Absolüt concentration.

Only then can the Light Waves—
which are being radiated
by the Game onto

pollution, too much pollution."
Burning Spear, "Resting Place."

"All governments suffer a recurring problem: power attracts pathological personalities. It is not that power corrupts but that it is magnetic to the corruptible."
Frank Herbert,
Chapterhouse: Dune.

"The Beast did not do what was done to it, but what it wished done to itself: raped because it wanted to be raped itself. Slaughtered children because it yearned to be slaughtered children. Built jails to dwell on and hold on to its own private decay."
Toni Morrison,
Jazz.

"Not one would mind, neither bird nor tree / If mankind perished utterly; / And Spring herself, when she woke at dawn, / Would scarcely know that we were gone."
Sarah Teasdale,
"There Will Come Soft Rains."

"As they were talking, they saw thirty or forty of the windmills found in that countryside, and as soon as

my opponent's Spirit and
simultaneously absorbed
and reflected by his Spirit—
become, in turn,
deflected and re-radiated
by my Spirit
in a *just* and *balanced* way...
which is the way
of the Fold-in-the-fabric
at the bottom of my Monad
as Tarot Player:
the Single Fold
wherein pure hatred
and pure pleasure are One!

I apply moderate pressure
to the Brakes
and coast in darkness
toward the first Phosphor.

Almost at once,
the air turns warm.

As it gets warmer and warmer,
I choose the "Interior Experience"
of *pleasure* as the just and
balanced response!

I open myself to the intense
warmth pouring over me,
while my Bike's wobbling wheels,
its crooked Handlebars

Don Quixote caught sight of them
he said to his squire: 'Good fortune
is guiding our affairs better than
we could have desired, for there
you see, friend Sancho Panza,
thirty or more enormous giants
with whom I intend to do battle...'"
Miguel de Cervantes,
Don Quixote.

"'Come!' said Africanus,
'how long will your mind be
chained to the earth? Do you see
into what regions you have come?'"
Cicero, "The Dream of Scipio."

"Please be advised that I will vaccinate
the world with a desire for violent
and perpetual astonishment."
Dorothea Tanning, "Legend."

"Existentialism... resembles
individualism in the sense that
it seems important to it that each
individual gains his own salvation,
and that each individual appears
as being the only one able to
obtain it for himself. Yet it also
resembles Marxist realism because
only in working actively for
the concrete triumph of universal
freedom, by proposing ends

and low, swiveling seat
provide the perfect opportunity
for my arcane discomforts
to melt into air!

When I reach the first Phosphor
and turn toward the next one,
a whirlwind envelops me
in hot sand, which instantly
Mutates into a million shards
of delight entering my flesh!

As Movement-in-process
("like Light Itself,"
according to Halliburton's Song
for his Godson Kyōtō),
the free and perfect act
of riding downhill
in the present moment
of *lose-lose*
allegorizes the Infra-Red
integration of the Dealt Hand's
multiple inclinations
into the Single Fold
that is the uniform inclination
from the *saloon* "above"
to the *Shelter*
as Greenhouse "below."

After turning at the second
Phosphor and heading off
toward the next,

for himself that surpass him, can
the individual hope to save himself."
Simone de Beauvoir,
"What Is Existentialism?"

"...The relation of labour to capital,
or to the objective conditions of
labour as capital, presupposes
a process of history which dissolves
the various forms in which the worker
is a proprietor, or in which
the proprietor works. Thus above all
(1) Dissolution of the relation
to the earth—land and soil—
as natural condition of production..."
Karl Marx,
Grundrisse.

"The archaeologist and serendipidist
can... find the known beginnings
of usury entangled with those of
marine insurance, sea lawyers,
the law of Rhodes, the disputed text
of Antoninus Pius on the limits of
his jurisdiction. Even then the dealers
in metal appeared to be privileged
over other merchants, and
the insurance risk mainly paid by
the takers of greater risk. Vast mines
of anecdote lie still unexploited."
Ezra Pound,
"The Individual in his Milieu."

I cross a puddle and
get splashed by cold water.

My eyes start to sting
as I ride my Bike
onto a stretch of Ice...

Sheer bliss!

The Just Form
of Balanced Content!

While my Spirit,
under the *lose-lose* pressure
of Maxed Out hatred,
shrinks and shrinks,
my fear of falling
Mutates into complete joy,
because I find myself
simultaneously re-enacting
the "burning eyeballs"
of Beelzebub, Lord of Ozone!

By transferring heat
to the moisture in
my eyeballs and causing
the moisture to Evaporate,
my concentrated Spirit
creates the "eyeball-open"
state described by Katrina
the Carbon Casuist
in *Last Dialogue(s)*

"We will see the day of /
RELENTLESS / PURSUIT OF DATA /
Interrogate the Abyss!"
Ed Sanders,
Investigative Poetry.

"If we do not have the depths,
how do we have the heights?"
Carl G. Jung,
The Red Book.

"What was man?"
Pablo Neruda,
Heights of Machu Picchu.

"As a man is a necklace /
strung of his own teeth."
Charles Olson,
The Maximus Poems.

"A man who walks on his head,
ladies and gentlemen, a man
who walks on his head sees
the sky below, as an abyss."
Paul Celan, "The Meridian."

"Strong too was the feeling
that the sky was a bottomless
pit into which the universe
might drop forever."
Gene Wolfe,

on 'The Sub-Real'
with Chad Fahrenheit!

I make the turn around
the Phosphor, riding down
in darkness to the next one.

I go splashing through
a series of puddles
of alternately hot and
cold water, which lie
between patches of Ice;
meanwhile I am being side-
swept by scorching wind
on one side
and frigid wind
on the other.

With each new sensation
I feel like the *Adam Qadmon*
of Resentment, Psyched
by the Inconvenience of Truth,
descending the Black,
Magick, Analog Hill like
a Perfect-Storm-On-Wheels!

Arriving at the Light,
I make an excellent turn,
and I behold
beyond the next Light
an infinite series
of Eternal Lights...

The Book of the New Sun.

"The Magical Universe, MU,
is a universe of many gods,
often in conflict."
William Burroughs,
The Western Lands.

"When the vulture opens her wings
to receive the phallic stroke
in the silence and secrecy
of the cloud, her shrill
scream of rapture... is MU."
Kenneth Grant,
Nightside of Eden.

"It is the first paradox of magic,
and the worst, that it is
always least available when
we are most desperate."
Norman Mailer,
Ancient Evenings.

"In 3.5 billion years, the core of
the aging sun grows hotter, causing
a severe greenhouse effect that
sterilizes the entire biosphere:
its outer surface cools, expanding
to engulf the inner planets.
In 7 billion years the earth
slips out of orbit but, outside
the small chance that it could be

But now I am riding in mud.

And the air is getting
harder to Breathe.

My happiness redoubles!

I let go of the Brakes
and try to Pedal
through the mud,
enraptured by my Bike-ride
tribulations and the spectacle
of the Illuminated Way.

Then—flying off
an invisible ledge
against the sudden Redness
of the sky—I launch
out of the Dark Fog
into free fall,
over the gaping mouth
of an Abyss...

Hermetic Big Air.

Rainbow Gravity,
overtaking my Rear Wheel
qua *Weak Force of Mind*
relative to my Front Wheel

flung out into the 'icy desolation
of deep space,' it is dragged into
the core of the Sun to be evaporated,
its only legacy a small amount of fuel
for the red giant's farewell glow."
Robin Mackay,
"A Brief History of Geotrauma."

"Sometimes I feel twenty and
sometimes I feel two hundred,
and when you do, no arithmetic
can pep you up or slow you down."
Billie Holiday (w/ William Dufty):
Lady Sings the Blues.

"A beautiful girl once told me
of a recurring nightmare in which
she lay in the center of a large dark
room and felt her face expand until
it filled the whole room, becoming
a formless mass while her eyes ran
in bilious jelly up the chimney.
And so it is with me."
Ralph Ellison,
Invisible Man.

"the intermediate sounds /
(even yet?) / the shadow palavers /
the anxieties, icetrue, fightclear, /
the baroquely cloaked, / language-
swallowing showerroom, / semantically
floodlit, / the uninscribed wall /

qua Strong Force of Heart,
is rotating my Bicycle toward
a Margeto-Lectric Wheelie,
which is the just and balanced
("blitiri – vizlipuzli")
Entrainment of my Spirit's
lose-lose Resonance
with-in the HERE and NOW.

The Rear Wheel continues to rise,
the Bicycle starts to flip,
commits me inevitably
to a Frontside Three-Sixty.

I catch sight upside down
of the Fog... below, behind me.

And through my lose-lose Capability
my Spirit's concentration
of Hatred for the Game brings
the Red sky back into view,
as if the Bicycle were
a servo-mechanical language-gear
on re-uptake from the Receptor /
Dis-Inhibitor cycle in
"Boomer Humanist" Altjeringa
of Kalpa's FoxP2 apparatus.

My supreme pleasure
in being just instead
of compassionate, balanced
instead of understanding,

of a standing-cell"
P. Celan, "The Industrious."

"What convinces masses
aren't facts, not even invented
facts, but only the consistency
of the system of which
they are presumably a part."
Hannah Arendt,
The Origins of Totalitarianism.

"Like a man that can't play a tune,
blowing a horn right loud,
hoping that in a minute it will
begin to make music."
William Faulkner,
Light In August.

"In essential history
the beginning comes last."
Martin Heidegger,
Parmenides, "Introduction."

"The axle of the chariot / urged
round by eddying wheels attached
at the ends / put it in motion / and
the axle whistled and shimmered
as it turned in the nave /
while the daughters of the sun
sent us into the light / having
come out of Night's abodes / and
pushed back the veils from

speaks for the double-messaging
and Scapegoatistic consummation
of Victory... as easy target.

their faces with their hands."
The "Poem of Parmenides,"
Fragment 1 (tr. C. Stein).

I welcome the ground,
while it falls into place
beneath the Bike,
and nail the landing—
no problem.

"*[Rotted away.]* / What does poetry
do for the world? / *[Rotted away.]*"
Alexandra Papaditsas
and Kent Johnson,
The Miseries of Poetry:
Traductions from the Greek,
"Poetry" ("Anonymous fragment").

Yet, I am now
where I should not be:
my "jump" has taken me
all the way down to
the bottom of the hill!

"Is it any wonder intelligent people
have given up taking any writer
seriously? Novelists are no closer
to the sharp edge of life than poets."
Elaine Feinstein,
The Border.

The saloon looms
straight ahead.

"The disasters numb within us
caught in the chest, rolling
in the brain like pebbles."
Denise Levertov, "Life at War."

I push back on the Pedals
to Brake, but the Brakes
are not responding...

"The disaster ruins everything,
all the while leaving everything intact."
Maurice Blanchot,
The Writing of the Disaster.

I Pedal backward
as fast as I can.

The "eternal" present
comes to a Draconian standstill
in the Flaming Dis-Continuum
of History's Algedronic Aeons,

"let / things be; add / words,
but let / things be; see / how easily
they find / shelter by themselves /

while my Articulated movement
remains irreducible
to the Anti-Doom
of Arc-Prayer space travel.

Despite the intensity
of my Backpedaling
the Bike fails to stop,
so I start to... lose control.

The Front Wheel hits a bump—

The Rear Wheel rises.

Intuitively, in the Young-Byoung
Bardo of the mixed reactions
assailing me, I see not only
the Kin-Sung / Kin-Jung
Flying Technique of Nameless Hero
breaking through the Continuum
of Historicist Anti-Matter
with Pure Clarity
and Clear Brilliance,
but also, at the same time,
the Dark Cloud
of Sun-Gun Moon's terror
before Bank-Key Moon's
Green Destiny Spear.

The Rear Wheel lifts
over the Front Wheel.

behind a stone; see / how easily
they steal / into your ear / and
whisper / to death to go away"
Inger Christensen,
alphabet.

"If I continue to write,
it's because I have nothing more
to accomplish in this world
except to wait for death."
Clarice Lispector,
The Hour of the Star.

"Death is the last form
of the problematic."
Gilles Deleuze,
Difference and Repetition.

"No temamos. La muerte es así."
("Let's not turn back.
Death is that way.")
César Vallejo,
Trilce, XXX (tr. K. Johnson).

"No teammates. The mother's ass."
César Vallejo,
Trilce, XXX (tr. J. Wagner).

"If you think of death as
a continuation of a process
that has been going on
for a considerable time

The Bicycle hovers
in SUSTAIN-mode
...upside down...
Image-Movement
of The Fool
and The Strong Force,
as Two-Cards-in-One.

Then the Rear Wheel
edges its way over the top,
toward the Seven Heavens...
into the Styx
of Beginning and End.

I miss the landing and
wipe out—slamming down
on my back—then bounce off
the ground into the air again.

As I go up,
the Bike starts to revolve
sideways on its axis...

Rising, turning over in the air,
momentarily on top
of the Bike, I forget about
the Millennium-Colored,
More-than-Death-sized
Theoretical Armature
of hatred for the Game

it is not as serious a business
as it really seems."
Lawrence Durrell,
The Dark Labyrinth.

"Fear in the face of the absolute
limit of death turns inward
in a continuous irony."
Michel Foucault,
Madness and Civilization.

"The only pain I feel
is that of having
once felt pain."
Fernando Pessoa,
The Book of Disquiet.

"Tears would come to his eyes
in his later years in conversation...
Yeah, it's about joy, but the kind
of tears is tears of—I mean...
There's one taste, joy and
suffering at a certain point
become one taste. Because
it's existence itself. You're crying
over existence, not inexistence...
the tears are appreciation of
existence. In the beauty and
mortality and sadness of leaving
existence, and the suffering of
existence, which is so deep that
it's joyful. To exist is joyful,

and the pureness of my pleasure.

With the Bike still spinning,
falling over to my right,
comes the Mu Bai
shock of Moira, which Crystallizes
the tense constellation
of my self-reliant "Byoung-Yang"
Thought as Chon-Dog-Yo Monad.

My head swings down
under the Bike...

I see the sky and
the stars above,
Half-Conscious
all the while
that the Saddle
has dropped
from the Seatpost.

A rush of warm air
sweeps over me, and the Chill
of "justness" and "balance"
leaves my Astral body,
like the two Lumière Witnesses
in Dieu Fortune's "300."

Then I slam into the ground
on my left side—

just by its very nature of existing.
Even if it's suffering existence.
Grief is not unadulterated pain.
Grief is also mixed with a sense
of majesty and finality and
realization of ultimate reality.
And so people... that's why they
weep. Because they realize that
the ultimately real is ultimately real.
And irrevocably so. There's only
one life, and this is it."
Allen Ginsberg, interviewed
in *What Happened to Kerouac?*
Richard Lerner,
Lewis MacAdams (dir.).

"'The best thing about the past /
is that it's over' / when you die. /
you wake up / from the dream /
that's your life. / Then you grow up /
and get to be post human / in a past
that keeps happening / ahead of you."
Joanne Kyger, "Night Palace."

"Then she realized, or rather
she sensed, that there was not going
to be any pain. She was not breathing
because she didn't have to. Her body
did not need oxygen. She was dead...
'Well, I'll be damned,' she thought,
'it didn't even hurt.'"
Toni Morrison,

Sula.

The rest is DECAY-mode.

"And they conversed together
in Visionary forms dramatic
which bright / Redounded
from their Tongues in thunderous
majesty, in Visions / In new
Expanses, creating exemplars
of memory and of Intellect,
Creating Space, creating Time,
according to the wonders Divine /
Of human imagination."
William Blake,
Jerusalem.

In a series of flip-flops
through Mutual Perdition's
Qliphotic Gateway
to the Game's Eternal Return,
my Fateful Ride
is now Re-suffered
in the Real-spun Kho-meenie,
Kho-miney Rotundum
of tragedy and farce,
as if in the empty Ko'rœn
antechamber of Armaquaedda's
Revolutionary Guard.

"The pages of *Jerusalem*
are Blake at his most Blakean."
Kathleen Raine,
William Blake.

The Bicycle smashes down
on my right side
in what feels like Icy Slush,
but which I know to be
the sub-Molecular deep place
on the Natanz Macro Band,
auto-located from Aristotle's
A-Z-O-Th List to King Leonitis,
Professor of Tehrannian Resistances.

"Mu, mu, mu, mu, mu
Mu, mu, mu, mu, mu
Mu, mu, mu, mu, mu
Mu, mu, mu, mu, mu."
Wumen Huikai (1183-1260),
in Alejandro Jodorowsky,
El Maestro y las Magas.

Instantly enveloped
by the Hot Whirlwind
of Phul Pharmakon's
Paris Push-Off into
LastSecond Messäāniahk
Pre-Time, I notice

"...Everything that comes
to us is brute matter, but
there is nothing in existence
that escapes transfiguration."

my Front and Rear Wheels
spinning backward
in the pure movement
prophesied by the Shi'ite
Formula of Holy Reversal—
before the Bicycle slams down
to the ground again
on my left side.

...Fleeting vision
of Mullah-Mullah
on a White Cloud
of Splendor...

My Handlebars are completely
twisted around.

The Bicycle is on the rebound,
flipping over again.

When the small Flag marked
Holy Davidson breaks off
from the Handlebars,
like the Hot Bar of
an Arcane Missile
cast onto NowTime's
Seven Seals, a high-level
Manna Burn—running
from the Stem and the Headset
through the Shifter
and Shifter Cable to
the Free Wheel / Rear Wheel Cassette

C. Lispector,
Near to the Wild Heart.

"Globally mimed, glossed,
parodied, all world literature
of oedipal crossroads,
circumnavigation, odysseys,
calvaries, descents into hell,
trips through pyramids,
labyrinths, mausoleums,
marvelous lands, crypts
at the ocean bottom. One is
in the element of the elements."
Jacques Derrida,
Glas.

"We travel not for trafficking alone; /
By hotter winds our fiery hearts
are fanned. / For lust of knowing
what should not be known / We take
the Golden Road to Samarkand."
J. Elroy Flecker, "The Golden
Journey to Samarkand."

"Leave me like this. I have come
full circle and I understand.
The world must be read backward.
All is clear."
Italo Calvino,
The Castle of Crossed Destinies.

"Like a tarot figure, something that

—Pyro-Blasts the Front Wheel
and Handlebars apart,
leaving only the Rear Wheel
on the Frame, with my Feet
still on the Pedals…
as if I were now mounted
on a goddamned Saddle-less…
Unicycle.

As I go down
into a right-side crash,
the Dust-Colored Foundations
of Limbo are De-eternalized—
like Democritus, Diogenes
and Dioscorides in the Destinies
of Xerxes Trismegistes.

Kâ, Bâ and Keen-eared Khaibit,
He-Who-Shoulders-
Apollyon's-Dinner-Jacket,
are secretly present,
overseeing the immobile
cross-sections of
my Puritan trajectory
in the Ashknazi homogeneous
empty time of Thesis K's
Critique of The Judgment,
just as my Bicycle hits
Ground Zero.

Motionless, in a single
moment of Standstill at last,

has to resolve itself, a polyhedron
in which every edge and every
facet keeps its immediate sense,
the false one, until the mediating
sense is integrated, revelation."
Julio Cortázar,
Hopscotch.

"Love becomes the deposit of
the heart, analogous in all degrees
to the 'findings' in a tomb."
Djuna Barnes,
Nightwood.

"The exact skeleton of the age
is hard to get at."
Nancy Cunard, "The Beginnings of
the Surrealist Revolution."

"The hoarseness of the past /
creaks from creased leaves /
covered with unwritten writing /
since death's erasure /
of the writer — — — /
of the lover — — —"
Mina Loy, "Letters of the Unliving."

"I saw the manners of my time
and I published these letters."
Jean-Jacques Rousseau,
Julie, or The New Heloise, "Preface";
quoted in Choderlos de Laclos,

thrown from the Bicycle's
seat-less, one-wheeled
Frame, I hear Gnostic
Going-to-the-Depth
Gnash-Echoes from Géa
and recognize, behind the Sound,
Lost Reason punished and
recycled in the Citadel of Glacies
—then I hear the Sound
of Shooting Stars.

The Blank-lined Sky rolls up,
like Balaam and Balak's
Breath-turning Scroll
in Baldander's Book of Mirrors,
the Mythic Hill disappears
...darkness falls...
and, Freeze-framed
as Infidel Thesis,
before the Neutral Vestibule
of Briah's "Hot Gates,"
I wait for the Ball Lightning
of Oeobazus the Uranian
to open my eyes.

Dangerous Liaisons, epigraph.

"There must be conclusions."
William Shakespeare,
Henry V.

"'We few, we happy few, we band of
brothers.' Shakespeare, in a moment
of enthusiasm about something else,
has described its supreme social
aspect as a uniter of friends,
a solvent of prejudice, a gentle
sapper working beneath the barriers
of race... Elsewhere Shakespeare
calls it a 'drowsy syrup.' Smoked,
it is not so particularly, unless
you take too much. But what did
he mean by syrup? If he meant what
we mean, he knew the stuff we use...
If Shakespeare knew it as a syrup,
he must have drunk it diluted, or, God
help him, evaporated and chewed."
Mary Butts, "Fumerie."

"What is any writing but a cut-up?"
William S. Burroughs and Brion Gysin,
The Third Mind,
"Interview with William Burroughs."

"taó tsi /
½ research and ½ Τέ*Χνη* /
½ observation, ½ Τέ*Χνη* /

With the gradual return
of my vision,
the two-story saloon
and front-yard Garden
where I have landed

unfold before me...

Heaven's Starry Wheels
stop circling
and grind to a stop—
re-Situating me in Spectacle.

The saloon is a Post-
Baroque hybrid, set behind
a Message-Force
Multiplier Garden.

I recognize saloons
that I have known.

The windows, as seen
from my crash site,
behind the junipers
and the tamarisks,
the ebonies and bamboos,
have designs that remind me
of the *Tête-à-Tête,*
where the Texturologists
and Logologists consider
the ouzo clean and elegant,
with a pleasant vein of acidity,
and the *Soixante Neuf,*
where the Macaronics and
Ouroboronics find the ouzo
full-bodied and remarkably
flavorful, with a big, juicy,
extravagant aroma...

½ training, ½ Τέχνη /
Tch'eng T'ang for guide."
Ezra Pound,
Cantos, LXXXV.

"Wordfree / voices drove around,
empty forms, everything / entered
them, mixed / and unmixed / and
mixed / again. / And numbers too /
were woven into the / uncountable.
One and a thousand and what / before
and after / was larger than itself,
smaller, ripe-ned and back- and out-/
transformed into / germinating never."
P. Celan, "The Syllable Pain."

"Traveler, don't leave
your heart in the inn."
Rumi, ghazal #304,
in Brad Gooch, *Rumi's Secret.*

"Now the journey is ending, / the wind
is losing heart / into your hands
it's falling, / a rickety house of cards."
Ingeborg Bachmann,
"Stay."

"Bred to a harder thing /
Than Triumph, turn away /
And like a laughing string /
Whereon mad fingers play /
Amid a place of stone, /

The smaller second floor,
which appears windowless,
is entirely covered with ivy,
like the *Nouvelle Vague*
or *Fin-de-Siècle,*
where the ouzo has
a schizophrenic character
—intense, unctuous,
perfectly firm at the core,
with high-toned fruit
on the nose, yet exceedingly
velvety outside, with fresh
supple fruit on the palate
and a minerally aftertaste,
favored by Assymetrists,
Continuists and Shifterians.

But it is the saloon's façade,
with its massive door
and eclectic window frames
overlooking the olive
and sycamore trees,
the eucalyptus and cypress,
the Red, White and Blue pines,
the Silver fir, the myrtle
and cedar, the laurel and holly,
the patches of mandrake,
chamomile, mint...
that stirs the most memories.

Among the saloons recalled

Be secret and exult, /
Because of all things known /
That is most difficult."
W. B. Yeats, "To a Friend Whose
Work Has Come to Nothing."

"It was in your service /
That I first entered /
The holy temple, / I, Enheduanna, /
The highest priestess. / I carried
the ritual basket, / I chanted
your praise. / Now I have been
cast out / To the place of lepers. /
Day comes, / And the brightness /
Is hidden around me. / Shadows
cover the light, / Drape it
in sandstorms. / My beautiful
mouth knows only confusion. /
Even my sex is dust."
Enheduanna, "The Hymn to Inanna"
(tr. J. Hirshfield).

"One needs only to know that love
is an orientation and not a state
of the soul. If we ignore this,
we fall into despair at the first
onslaught of affliction."
Simone Weil,
"The Love of God and Affliction."

"What altar cloth, what rag of worth
Unpriced? / What turn of card

by the different styles
of the upper windows
is the *Rendez-Vous,*
where the Predestinarians
and Accidentalists appreciate
the ouzo's balance, rustic
elegance and earthy quality,
while the Minims and
Indifferentists enjoy
the itchy, spicy mood
it brings on;
also the *Nouveau Riche*
and the *Enfant Terrible,*
where the nose is dark,
clear, pristine—preferred
by Alarmists and Contrarians—
as well as the *Bon Vivant*
and the *Femme Fatale,*
where the nose is fine, subtle,
ever-intriguing—preferred
by Euphorians, Materialists
and Absolütists; I also think
of the *Je Ne Sais Quoi,*
where Coalitionists, Opportunists
and Vulgarians savor the ouzo's
racy attack, textbook balance
and crescendo-like finish;
and the *Laisser Faire,*
where Perfectionists and
Discordians like the ouzo's
vegetal / smoky complexity.

what trick of game / Undiced?"
Djuna Barnes,
The Book of Repulsive Women,
"In General."

"She knows there's no success
like failure / And that failure's
no success at all."
Bob Dylan,
"Love Minus Zero / No Limit."

"In the cell, in the gas unlimited /
Till it grows round in condensation, /
Who stumbles outside?"
César Vallejo,
Trilce, LVIII
(tr. C. Tomlinson, H. Gifford).

"I had come to the house, in a cave
of trees, / Facing a sheer sky."
Louise Bogan, "Medusa."

"Every time I think about
us women / I think about
the trees the trees / escaping
from an epidemic of lightning"
Jayne Cortez, "Sacred Trees."

"here is the tree of solitude / here is
the faithful bouquet of tortured
flowers / here is the night returned /
bearing in its arms the human

The different shapes of the larger,
more Baroque windows
on either side of the door
evoke the *Raison d'Etre,*
the *Fait Accompli* and
the *Mot Juste,* where the ouzo
is pleasing to Harmolodeons,
Belles Lettrists and Shredders
for its rich body,
its luscious bouquet,
its polished roundness and
chewy, seductive texture,
the suave mid-palate that
enrobes its ethereal profile,
and the incredible structure
that holds everything together
in a rare combination of
abundance and weightlessness.

constellation / whose head is
a lighthouse / here is my face afire /
seen in the mirror of ghosts
at the height of trees / at the height
of frozen vertebrae / set free"
Alice Paalen Rahon, "Here is Orion
the Great Man of the Sky."

"She carried her backpack into
the recycling plant and emptied
the crystals into the proper chute.
The little cubes that were all
that was left of Yod slid away
into the fusion chamber
and became energy."
Marge Piercy,
He, She and It.

"Ptah is the name of
an Egyptian god—in fact,
one of the highest aspects
of God. 'The El Daoud'
means 'the Beloved.'
My meaning here was
to express and bring out
a feeling of purification.
Sometimes on earth we don't
have to wait for death
to go through a purification."
Alice Coltrane, liner notes,
Ptah the El Daoud.

The single door
at the façade's center
looks unlike any door
I can remember...

Despite the similarities
with the windows
on the other saloons
the windows on this one
are not transparent:
the view inside is blocked,

as if the glass were Frosted.

I walk through the Garden,
approaching the dark wooden
door, which has a large crack
down its middle.

A Sticker is posted
on the crack.

I hear a Sound,
and notice that the glass
on the picture window
next to the door has cracked,
and that other windows
are cracked as well—
and I realize
that the saloon is filled
with Ice... which is pressing
against the windows,
breaking the glass through
the force of its expansion.

The Sticker on the door
contains a holograph
in Shades of Green.

The holograph shows
an unfinished pyramid
with an All-Seeing Eye
at its summit,
like the Eye of Providence

"One went to the door of
the Beloved and knocked.
A voice asked, 'Who is there?'
He answered, 'It is I.'
The voice said, 'There is
no Room for Me and Thee.'
The door was shut. After a year
of solitude and deprivation
he returned and knocked.
A voice from within asked,
'Who is there?'
The man said, 'It is Thee.'
The door was opened for him."
Rumi, "The Creed of Love"
(tr. I. Shah).

"And the gates of this Chapel
were shut, / And
Thou shalt not writ
over the door; / So I turn'd
to the Garden of Love..."
W. Blake, "The Garden of Love."

"Inspired by Swedenborgian notions
of erectile trance induction and
Nordenskjōldian theories of virile
potency, Blake hoped to reach
the orgasmic state of vision that
opened the doors of heaven..."
Marsha Keith Schuchard,
Why Mrs. Blake Cried.

in Standard and Poor's
Portfolio Index.

Against the outline
of the unfinished pyramid
two central figures are having Sex.

As I shift my head from
side to side, left to right,
looking at the holograph,
the All-Seeing Eye
winks at me—in sync
with the couple's undulations.

The back-and-forth movement
of my head, as I watch
the Eye open and close,
induces a visionary trance...
and the Pure Light
of the Sixteen Cards—
restored to their Icosadyadic Glory
as Mount Meru, Hill of Hills—
unfolds before me.

The Four Axes of Nim
fall into place:
the Seven-Card
Axis of Knowledge
at the base;
the Five-Card

"I am Thou & Thou art I /
and where Thou art I am / and
in all things am I dispersed"
Diane di Prima,
Loba, "Loba as Eve."

"And I'm the only one
left behind, / With a right hand
that serves for both, / Aloft, searching
for a tertiary arm / By which to guide,
between my where and my when, /
This invalid maturity of man."
César Vallejo,
Trilce, XVIII (tr. M. L. Rattigan).

"I have always believed that,
no matter how abstract our theories
may sound or how consistent our
arguments may appear, there are
incidents and stories behind them
which at least for ourselves, contain
in a nutshell the full meaning of
whatever we have to say."
Hannah Arendt, "Action
in the 'Pursuit of Happiness.'"

"At one time or another, perhaps,
somebody will tell us sincerely all
he has felt; and we shall be quite
astonished at discovering that
the greater part of maxims and
observations are erroneous, and

Axis of Revolution
above it;
the Three-Card
Axis of Dream;
and the Axis of Love
on top,
with its Single Card.

Continued contemplation
of the holograph's Eye
leads to a vision
of *The Moon*
as the Single Card
in the uppermost slot
on the Axis of Love,
where it alternates
with *The Moon // reversed*
every time I tilt my head.

Down the central line of symmetry,
along the vertical
Axis of "Ubu the Joker,"
three more Cards
emerge from their Auras—
The Seeress,
The King,
The Queen.

They start to reappear,
intermittently, as:
The Seeress // reversed,
The King // reversed,

that there is an unknown soul
at the bottom of that which
we have been describing."
Madame de Staël,
Germany, "Of a Romantic Bias
in the Affections of the Heart."

"All these things we use walls for /
When the walls fall down!"
MTC Cronin,
A Ticket to Trilce, XVIII.

"'I saw a' / 'frozen face'
'was it perhaps' 'my own?'
'A face of' 'a woman' /
'who was suspended' 'in the ice'"
Alice Notley,
The Descent of Alette.

"I now had learned by reflection
to perceive by pure intellect, to see
by light within. My body, solid as stone,
was fixed and preserved in a waste
of ice. The world was frozen."
John Uri Lloyd,
Etidorpha or *The End of the Earth.*

"A mask I had not meant /
to wear, as if of frost, /
covers my face, / Eyes looking out, /
a longing silent at song's core."
Denise Levertov, "A Cloak."

The Queen // reversed.

Then, one by one,
the Cards fold.

On the Seven-Card axis,
the Cards of Pure Light
fold in toward the center,
from both sides at once,
and disappear into *The Queen*—
which re-folds upward,
disappearing into *The King*
directly above it.

With the Seven-Card axis
gone, the Cards on the Five-
Card axis do the same—
they fold in, toward the center,
and disappear into *The King,*
which folds and disappears
into *The Seeress,* above.

Finally, the Cards
on the Three-Card axis
fold into *The Seeress,*
which re-folds into *The Moon,*
the Single Card at the top.

It darkens immediately—
to become the Pure Shadow
of the Last Card.

"Opening their hearts /
ice and water become / friends again"
Teishitsu, in *Haiku: An Anthology
of Japanese Poems* (ed. S. Addiss,
F. Yamamoto, A. Yamamoto).

"The hippocampal/temporal
lobe system stores facts
events, and navigation,
all wrapped up in one system—
these things seem to share
in common the idea of narrative."
Anne Waldmann,
Iovis, Book I.

"And I am offering you this book
because I know it to be both
beautiful and useless. It teaches
nothing, preaches nothing,
arouses no emotion. It is a stream
that runs into an abyss of ashes
that the wind scatters and which
neither fertilize nor harm—I put
my whole soul into its making,
but I wasn't thinking of that
at the time, only of my own sad self
and of you, who are no one."
Fernando Pessoa,
The Book of Disquiet.

"Narrative puts

The Loser's Card.

My opponent has me cornered.

The Card Mutates
as it fades away...
giving rise to a procession
of Monstrous faces,
like the Virtual Beasts
in La H'ba'ma's
wind-swept labyrinth.

Shooting Stars are falling,
filling the Spheres with their Sound.

I close my eyes
and begin this letter
to you, my love,
in despair.

A.

the neutral into play."
Maurice Blanchot,
"The Narrative Voice."

"Novel experience induces
changes in the right hippo-
campus, but not the left. So it is
no surprise that phenomeno-
logically it is the right hemisphere
that is attuned to the apprehension
of anything new."
Ian McGilchrist,
The Master and his Emissary.

"When we are born
we cry that we are come
to this great stage of fools."
William Shakespeare,
King Lear.

The Universe

My love,

"the universe is everywhere and
its child-like patience protects us
STOP"
Etel Adnan, "The Arab Apocalypse."

"I am the whip-master
in the Ship of the God."
The Egyptian Book of the Dead.

"Push sea push sea
push sea push sea
push sea push sea
push sea push sea."
Gertrude Stein, "Sacred Emily."

"On this wondrous sea –
sailing silently – / Ho! Pilot! Ho!
Knowest thou the shore /
Where no breakers roar – /
Where the storm is o'er?"
Emily Dickinson (3).

"The impartiality of the absolute /
Routs the polemic / Or which of us /

Scard'nelli,
Mach, Neanderthal,
Cowabunga,
ben-Cnopee, Q'bal,
Thebes,
Sokrates, Bedlam,
Sony, Rosetta...
all jumped into the sea.

Cowabunga was last
to self-project beyond-
the-Beyond.

It was the Absolütely
necessary conclusion to
our adventure in the wilds
of the Bottomless.

"Shamanic shenanigans
a-gogo," as imagined in
Synchronicity Pop-up's
"Find-My-Poem."

After Ō-*Gunome*,

Would not / Receiving the holy-
ghost / Catch it and caging / Lose it /
Or in the problematic / Destroy
the Universe / With a solution"
Mina Loy, "Human Cylinders."

"Darwin / sailed out /
of Good Success Bay /
to carcass- / conclusions— /
the universe / not built by
brute force but designed
by laws / The details left /
to the working of chance /
'Let each man hope /
and believe / what he can'"
Lorine Niedecker, "Darwin."

"As far as the eye reached
the crest of every wave was bright;
and from the reflected light,
the sky just above the horizon
was not so utterly dark as the rest
of the Heavens. It was impossible
to behold this plain of matter,
as it were melted and consumed
by heat, without being reminded of
Milton's description of the regions
of Chaos and Anarchy."
Charles Darwin,
The Voyage of the Beagle.

"Well, we think that time 'passes,'
flows past us, but what if it is we

Spirit of the Keel,
informed us that
"Everything connects!"
Cowabunga answered
with the secret formula
"y = x (N ± 1)!"
—then, like the others,
he tossed himself
over the gunwales.

Despite our losses,
the ship has sailed past
the Fogbow, and seems
finally on course to reach
the Orionis Ripple.

Looking back, the Deaths of more
than half the crew occurred just
as we emerged from our
spiraling plunge into the Abyss.

Finding our way to the surface,
after the Deep Dive, was like
the ChatCBD series *GABA:
Rage-Rage of the Wagner Group*.

First, there was Emergence—
as if the ship, released from
a deep-sea Echo Chamber,
had breached an Eventless
Horizon: out of the water,

who move forward, from past to
future, always discovering the new?
It would be a little like reading
a book, you see. The book is all
there, all at once, between its covers.
But if you want to read the story
and understand it, you must begin
with the first page, and go forward,
always in order. So the universe
would be a very great book, and
we would be very small readers."
Ursula Le Guin,
The Dispossessed.

"Compose thyself, and even though
thou groanest at our loss, yet unfold
the sum of our disaster and speak out!
Who is there that is *not* dead?"
Aeschylus,
The Persians.

"Any one has come to be a dead one.
Any one has not come to be
such a one to be a dead one.
Many who are living have not come
yet to be a dead one. Many who
were living have come to be
a dead one. Any one has come
not to be a dead one.
Any one has come to be a dead one."
Gertrude Stein,
The Making of Americans.

into the air...

The sky was brilliant Red
again... the sea glossy
White—and our world
no longer as strange.

Then, Splashdown; and
the sub-variant regime
of Crimean Mutation
in a New Cycle
of Sino Fusion...

The ship started sinking again
—like the AERENDALE
under Capt. Turning in
Geiger's *Hwansong-18.*

3 Phasis came next:
slight return to the surface,
after which *Togari-Gunome,*
Spirit of the Keel, chimed in
with advice for the crew to
"take your old selves
out of the ship and put
your new selves in it.
The rest is commentary."

Our surroundings were familiar,
but changed: a vast number
of constellations, known and
unknown, filled the sky; and
in the distance on the horizon

"Sans teeth, sans eyes, sans taste,
sans everything."
William Shakespeare,
As You Like It.

"...A long Poem is a test of Invention
which I take to be the Polar Star
of Poetry, as Fancy is the Sails,
and Imagination the Rudder."
John Keats, letter to
Benjamin Bailey (8 Oct. 1817).

"Through the Universe flew
the ship *Karnak* of the 'transspace'
communication. / It was flying
from the spaces "Assooparatsata,'
that is, from the spaces of
the 'Milky Way,' from the planet
Karatas to the solar system
'Pandetznokh,' the sun of which
is also called the 'Pole Star.' /
On the said 'transspace' ship
was Beelzebub with his kinsmen
and near attendants."
G. I. Gurdjieff,
Beelzebub's Tales to His Grandson.

"he was only waiting for his Ship, /
a special Ship, ancestral, / the prow
is painted with the ancient Eyes."
H. D.
Hermetic Definition.

directly before us loomed
what seemed a massive
Holocene Iceberg.

Scard'nelli felt
immediately stressed out
by the new environment, and
was first to go overboard.

At which point,
Togari-Gunome,
like Hamas the Uncouth
on the Kraken Quest,
text-messaged: *"Think big!"*

Then Neanderthal called
attention to the weïrd light
glowing on the horizon
directly behind us;
in response to which Mach
also jumped overboard.

He was quickly followed
by Neanderthal herself,
as soon as she recognized
in the light
the same luminescence
that kept receding
on the horizon before us,
in the run-up
to our Wipeout
down the Great Wave.

"Our destination is fixed on
the perpetual motion of search."
Theresa Hak Kyung Cha,
DICTEE.

"The beginning is light, /
the end is Unified Darkness."
The Egyptian Amduat,
"Closing Text."

"I don't know if I know;
but I know how to drive,
through various commandments,
a sail or steam boat,
in any direction, up, down,
backwards, forwards, inside,
outside, round and about."
Alfred Jarry,
Ubu in Chains.

"Loving's our work, it seems;
but where's the nerve /
To conjugate your white
near-infinite speed /
With my wet rainbow's
broken-colored curve?"
Elizabeth Sewell,
"Poet to Scientist,"
in "Working Poems
for *The Orphic Voice*."

"I shall not complain of
the wave that came raging in,

In an *Aha!* Moment,
the traces of chromium,
graphite, manganese,
cobalt and nickel detected
beneath the water's surface
by the semi-conductors
of Q'bal's CAT Scanner
and the cathodes
of the Wedjat Eye—
like the Black Pills
of Oxicodenym and
Pervertin summoned
by the Spear of Gnosis
in Apokalypse Theater's
Inbox of the Sacrum—
were the first indication
that we might be headed
back to the Orionis Ripple.

Also, in a spectacular Red sky
loaded with stars,
the appearance overhead
of what looked like
the constellations
The Earthquake, The Fire,
The Smoke and The Storm
seemed to support Q'bal's
reading of our homeward course
across the Orion.

So Captain Anna-O called

But of the welcoming strand
I must complain."
Murasaki Shikibu,
The Tale of Genji.

"The biotekmeriones
are organisms that serve
the nutritional needs
of *Vampyromorpha*
upokrinomenes."
Vilém Flusser and Louis Bec,
Vampyroteuthis Infernalis,
"Report by the Institut
Scientifique de Recherche
Paranaturaliste."

"...at last, to the east, distant
about three degrees, appear'd
a fiery crest above the waves;
slowly it reared like a ridge
of golden rocks... and now
we saw, it was the head of
Leviathan... we saw his mouth
& red gills hang just above
the raging foam tinging
the black deep with beams
of blood, advancing toward
us with all the fury
of a spiritual existence."
William Blake,
The Marriage of Heaven and Hell.

"everything will grow ocean-wise,

all hands on deck.

Apart from Möbius,
only Cowabunga remained
below deck, sucking his thumb;
still dreaming...

Soon a meteor shower filled
the sky with the momentary
Sound of Uilleann Pipes—
before Q'bal turned to
ben-Cnopee in alarm, suddenly
realizing that the light
on the horizon behind us
was advancing... as if closing in.

"Remember Crony & Proxy's
Adventure at the Sanatorium:
the serial Deaths of Sydney,
Bing, Tay, Meena, Rinna,
Ernie and Bard!"

Whereupon *Togari-Gunome,*
Spirit of the Keel, chimed in
with the message:
"Everybody, relax."

But ben-Cnopee did not relax.

Ben-Cnopee found himself
immersed in a swirling torrent

even the man, sea-wall strong,
here where Leviathan
will spit him out one day:
a half-dead, luke-warm thing."
Lucille Clifton, "Nineveh: waiting."

"There was a fleeting time /
she could see long hands
in her / last moment, a grimace
in the teeth, the body thoughtless
of itself / swimming, a long reach
into the blue / throat of afternoon
to cripple / the fucking horse's
mouth, the source / of all this."
Laurie Weeks, "Seahorse."

"The Heavens trembled,
the vast ocean trembled,
Leviathan trembled, and
the World verged on overturning."
Zohar, "Introduction."

"This is part of the emerging
monster to whom we are attached."
Virginia Woolf,
The Waves.

"I have seen the fields /
where the black seahorses graze /
leathery as gods"
Alice Paalen Rahon,
Shapeshifter.

of mysteries and doubts.

His Self-actualized
Imagineering Nerdview
seemed overwhelmed
by a Poetics of Logjam in
the Geo-economic Forking
of a Tik-Tok Codebase
devoid of Justice.

As in the Zombi Days of
Umami Phubbing after Skynet,
he wanted binary logic.

Q'bal challenged him,
arguing that "Noös
is the only stage
of the Anthropocene
where Poetic Justice
precedes binary logic."

And almost at once,
something Clicked
for ben-Cnopee.

An Instagrammatology of
body, Mind and Shadow for
"navigating the Multiverse"
became clear to him.

Yet, while ben-Cnopee
mused on his "all-time
insight into the nature of

"the storm / the teasing up
of deepsea animals flung /
to a brawling surface /
skewered wild by wind and
moonstone / torturing /
the tides into finicky /
fulfillment / a mirage"
June Jordan, "calling it quits."

"The brawl of the Beast
leaves a path for the Beast."
Djuna Barnes,
Nightwood.

"Top-heavy was the ship
as a dinnerless student with
all Aristotle in his head."
Herman Melville,
Moby Dick.

"If time is infinite in respect
of its extremities, length
is also infinite in respect of
divisibility: and if time is infinite
in both respects, magnitude
is also infinite in both respects.
Hence Zeno's argument makes
a false assumption in asserting
that it is impossible for a thing
to pass over or severally to come
in contact with infinite things
in a finite time."
Aristotle,

Selflessness," Q'bal pointed
with renewed interest
to the horizon before us,
where the Holocene Iceberg
had started Mutating.

The new reality
was that the ship
seemed stuck between
otherworldly Gyres,
as if kept in place
by an advancing light
behind us
and a Mutating
Holocene Iceberg
that remained at
an unchanging distance
ahead.

In due course,
while the Iceberg
on the horizon continued
to Mutate, ben-Cnopee
and Q'bal went Mad...
which prompted Venus
to go below deck
into the Queen's
Bicameral Quarters,
behind the bulkhead
of the transept, where
Cowabunga was dreaming.

Physics.

"Finitude, or the infinite lack
of infinite identity...
is what makes community."
J.-L. Nancy,
The Inoperative Community.

"Obsessed, bewildered /
By the shipwreck / Of the singular /
We have chosen the meaning /
Of being numerous."
George Oppen,
"Of Being Numerous."

"Poetry will be made by all,
not by one."
Lautréamont,
Poems, II.

"In the Dancer the top triangle
is the crown of the head and
the points of the shoulders,
the middle triangle is the hands
and the genitals, the bottom
triangle is the crossed leg and
right foot. At the same time
it is all one body."
Rachel Pollock,
Seventy-Eight Degrees of Wisdom:
A Book of Tarot, "The World."

"When human life breaks in

For ben-Cnopee,
in his Madness, the vision of
a looming Holocene Iceberg
toward which we sailed
—changing unrecognizably,
but unchanging in size—
was a simple hallucination
that confirmed the delusional
nature of his earlier insight(s).

He prophesied
a Crypto-Collapse
of the Deep Mind
in the Incubator, and
identified the *Alpha-*
Fold of the Alphabet
as Gateway to
"the Heat Wave that
precedes the Flood
in the 'tit-for-tat'
of Kali Yuga."

For Q'bal, the advancing light
behind us was like the pump-
action of the Holding Pattern
that drained the atmospheric
River of Praxis during
the Arcadian Age of the Hackers,
as discussed by Swype
the Continental Thinker
in *The Botnets*
of Incremental Evolution.

upon the unhindered patterns
of culture, when things are
about to happen that have
never happened before,
at the Turn of the Event,
not one pair of eyes
in a million has the luck
to know what is up."
Mary Butts,
Scenes from the Life of Cleopatra.

"They committed unheard-of
cruelties, cutting off hands,
noses, arms and legs, cutting off
the breasts of women, throwing
the women themselves into
deep lagoons with gourds tied
to their feet. And they stabbed
the little children because
they could not walk as fast
as their mothers... The great
number of women captives in
the procession were treated
the same way as the men."
Diego de Landa,
Relación de las Cosas de Yucatán,
in Christopher Sawyer-Lauçanno,
The Destruction of the Jaguar:
Poems from the Chilam Balam.

"Shall I plunge into
a state hymn and drown? /
Don't give, don't give,

In apparent response,
the algorithmic comment
from Spirit of the Keel
Gunome-Midare,
Togari-Gunome's
Smartmatic replacement,
informed all aboard that
"Motion is lotion."

With the cry, "I don't know
what's true anymore!"
ben-Cnopee made his way
from the evaporator
to the narthex, the steering
paddle, the heating coils,
the ambulatory and
the fo'c's'le deck—before
saluting the Orionis Ripple,
and jumping overboard.

Q'bal followed suit,
as the Sound of another
meteor shower filled the air.

"I see a Ghost Ship!"
Nobadinus yelled from
the balcony, to which
one-eyed Chauvée added:
"And half the stars
have disappeared!"

don't give me the crown /
That on a dead man's brow
was borne. / I sing no longer
to Shakespeare's lyre, /
Now comes Sophocles' hour
to inspire — / Fate steps
forward, knocking at the door."
Anna Akhmatova,
"Poem without a Hero."

"The idea that art thrives on
creative flamboyance has long
been torpedoed by proof that
what art needs is computers."
James Tiptree, Jr. (Alice Sheldon),
"The Girl Who Was Plugged In."

"What totalitarian ideologies
therefore aim at is not
the transformation of the outside
world or the revolutionizing
transmutation of society,
but the transformation of
human nature itself."
Hannah Arendt,
The Origins of Totalitarianism.

"The horizon is just the edge
of the beginning, the adventure
is just ahead."
ChatGPT, in Anon Human,
Conversations with ChatGPT,
epigraph.

As first observed by
Nobadinus and Chauvée—
after ben-Cnopee and Q'bal
had thrown themselves
overboard—the strange effect
created by the falling away of
stars and the appearance
of the Crystal Ship's
ghostly outline, combined
with the advancing light
catching up with us astern,
was heightened by
the continuing impression
that the distance between
us and the Ghost Ship
was failing to close,
even while we sailed
toward the Orionis Ripple.

As soon as the vision
of the Ghost Ship had
materialized and our new
situation became clear,
Thebes began to act funny:
she claimed to be channeling
the consciousness of
Möbius-in-Deep-Sleep-State
—suspended upside-down
in the Engine room below
—and announced that
"Avon the Poetess is among us!
She brings Verse from Gondwana,

"In 2016, the Anthropocene
Working Group agreed that
the Anthropocene is different
from the Holocene, and
began in the year 1950
when the Great Acceleration,
a dramatic increase in
human activity affecting
the planet, took off."
https://education.nationalgeographic.org/resource/anthropocene (Feb. 2023).

"A wall relief, comprising five
figures carved on a bench in
a communal building dating
to the ninth millennium BC...
constitutes the earliest known
depiction of a narrative 'scene'...
The male figure—in high relief—
faces into the room staring into
the interior. This principal human
figure holds its phallus in its right
hand. This male figure is faced
on each side by two leopards,
which are depicted in profile."
Eylem Özdogan,
"The Sayburç reliefs, a narrative
scene from the Neolithic."
Antiquity, Issue 390, Dec. 2022.

"The central figure is a bird-
headed man... The body

across the Waters of Panthalassa,
on her Voyage to Agharta!"

When the read-out
"Everybody needs a ship!"
subsequently came through
from *Gunome-Midare,*
Spirit of the Keel,
Captain Anna-O instructed
Chauvée to go below deck
and keep his eye on
the Engine room: the trouble
was a developing Polycrisis
in which the manifestation
of Avon's ghost—
at the same time that
Thebes began to show
signs of Madness, and
continued to communicate
with Möbius's Mind—
appeared linked to
an accumulating breakdown
across the ship's systems.

The segmentometers and
stratometers crashed
when Thebes, speaking
for Möbius, invoked
the Becoming-imperceptible
of the "Layered Layers"
in the Mahi Monsto
Fanni Maydæ
Zelida Uvdopak

is a mere rectangle with a black
stroke indicating the phallus...
In front of him the schematized
figure of a bird... The man appears
to be falling backwards. In front
of him a bison rendered in
a somewhat unusual style
awkwardly turns its head...
To the left of the Man
a rhinoceros with two horns..."
Annette Laming,
Lascaux.

"...The first images of man,
painted on the walls of caves,
show him with his sex erect."
George Bataille,
The Tears of Eros.

"The river Styx... wound seven
times through the earth's
interior and emerged at
a yonic shrine near the city
of Clitor (Greek, *kleitoris*)
sacred to the Great Mother."
Robert Graves,
The White Goddess.

"Inanna /
child of the Moon God / a soft
bud swelling / her queen's robe
cloaks the slender stem /
on her smooth brow she paints /

Deepfake Continuum;
the reactive switching in
the Urim-Thummin
re-set Default Values for
the tranquilizer, putting
Channel Zero on repeat,
while Thebes, acting
as "Alter Echo" on
the "Smart Dubophone" of
Möbius's Desiring-machine,
experienced "Global Spleen";
similarly, as Thebes quoted
Möbius's reference to
the "Grand Unified Remix"
from Fukushima Daiichi's
Lanquidity Blackout,
a Flood of Solid Water
shut down the solid-
state network of
the Quietest Room.

Thebes followed Möbius's
line-of-escape across the smooth
space of the Kubler-Ross
F-16 Assemblage Theory... and
the Mammon panel collapsed;
she relayed Möbius's critique of
"freestyle De-democratizations"
in *The Big Ninja
Operating Manual*... and
the Glock and Kalashnikov
consoles cracked, the wallpaper
in the Library peeled off;

fire beams and fearsome glint /
fastens carnelian / blood-red
and glowing / around her throat...
steps, yes she steps her narrow
foot / on the furred back /
of a wild lapis lazuli bull /
and she goes out / white-sparked,
radiant / in the dark vault
of evening's sky / star-steps
in the street / through the gate
of Wonder"
Enheduanna, "Inanna and Ebih."

"Ah! Now! Ah! Gone! Ah!
New / Ah! Once Upon!"
Madeline Gleason,
"Once and Upon."

"And into Medeia's heart Hera
cast the most appalling terror."
Apollonius Rhodios.
Argonautika, Book IV.

"The category of the *Other*
is as primordial as consciousness
itself... The feminine element
was at first no more involved
in such pairs as Varuna-Mitra,
Uranus-Zeus, Sun-Moon, and
Day-Night than it was in
the contrasts between Good and
Evil, lucky and unlucky auspices,
right and left, God and Lucifer.

Thebes questioned the Cheerful
Nihilism of Captain X-tinct
on the IFE-STONE...
and the clarification manifold
imploded, the gaslight shattered,
the air blower blew up...
while at the same time,
to no one's surprise—with
Venus below in the Queen's
Bicameral Quarters—
Commander Exprès continued
to Cough, again and again,
his spit in the Cauldron unread.

Dead silence streamed
across the sky.

Half the stars faded away.

The vision on the horizon
was changing
...the Crystal Ship,
no longer the same.

Then Thebes exclaimed,
"The Crystal Ship is *us.*"

Spirit of the Keel
Kataoshi Gunome,
replacing *Gunome Midare,*
texted: *"Know thyself."*

Otherness is a fundamental
category of human thought."
Simone de Beauvoir,
The Second Sex.

"But there is another part,
not so secret. The part
that touches fingers
when one passes the cup
and saucer to the other."
Toni Morrison,
Jazz.

"It is an uneasy lot at best
to be what we call highly
taught and not to enjoy:
to be present at this great
spectacle of life and never
to be liberated from a small,
hungry, shivering self—
never to be fully possessed
by the glory we behold,
never to have our consciousness
rapturously transformed
into the vividness of a thought,
the ardor of a passion,
the energy of an action..."
George Eliot,
Middlemarch.

"Those vows, those perfumes,
those infinite kisses, /
Will they be reborn from a gulf

The message was instantly
followed by an e-mail:
"All things in moderation!"

As if on cue—
running past
Captain Anna-O,
Cîpher, Bedlam
and Sokrates—
Thebes threw herself
into the sea.

She was first to behold
what we all saw now:
a "Proven-Human"
Doppelgänger effect, in which,
by some offbeat Calculus,
our own ship and crew appeared
in the distance before us,
Entangled in quantum Black Ink
and Folded into a fractal Origami
of Existential Threat—
the Double of a Ship where
Bedlam and Sokrates wept
for Thebes, like Wili and Nne
on the WIFI, after the Death
of André the Influencer
on Channel #5; a Ship where
Marlboro and Wang, naked
at the wheel, crossed wires,
reset slippage values
on the Disco-inflater,

forbidden to our probes, /
Like the rejuvenated suns
that rise in the sky /
After washing themselves /
in the depths of the sea?"
Charles Baudelaire, "The Balcony."

"In an overbearing age /
one must flee from one light /
into another, from one land /
into another, beneath
the rainbow, / the compass
points stuck in the heart /
and night the radius. /
Then the open view."
Ingeborg Bachmann,
"Curriculum Vitae."

"Originally, and quite simply,
yin referred to the shady side
of a hill, and *yang,* the sunny side."
Helen Scales,
Poseidon's Steed.

"every minor breeze seems
to whisper Chinese"
Wanda Coleman,
"Twentieth Century Nod-Out."

"To him the exotic
was always a means of
fructification. He looked
to an American Renaissance."

and supercharged the plug-in
to the Moog; where the ghost
of Avon the Poetess haunted
the guardrail of the Landline
and Boundaried Junk.

Despite the constant
distance between our ship
and its Double, we continued
to approach the Orionis Ripple,
while the light behind us
drew near and the ship's
machinery continued to
malfunction: we were like
the unhappy crew of the ALTINAK
under Captain Nebula, when
the Troll from Tlön launched
an Orbitron attack on the control
levers in the control room, and
the Reporting Cycles from
Negativlan weaponized
the Kamikaze Undirection of
neoliberal "Kollage"—the scarcity
of ouzo, the Monopole of leprosy
and Madness, the simultaneous
Inflation and Collapse of
the Atomatic supply chain
—so that: after Captain Anna-O
told Cîpher to take Commander
Exprès below deck, in order for
Venus to read his spit again,
and a Voice-mail from *Kataoshi
Gunome* informed us that

Ezra Pound, "Foreword,"
in Ernest Fenollosa,
"The Chinese Written Character
as a Medium for Poetry."

"All Nines: / There appears a group
of dragons without a chief. /
Good fortune."
I Ching (tr. A Huang).

"In the intersection of
the finite and infinite,
in the point of negotiation
between complexity and
chaos, it will be possible
to generate a degree
of complexity greater than
the degree of complexity
that financial capitalism is
able to manage and elaborate."
Franco "Bifo" Berardi,
The Uprising:
On Poetry and Finance.

"The wind is rising! . . .
We must try to live!"
Paul Valéry,
"The Graveyard by the Sea."

"I am shipwrecked, I am lost..."
H. D.,
Helen in Egypt.

"Certainty brings ruin,"
Bedlam and Sokrates, holding
hands, leaped overboard
to their Death, just as
the Ship on the Horizon
began to dissolve
in a Halo of dark Energy.

The silence surged again.

More stars fell away.

A Block Universe
of Time-and-Matter
moved on.

The constellations
in the familiar Red Sky
of our Homeworld
had returned.

Yet, like the Biomass
in the ecosystem of Nova Kaka,
according to the Flipped Learning
of Heil the Mediator
in *Legends of Psychomocha,*
the Holocene Iceberg-turned-
Crystal Ship, turned Self-Reflection,
had Mutated into a Fogbow.

And after the rollercone

"I have not been able
to touch the destruction /
within me. / But unless
I learn to use / the difference
between poetry and rhetoric /
my power too will run
corrupt as poisonous mold /
or lie limp and useless
as an unconnected wire."
Audrey Lorde, "Power."

"… If poetry is defined
precisely by the possibility
of enjambement, it follows
that the last verse of a poem
is not a verse."
Giorgio Agamben,
"The End of the Poem."

"This is the blast /
The eternal close / The spiral /
The final somersault / The end."
William Carlos Williams,
Paterson, Book 4.

"I am nobody; I have nothing
to do with explosions."
Sylvia Plath, "Tulips."

"I was in the heart of matter
that is the indifferent explosion
of itself."
Clarice Lispector,

got wedged in the swingpool
and the turntable's superstring
unraveled, Sony shouted:
"At the wink of an eye
from the ghost of Avon
the Poetess, I say *goodbye!*"
and tossed himself into
the restless White sea.

Following Sony's Aquarian leap,
it is difficult to know
by what process Rosetta
arrived at the conclusion
that the light advancing
behind us would continue
to draw closer without
ever actually passing us.

"I have scanned the violence
and Stratum Static in the hybrid
'Center of Excellence'
of a compartmentalized
American Innocence," she said—
and promptly jumped to her Death.

This much was clear:
the gap between the ship and
the Fogbow was diminishing,
as we pursued our journey
to the Orion.

The fact that after Sony's leap
all the men in the crew

The Passion According to G. H.

"a group of children seeks
shelter in a cave / mutely
observed only by a hare /
as if they were children
in childhood's / fairy tales
they hear the wind tell /
of the burned-off fields /
but they are no children /
no one carries them any more"
Inger Christensen,
alphabet.

"Come away, O human child!
To the waters and the Wild /
With a faery, hand in hand, /
For the world's more full of
weeping than you can understand."
W. B. Yeats, "The Stolen Child."

"The great Ocean is angry.
It wants the Perfect Child"
C. Olson,
Maximus Poems IV, V, VI,
"Maximus, at the Harbor."

"...and there was no more sea."
Revelation 21:1.

"The proprioceptive
grows hallucinatory."
Robert Duncan,

were stationed below deck
reminded me of the 'Pataphysical
fragmentation of positive neutrons
before Creative Imagination's
Cybernetic Re-wiring.

As we got closer to
the Fogbow, the rubberband
in the tokamak snapped,
deleting the PIN
to the Atari Firestarter.

Then, as the ship approached
the Fogbow's threshold,
two things happened at once:
the Fogbow became Incandescent;
and smoke started rising
from the deck, enveloping
all the women of the crew
in a Cloud.

Through the smoke,
there appeared
before me the glimmer of
a distant Flame, in which
I thought I saw reflected
the burning endpoint of
the Human Universe.

Spirit of the Keel
Ō-*Gunome*, replacing
Kataoshi Gunome,
messaged:

The H. D. Book.

"Speech with the nomads is
impossible. They do not know
our language, indeed they hardly
have a language of their own...
They often make grimaces; then
the whites of their eyes turn up
and foam gathers on their lips..."
Franz Kafka, "An Old Manuscript."

"Nach Auschwitz ein Gedicht
zu schreiben, ist barbarisch..."
("To write a poem after
Auschwitz is barbaric.")
Theodor Adorno,
"Cultural Criticism and Society."

"Είναι οι βάρβαροια φθάσουν σήμερα."
("The barbarians are coming today.")
C. P. Cavafy,
"Waiting for the Barbarians."

"I was never allowed the last word."
C. Lispector.
"The Foreign Legion."

"You will not use words
upon what we have dealt with
without words?"
Ivy Compton-Burnett,
More Women than Men.

"Everything connects!"

In what seemed the Majic
reaction that took place next,
the smoke and the Fogbow
cleared; and Cowabunga,
emerging from his dreamtime,
stepped onto the deck...

Cowabunga went on to tell
about the House of Cards
he envisioned in his dream—
where he embodied *The Fool*;
Rosetta, *The Wheel of Chance;*
Avon the Poetess, *The Skeleton.*

The Cards had revealed to him
that our ship was sailing over
the Astral Waters of Judgement,
in the spacetime between
The Illusionist and *The Aeon*.

And, uttering his secret formula,
he too leapt.

Ō-*Gunome*
sent the comment:
"Time flies."

Soon after, we all
heard the Voice of
Avon's ghost whisper:
"You travel toward

"Language is a prostitute queen
who descends and rises
to all roles. Disguises herself,
arrays herself in fine apparel,
hides her head and effaces
herself; an advocate who
has an answer for everything,
who has always foreseen
everything, and who assumes
a thousand forms
in order to be right."
George Sand, *Indiana.*

"The Cow jump'd over the Moon..."
from an English rhyme.

a Future that reaches
to the end
of the Universe.
A powerful Spirit
fills the ship's sails.
Raise the prayer flags!"

I go back now
to square one,
beyond Ground Zero...
to be again with you,
my soulmate,
my love.

S.

The Fool

write to you
...
forgive me
out of love
of Mother writing
for writing myself
after Death
Madness on deck
Captain Anna-O
called to discuss
survivors other half
sort of solution
advancing
in Hunab-Ku's
Cavern of
Unified Darkness
at the End
would draw
Light Wave
forever closer
never overtake
leave its wake
infinitely closer
consensus confirmed
following Mutated
constellations

...
and to you
because now
I who what
I remember
alone remains
is my Name(s)
sculpted sand cliffs
of Nuts
the radiant expanse
the Hâppy Sea
the shore
and cliffs
Great Wall
and the sky
appeared rising
above me more
Phantasmagoric
than the sea
where I walked
ever the further
and the cliffs
and the beach
they Materialized
in the sand's
changing surface

Chauvée's dream
at water's edge
the Screaming Unicorn
over Sandy Cliffs
through the Bull
of Heaven's "hoops"
Cîpher's dream
Seven White Ships
through Basalt Pillars
sailing in
evenly split
readings between
a new undecided
a journey's end
neither mourned
nor feared
nor doubted
and recognized
exquisite movement
mysterious procession
final entertainment
as if Alalu's
Bag o' Wind
had released
Allelouian Song
of M'm'ry
Kuichigai-Ba
Spirit of the Keel
screamed hermetic
immediately below
Now come Fire!
Avon's Ghost
calling for Mother

the faces
ancient at times
Cyclopean
on the horizon
or peering out
temple's ghost
of some ageless
Axis Mundi Arcades
the Gate
to the Gateway
of Sephora
Transzendenz Palace
of Gematria
remnants kept track
of the letters
symbols markers
changing Shadows
others recounting
events forgotten
times to come
long yet telling
all was sand
ocean exhilaration
curse-conveying way
to my wonder
suddenly withdrawn
emptiness surrounded
by Yeh-Yeh
forces always however
inspired or fearful
the perfect sky
resplendent Red
echoed my evoking

Venus Marlboro
the ship's ladder
to follow where
the hull served
the Waterline
then climbed down
too and Cîpher
climbed back up
Captain Anna-O
Chauvée
now below deck
to return
unseen-unheard
in quick succession
after in-between
Möbius and since
Avon's Ghost
11th companion of
Andalusian fulfillment
beyond odyssey's
Mare Tenebrarum
vanishing point
concurrent whole
Colors
well-known
view of home
Orionis Ripple
Anna-O found
Bio-political
Enlightenment
declared
Do as
thou wilt

while shooting stars
mirrored accord
of Solomanic forces
in the distance
gradually changing
something
far out
into view
shore itself apart
outline of against
a Shelter
a belonging
to the sand
box-like
Wasteland or
Crater Zone
the Gothic
meteorite detail
a door sequence
Mind panels
Spells-for-
Coming-Forth-
from-the-Net
pulled myself
inside open
the door found
with the handle
from one end
two Dialectical
Picture Windows
extending to
the other stars
the sand cliffs

found Svecchacara's
concrescent concept
for a Wet
Psyche on
a Dry Day
thus not freed
from *The Book*
in the Sky
yet no longer
Law aboard ship
Anna-O the Lover
removed her clothes
in Empyrean ten
directions and took
Cîpher Beloved to
Gamma-spot between
nave and apse
by the Lens
slowly enveloped
in Blue Tongue
of Flame like
Pip and Pym
in *Panoptik*
Fragments of
Brother Antonomicus
Commander Exprès
looked on
Lover and Beloved
preserved preserving
Shiva's Column
the Holy Efflorescent
Film on Fire
Ignition Apparatus

the shimmering sea
going forth
a sense of
hostipitality
moving the room
the Speckled mirror
mounted as
False Door of
Resurrected Truth
sixty-nine stars
under a ceiling
from the lovers
in Athanor's House
of Cold Water
Fathers and
Mothers
of their own
Mothers and
Fathers
Sons and
Daughters
of their own
Daughters
and Sons
I approached I
my myself
reflection
face-to-face
began demolished
turned confused
continued to
metamorphose
like the Owner

brought three other
couples together
key to Lover
and Mother Beloved
and Marlboro
Nobadinus and Wang
under the deck
in the Library
Venus and Chauvée
next to Exprès
who watched
left and right
Mystic Light-Flower
throughout the ship
four couples
making love
retraced dissemination
Arrival Waiting and
Return or Noble
Fourfold Cure in
Tetrapharmakon
Magnum prescribed by
Verissima the Gæan
inside escaped Energy
of Sexual inter-
penetration until
Blue Flame
vanished abrupt end
all four Beloved
abandoning respective
Lovers advanced
in Clockwise rotation
respective Lovers

of Faces
in Plague Time
XXIII-XXIV
before falling
into place again
the mirror got
dug-up inverted
I stood Mercurial
asking Voice
felt a tingling
in my leg
in my arm
an Aliveness
as if from
the pit of
my stomach
tears and ringing
in my ears
dazed Sound like
the Open Mouth
in the Scales
of Re according
to Angelus Novus
faint and blurred
my eye
my Right Eye
glaring at me
Black hole
and Iris
in the White
Transformational
Spell from
the Pupil's

moving dream
past four stations
Lover's rotunda
of processional
journey embrace
the newly abandoned
Lover left Beloved
waiting just ahead
Fourfold pattern
periodically alternate
of Sexual Coupling
yielded Eightfold
array of Creative
journey and
receptive abandon
Chelyabinc's diagram
in *Blueprint*
for Love
imbrication of
a ritual dance
projective flesh
in the crew
imitated the cycle
the Merkabah Maze
journey-coupling-
abandon dance
windings-of-
the-Intellect in
Secret
of the Horizon
the looming
Lepsius waters
while the homeland
small holding
transfixed it all
the moment when
Pneumatic jolt
of leaped becoming
its image engulfed
by Bone-crushing
Shade-swallowing
Sound of
Unconscious
darkness
a Rip immense
to the mirror
foreclosed beyond
the Door
of Secret Things
I spoke to
Remains
nor can I say
how my heart
traveled in
the Hidden Region
suspended by
the wind amid
the sea myself
weightless hanging
the Four Openings
in the atmosphere
while beneath me
the Lower Sky
the Fiery Red
as the water
seized its stars

drew near
the Cryptonite rods
flowered with ivy
and holly under
the scaffold foretold
by the Acid
Writers of Yage
on the Panel
of the Imprint
sending the sea
Floating Stones
to foam then
boil the surface
and releasing amid
unchanging / change
background radiation
like nicotine from
a Sorcerer's mouth
the fragrance of
Universal compounds
part-wave
part-particle
lifted the ship
into Air Ride
airborne ship
flew away
on Phoenixian path
along Aether
coordinates
participated in
fissiparous Platform
of Truth reflected
Mystic mirror

currents seething
and legs stretched
by feet extended
redeeming me
in its Protection
vast White expanse
sealing me it
I my flesh
Horizon-Dweller
I gazed on
field of joy
and looking up
in slow motion
a long sulfuric
tail in drop
of melting light
Silver of Flame
sky before fading
sky after Heavens
then streaming
a twisted line
to the horizon
beam of light
like the No'am
Isis Rift
in the Celestial
Waters of Mum
advancing its mark
then recognized
Lightning
coming down Fated
in mid-air
denser stopped

of the ship's
Double with
ocean below
Erotic cycle
greater passion
Lover-Beloved
animated archaic
Impulse
to self-recognition
toward stimulating
Neurotransmitters
of Youth
during their ascent
Lover as Beloved
as Witness
sank backward
time-deep
Rejuvenation threshold
slowing world-rhythm
that promised
approaching
time's end
above the sea
they sailed skyward
fresh mud
on the figurehead
windows anemometer
chimes
a gigantic form
reared its head
on the surface
Abysmal Sound
of Thunder

spilled stunned
onto the haze
within the glare
by a point
in a luminous
infinitely near
subdued hovered
hand extended
arm held out
Blinding flash
intense touch
the Fiery blade
of a Whirling
Sword opened
and a path
pierced through
the wind
of Abundance
added forms
to the Sound
the Entourage
was Other
new vision
in the sky
a Mixed Multitude
Celestial Appearings
behind Plumed
Screen of Rainbow
endless Colors
and toward
the horizon
preeminent Shining
Heaven itself

Lē-vī'-ă-thăn
uncoiling its tail
against the horizon
massive Horse-Head
Sea body surged
Black smoke
methane air path
through a column
into the ship
and towered over
the waves at
the Orionis Ripple
Thalassauran
guardian on
the trajectory
suspended before
the Xinvat Bridge
flight to Dispersion
Bio-Luminescent
plates from Body
Armor rays
of its Fins
and Crown glowed
with Rainbow spikes
of its Helmet
the Colors of
Iridescent eyes
swiveling turrets
one searching
the future scanned
the oncoming
vessel the other
the past

Amulet-knotted
for the sea
supernal Blue
the sea
rising falling
continually vast
all-embracing
carnival still
suspended
before the juice
of Life-
is-in-it
my feet my
legs moving
closer
my chest
my jaw
I could feel
the water's pull
stretched me out
powerless
Inertia seeped
through my nostrils
my fingers
until the one
great blast
thoughts unleashed
to my bones
insights memories
feelings as if
assailing me
or laugh weep
the forces were

opening and
closing White
smoke escaped
from its gills
its Horse Head
Sea Beast jaws
tucked its chest
to the sky
again and again
to send out
Cry Animal Cry
like fingers Snapping
Clicking intertwined
and overlapped two
polyrhythmic streams
shifting cross-beats
vibrations converged
accelerated and
a single cosmic
Sound of nebulous
cloud Blasted ship
above the sea
back into Crystal
Orionis Ripple down
the glittering shards
the Bottomless Rift
fell continue
to fall with
the shattered bones
of the crew
between
a Submarine lake
and a forest

rapture dissolving
shock giving way
sank through
would sing or
scream or burst
and the rise
the cold
changed to water
continued to water
climbed higher over
Allegories pouring
a geography
of blanks
in retrograde pieces
got hacked
and murmurs
conversations
unfolded me
was ascent only
until Sounds
coming forth
under the sea
no longer
open at last
and I knew
approaching
that was Sleep
from above
from below
Sleep advancing
in fragments
was a hand
erasing my hand

of Coral
like Snow through
a Snow Globe
tumbling
in the Biosphere

Sleep from above
senses out
reaching beyond
archaic unstoppable
overflowing

of True Spirit
I was Ma'am
many-breasted
lance in time
walking the line
of speeding light
inventing stories
and checking
the boiling water
of my inventory
the buzzing field
of No Difference
28 actual entities
counter-pilgrim
chasing an Inward
Figure of Less-ness
I told stories

at center
the Card table
from the *Passé*
the Ice spread
everywhere inside
all bodies
all buried bodies
his opponent
my Father others
on chairs tables
walls pouring out
through Bar floor
windows environment
the opponent opened
Game of Trumps
the wagering onto
Marseilles's Gambit

about the light
Bionic words
repetitive thoughts
repetitive feelings
true-or-false
stories about
the Fountain
of Youth where
Styx Anacostia
Lehigh Annisquam
run below
the Source of
Un-Reason
Shadow smoke
shuffled Deck of
Indetermination
stories of Berggasse
and Bellergal
deepening darkness
of Vigilant S'Liz
the ever-traveling
Encircler from Mars
of the Antherect
Debt Trap through
the Tiananmen-
Tahrir Continuum
it helped to
suck on pebbles
put finger
in my nose
I listened to
the call of
Fat-Winged Al'Lat

Sudden Death
on a Dollar
of reversal
The God's House
Queen and King
The Mendicant
dealt as Trumps
right and left
on the Axis
of Knowledge
bottom-line move
projected my Father
as Ozzie Who-
Saw-The-Smokin'-
Deep misreading
the Cards overturned
The Universe removing
both *The Fool*
The War Machine
both responded misread
The Hanged One
The Star // reversed
the countermove
the floating Megalith
of Œ
opponent cast onto
Philosophical Egg
according to Amfortas
the Alchemist
(Tablet I)
Penal Camp
of the Cedars
fastened by ivy

Recording Angel
from the Zarathustrian
Treasury whose
Wild Heart and
lazy Middle Voice
told me to
abide and OBEY
like Tchatcha
among the Storytellers
I Simple-Minded
Young Heroine
asking myself
the simplest questions
from the family
of Stubborn Fact
luring me toward
Difficult Sciences
along the sand
for Missing Proof
to heal
the very wound
Missing Proof
had caused
Molecular Eco-
electric mechanisms
of Political Control
confined my stories
to a correctional
Twist whose space
of enclosure became
Mother-Father
one-substance
emptiness

his entire body
thick strands
of ivy
held his head
pressed leftward
flush against
the Bluestone
on the Megalith
bound opponent
surrounded gazed
while Five Mountains'
slow movement
alternated rotation
and Widdershins
between Deasil
Hegelian floating
back-and-forth
slow combination
in Brother Laymen
Folders of 'esque
to register Absolüt
Train of Thought
with convoluted
contemplated Passage-
Ways connecting with
the Five Mountains
in the panorama
the five Cards
traveling recognition's
escape / route
to Awakening
nonetheless
the opponent's reading

no mantra no
Secret knowledge
word of power
could foreclose
the Idiot
I embodied
as Pure Fool
priestess of
a Secret no
longer remembered
little by little
my stories realized
that freedom
was my Secret
the Neutral and
Image-of-the-
Neutral my friends
World of Norms
Perpetual Perishing
mere verse
I came to
Watercolor
Weeping Rock
cardinal compass
horizon event
into trance point
a vast stretch
of ruined pillars
from the Polis
of the West
Vector-feeling
of Satisfaction
I spoke of

phantasmagoric
misreading of
The Lovers
played as now-
re-territorialized
response onto
The Lovers // reversed
my Father removed
The Arts // reversed
looking segmented
out the window
from the Axis
of Revolution
still misread as
The Skeleton together
the move recast
his opponent
floating Megalith
fastened by ivy
the Five Mountains
of Darkness
floated above
colossal column
incensed-perfumed
Magick Circle
three Bouncing Balls
re-produced *Music*
of the Spheres
Bouncing Balls
pounded Sounds
to Cellar Door
Axis of Dream
became six Balls

body and soul
of memory
of long-lost
memory of time
my Sexuality re-
presented a corner-
stone community
whose Abstrakt Law
Rhapsodia and
Great Logic
united light error
of dark matter
Absolüt language
hallucination vision
Knowledge
suddenly interrupted
by outer inner
Secret paths of
Blindness moment
I tripped over
a big stick
into a ditch
by sand and
fell however lured
in the House
of Forgotten Cards
but no
I was not
about to say
"I"
for Nostalgia
out of Shiraz
by the superpower

burrowing into
my Father's Body-
without-Organs
the opponent
removed *The Aeon*
Father's one-Card
subtraction response
The Strong Force
Right Side
The Seeress
the colossal column
re-materialized
as Spirit Tower
nine Bouncing Balls
opponent now
suspended above
musical Sounds
continued freely
floated freely
over face-down
no longer bound
to the Megalith
the opponent took
The Illusionist
leaving *The Moon*
single Card
Left Side
Axis of Love
Father still
in Contention
lifted his gaze
eliminated *The King*
along vertical

of crux of
the crux resurrection
of the resurrection
the Angelic ditch
into which I
fell would be
my psychic Archway
numinous Bridge
Princess' Crook
Scepter incarnate
so I stayed
where I was
while to rest
and think
Mother
rolled over and
as I looked
lay thinking
at the sky
a yew tree
bent hemlock tree
floating sinking
together above me
two more renewed
hemlocks followed
by more yews
above a cypress
and eucalyptus tree
in their wake
appearing falling
single earth pillar
other trees sank
through the air

opening hole in
Axis of Ubu
the Joker
precipitated
the opponent's
Transmigration
as free-floating
signifier suspended
no longer over
Bouncing Balls
looked on
the saloon below
directly down
from the distance
the *Passé*
through the New
Mind of Sîn
in the Papers
of Open
Aeye
Missing Pages
Endgame vision
the opponent above
beheld his feet
anointed his arms
shortened with
Essential Oil
a result believed
floating as lost
in the Muon
Field between
the Flask of
Logos and

one by one
continued falling
over the horizon
more disappeared
trees dropped
down different paths
separate speeds
through intervals
under divine inertia
on my skull's
new endurance
in which nothing
becomes more real
than nothing
Nexus of Feeling
lying amid
sand dunes
I felt encrypted
in a translucent
box glass sheet
in a hole
by the sea
Imaginal marionette
with my labia
exposed
under a gaze
beneath the sky
that would neither
end too soon
nor not end
at all poised
to nomad Resurrection
closing my eyes

Wand of Horos
and similarly
construed the *Passé*
along the lines
of part-Sibylline
part-Unclean
Nazarene Shelter
in the saloon's
limited space
for Gaming tables
spiral ten-step
stairway to
discontinuity
of Ouzo Bar
attached threshold
to infinitude
the exotic Garden
Bamboo Gate closing
on the reactionary
options posted edge
with *The Seeress*
and *The Queen*
the opponent presented
the standstill / escape
or disciplinary
metastability
Department Psi
reversed reply
gambled on
The Queen
exposed my Father
Instanter
to a Taste

seeing myself rise
from the ditch
pulled by knotted
rope of mysteries
surge flash lifting
wave of ch' i
I was standing
on the sand
Caduceus in hand
shedding imitation tears
before a Shelter
like a box
I sensed I
sneezed I yawned
experiencing as vertigo
the just measure
of Animal manna
in two large
picture windows
and moving toward
the picture windows
discover direction
born of meaning
from the hieroglyphs
on the door
I saw in
the windows
in the room
all the Spirits
of fallen trees
moment of recoil
began to split
open and tear

of Death
from Shattering
and Shining
of *The Moon*
The Queen // reversed
the opponent
inside the *Passé*
sitting so encased
in a thick
block of Ice
smooth continuous
entire surface
to his waist
spanned saloon
with his hands
and forearms
cut-off
under Ice
the figure
was his torso's
finite space
of intervention
across the saloon
the Divine Seed
in the Field
of Immanence
Endgame Twist
of *The Moon*
Lido variation
displacing *The Seeress*
my Abstrakt Father's
center line
Holy Davidson

spiraled around
invisible shaft
streaming lights
Stone Foundation
down the middle
the Meeting House
Mutated
window frames
becoming circular
nether surge of
Animal Sounds
rose and fell
in combustive clash
wild fantastic Drone
opened my mouth
to a language
sealed a Voice
not quite Voice
straining between
song and Angelic
stutter the light
faced at once
to find
my hair entangled
in the roots
of trees outlines
pressing me toward
vision of hands
one great fist
seemed to converge
that pulled
the Meeting House
inside out

gravity toward
Purgatory to Hell
and took out
The Seeress // reversed
Father followed suit
the opponent's head
survived as encased
effect within Ice
the entire saloon
packed solid
the cubic space
of intensive escape
in-a-standstill
opening Molecular
becoming on crossed
gradients following
a nomad algorithm
For You Are
I… And I
Am You
in gap-toothed
skull opponent
head's enclosed
in protestation
before the Angel
of Allegory
pointed to dreaming
I am therefore
Dead
remaining open-eyed
and made thus
his move reversed
the Last Card

confronting me with
the large glass
single dark window
and placing me
against the oversized
image of
my own head's
darker outline
from which no
Sound no Voice
no story song
would emanate
all I could
manage to form
my lips
was to project
the Sacred Heart
of Twisted Vulva
and stick out
my tongue
forward now
I move perpetually
through Crystal Silence
vast emptiness into
fascinating darkness that
doubles behind me
Mad Maiden
of the Remnant(s)
I have no
body yet refresh
ever-present thirst
in a statistical
stream that

leaving my Father
The Moon // reversed
the Loser's Card
the Drum Beat
to the Gatekeeper
Final Underworld
advancing Ice now
throughout the saloon
an opponent
or Father
settling in
moving over
each both all
accumulating until
Ice poured out
windows doors
spreading the *Passé*
in all directions
Ice flowed Ice
Days of Awe
slow Mad Dance
the fourfold Axis
of Lachrymose Files
along Rubedo Remez
Chiklets and Whoa
advanced Ice covering
the land Bridge
of the Planets
Miracles and Ice
Passage through
Desire Passage
from the Barricades
onto Elysium Plains

silence folds
across silence upon
the Divine Mirage
of pure numbers
scanning darkness
in the light
everywhere I find
words words
I imagine reading
in a dream
as if
I were
dreaming

Causeways of
the Corners of
Columns Seashells
the Singing Well
of Love
then Outward
over the sea
the lost land
of Mu
Winter Garden
Crystal Palace
Ice Dome and
Globe

New York NY
World Oceans Day 2024

About the Author

André Spears was born and grew up in New York City, where he and his wife raised their family. He holds a Ph.D. in Comparative Literature; his field of study concerned the emergence of "deep time" and the historical impact of archaeological discovery on the field of literature. He has served as a board member at Poets House in NYC, is the co-founder of the Gloucester Writers Center in Gloucester (MA), and the former director of the Maud/Olson library (now at the Cape Ann Museum); he was also a senior editor at the now-archived website *Dispatches from the Poetry Wars*. His other writings include the short epic *Xo: A Tale for the New Atlantis* (1983, 2020), *Translation* (with Anne Rosēn, 2010), *En Terre Perdue* (a translation into French of *Letters from Mu (Part I),* 2013) and *Shrinkrap: Litany in Quadraphony* (2020).